Challenging Anthropology

LIST OF CONTRIBUTORS

Bernard Arcand—Laval University
Michael Asch—University of Alberta
Bernard Bernier—University of Montreal
M. Louis-Jacques Dorais—Laval University
Jim Freedman—University of Western Ontario
Max Hedley—University of Windsor
Susan Hurlich and Richard B. Lee—University of Toronto
Chantal Kirsch—University of Montreal
Roger McDonnell—University of Toronto
Jerome Rousseau—McGill University
Gillian Sankoff—University of Montreal
Martin Silverman—University of British Columbia
Gavin Smith—University of Toronto
David Turner—University of Toronto

Challenging Anthropology

A Critical Introduction to Social and Cultural Anthropology

Edited by:

David H. Turner
Department of Anthropology
University of Toronto

Gavin A. Smith
Department of Anthropology
University of Toronto

McGRAW-HILL RYERSON LIMITED
Toronto   Montreal   New York   St. Louis   San Francisco   Auckland
Beriut   Bogotá   Düsseldorf   Johannesburg   Lisbon   London   Lucerne
Madrid   Mexico   New Delhi   Panama   Paris   San Juan   São Paulo
Singapore   Sydney   Tokyo

CHALLENGING ANTHROPOLOGY

ISBN 0-07-082807-5

1 2 3 4 5 6 7 8 9 0 D 9 8 7 6 5 4 3 2 1 0 9

Printed and bound in Canada

Canadian Cataloguing in Publication Data

Main entry under title:

Challenging anthropology

ISBN 0-07-082807-5

1. Ethnology—Addresses, essays, lectures.
I. Smith, Gavin A. II. Turner, David H., date.

GN325.C43   301.2   C78-001549-5

Cover design: Sharon Black

TABLE OF CONTENTS

ACKNOWLEDGEMENTS

Besides the contributors themselves, a number of people were as crucial to the publication of this book as the editors, and we would like to express our sincere thanks to them. Guy Lanoue and Lise Lavoie helped in the essential work of translating from the original French in the case of a number of articles. Also thanks to Alison de Pelham who compiled the index and glossary. Ruth Turner and Joanna Sworn helped us in so many ways that we could not list them all here and we hope that they will get as much pleasure out of the book as we do. Finally, we would like to thank Jane Abramowitz whose enthusiasm in the early stages was what led to the initiation of this book, and Timothy Griffin and Joanne Culley who have seen it through its later trials and difficulties.

INTRODUCTION

Most people who come to read this book will not be specializing in social or cultural anthropology, nor have any intention of doing so. This is, however, a collection of essays written by people who have chosen to earn money as professionals in the field of anthropology. If we, as the editors writing this Introduction, look along the shelves of our studies, we can count—off hand—at least fifteen textbooks on anthropology all published within the last ten years (though none published in Canada and written by Canadians). In each of these the writers seem to have set out to tell people who are not specialists in the subject what "anthropology" is and how it is done.

Many readers of this Introduction will just be encountering texts such as these; others will be familiar with them from the past. These are books which explain to outsiders what anthropologists do. The professional anthropologist, however, is not really like the professional engineer or professional medical practitioner. For these people the task is less one of explaining to others the inner workings of their profession than the providing of a service for society—to build highways or attend to sickness. Therefore, while for informational purposes there may be texts which explain to outsiders what these professions do, the task which these professions perform for society is not seen to be primarily to explain and analyze, but to perform.

The book about anthropology, however, does not stand in quite the same relation to the profession as does the book about what an engineer or a medical doctor does. This is because, whether he or she likes things the way they are today, most professional anthropologists are making careers out of the analysis of society and the communication of that analysis to others. This puts the anthropological textbook in a rather different position vis-à-vis "outsiders" than would be the case in many other professions. Conventional textbooks on anthropology may be necessary to introduce others to the trade and the tools of the trade—indeed this book makes something of an assumption that the

1

reader will have had some kind of exposure to such texts—but there is a call for something else as well.

In short, the state of the profession and the state of the society we live in are such that people who are not necessarily going to become "professionals" can gain from exposure to a provocative and critical look at social and cultural anthropology because, in view of its subject matter, this means a provocative and critical look at society itself.

So, besides introducing people to the tools for the study of societies, an anthropology textbook should also take into account the effects on the reader of exposure to anthropology. The view of the editors and the contributors in this book is that the materials of social and cultural anthropology should provoke reader and writer alike by drawing them out of the claustrophobic and myopic atmosphere of their own world and thereby allow them—even if only momentarily and in the rarest of glimpses—to see themselves "as through a glass darkly."

We say both reader *and writer* because the contributors to this volume have quite intentionally tried to go out on a limb with the anthropological tools they have at their disposal, to take a critical look at the people about whom they write, at the discipline of social and cultural anthropology and, of course, ultimately, at themselves and their own society.

This is a quite different attitude to the process of learning than that which is found in conventional textbooks. Inasmuch as it brings the writer into the direct line of vision of the readers, it forces him or her into an exposed position which the grammar of most social science writing specifically avoids. We have asked the contributors to say things which—perhaps in other circumstances—they would be more hesitant about. It is important to recognize this as you read the book. We have done this intentionally. Against what has sometimes been referred to as "the banking concept of education," in which knowledge is deposited into the student like money in a bank, we have presented here a kind of document which respects the potential of readers to be provoked and to gain through the critical perception which thereby emerges.

This means harder work for the reader, at least in the initial stages of exposure. Anthropologists are especially aware of the "costs and benefits" of this kind of thing through knowledge of initiation rites. Their intensity and duress demand a certain commitment and exposure on the part of the initiate which momentarily make him or her personally vulnerable and sensitive. Because of these (often shared) moments of heightened awareness and unease, the person who emerges thereafter is a different person than the one who entered the "passage." There is no need to carry the similarity too far. It is enough to say that learning is about this kind of thing, and that the degree of learning is at least partially connected to the degree to which the people involved are prepared to "get involved," make themselves momentarily vulnerable and, at those moments, draw in

2

the anchors which chain them to their own preconceptions of the past. Such is the kind of demand this book makes on the student. We believe that the rewards are worth it.

In seeking out contributors we had one over-arching priority: that they in some way took a critical stance toward their subject matter. What form that stance took was a matter of their own concern, and you will find a variety of views expressed here. Criticism does not mean destruction, though it does mean a kind of negativity toward what is being perceived. In this sense social anthropology is not unlike philosophy. It differs in that where the latter is "a kind of aesthetic contemplation of consciousness by consciousness," (Lévi-Strauss) the former takes as its subject matter—as its point-of-focus—the social world. If this social world were unproblematically available to matter-of-fact perception, there would be no need of a science called social and cultural anthropology. It is by devising means for breaking through this matter-of-factness that social anthropology becomes critical.

If our contributors believe this when faced with their own ethnographic data then, by logical extension, they should write in such a way as to provoke a critical spirit in the reader when faced with these texts. There is nothing new about this for a large body of anthropological literature, of course. What is new is that this should be used in the writing of a textbook. It is for this reason that the book provides an important bridge between introductory texts written for "outsiders" and the body of anthropological literature written, for better or worse, largely for "insiders."

The book is set out so that it can be used in a fairly straightforward way in the teaching of a second year social and cultural anthropology course, having sections on Institutions, Language, and Ethnographies. But it begins and ends with two themes that we feel are appropriate. It begins at the beginning, i.e., by addressing the question of how social and cultural anthropologists acquire and order their data. And it ends by addressing the question, "To what use can the anthropologist put the concepts and perceptions discussed in the body of the book?" It does this by taking a number of "current issues" and having anthropologists talk about them.

ANTHROPOLOGY AND THE HISTORY OF IDEAS

Social and cultural anthropology has traditionally been conducted through fieldwork, that is, through the direct encounter between the anthropologist and "the other"—their practices, their ideas, their present moment. Having no written traditions of their own, most of the diverse peoples studied by anthropologists are unable to trace out their own histories and their own intellectual development. But they have been able to enter ours and occasionally make a profound impact on our own direction, or lack of it. To those of socialist persuasion, the Australian Aborigines have been used to demonstrate the primaeval nature of cooperative organization and economic and social planning; to those of capitalist bent, a counter offensive is mounted with the example of the Mbuti pygmies to show that competition and pragmatic self interest are rooted in the nature of things. The example of the Inuit is raised to prove the eternal nature of the nuclear family by those who would defend it today, while the Nayar of India are used by its detractors to demonstrate the opposite, and raise questions of alternate lifestyles and relations between the sexes.

Both Locke and Hobbes, the founders of modern liberalism, drew on what were, in effect, ethnographies of their own civilization's antecedents (Greece, Rome, Egypt) and on travellers' accounts of other peoples discovered through the expansion of Europe in the sixteenth and seventeenth centuries. The articulation of their philosophies was particularly crucial in the early stages of mercantile and industrial capitalism when freedom of movement and association were necessary to this economic development. Similarly, both Rousseau and Marx drew on ethnographic accounts, the latter particularly on the examples of the Iroquois and Australians, in formulating their ideas on democracy and socialism.

The above traditions of thought are now firmly established in the West and the relation of anthropology to their continuance is complex and subtle. In Part II of this book, for example, the authors rework established ideas in "schools," such as Marxism and structuralism, by interjecting into them ideas developed out of the encounter with "the others." Just how this encounter is itself accomplished is yet another issue and is dealt with in the first section of the book "Fieldwork." However accomplished, this encounter has affected our authors in basically similar ways. They communicate an uneasy, and at times difficult-to-articulate, awareness that anthropology itself has for most of its history been imprisoned within the folk and theoretical models of Western society. This is not surprising considering that anthropology grew out of the highly ethnocentric and imperialistic civilizations of Europe and North America. The rise of anthropology was, indeed, made possible by the incredible growth and expansion of capitalism, first in Britain and France, and then in the United States, from the middle of the last century to the 1960s. Not only did this system provide the wealth, opportunity, and leisure (for some classes) necessary for travel to exotic places, it also provided the colonies as an object of study. Here the academic or the traveller could enthusiastically pursue his or her interests under the peace and security furnished by the colonial regime. In return for his or her friendship and enlightened appreciation, the anthropologist or traveller received a wealth of information leading to a lucrative academic career or to a promising future as a popular writer. At worst the encounter left the Westerner with a deep feeling of alienation from his or her own society and a critical (in the conventional sense) obsession with that society's most cherished institutions.

As the economic and political power of the West has waned, however, so has the anthropological quest through fieldwork, and so, it might be predicted, will anthropology's grip on the public imagination. Not only are the "natives" now restless and moving to shred the last vestiges of colonialism in the Third World, but colonial-type regimes in settler societies such as South Africa, Brazil and Rhodesia have now come to see anthropological research as more of a threat to their stability than an aid to administration—the prevalent attitude during the height of the colonial period. And they have reason to be concerned, for anthropology has now matured sufficiently as a discipline to be able to account for its own existence. Having done so, its practitioners find themselves increasingly critical, again in the conventional sense, of the colonial connection.

As Turner shows in his paper "From the Outside Looking In," even in a "civilized" and secure country like Australia, there is considerable resistance on the part of mission and government agencies to anthropological fieldwork. Fieldwork, by its very nature, upsets the normal routine of administration, and raises issues which question the very administrative connection itself. As McDonnell illustrates in the essay that follows, the encounter with the "other" the anthropologist experiences, alters the fundamental basis on which one's own standards of right and wrong, good and bad, appropriate and inappropriate, rest. And these standards are shared by others of one's own society, including those encountered "of one's own kind" during fieldwork.

Reconstituting this breakdown of assumed truth is, as Smith shows in the third section of Chapter 1, perhaps the anthropologist's most difficult and frustrating task. It means comprehending the process and the new knowledge gained in terms of one's own intellectual traditions. And these traditions have been closely tied to the biases of one's own society. Some anthropologists have been unable to bridge the gap and have gone the way of Don Juan (see Castenada 1968, *The Teachings of Don Juan*, Harmondsworth: Penguin); others, however, have been more successful. But one of the consequences has been to undermine the ideological underpinnings which hold relationships together in one's own society. The unsystematic half truths people invent and inherit to justify particular interests become subject to a new standard—the half truths of people with opposite interests. In the anthropologist's situation, the folk models of the rulers are now juxtaposed with those of the ruled; those of the powerful with those of the powerless and those of the wealthy with those of the poor. And this very juxtaposition raises the issue of whose version comes closest to comprehending the larger reality which encompasses all the diverse individuals, groups or classes constituting the society in question.

"Bridging the gap" in these terms is really the theme of Part II as a whole: "Concepts and Problems." The articles of this section deal with the way anthropological research and thought has modified or extended western ideas and western intellectual traditions in order to allow a more comprehensive understanding of the diverse realities anthropologists have encountered. And part of this process has been to modify anthropologists' own ideas about the nature of what they are studying and about their own society.

In Chapter 2, "Kinship," Silverman takes this issue right into the very heart of conventional social and cultural anthropology. His studies of Banaban kinship in the South Pacific and his critical reading of the literature have led him to wonder whether the basic concepts "kinship," "marriage" and "family" are meaningful at all outside the Western experience. And even within it, their analytic value is far from clear. "Family," for example, is normally taken to mean a small group of people related by kinship and marriage, basically a man, his wife, and their children. However, in medieval England, the same word meant, "household" or "domestic group." It took on the "kinship" aspect, only with the rise of industrial capitalism. How then, asks Silverman, can we universally apply concepts such as kinship and family, individual and group, rule and principle, when they are so closely tied to the historical development of a particular civilization in Europe?

Asch, in Chapter 3, makes much the same point in respect of the way anthropologists approach the study of economic systems and the relation of people to the environment in his paper comparing the cultural-ecological with the "mode of production" approach. For Asch, the main failure of the traditional ecological-evolutionary approach to economic anthropology has been its adherence to mainstream "free-market" modes of thought. The social Darwinism of a developed capitalist system is raised to the status of anthropological theory—societies develop by successfully harnessing greater supplies of energy from their environments through more efficient technological means and an increasingly specialized division of labour. Social relations of production are ignored in favour of a simplistic model of the economy, linking environment (available resources), people (population density), technology (energy harnessing apparati), and consequent social institutions. The dynamic in this chain is the relation of available resources to population pressure. As crises are occasioned by the inability of existing technology to supply the energy needs of an increasing population, pressure for technological change occurs. Social forms developed around existing technology (social service industries, for instance) may prevent the changeover to new technology by absorbing the capital needed for its accomplishment. These then must be abandoned to allow the transition to the new technology. This may seem logical because it is in fact the logic our policy makers follow. But they follow it because it is within the logic of capitalist enterprise not because it reflects an objective analysis of the economic system as a whole. And it certainly does not reflect an analysis of non-Western economies. What is missing from the account is the crucial role of the social relations of production in determining the very pressure on resources which is at issue.

6

For instance, the existence of a capitalist economic system based on a division into owners pursuing profit and workers pursuing wages (to simplify) leads to an economy based on fulfilling artificially created needs in order to sustain both profit maximization and wage increases following on it. It is the resulting "growth" which, in fact, creates the ecological crisis not the inadequacy of the existing technology to extract more energy from the environment, although this may become a proposed solution to the crisis. But given the same population, the same resource base and the same technology—but different relations of production—such crises could be avoided. As an alternative to the ecological-evolutionary approach, Asch offers a more flexible one based on an appreciation of the dynamics and complexity of a mode of production. This approach focuses on the social relations of production and their dialectical relationship to technology and environmental factors. The model, he finds, applies adequately, not only to our own type of economy and society, but to many others as well.

Paralleling this critique of traditional economic anthropology (or at least a dominant branch of it), is McDonnell's examination of anthropological approaches to the study of religion. He traces through a tradition of anthropological thought from Tylor, Frazer, Durkheim and Malinowski through to Van Gennep, Douglas, Lévi-Strauss, which is tending toward a certain conclusion—or at least a new starting point. This is the realization that religion is less a "thing," (object, institution) defined by a particular type of content (belief in the supernatural; attribution of cause to nonhuman, nonnatural sources) as a mode of apprehension.

Religious thought and ritual practice are the symbolic expressions of the very nexi of human existence—points of transformation, zones of transition, the grasp of paradox. Human existence and human consciousness intersect, encounter, and separate; the mind reflects on an unintelligible event; "unnatural" symbols emerge to comprehend it. Ghosts and gods, totemic beings and miraculous creatures merge the experienced with the imagined in an attempt at understanding and explanation. The essence of this perspective on religion is expressed by Van Gennep in his treatise on rites of passage: a person wavering on the boundary or margin between two positions reaches an imaginary point in which he or she is neither in one position nor the other. Ritual activity formalizes the transition but does not explain it. Religious thought attempts to grasp the moment itself, but that moment always escapes.

In the paper that follows, Turner examines one format for thought along these lines—myth and folklore. The examples he selects show people reflecting on the paradoxes of their own arrangements for living, though in such a way that the status quo is ultimately justified. However, the experimentation employed to reach this conclusion is at least evidence that doubt is being entertained. What distinguishes folklore from myth is the degree to which this experimentation proceeds outside the bounds of tradition. Turner illustrates this with an analysis of the film *Jaws* alongside the Tshimshian myth of Asdiwal. The supernatural "touch" to the Asdiwal story—something characteristic of myth in general—perhaps indicates respect for a certain quality of human thought which transcends normal human ability.

In the essay on class analysis that follows Smith looks at one of the focal points of critical activity throughout human history—relations of domination and differential access to power and wealth. The model of class he offers transcends the particular situation of western capitalist countries to encompass a wide range of societies, including those of the tribal and peasant variety. Rather than take class relations in their western form and generalize them to other societies, Smith *transforms* them into a series expressing a number of possible combinations of elements and relations. This involves an examination of producers and nonproducers in terms of whether they control or are separated from the means of production. Smith then examines class relations in peasant society in terms of this model as a whole without committing the *assumption* that class relations there are structurally more similar to class relations in capitalist society than they are to those in, say, a tribal society. This approach avoids the temptation so prevalent in anthropology of seeing other societies or at least aspects of them as merely elementary versions of our own.

In the final part of this section, we return to the question raised initially by Silverman at the beginning of Part 2, namely the adequacy of Western categories of thought to define both the diverse realities we encounter as anthropologists, and those we experience in our own society. According to Dorais, language as such may, in fact, force an interpretation on reality for us by predefining and differentiating it. Language can thus serve to maintain existing differences in class, ethnicity and occupation; and insofar as it does, intervening in reality to maintain a certain interpretation, it becomes ideology. The use of the distinction between "joual" and "Parisian French" and between "Ottawa Valley" and "proper" English, come immediately to mind as examples. They conjure up distinctions between unsophisticated and sophisticated, uneducated and educated, backward and progressive which either have no objective foundation or do simply because of the imposition of this categorization. There is an "upper class" standard to which we all must aspire, and in doing so we legitimate the distinction between that class and the others.

Sankoff follows Dorais with a case study of language use in Papua-New Guinea. She shows how a language hierarchy developed with colonial rule amongst native people who had previously considered languages as merely being different. The languages of other tribal groupings defined them as "aliens" but they were not ranked according to their superiority or inferiority. In the contact situation, however, new dialects emerged, associated with the Europeans, which eventually came to be used as a means of asserting differential access to power and resources. The role of linguistic and rhetorical competence changed as the most important resources shifted from confinement to the land and labour of the neighbourhood, to access to the colonial missions, administration and businesses. The ability to use certain linguistic tools—such as *pidgin*—became crucial for gaining access to the valued resources emanating from these sources. So the role of certain kinds of linguistic competence—rhetoric, multilingualism etc.—was transformed as a function of the changing social relations of which it was part. Sankoff is then able to propose some predictive hypotheses about the way in which New Guinea's newly-gained independence will lead to a new transformation, this time in the differential uses of English.

In sum, the contributors to the first two parts of the book direct our attention away from the folk models and theories that dominate the internal scene of any society, including our own, toward a more objective understanding of the human condition.

THE ETHNOGRAPHIC PAST AND PRESENT

In the first chapter of Part 3 (Chapter 9) "Ways of Life," Turner shows how hunters and gatherers have developed their social relations into a "technology," capable of sustaining people's existence under a wide range of ecological and demographic conditions. At one end of a continuum are peoples like the Cree who have organized themselves in such a way that maximum productive effectiveness is achieved within a network of relations, usually located within a definite territorial range. Within this kind of society coproduction ties are formed on a pragmatic basis within a network of people with whom one has had some contact during his or her early years, and with whom one comes into contact after marriage through the working relations of his or her spouse.

At the other end of the continuum are peoples like the Australian Aborigines with their "rule" governed social relations and intricate systems of clan alliances through totemic brotherhood and intermarriage. Establishment of an abstract, possessory, relation to the land rather than a concrete residential one, and formal alliances between the possessors of land allows for the planning of production relations both in the present and for the future. Actual movements of people over the landscape in production groups composed of members of different clans is achieved via rules of access determined by the marriages of one's clanspeople, past and present. Ties of brotherhood expressed through ritual association beyond the cluster of clans one is involved with through marriage provide an institutionalized means of dealing with remote people and an opportunity for access to a still wider range of resources and trade items.

Once established, these two arrangements contain very different internal contradictions and are, theoretically, propelled along very different historical paths.

In Arcand's paper we have a more detailed examination of a people at Turner's Cree end of the continuum—the Cuiva of Columbia. Arcand shows that the Cuiva do not fit the conventional definition of a "band" society as established by Julian Steward and others, with its presumed patrilocality and political authority embodied in the elders. The Cuiva are able to function quite adequately through associations established by kinship, domestic living arrangements and the ideology of common band membership. The latter is rather vaguely defined in terms of "common origin" but provides a framework or "pool" within which ties of friendship and marriage are worked out on a personal and pragmatic basis. Activities here are rather coordinated than directed and freedom within the band works against the emergence of authoritarianism.

Arcand's paper does, however, point to a potential paradox in human societies where the "common good" is achieved by basically leaving people to their own devices within a defined jurisdiction. Here, freedom may turn to licence and activities may not always coordinate themselves in such a manner that all people benefit equally.

In the two papers that follow we see the realization and elaboration of hierarchical structures in three quite different and widely separated societies, the Kwakiutl of British Columbia, the Kayan of Borneo and the Kiga of Ruanda. In Chapter 2 Rousseau shows that within the Kwakiutl village production community are descent groups called *numayma*, each with a chief and each ranked with respect to other *numayma* within the village. Villages are in turn ranked. In addition to this ranking system, the Kwakiutl as a whole are stratified into nobility, commoners, and slaves. While commoners and slaves remain more or less confined to their particular villages, the nobility often intermarried with the nobility of other villages. This latter development presents an interesting paradox—ties outside the village production community among the nobility potentially modify or weaken ties within. A brake on the development of classes along these lines, however, was the potlatch. Potlatching redistributed or even destroyed surpluses produced within the village and achievement prevented the consolidation of chiefly power. Through the establishment of hereditary positions, descent groups were also somewhat fluid in composition and one could negotiate membership in one's mother's or father's, or even both.

By contrast, among the Kayan, the system of ranking was indistinguishable from the stratification system. The Kayan were divided into villages and each village had a chief, but the chief was not the head of a descent group within the village but of a general category—the "refined people." All people who were not "refined" were "inferior people." The first category was in turn subdivided into *marens* (rulers) and *hipuys* (commoners) and the second, into *panyins* (commoners) and *dipens* (slaves). These categories included all Kayan and were based on common ritual association and duty. In fact, the Kayan paradox seems almost the reverse of the Kwakiutl one—external ties beyond the village on the basis of membership in a common category inhibit the internal functioning of the village as a collective unit. The

Kayan chief is an adjudicator between villages and appropriates labour in support of this function; the Kwakiutl chief is an organizer of production activities within his village and descent group.

In Chapter 12 Freedman shows the way in which a system of inequality based on class divisions emerges in a Ruandan society where previously checks to inequality were institutionalized. These social constraints on inequality were undermined by the development of capitalism in the larger society. His suggestion is that "development," far from reducing inequalities, has in fact increased them. Moreover, insofar as it is inequality which hampers an overall rise in productivity, the advance of capitalism in certain sectors of a Third World social formation actually negates the stated goals of development in other sectors. He illustrates this by reference to his own fieldwork among the Kiga.

Freedman suggests that in the traditional social relations of the Kiga, the individual acquires the resources necessary for livelihood through demonstrating his legitimacy. On the one hand this means being born into the membership of a certain group, and on the other hand it involves a certain social performance. Access to both productive means and the labour necessary to give value to those means depends upon the individual's social performance. In this sense, "property" and "labour" are essentially *social*. Insofar as money acquired in the capitalist economy allows individuals to acquire both property and labour without having to perform any prescribed social activities among the Kiga, these valued resources lose their social character and become commodities. And as social things become asocial commodities, so social people become asocial individuals. "Exploitation of nature becomes thereby exploitation of other people," and the fetters which keep inequality in check are broken.

In Chapter 13 again we see the processes of change occurring in a "peasant" community as a result of the peasant's relationship to a changing capitalist system. But the historical background from which emerge the social relations among the *huasicanchinos* is quite different to the history of the Kiga. And, similarly, the historical development of capitalism in Ruanda has features distinct from its development in Peru. So the nature of the transformations discussed are different, though there are common elements to both. Smith acknowleges the element of power which is a part of the domination of the *huasicanchinos*, but lays emphasis on the element of "disguise" which occurs in the relationship between the subsumed peasantry and the dominant economic system. The idiom of social relations among the *huasicanchinos* is used by others as a means of extracting surplus from them. But the tension which results from this kind of "disguise" results in continual transformations in social relations.

Hedley's discussion of small farmers in Alberta (Chapter 14) is a detailed discussion of the crisis which results from contradictions in what he calls "the domestic commodity mode of production" as a result of its articulation with advanced capitalism. The process is one in

which the strategies of small farmers to preserve their system of production are precisely those strategies which undercut the viability of
the small farm. The sale of the family's labour power to non-agricul-
tural enterprises in order to acquire funds for the continued operation
of the farm, reduces the amount of labour-time available for the farm.
By investing in costly equipment, the farmer attempts to resolve the
problem, but this dependency on machinery produced in the manufacturing sector, drives up the need for liquid assets, so that the
farmer is left like a fly in a web: each struggle he makes to free himself
entangles him more.

In the final chapter of this section (Chapter 15), Bernier brings together many of the threads which have been developed through the
previous chapters of the book. Confronted with the fact that increasing numbers of the world's population are becoming urban dwellers,
social and cultural anthropologists have had to address themselves to
the question of how to conduct ethnography in the city. The tendency
has been to carve out elements of city life which are seen to be the legitimate area of anthropological enquiry. Bernier suggests that such
studies should be careful to take into account the entire process of the
effects of capitalism on the form of the city, and he then lays out the
major issues which such a holistic view must take into account. As he
points out, so interlaced are the developments of one issue, e.g.,
property speculation, with those of another, e.g., the role of the state,
and the problems of housing, that it becomes difficult to write about
the city in terms of simple cause and effect. A number of balls must be
thrown into the air and kept in motion, while we attempt to concentrate attention on just one of them.

Just as the application of Western concepts to the analysis of the
peoples discussed at the beginning of Part 3 acts to challenge the assumptions behind such concepts, so that, in the final chapter of the
section, we find, too, that many of the assumptions which we make
about the operations of our own urban society must be challenged
and new concepts developed. This critique of our own conventions is
the challenge of anthropology.

DOMINATION & DEVELOPMENT

Social/cultural anthropology has come to study issues and peoples
quite different from those of its original founding fathers such as
Frazer, Tylor, and Mauss. To paraphrase the words of Peter Worsely,
the ends of anthropology have had to change for anthropology to
avoid its own end. The implications of this book are that it has not
been hard for anthropologists to continue to play an important role in
the development of thought. But as the world has changed, so the
topics of concern to anthropologists have changed too. That is why,
for the last section of the book (Part 4), we asked a number of anthropologists to speak out on the issues which concern them. To some extent, this is the final challenge to contemporary anthropologists—to

be able to cast an original light on the issues which concern them and nonanthropologists alike.

Four issues are discussed in this last section: the inequality of men and women, autonomous development for Canadian Indians, the policy of *apartheid* in southern Africa, and the national question in Canada. The four chapters have in common their stress on the dangers of isolating social groups and categories from their larger context. Kirsch's article (Chapter 16) stresses the importance of studying the origins of women's subordination by relating it to the development of social relations as a whole. Asch similarly stresses the danger of isolating the study of the Dene mode of production from its articulation with the total Canadian society, in Chapter 17. In Chapter 18 the political implications of this become clear when we are reminded that the South African government translates *apartheid* as "separate development." And Bernier re-emphasizes the importance of a holistic analysis by examining the nature of the Canadian nation-state through historical study of the class antagonisms that led to its formation.

It almost goes without saying that all of the peoples studied by our authors have been in some way influenced by their position within the nation state. For the Cree, there is the fur trade, for the Dene, "northern development," for the !Kung San, the *apartheid* system, and so on. But for some of our authors the connection was sufficiently dominant that the social relations among the people studied could not be undertaken at all without making some reference to the operations of the larger society. The Kiga of Ruanda, the *huasicanchinos* of Peru, and Alberta small-scale farmers, for instance, appear simultaneously "traditional" and "modern." But the situation is not as simple as this. The difference between one sector of the society and another in each of these situations is not merely a matter of degree, nor a matter of the persistence of "tradition." If this were so, then, as "acculturation" ran its course, so the degree of difference would lessen and the social relations of the entire society would become generalized. But the data do not support this view. Rather, the authors suggest that the social relations among the people they lived with were partly developed in opposition to forces lying at the heart of the larger society. This is even the case with Hedley's Canadian farmers. The image is not so much one of destructuration, as one of reformulation of the significant oppositions in a social formation.

Our ethnographers then find themselves faced with the fact that ties with the larger system have a dominant influence over internal social relationships, and that intra-group relationships appear to have qualititative differences from those at the heart of the nation-state. Moreover, the subsumed system is not necessarily undynamic or incapable of autonomous development. This means that social change cannot be referred to in terms of a unilinear assimilation of "traditional societies" to "modern societies." Instead, it is possible to suggest that, to some extent, the structure of the social relations of the group being studied occurs as a function of the group's articulation with the dominant system. But "restructurings" do not *necessarily* lead to a reduction in the degree of difference between the subsumed system and the dominant one.

Thus, even if, from a historical point of view, it were possible to *observe* a tendency toward the generalization of social relations throughout the "Third World" in response to colonialism and capitalism from the ethnographer's point of view, it is not at all useful to *assume* such a tendency. This is because any moment in history is the product of the working-out and the endlessly-renewed positioning of systems vis-à-vis one another, and this process is the object of study for social anthropology.

It is a growing awareness of this problem which has led to renewed interest in the concept of the *mode of production*. Despite the fact that authors appear to use the concept in a variety of different ways—often in a single article and often only loosely defined—there appears to be agreement that the concept helps us to deal with the variety of interlocking, but qualitatively different, social relations of production, which exist in virtually all societies. Indeed, one of the features which distinguishes the contemporary nation-state is the complexity of the combination of distinct modes of production within.

But, since the formation of the nation-state is itself a question for study in anthropology (see Chapter 19), the combination of a number of modes of production needs some other referent and the term which is increasingly coming to be used for this is that of the *social formation*. The way in which modes of production combine in any one social formation are practically infinite, however, so we must go beyond designating particular social formations as "communal," "capitalist" or "socialist" to an empirical study of each social formation in its own terms.

We have all tried, throughout this book, to raise arguments and to provoke debate. We hope that the reading of the book will initiate a dialogue and we hope that out of that dialogue will emerge new ideas and new issues which are not contained herein. Insofar as the last section addresses questions about which most people have an opinion one way or the other, the articles therein may appear especially provocative. But this has, in fact, been the theme of all the writing in the book. The measure of its success will be the extent to which it encourages students and teachers to engage in debate and the extent to which that debate leads to a greater critical awareness of the social world.

GAVIN A. SMITH
DAVID H. TURNER
APRIL, 1978

PART I
FIELDWORK

CHAPTER 1

FIELDWORK

1. On the Outside Looking In

DAVID H. TURNER
University of Toronto

In 1971 I was refused a permit by the Australian Government and forced to leave Groote Eylandt, an island off the Arnhem Land coast of northern Australia. I had just arrived back again to continue the research I had begun there in 1969 into Aboriginal social organization and symbolism. The island lies in a federal Aboriginal Reserve under the jurisdiction of the Northern Territory Administration and it is they who determine just who comes and goes through the area. The permit was denied even though I had secured written permission to stay from the Aborigines at the local mission and government settlement and even from the Administration's own representative on the island.

I was not the first to experience such difficulties. Fred Rose, a noted Anglo-Australian anthropologist, had worked there in 1940 and again, briefly, in 1948 with the Australian-American joint expedition to Arnhem Land. He was refused permission to reenter the Reserve in 1968, the year before I arrived. His refusal seemed related to the fact that he had since "defected" to East Germany and had been closely tied to the Australian Communist Party and Trade Union movement (see Rose, 1968). My admission, after his refusal, also seemed related to this situation—the Liberal-Country Party government had to demonstrate that it was not against research as such, but only subversive researchers. At the time of my application, I was a Ph.D. student at the University of Western Australia, a Commonwealth scholar, and held a grant from the Australian Institute of Aboriginal Studies (A.I.A.S.)—in short I was "clean." And so I was admitted. But in 1971 I was denied access by the same Administration. The reader is almost forced to draw the conclusion that I had done something during my fieldwork to offend the authorities or I had published or said things publicly afterwards which would render me politically suspect. But at the time I could think of nothing which would support either interpretation.

Like most anthropologists, I had been rather conservative in my attitude to the situation I encountered and had accepted the Administration's (government, mission, and business) presence as "given." My project was sponsored by the A.I.A.S., a "Crown corporation," and I had even been asked for advice, after my fieldwork, by the then Minister of Aboriginal Affairs. And I had not published anything, nor made any statements. So my difficulties posed something of a problem as far as explanation went.

Certainly the island was a sensitive area; the Government and Church Mission Society had been involved with the local inhabitants since the early 1940s (a mission had been established in 1921 but none of the local Aborigines had bothered to move in): a manganese mine had been established in 1966 and a prawning factory was just getting underway in 1969. At that time, the Aboriginal population was some 800 and the White 200, but the latter was rising. The only explanation I could come up with for my unacceptability was that the procedures I was forced to follow in my attempts to gain a permit were in fact designed to gain certain kinds of information which could be used to judge me against some standard of acceptability or unacceptability. I reasoned that previous information was inconclusive and that additional data were required.

It was this interpretation that appeared in my 1972 *Nimda Rites of Access* paper, a paper written very much in the "Nacirema" tradition (Miner 1956) in terms of style. In it I set about comparing the way decisions were made on the status of strangers in two societies—Groote Eylandt Aboriginal and Nimda (Administration). In the paper, I was the stranger in question. The paper was oblique, but it was also analytic and academic. At the time, this format seemed to suit the occasion and subject matter: I was, after all, being denied access to "my people"; the research I had put so much of myself into was being threatened; and I had travelled some 10 000 miles to carry out the project. The style served to tame some strong impulses which might have become uncontrollable had I broached the subject directly.

Here, with some editing, is part of what I wrote in that article:

A stranger sent word to Nimda leaders informing them of his reasons for wishing access to their territory. The Nimda concerned, however, failed to acknowledge the message, thereby forcing a direct encounter between the stranger and themselves—that is, if he did not at this point cancel his visit. This stranger, however, not knowing how to interpret this silence, approached the Nimda leaders in person to restate his case—namely that he wished merely to pass through Nimda territory to reach the neighbouring aborigines.

The initial Nimda reaction was to deny receipt of the stranger's message and criticize him for failing to forewarn them—this despite

18

assurances to the stranger by intermediaries that his communication had, indeed, been delivered. Next, the stranger was told that consultations regarding his proposal would have to be held between Nimda leaders and that he would be informed of their decision at an appointed time. When this time was passed and no news had been received, the stranger again contacted Nimda leaders who told him that his problems were of only minor concern to them and that they had much more important matters to deal with. A decision would be made at a later date and he would be informed of the results at a specified time.

After the above sequence was repeated for a second time, the stranger was finally informed that a decision had been reached and he would have to prove that the members of the group he wished to visit were willing to receive him before he could proceed through Nimda territory. As he would not be allowed through Nimda territory to obtain this in person, and as no other form of communication other than word of mouth was possible, the "proof" would have to be obtained by Nimda representatives there. The eventual reply was that the people in question were opposed to his visit. The stranger's immediate reaction was, of course, to deny the reliability of this report and demand that he be permitted to solicit in person the people he wished to visit. This demand was refused by Nimda leaders who again argued that to do this he would have to pass through Nimda territory, in which case he would first have to demonstrate that he was welcome among them.

Having reached this impasse, the stranger changed his approach. The territories of some of the clans he wanted to visit could be reached by passing through the territory of a certain Nimda subgroup (that of the Church). By bluffing one leader of that group into support, the stranger, in defiance of the earlier instructions, set off through Nimda country and succeeded in reaching his objective. In the meantime, however, other Nimda leaders discovered what had happened and sent word ahead to their representatives that he must be sent back. This was accomplished, but not before the stranger had learned from the people he wished to visit that they had been eagerly awaiting his arrival. Despite his protests that he now had proof of his acceptability, he was nevertheless forcibly removed by Nimda representatives and forbidden from recrossing their territory and revisiting the other group.

This sequence of events makes sense only if it is seen in the same terms as the response of the Groote Eylandt Aborigines to the same situation—that is, as an attempt to identify strangers in indigenous terms in order to locate them within existing social organizational categories.

Unlike the Groote Eylandt people, however, the Nimda rarely pose straightforward questions to strangers in order to establish their identities. Rather, they seem to employ a series of strategies designed to yield the required information, yet keep the person concerned unaware of their objectives and criteria of acceptability. Nimda leaders apparently feel that strangers will evade and fabricate answers in order to hide information which might result in a negative identification. On the other hand, many people acquainted with the Nimda feel that the beliefs and values the Nimda *say* form the criteria for acceptability and membership in their groups are in any case inconsistent, and at times contradictory, particularly when evaluated against their actions.

Informants say the Nimda try to convince neighbouring people that they are like their brothers, yet they subjugate and dominate them; that neighbours should be given access to Nimda knowledge and beliefs, yet they exclude them from all but minimal contact, and at the lowest level; that all people should have the freedom of choice to determine their own future, yet they insist that the neighbours be guided by Nimda representatives sent to live among them. Consequently, not knowing what to make of this, neighbours and strangers who learn of the peculiarities of the Nimda from these neighbours find it best to yield as little information about themselves as possible beyond stating their acceptance of whatever overt ideas and practices the Nimda hold, even though they appear inconsistent.

There are three possible explanations for these inconsistencies. Firstly, they may be evidence of what Lévy-Bruhl (1966: 63) has called the "primitive mentality" which "does not bind itself down, as our thought does, to avoiding contradictions." Secondly, subgroup differences may exist within Nimda society which cannot be resolved. Thirdly, certain principles may exist which are shared by all Nimda but which are not stated explicitly, particularly to strangers, and which synthesize these apparent contradictions on a higher level, or at least render the contradictions trivial to the Nimda. In the case study of the stranger-Nimda encounter mentioned above, the circularity of their reasoning over the "proof of welcome" issue, and their inconsistency once this proof had been demonstrated, would make sense once these happenings were seen as strategies designed to elicit information relevant to identifying the stranger in terms of more crucial and consistent Nimda beliefs and interests which remain unstated to outsiders. The strategy reflected here could be labelled "the strategy of contradiction." In the case study cited it was used to so frustrate the stranger that he disobeyed the collective authority of the Nimda and attempted to secure his ends by devious means. Whatever the underlying standards held by the Nimda, this act must have been interpreted by them as evidence that he could not be aligned with any of their subgroups, as they removed him from their territory and denied him future access.

A second strategy was also illustrated in the above case study which I will call "the strategy of harassment." It seems designed to make the stranger lose his temper and retaliate, thus perhaps making him reveal ideas he might otherwise have kept to himself. In the example given, this strategy proved unsuccessful. A third technique also employed here can be called "the strategy of delay" which, like the "strategy of contradiction" seems designed to provoke the stranger into acting prematurely. A fourth technique can be located in the case study and this is "the strategy of accusation." Here, the stranger is permitted temporary access of Nimda territory or to an adjacent country and then is repeatedly accused by the Nimda people residing there of attempting to turn the locals against their Nimda neighbours. Rumours are also circulated among the inhabitants that the stranger is there to exploit or in some way endanger them. The Nimda seem to feel that hostilities generated by this situation may eventually lead the stranger to act in such a way that he will be admitting guilt. In point of fact, there is little the stranger can do to avoid this. On the one hand, he may respond by attacking his accusers and thus appear to the local people to be trying to endanger their relations with the Nimda. On the other hand, he may choose to remain silent, a course of action that to these Aborigines would be considered a sign of guilt.

*   *   *

In my "Nimda" paper, I went on from here to "discover" the standard against which I was being judged by the Nimda and found it to be a capitalist, fundamentalist-Christian, colonial one. I concluded that my actions had been judged, "not in the interests of maintaining 'the system' ".

Six years later, however, the Nimda paper seems overly paranoid and conspiratorial. It now seems to me, after rethinking the events and after talking to other anthropologists with similar experiences, that the so-called "strategies" were very much the product of mismanagement, misunderstanding, and indifference, some of it of my own making. I could have been more patient and followed channels even if it had meant months in Darwin. But still, no one really wanted to help me in my efforts and I was removed at the first excuse. There must have been something in the way of a standard against which I was being or had been judged.

And then it struck me. What was wrong with my first interpretation, apart from missing the "bureaucratic factor," was my level of analysis. These were not political scientists, economists or theologians armed with formal models of Western categories of thought and action, able to judge people in terms of where they stood in the Great Debate between Right and Left; Capitalism and Socialism; Atheism and Christianity. They were merely practical people trying to do a job with as little interference as possible: larger philosphical issues were subordinated to this basic interest. The fact that "doing one's job" may have been objectively related to upholding the interests of capitalization, colonization and christianization, was irrelevant to them and to my interpretation. And just as the actions of these people were not *intended* to defend these processes, so mine were not *intended* to interfere with them.

21

What I had done in my day-to-day activities during my fieldwork, and even in my efforts in Darwin to gain a permit, was to interfere with officialdom's ability to carry out its own job, also on a day-to-day basis. I had done this by undermining, quite unintentionally, the basis of an established routine which had been in process long before I had arrived and which continued after I had left. Judged against this standard I was a "subversive" as surely as Rose. The difference was, Rose had insisted on his status from the start—I had at least had a chance to work it out in the field. A number of events come immediately to mind which at the time seemed fairly innocuous—some of them even funny—but which, when examined in terms of this standard, could have been partly responsible for some of my later difficulties.

First, just the fact of my living with the Aborigines must have presented a problem for the Administration. I knew the local language and they, by and large, did not. This gave me access to privileged information. I was also trying to understand things from the indigenous point of view which they generally found incoherent and even disgusting. Insofar as I succeeded in some measure I was undermining a fundamental principle on which the exercise of control rested—that these were "primitive people" incapable of managing their own affairs. In simply talking to the Whites on the island during my fieldwork I increasingly was able to communicate that Aborigines were thinking, feeling people whose actions and thoughts were understandable, given we accepted certain premises. I could show that they had the capacity to change and create of their own accord and were fully capable of reaching their own understanding of the White man and his ways. Approached democratically rather than paternalistically they could work out their own future.

The agents of the Administration and mission were there to "help" these people—they were not there to endanger and exploit them. Undermine the basis of this philanthropic humanitarian motive and you undermine the whole apparatus which has been established to persuade people to do this kind of work. The closer your ties become to individuals in the Aboriginal or White community, the more your "findings" penetrate, and the more impact they have. Had the majority of the White people I met come to accept the native standard of development—social rather than economic—I venture a guess that most of them would not have continued to do what they did; at least they would not have done it so uncritically.

One's very presence, then, upsets two relations basic to the smooth functioning of the Administrative regime—that of head office to branch plant, and of branch plant to subjects.

The second "irritation" that comes to mind involved a survey of the coastline by the Australian Navy. It all started rather innocently. I was interested in recording some cave paintings near Central Hill, the highest point on the island, a mount of rock some 600 feet above sea level, and had been able to persuade a young man from East Wind

22

clan to take me there. I had a motorbike (a requirement of the Administration) and as it was the end of the dry season, the bush tracks were fairly easy to negotiate. We had not carried any water as my companion said we would find some when we got there. Half a day's journey brought us to Central Hill. On our approach, however, my guide spied something which deflected his attention away from the cave paintings and was to prove a thorn in my side for many weeks to come—atop the hill there stood a huge black flag. My Aboriginal friend was so perplexed by this—the hill was a sacred place and any interference with it was a very serious matter—that he insisted we climb up and take a look. The climb was long and hard and we had no water so that by the end of it I was pretty well exhausted. We examined the flag and from the markings on it I was able to tell him that it was a survey marker from the ship the "Moresby," currently anchored off shore. It had been brought there by helicopter. My friend became very agitated and said we had better climb back down to look for the paintings as we had to get back to the settlement before dark. Unfortunately for my purposes the climb down left me thoroughly bushed and as my guide was unable to find water, we decided to set off back to the settlement.

By the time we reached home I was feeling sufficiently recovered (we had found some water on the way) that I decided to continue with my plans to visit the southern part of the island the next day with a hunting party. I arrived back two weeks later to find all hell had broken loose in the interim.

The night I had returned from Central Hill a meeting of the Aboriginal men had been called to discuss the question of the flag. After deliberating for a few days, a decision was made that either the flag should be taken down immediately or they would prevent the Moresby survey crews from setting up camps on the island. The ultimatum was taken to the settlement superintendent, from there it went to the District Welfare Officer, from there to the Administrator of the Northern Territory Welfare Branch and from there to the Vice Admiral of the Australian Navy. By the time enquiries had been made, some of the blame had fallen on my shoulders—after all these people were too unsophisticated to think of this themselves; there must have been someone pushing them. And I was the logical candidate. A hostile situation; but fortunately for me, a local patrol officer had interceded on my behalf, pointing out that I had not even been around when the meetings took place and that these same people had shown an independent spirit on many occasions before.

With the aid of some of the Aboriginal men I was able to convince the settlement superintendent I really had had no part in the "uprising" and he even later apologized for jumping to certain conclusions prematurely. Both of us, as he later concluded, had been used as scapegoats by a more senior officer trying to cover up his own inability to control the situation. It was not long before the superintendant quit and left the island. But I *had* been there to provide the initial information and did not forewarn local officials about what might transpire.

The final example of interference that comes to mind directly involved the mission and, although at the time, the incident seemed quite humorous, it probably proved the most damaging. About a month into my fieldwork I was sitting in my tent in the Aboriginal village talking to a group of young men about their ceremonies. The conversation proceeded in a mixture of simple English and, due to my inadequacies, even simpler Anindilyaugwa, the local language. We had gone over mortuary rites, increase ceremonies, and the gatherings held to honour the ancestors of the clans, when one of them stepped in and said, "Alright, we've been telling you about our ceremonies, how about you telling us about some of yours?" And so I proceeded to describe to them as best I could, those quaint customs, Christmas, and Halloween. Christmas wasn't too difficult—they knew about it from the mission and were already convinced of its significance. It was a time for receiving free food and clothing from the mission and it was not unreasonable to allow their interpretation that Santa Claus was a returning ancestor. Since their minds were made up about Christmas and I was not about to change them, I went on to Halloween. At least here they would have no previous information on which to base an interpretation—it isn't even an Australian custom. But I was in trouble right from the start:

"In my country we take these yams (there is no word for pumpkin, and yams are the closest equivalent), hollow them out, and carve faces in them. Then we put a candle inside and stand them in the window for everyone to see."

At this point my audience was gravely serious.

"Then we dress up in costumes resembling ghosts and sorcerers and go around to people's houses knocking on their doors."

This occasioned some laughter.

"Then we say to the person who comes to the door, 'trick or treat,' "

More laughter.

"If they give us some sweets (they don't know the word 'candy') we go on to the next house. But if they don't, or they won't even open the door and let us in, we play a trick on them, like throwing eggs at their windows, or letting the air out of the tires of their cars." (I don't know what you did, but this is what we used to do).

At this point my audience burst into howls of laughter, and the more detailed I got the worse it got.

"My ancestors used to believe that the spirits of the dead returned to earth for a night every year to visit their homeland. People were afraid and stayed indoors. If they ventured out or didn't show the proper respect the spirits would punish them. They dressed up to copy the spirits and what they did; we still do it today because it is our custom."

By the time I had finished they were literally rolling on the floor, and I was left wondering what was so funny.

The problem was not that they didn't understand what I was saying; it was that they had understood it all too well. What I had been describing was the logic of their own ceremonial activity, but in the context of the White man's society. Here were totems, rewards, and punishments for proper and improper ritual activity, returning ancestral spirits, the sanctity of tradition, people "painting up" to resemble spirits, and so on. The European and the Aborigine were not so different, theologically, as the missionaries had led them to believe. And why on earth was I trying to find out from them things which I already knew?

Time passed and about three months later I received a message from the mission superintendant that he wished to see me—urgently. When I arrived in his office, he greeted me abruptly and we sat there in uneasy silence for a while, as he tried to find the appropriate words to introduce the subject he wanted to discuss. Suddenly, out of nowhere, he blurted,

"You are keeping a number of women in the village and you worship vegetables."

My mind went numb and it took me a few moments to recover my senses. What in heaven's name did he mean? Then I started to laugh, which only made things worse.

"Oh, the wives," I said, "is that what you've heard?"

"Yes," he replied, "the men say you have a number of wives in the (Aboriginal) camp."

"That's perfectly true," I answered, and proceeded to explain that since I had been assigned a clan by the Aborigines I therefore called people in that clan 'brothers and sisters.' It also meant there was another clan whose members I had to call 'wife and wife's brother.' My own wife, I explained, had been assigned to that clan. The superintendant nodded in agreement but did not seem altogether convinced. There was still the vegetable worship. This had me stumped until I recalled the episode in the tent. The Halloween story must have circulated through the entire village until it finally reached the superintendant as a statement of my own religious beliefs. I explained all this to him, but he was not amused; after all, I did not attend Church and was providing information about the White Man's religion which did not coincide with the official version, which to this point was the only information the local people had to go on. Although we parted on uneasy terms he was, I think, convinced at least that I was not a philanderer.

Many other similar events occurred during the course of my fieldwork—some of them humorous, others more serious: I had responded with anger when I discovered, from a local official, that the Administration and mission had information on my background and family which had been obtained, he said, from an RCMP file, compiled for the Australian intelligence service. This was done as a matter of routine on people working in "sensitive areas." I had also refused to deal with Federal agents after the government had "bought into" my study through the supervising agency in order to have access to me and my research.

There were other things that made me suspect even from the Aboriginal point of view. With my permit up for renewal every few months, there was the pressure of a constant deadline—much as I had experienced in the newspaper business—which meant getting as much work done in as short a time as possible for fear I would not be there the next week. But unfortunately, my informants were not always as eager to work as I was. Then there was the time I got annoyed and later angry with the ritual leaders for telling me every week that "this will be the weekend when the circumcision ceremony will be held." The one weekend I was away was the weekend it was held.

These were hardly subversive activities—the flag episode, the story swapping, just being there, and the overwork—but they were sufficiently outside the normal pattern of things in the context of the day-to-day life of the community that they added up to a constant irritation. And perhaps an irritation a week is equivalent to one act of subversion. But, if you, as an anthropologist, are doing your job properly, trying to keep a foot in two societies and cultures, such things are bound to happen.

One of the ways the people you interact with, on both sides, have of dealing with this is to draw you more fully into their own society—forcing you to behave like a normal person, subject to the same constraints as they are. In the event this happens and you become a functioning member of the native or the colonial society, your work as an anthropologist ceases. In the first case, you lose your detachment and research interest as well as your ability to move through a cross-section of the whole society; in the second case, you lose the trust of your informants and your ability to move as a relatively unacting observer through the day-to-day life of the community. But by the very nature of your work you are drawn more to the native side than to the administrative side and, insofar as you are drawn in on your own terms, your alliance with the indigenes is an uneasy one. Having experienced you once, it may simply be more convenient for everyone if you were not experienced again—at least not as a long-term resident doing the same kind of work. "Subversion," it seems, is built into the nature of the enquiry.

2. Understanding the Encounter

ROGER McDONNELL
University of Toronto

Anthropologists have the curious custom of contrasting an "armchair" to a "field" when describing their two main types of work. The first is suggestive of a quiet study and the unharried, regulated ambience of a university college. It also carries with it the pejorative connotation of naive judgements and a stay-at-home parochialism. The "field" conversely is understood as an unregulated and somewhat untamed situation. It is known by its lack of patterned familiarity and appreciated for its shock value as well as its capacity to seriously jumble familiar ways of thinking and place in doubt ideas about what it means to be human.

To a very large extent this contrast between "armchair" and "field" is more folklore than fact. As often as not these days, the university setting is far more unsettling than many field situations. In addition, an increasing number of tidy, problem oriented monographs do not provide strong evidence that "field work" necessarily challenges prior judgments to any significant degree. Still "field work" continues to carry on extraordinary importance for many anthropologists and so I will briefly address its understood promise.

It can be a salutary exercise to view an ethnographic film, say the second reel of *Dead Birds,* without the sound. In some respects the experience approximates what happens to the anthropologist entering the field or indeed any person exposed to a culture other than their own. A sense of distance and incoherence is achieved and, in terms of this estrangment, a people may appear bizarre and their activities take on a certain intransitive quality. Events do not unfold according to expectations, familiar sentiments are displayed in unfamiliar settings, it becomes difficult to infer purpose, and there is no obvious indication of shared assumptions, values and understanding. In short, like the viewer of the silent film, the anthropologist lacks a ready script which ties events together and informs an experience of them. Detachment in such circumstances is not a matter of discipline or training; it occurs necessarily and frequently results in a period of disorientation in which the fieldworker simply does not know what is going on. He is overwhelmed with a jumble of partly intelligible detail which challenges all those highly developed senses which characterize him as a person from a specific culture. His sense of fun and propriety, his sense of dignity, his sense of pity, of shrewdness, of beauty, of etiquette, and so on may all receive a frontal assault during fieldwork.

It is at this point, when the senses are "battered," that a detachment of a special kind is required. But it is not a detachment from the object of investigation; it is a detachment from the subject (i.e., the anthropologist from himself) that must be attempted, and it is this which distinguishes the "fieldworker" from the tourist. In various respects this is a daunting and somewhat contradictory task for which there is no entirely satisfactory solution.

Work in most field situations requires a certain cultural relativism and the anthropologist is compelled to grant an authority and privileged position to alternate ways of experiencing the world. What the anthropologist must place in parentheses, so to speak, are those disconcerting prejudices one discovers in oneself during the course of fieldwork. This involves going beyond those spontaneous and, to some extent, inescapable moments when one might be prompted to characterize the appearance or activity of a people to be "undignified" or "noble," "relaxed" or "lazy," and so on. The task is not to judge events in familiar terms but to research how those same events are recognized as a kind of experience by the participants in the field.

The point here is straightforward enough. It is futile to pick up a book in German, try to read it as if it were in English and then conclude that it is badly written. This sounds silly, but it is exactly the sort of thing many people do when confronted with a cultural milieu they find strange. The anthropologist, by contrast, must achieve the equivalent of determining the meanings of the words and discovering the rules of grammatical construction. Throughout, however, one is always subject to the dangers of over-determining the character of what is observed. This is no more evident than in the investigation of social relationship and it will be instructive to review briefly a few of the considerations involved by examining the following sequence of behaviour.

Individual A enters a given room on Thursday evening at 7:00 P.M. In the room are ten other individuals, B, C, D, etc., all of whom are seated around a large table. A walks to one end of the table and turns and faces the others, s/he then speaks for about thirty minutes. During this period some of the others take notes and all appear to listen to what A is saying. After speaking, A sits down. The others then ask A questions and during this period, lasting about an hour, A occasionally gets up and writes or draws a diagram on a blackboard. At 8:30 P.M. everyone leaves the room.

Now this sequence may seem familiar and you may be half thinking you recognize a form to the interaction. The ethnographic impulse is to always doubt the relevance of such spontaneous moments of recognition since there is very little about any behavioural sequence that necessarily indicates the nature of relationship. Consider the following possibilities: Individual A is a "teacher" and all the others are "students." It is assumed by all participants that A has the initiative in the interchange; A can pass students or fail them, etc.

Conversely, B, C, D etc. are a group of executives who have hired A as a consultant. In this case A, as employee, does not have the initiative and if the Thursday evening advice proves to be poor, s/he can be fired.

One can, of course, create additional scenarios to fit the sequence as described. The point, however, is fundamental; the relationship, in this case between A and the others, can be radically different without any change in the observed sequence behaviour. A corollary of this is that the behaviour can vary without there being a necessary change in relationship. The fieldworker's task is to determine the nature of the relationship and this cannot be known without further information. Clearly, it makes a great difference whether the room is thought of as a "boardroom" or a "classroom," whether the difference between A and the others is understood as "teacher"/"student," or "employee"/"employer," and so on. In a typical "field" situation such necessary information is usually unstated.

In addition to what is unstated, there may be much inscribed within a situation which is explicit but intelligible only from the vantage of the participants; gestures, differences of dress, tones of voice, etc. may all be indicative and relevant to a proper understanding. In a substantially novel cultural milieu, however, the ethnographic problem is to determine what to include in a description of events, so that, later, inquiries about specific aspects can be made. There are, in principle, no grounds for excluding anything and for this reason, at least during the early stages of work, the anthropologist's notebooks are typically crammed with details the importance or unimportance of which may not be appreciated until long after.

The usual example given by those commenting on fieldwork involves events that are dramatically odd. My suggestion concerning the ethnographic film is in this vein. The reason I have used a more or less recognizable example above is to introduce an increasingly important feature of fieldwork in Canada and, in varying degrees, many other parts of the world. This involves the fact that very frequently the immediate shock value of being plunged into an utterly strange cultural situation no longer occurs. It is not a matter, therefore, of the fieldworker recognizing or thinking he recognizes rough similarities to things with which s/he is familiar, rather it is a question of recognizing events, activities, and objects in the field that are in certain respects, identical to that which s/he knows from his/her native milieu. Currency, forms of wage employment, types of clothing, forms of recreation may all be identical in many important ways. It is this identity, however, that can camouflage profound cultural differences and in this regard I would like to describe an event from my own field experience with a group of Athapaskan Indians in the Yukon. It involves a "poker game."

I had been in the field only a short time and was still a long way from getting my bearings. It was mid-winter and the warmest it had been for three weeks was −53°C. There was no employment in the

29

small community and because of the cold no one was pursuing the customary activity of winter trapping. During this period many men had taken to playing cards. Crib was the most frequently played game and, with much tobacco and endless cups of tea, a series, beginning at 9:00 P.M., would often continue until 5:00 A.M. Most games involved two to four men and were played in various cabins throughout the village.

One evening, a few hours after a crib session had begun, a young man entered the cabin I was visiting to announce that a poker game had begun in one of the other cabins. The news was greeted with enthusiasm and after finishing the game in hand we all walked over— some, like myself, simply to observe and others, it turned out, to participate rather seriously.

When we arrived there were about twenty people in the main room of the cabin. The players were kneeling around a blanket spread in the centre of the floor. The stakes were wooden matches and the cards were dealt onto the blanket. During the next few hours some players left the game and others joined. At any one time there were only five to six participants.

Among those who joined the game was one of my companions from earlier in the evening. Having no matches with which to enter he borrowed some from myself and others. During his first half-hour of play he accumulated a large pile of matches. During the ensuing hour, however, his winnings gradually dwindled until eventually he had not enough to follow through on a bet on the hand he was currently holding. He then asked the other players if it would be permissible to bet with some .22 rifle shells he had found in his pocket. All agreed to this and they settled on how many matches each rifle shell was worth.

This translation of matches into something else was, it turned out, but the first step of many. My friend soon lost the shells he had found in his pocket and sent someone off to get more betting supplies. During the course of a long night the number of players gradually decreased until it became a contest between two players; the one who had sent for more supplies and an older man who had recently returned from his trap line. Those who dropped out stayed to watch although the game went on until 8:00 A.M. It was, for the younger man, a complete debacle. In the course of the night he lost successively a case of .22 shells, all his large rifle shells, his .22 rifle, his large rifle, his traps, his sleeping bag, his tent, his snowshoes, his toboggan, his dog harness, and finally his dog team. With the exception of what he had on he lost all his material possessions.

Along with everyone else I was mightily impressed with the sustained tension surrounding the game as it developed. I was to discover, however, that I was being impressed in terms of considerations that were not of primary significance to the others present. What I saw happening was a man gambling with all he had—and losing all he had. Why the loss of material goods should strike me as so significant is doubtless a commentary on myself at the time and also on the culture of which I am a product. What everyone else knew was that the winner of the poker game was also the "uncle" of the younger man. The significance of this was apparent as soon as the weather warmed and the younger asked the older for material assistance in order to go trapping. This was immediately granted and the "uncle" gave the "nephew" everything from rifle shells to a dog team i.e. everything that had been won in the poker game. In other words, regarding material goods, the younger man had an ace-in-the-hole which he could not gamble away. This was his relationship to the older man outside the context of the poker game. It was this relationship that precluded any possibility of becoming totally alienated from the possessions he had lost.

This knowledge utterly defused my understanding of the "poker game." The unmistakable dramatic tension that had grown as events unfolded was now a problem. If it was not material that was being gambled, what in fact had been at stake? What had kept the contestants going for ten hours and, just as important, what had kept the others watching them? The answers to these questions, which we cannot begin to explore now, involve a distinctly non-Western view of what it is and means to be human. This took me a long while to appreciate. I simply introduce the matter here in order to point to the "field" rather than myself for an understanding of what, in this specific ethnographic context, I had recognized as a "poker game." If partly accurate, such spontaneous recognition was also impossibly skewed.

It can be seen, I hope, that a winnowing process occurs during which the anthropologist narrows the field as s/he learns its dimensions as viewed by others. This process is, in turn, subordinate to reductions that occur before field work begins. On the one hand, there are the barely disguised institutional biases of licensing and funding agencies. The story Turner tells of government agencies screening for a type of research and researcher is but one example of the sort thing involved. The field is, so to speak, diminished from the outside and in a manner extraneous to the culture and society to be studied. On the other hand, there is the "trained" anthropologist who is tutored in those concerns that poise him or her to appreciate the potential significance of certain matters and to pursue lines of inquiry that are intelligible, as such, within the tradition of the discipline. Without necessarily preconceiving the field situation, the tutored anthropologist is, therefore, very much predisposed. For example, if anyone should claim that humans place a high value on those things that are most useful to them we have, as Malinowski observed, a certain kind of problem "foreshadowed." A central promise and favoured rationale for fieldwork is that it provides the opportunity to find counter-evidence to such a claim, just as the claim is the means of recognizing the significance of such evidence should it be discovered in a specific field situation.

If partly true, this rather classical account of the relationship between theory and research is also impossibly narrow. Among other things, it does not emphasize that during fieldwork the anthropologist never observes what finally concerns him the most. What people say and do is only half the story and indeed it is no story at all to the anthropologist if he cannot describe order in these sayings and doings. It is this order, usually marked off by such notions as organization, structure, and system that is not subject to direct observation. Order (and the specific character and source of disorder) can only be appreciated after the event for the obvious reason that the culture and society of any people is never in place at any one time.

In a very real sense, therefore, the totality conceived of as a "social structure," "culture system," etc. is not to be found in the field. To some anthropologists this fact is a central concern for it prompts reflection on the source of those comprehensive concepts which bring order to field data. Does, for instance, a recognition of certain institutional domains promote in analysis a certain idea of man? Conversely, does a certain idea of man prompt the imposition of an institutional order which is indifferent to the order recognized and differentiated by the culture and society investigated? Such questions, however, take us beyond fieldwork. They engage a hesitation regarding how to emphasize, connect, and interrelate field data in a written document. One is back in the armchair—a potential author deciding on a readership. As Smith insists, the choice involves moral and aesthetic alternatives.

3. Writing about it afterwards

GAVIN A. SMITH
University of Toronto

BETWEEN ENGAGEMENTS

It was the fourth day here. The tension inside was uncoiling. I was worried about the vacuum it would leave. I was unsure.

One stage of fieldwork was over. The last weeks had been desperate ones: would I get those last few things I needed? What was that gigantic set of questions I had completely forgotten to ask? What had happened to the moment, the set of moments, the "jump" I had been waiting for?

The mountains I came from lay back over there. This was the pause I needed and did not want. A country house loaned. A pile of disorganized and fragmented notes. The company of bright, crisp people. Certain reckonings. The tension uncoiling like a fist. Or a snake.

The gardener, Pardo, was cleaning out the swimming pool. He stood in the empty, sloping pit pushing a broom up the stained walls. His arms were covered in burns from the chloride. Paulina, the woman he lived with, was walking towards the front door of the house. A pause. Walking towards me. She has something in her arms. A child? She stands quite far off. Does she want to talk to me? Is she looking at me? Surely not. Behind me? She coughs.

I say, "Buenos dias, Senora Pardo. Que tal?"

"There's no problem, Senor," she says, "It's just the child, Senor."

Is the child sick, I ask. Well perhaps just a little sick, yes, she says. I get up and come over to you, Luisa. What are you? A child? A shrunken mummy from a Nazca grave site? A newborn infant? This is the house of a rich man. One of the richest of them. What are you? How do you come to be here on this grass lawn, with the swimming pool there, just so. And over there the stables. And here the wrought-iron garden table with the parasol. Was this not to be the pause? Is not the filthy city down there?

Little Luisa. So little. Just twelve-and-a-half pounds and two-and-a-half years old for all that. Two hospitals we took you to simply refused to waste their time. At the Anglo American Clinic there happened to be two students visiting from Johns Hopkins University who were here to look at chronic forms of malnutrition. You were interesting. They took you in. We were asked to sign papers showing that we would be responsible for you (your bills?). We mentioned the name of our host. He was a Governor of the hospital so why didn't we call him? We did: it was absurd and embarrassing to take the child to such a hospital. Paulina has five other children; this one will either die after costly treatment, or survive and be mentally deficient. He wished that we had consulted him first.

We returned to the house. Paulina had left the children in the care of another employee of our host. When we arrive she goes off to her own house. I talk to Paulina about where she gets food from. I hope I do not understand what all this is about. I hope that there is a terribly clever and convoluted explanation of how I can be confronted with a child suffering from extended third degree malnutrition living in the garden of the president of IBM, Peru. I am also thinking about how much money I have left for moving into a rooming house down in the city. The neighbour returns. She has another baby in her arms. This I cannot believe. She uncovers the child, but before I can look at his face, she passes the bundle of rags into my arms. Paulina says, this one is no problem, senor, this one is dead. The other woman says, we must bury him. Yes, I say, trying to keep within the ordered logic of events. But we must report it, says the old lady. To whom? To the Guardia Civil.

The police. The old pick-up truck with the ragged bundle on the boards in the back. The morgue. The morticians handing out their business cards. The second phone call with the rich man ("I am to pay for a funeral now? What are you doing out there at my house?"). I remember very well that it was a pay phone.

Luisa was in a tent at the clinic. Paulina was in her shack at the end of a rich man's garden. Pardo had finished the pool and the water was running back in. Our host was talking this scandal over with his children at the town house. I was standing at the counter of a shanty-town stall drinking a glass of warm Cristal beer. This was where the second piece of fieldwork would begin. More tricky than the first part. How to bound it, make a unit for study? Then there would be the question of economic data. The tension began to recoil into a tight fist inside again . . .

THE POST-FIELDWORK EXPERIENCE

The nature of the crisis you face after the experience of fieldwork has a lot to do with why you chose to go into anthropology in the first place. This will vary from one person to another and even within one person a multitude of inconsistent, incomplete sentiments coexist. Like most anthropologists, I shall make the recognition of such diversity an excuse for talking only of the particular, namely myself. What follows is personal. But inasmuch as it is a communication, it stretches that intimate experience in an attempt to touch some common ground we share, and thereby change it: make it a little unfamiliar. It is the unfamiliar that leads to reflection.

My post-fieldwork crisis went through three phases: placing my actions in the context of the whole issue of "development-underdevelopment"; then placing my actions into the context of my own society to which I had returned; and finally, as time went by, evolving a more total kind of personal praxis. I hope that what I mean by this "personal praxis" will become clear by the end of this discussion. To some extent, I suppose that the sequence of the first two phases have now become conflated into the third and cannot therefore be reproduced quite as I felt them. In fact, I think that they both come down in the end to this final issue of personal praxis, but since many will regard a discussion of this final issue (to which the bulk of this essay is devoted) more ethereal than practical, I shall say something about the first two preoccupations in order to show why this is not the case.

In 1955 Claude Lévi-Strauss wrote the following passage:

> *If anthropology cannot take a detached view of our civilization, or declare itself not responsible for that civilization's evils, it is because its very existence is unintelligible unless we regard it as an attempt to redeem it (1969: 388).*

If you have acquired any special knowledge through your study and through your exposure to the Other, how are you to use it? If, for example, you believe that it should be used in some way for the benefit of the people with whom you have lived, how are you to operationalize that belief? If you believe that such a desire is simply a middle-class hang-up and that your actions need not therefore be directed to such ends, then what ends should they lead towards? If you believe that the first endeavour leads to a certain kind of practical anthropology, while the second leads to the advancement of anthropology as a science, then insofar as both come down to the advancement of your own career in the one or the other, then how are you going to set about that particular excercise?

The point of raising these questions in such a cynical way is to demonstrate that, whatever your circumstances, you are faced with a dilemma.

Some anthropologists have been fortunate enough to be able to turn their desire to be useful to their own informants into a practical exercise. A number of Canadian anthropologists working in Canada, for example, have recently put what skills they have at the disposal of native groups confronted by an avaricious capitalist state[1]. What is a less happy reflection is that their task is made the more necessary by the fact that there are other anthropologists who have chosen to work on behalf of elements of that expansionist capitalist state so as to explain the natives out of existence, to quite literally explain them away.

Here I shall pay no serious attention to this second type of "committed anthropologist." Personally I regard them as more or less skilled musicians. It is the oil companies and the various branches of the state apparatus who pay the piper and hence call the tune.

But while, for these second kind of consultants, the old question of the sixties, "Who are you working for?" is clearly answerable, it is nevertheless still a hard question for those who work on behalf of the people whose history and social relations they have been studying. For it is likely that, precisely through that study, it will be revealed that there are many currents and interest groups within "native groups" which can be served. While for political reasons it is important to assert that one is "working for the *huasicanchinos*" (for example), it would be blindness not to recognize that one is in fact only working for those *huasicanchinos* who have chosen to employ one's services.

A second difficulty has to do with your goals as a resource-person for the people. I am assuming here that you are not yourself a member of the group and I am further assuming that you have abandoned that form of arrogance which supposes that you can make policy decisions in a struggle from which you are definitionally excluded. The question still arises: what is your goal? Anthropologists have traditionally focused attention on small-scale community studies. Committed anthropologists brought up in this tradition have tended to assume that changes emerge externally and then they have supposed that choices can be made between one external change and another. This conceptualization, combined with excessive amounts of developmentalist arrogance, is what characterized the Cornell "Vicos Project" in Peru (Holmberg, 1959), which should remain a cautionary lesson to all outsider-anthropologists.

Nevertheless, I do not mean to criticize the vital work being done by such anthropologists as Asch, Brody, and Feit, who are resolving this issue by placing ethnography into the framework of a more broad political economy. Here I wish only to raise the question that even for those fortunate enough to find practical outlets for their skills, the dilemma remains with respect to focus and goals.

And the final question for this kind of committed anthropologist must be: "What precisely is my function?" The answer will vary according to the situation in which he or she is involved, but I want to suggest here that whatever its specifics may be, it will eventually have much to do with an ability *to communicate experience,* so that his or her own study goes beyond the mere extension of personal knowledge.

This same factor of communication is present for those who do not actually work with the groups of people about which they have a special knowledge; for them too, a personal praxis must also be found. One of the first things that struck me on returning from fieldwork was that the mechanisms which, on a world scale, created discrepancies between the West and the Third World, also acted to create and accentuate discrepancies within the capitalist nations themselves. Similar observations have led some anthropologists to take a particular perspective referred to as "studying up," i.e., using the skills of ethnography not to study the exploited, but to expose the mechanisms of the exploiters.

I have mentioned these two issues here, not with a view to tackling them exhaustively. They represent the first two phases of the crisis I

went through after my fieldwork. I have not overcome them or sur-
passed them. They lead me to present to you what is for me a most
personal and unresolvable dilemma which I wish to present as the
concluding part of this paper.

As a "committed anthropologist" (which expression I take with
many reservations) performing any or all of the above-mentioned
roles, or even merely teaching, how do you extend an experience, a
body of knowledge, or a theoretico-practical viewpoint beyond your
own self-edification? In my view, unless you can come to grips with
this question (by which I do not necessarily mean "answer" it) you
cannot face squarely what you are doing, and most specifically you
cannot confront properly the matter of how you set about writing
down anything for somebody else to read. What do you expect will
happen to them when they read it? And if this is of no concern to you,
why—beyond the structures of your own university career—do you
write at all? Unfortunately we have gone well beyond that blessed age
when mere exposure to "truth" was to have the desired effect. What
the "freedom of the press" has actually revealed is that no amount of
muckraking will change the average citizen's most cherished desire
which is, as one cynic once put it, "to be sure his toothbrush is in the
right place when he gets up in the morning."[2]

In light of this fact, the undying cynicism of the fourth estate—and
of anthropologists too, I suppose—becomes manifest. It was what,
back in 1941, drove James Agee beyond despair:

> *It seems to me curious, not to say obscene and thoroughly terrify-*
> *ing, that it could occur to an association of human beings . . . to*
> *pry intimately into the lives of an undefended and appallingly*
> *damaged group of human beings . . . for the purpose of parading*
> *the nakedness, disadvantage and humiliation of these lives before*
> *another group of human beings, in the name of science, of 'honest*
> *journalism' (whatever that paradox may mean), of humanity, of*
> *social fearlessness, for money, and for a reputation for crusading*
> *and for unbias which, when skillfully enough qualified, is ex-*
> *changeable at any bank for money . . . (1966: 7).*

I do not wish to condemn wholesale the project of writing as an element in what in the end I believe to be a political praxis. To the contrary, my argument remains that in nine cases out of ten, it is verbal
communication that is most immediately at the disposal of any of the
potential actors I have so far discussed—indeed that any avowal to
the contrary is merely self-delusion. But, this being the case, anthropologists, of whom I happen to be one, (and I have assured you that
this is a personal catechism) should examine very thoroughly the relationship between the content of what they are trying to transmit
and the style they use for its transmission.

I began this article with an account of a particular incident I experienced while I was on a fieldwork trip. In the remainder of this article I
would like that account to remain in the reader's mind while I try to

come to grips with how best I can communicate experience as part of the problematic of social anthropology. But I should make clear that I believe that the issue I face is not dissimilar to that faced by anybody whose task it is to communicate in order to fulfill a certain purpose: be it to provide historical research for an exploited people for them to use as they wish, or as a witness giving evidence to a Royal Commission, or sitting at a typewriter trying to write a book, or as a report to the Party's local subcommittee. Finally, insofar as, come the revolution, most practising anthropologists happen also to be teachers, it pertains especially, I suppose, to teaching.

THE ELEPHANT AND THE BOOKSELLER[3]

I find that the greatest challenge which I face when trying to reproduce the way I think now about my experience of a certain social world of some years back, is the challenge of how to communicate: the form of exposition.

There are various ways in which this is usually done and I will suggest two as illustrative of my problem: the travel memoir, and the ethnographic monograph. The one takes the reader along the route travelled by the author, with the occasional pauses for reflection and possible reminiscence; the other also presents the way that the author thinks about his experience, but does so in a manner which almost removes the author from the presence of the reader and thereby gives an "objective" impression of what is being written.

Since I have returned from the field I have read many scholarly articles about matters which have given me new insights into my experience, but these insights have not been so conclusive that they have succeeded in rendering my past experience coldly objective. On the other hand, because the confrontation of my past experience with what I have since read—about underdevelopment, about the structure of capitalist cities and so on—has strongly influenced the way I now think, I am unhappy with the personal style of a travel memoir. Memoirs seem to attend to a close reproduction of experience, while ethnographic monographs seem to have as their referent some broader "scientific" interpretation, and it seems to me difficult to bring these two "styles" together.

And yet the problem I face here, as an anthropologist "writing up" my fieldwork, is only a heightened form of the confrontation between experience and interpretation which we all face when we place our own experience—whether it be personal experience or the experience of, say the television news—alongside the volumes of scientific interpretive literature available to us in libraries as well as airport bookstands. So I do not think that the specific problem that I face here is confined to my role as a professional anthropologist. It is a problem which faces anybody who is trying to pick the right form of communication for, on the one hand, the reproduction of experience and, on the other, the expression of one's own interpretation of that experience, aided by one's own stock of knowledge (for the scholar: his theoretical training).

The problem is that, although the differing styles of the memoir and the monograph reflect the writers' emphases, in the first case on "subjective experiences," and in the second case on "objective interpretation," the two are in fact inseparable. What we find in one or other of these books is largely the result of a kind of professional convenience and division of labour. The memoir-writer sees his experience as problematic and attends to it through critical introspection, while paying little overt heed to his own "theoretical" position. The monograph-writer minimizes his own personal discomforts in the field; his book instead represents a rapid journey back from this experience, through the blinding jungle of "the established literature."

Let me try to go back for a moment, to the other side of that jungle; in fact to the other side of the experience of Luisa. If I look at the diary I wrote as I worked my passage out to Peru from Liverpool, I find that I was sufficiently aware of the ostrich-like nature of my life, buried in the sand of Western society, to believe that what was to come would be a shock to my emotional system. I seem to have hoped that this shock would have a meaningfulness beyond the anticipation of my meagre reasoning:

> No change, like this one is going to be, ends up being what you anticipate. The movement from the this to the that comes when you least expect it. Half our oppositions are false—created by ourselves to make us feel that we are making leaps. Such leaps are no test: merely self-indulgence.

Actually I find this embarrassingly naive. I can claim no spiritual or theoretical *afflatus*. But, this being so, my experience and my bookish knowledge remain separate and incomplete. And I believe that it is this incompleteness which lies at the heart of both artistic and scientific communication.

Social anthropologists are generally at pains to establish their credentials as scientists rather than artists, of course. Where anthropologists, as authors, have lowered the mask of their own scientism to reveal the personalities which lie behind, they have usually done so in the introduction to their monographs. They then relapse into that idiom of scientific expression which expressly removes the "experimenter-observer" from the reader's attention. Reader and writer alike are able thereby to collude in placing personal reflections behind them once the book "really begins." When problems are to be faced and thought over, this is to be done "within the bounds of the book," or at least within the bounds of the theoretical issues to which the author claims relevance. This after all is what good science is all about (Kuhn, 1970).

Or is it? Victor Turner, for one, seems to feel differently:

> Although we take theories into the field with us, these become relevant only if and when they illuminate social reality. Moreover,

> *we tend to find very frequently that it is not a theorist's whole
> system which so illuminates, but his scattered ideas, his flashes of
> insight taken out of systematic context and applied to scattered
> data (1975:23).*

He seems to be suggesting that "flashes of insight" are just as important for the anthropologist's understanding of society, as his more
consciously-recognized, structured theories. This comes as no great
surprise to the person who had done fieldwork, despite the fact that
later, as author, he may do much to obscure this "unscientific" form
of interpretation. But if the anthropologist-as-ethnographer is prepared to acknowledge this important role of "flashes of insight" for
himself why, when he becomes anthropologist-as-writer, is he not
prepared to grant the same process to the reader? Since the reading of
the monograph is, for the reader, a kind of confrontation with experience, why should not the style of writing in that monograph specifically attend to this fact? In short, what are we to make of a style of
communication which attempts to remove the reader from the direct
experience of participation by using a scientific idiom which presents
data as only theoretically problematic (i.e., to be solved "within the
book"), while remaining pragmatically *ex post facto*? By this last expression I mean that the work of interpretation is supposedly completed within the book and by the author, rather than beyond the
book and, at least partly, by the reader.

According to the principles of empiricist science, of course, this is
precisely what *scientific* communication should do. The laboratory experience must be perfectly objectified. But it does not follow that a
science concerning itself with social experience can, or should, follow
this precedent. Insofar as social science is a reflection of awareness,
the social science monograph is, for the reader, just one looking glass
in a hall of mirrors.

On a train from Cambridge, England, to London, a somewhat fan-
ciful sociologist friend of mine once remarked to Edward Shils that
the best work of sociology that had ever been written was *Les Re-
cherches du Temps Perdu* by Proust.[4] It might be interesting to compare
the different forms of communication chosen by Proust and Shils.
The one proceeds by way of metonymy in order to involve the reader
in the experience of reading;[5] the other appears to proceed in a common-sense sequential line of cause and effect, breaking things down
into their component parts. If "social structures are just as real as individual organism" (Radcliffe-Brown 1940), so they can be laid out in
this way.

The difference between the two lies in the fact that Proust's is an essentially *artistic* poetic device, which acts to involve the reader in the
"work" of reading. As a result, the reader is drawn into the book and
forced to reflect, be provoked, guess, feel, and so on. In Victor
Turner's terms, what Proust is doing is creating a *liminal state* for us
while we are reading (cf. Turner 1969; 80ff). The whole exercise of
Proust's *Memoirs* is one of *liminality*—by Proust and for the reader.[6]

The devices used by Shils and many other social scientists are, by contrast, attempts to be as nearly scientific as possible. To do so, however, they are no less constrained by their poetic devices than Proust (especially metaphor, simile, and analogy).

Most of us who have taken one or two social science courses are quite familiar with the poetic devices of scientific expression found in works of social science, but we can become far more aware of them by contrasting the *scientific* style I have described above with the project of *art*:

> *Habitualization devours objects, clothes, furniture, one's wife, and the fear of war . . . Art exists to help us recover the sensation of life; it exists to make us feel things, to make the stone* stony *. . . The technique of art is to make things 'unfamiliar,' to make forms obscure, so as to increase the difficulty and the duration of perception. The act of perception in art is an end in itself and must be prolonged (Victor Shklovsky quoted in Scholes 1974: 83-84).*

The implication of this statement is that we, the actors in society, are often so numbed by habit that we see without really perceiving. It requires a certain squint or discordance to make us reflect and become momentarily clear-sighted observers of our own selves in the world. Artistic devices serve to provoke in the reader such reflection, making he or she (not the writer) temporarily a philosopher. It is this which leads some artists to fetishize their own art in the expression, "My art is greater than I am," in the sense that the work appears to be beyond the artist's direct control, once completed.

For Shklovsky then, art is less ambitious than science: it seeks only to brush the fur the wrong way occasionally, not to skin the cat.

For Lukacs, the artistic project is somewhat greater than this, because for him our daily experiences do not merely numb us: they actually deceive us into thinking the opposite of what is true. As we live life from day to day, making common-sense assessments and decisions, the pattern of social relations which we see on the surface is very different from—and often quite the opposite of—the deeper, concealed, essential rationality of our social relations (Marx, 1970: 80 and *passim*). Lukacs therefore strongly criticized those writers who attempted to reproduce the ordinary, common senseness of daily life. Placing the commonplace in the foreground, he said, prevents the author from,

> *drawing the deeper objective and subjective social definitions out of people and situations [because] the social definitions that are at all perceptible in the commonplace necessarily lie upon the immediately perceptible surface (1972: 107).*

The question I ask therefore is this: to what extent is this exposure to strangeness amidst the ordinary, different from the project of the social anthropologist writing about the social world of "the Other," in such a way that it becomes real in some way to "the We" for whom he is writing? Such a person surely faces the same dilemma: shining a light on the commonplace of other peoples, so as to uncover the extraordinariness of our own commonplace (as well as the commonplaceness of their exoticism). What difference is there between the underlying assumptions about social experience held by Shklovsky and Lukacs, and that of Lévi-Strauss, when he writes,

> *Understanding consists in the reduction of one kind of reality to another; that true reality is never the most obvious of realities, and that its nature is already apparent in the care which it takes to evade our detection (1969:61).*

And, if this is the case, what does it imply for the *content* of what the anthropological author wishes to say, the *purpose* he has for saying it, and the *form* he uses for communicating with others? It is obvious that the effect on the reader of particular poetic devices is very significant in contributing to what s/he "receives" from a particular reading, and yet social scientists—even those who purport to study culture as communication—seem to be generally unaware or uninterested in this relationship. It is where the closure of convenience takes place.

To return to the issues which I raised at the beginning of this section of the Chapter, I find this to be the most pressing crisis of personal praxis which I face: whatever I do, I am faced with the question of how to communicate. So, in my view, while all of the foregoing may be treated to a dismissive and sophisticated chuckle by the scholar-academicians of social science, the issue cannot be so easily eliminated by those who claim to use their anthropology—or any particular skill, knowledge or experience, for that matter—to change, as well as understand the world. For them the issue of communication, the question of the degree to which they are prepared to involve the reader in a particular "reading," is a significant one. It requires at least as much reflection as the analysis of two different kinship systems, or two different ways of categorizing firewood. Hitting the target squarely and effectively is as important for the intellectual as the revolutionary guerrilla fighter, if the role of intellectuals is to have any significant praxis at all.

NOTES

1. *See Asch's article in the final section of this book.*
2. *The cynic in question was Pierre Elliot Trudeau, in a television interview in the early seventies.*
3. *The subheading refers to the title of a poem by the early eighteenth century poet and playwright John Gay, of which the following is an excerpt:*

    The man who with undaunted toils,
    Sails unknown seas to unknown soils,
    With various wonders feasts his sight:
    What stranger wonders does he write!
    We read, and in description view
    Creatures which Adam never knew;

> For, when we risk no contradiction,
> It prompts the tongue to deal in fiction.

4. *Victor Turner, for his part, pays his respects to the anthropology of Jean-Paul Sartre, who tried to delve within himself to examine the crisis of being Man. He then asks of the existentialists precisely the question I now ask of the social anthropologists: "One might ask who is the audience of these prolific if alienated profits of uncommunication?" (1975: 55-56).*

5. *That is, stepping from one idea or phenomenon to another, the connections between which are tenuously made clear to the reader.*

6. *I am reluctant to give any precise definition for* liminality. *The reader is referred to Turner 1969, Chap. 3; 1975 Chap. 6., from which I select the following:*

> "the attributes of liminality or of liminal *personae* ('threshold people') are necessarily ambiguous, since this condition and these persons elude or slip through the network of classifications that normally locate states and conditions in cultural space" (1969; 81).

> "I see liminality as a phase in social life in which this confrontation between 'activity which has no structure' and its 'structured results' (Sartre 1969: 57-59) produces men in their highest pitch of self-consciousness" (1975:255).

BIBLIOGRAPHY

Agee, James & Walker Evans 1966. *Let us now praise famous men.* New York: Ballantyne Books.

Holmberg, Allan 1959. Land Tenure and planned social change: a case from Vicos, Peru. *Human Organization* 18:1.

Kuhn, Thomas S. 1970. *The Structure of scientific revolutions.* Chicago: Phoenix Books.

Lévi-Strauss, Claude 1969. *Tristes Tropiques* Translated from the French by John Russell. New York: Atheneum.

Lévy-Bruhl, Lucien 1966. *How Natives Think.* New York: Washington Square Press.

Lukacs, Georg 1972. The intellectual physiognomy of literary characters in *Radical perspectives in the arts* (ed) Lee Baxandall. Harmondsworth: Penguin.

Marx, Karl 1970. *Capital* Vol. I. Moscow: Progress.

Miner, Horace 1956. Body Ritual Among the Nacirema, *American Anthropologist,* 58; 503-507.

Radcliffe-Brown, R. 1940. On social structure. *Journal of the Royal Anthropological Institute* Vol. 70.

Rose, F.G.G. 1968. *Australia Revisited.* Berlin: Seven Seas Publishers.

Sartre, Jean-Paul 1969. Itinerary of a thought. *New Left Review* Vol. 58.

Scholes, Robert 1974. *Structuralism in literature.* New Haven: Yale University Press.

Turner, D.H. 1972. Nimda Rites of Access, *Anthropological Forum* Vol. 3, no. 2.

Turner, Victor W. 1969. *The ritual process.* Harmondsworth: Penguin

Turner, Victor W. 1975. *Dramas, fields and metaphors.* Ithaca: Cornell University Press.

ADDITIONAL READINGS

Culler, Jonathan 1975. *Structuralist poetics* London: Routledge & Kegan Paul.

Genette, Gerard 1972. *Figures III* Paris: Seuil. (On Proust)

Jongmans, D.G. and P.C.W. Gutkind 1967. *Anthropologists in the field.* Assen: Van Gorcum.

Read, Kenneth 1965. *The High Valley* New York: Charles Scribner.

Shklovsky, Victor 1965. Art as technique in *Russian Formalist criticism* (ed) L. T. Lemon & M. J. Reis. Lincoln: University of Nebraska Press.

Shklovsky, Victor 1973. *Sur la theorie de la prose.* Lausanne: L'Age d'Homme.

Traditional hunting techniques are still followed by many Aboriginal peoples in Australia. In Northern Coastal areas turtles and dugong are harpooned from dugout canoes.

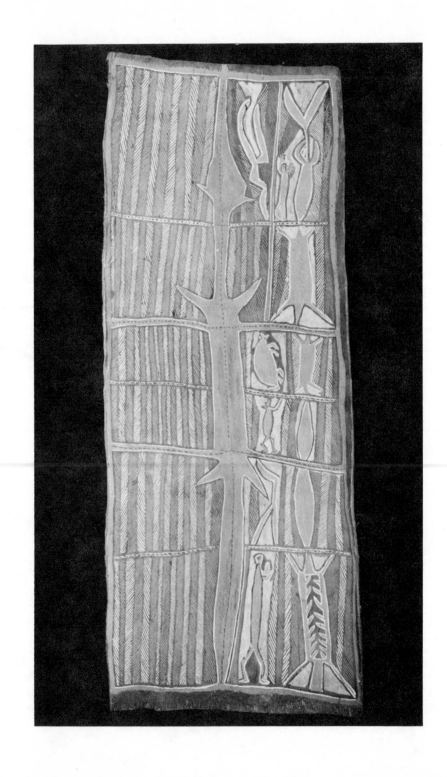

◁*Aboriginal art in Australia depicts the events of supernatural beings of the Dreamtime. In this bark painting from Groote Eylandt, the artist portrays the path followed by the departed spirit on its journey to the land of the dead.*

Ritual actions dramatized the events of the Creation Period in Aboriginal Australia. Still today in many parts of the continent, the totemic ancestors are celebrated during mortuary ceremonies and circumcision rites.▽

Livestock husbandry in Peru is the community's primary occupation. For the shepherds—nearly all women—life in their remote huts is lonely and hard. Spinning is a constant occupation for most women.

In Peru most food for local consumption is processed in the village too. Here are women separating grain from husks, prior to grinding.

The Territorial Liquor Store in Fort Simpson, N.W.T., Canada.

Today in the Yukon and Northwest Territories the hunt is carried on with the aid of rifles, motor boats, and store-bought foods. The social relations of hunting, however, remain very much traditional.

Camps like this one in the Northwest Territory house the small groups of hunters who have dispersed over the band range for the winter season.

Many of the descendants of Aborigines are today fringe dwellers living on the edges of White settlement. They have been forced out of one way of life but not brought into another.

In eastern Arnhem Land Aborigines still celebrate the events of the Creation Period in the ancient manner despite the presence of missions and other White enterprises in their midst.

Rites of Passage mark important changes in an Aborigine's life cycle and are celebrated with all the totemic pomp and circumstance appropriate to such occasions.

Towns on major transportation routes throughout the Peruvian highlands come alive with activity when the people of the surrounding area arrive to market their produce.

Fairs held on religious holidays in highland Peru provide an opportunity for people to come from far and wide to renew old ties, establish new ones and conduct business.

PART II
CONCEPTS AND
PROBLEMS

CHAPTER 2

"KINSHIP"*
An informal, critical guide to some problems[1]

MARTIN G. SILVERMAN
University of British Columbia

INTRODUCTION

One's approach to "kinship" depends very much on one's larger conception of anthropology. To me, one of the tasks of anthropology is to help us understand the interconnections between the events going on around us (including those we participate in), and to help us think through the question of the necessity of these events and their implications. This naturally, then, raises questions about Canada in its internal and global contexts today, as years ago a similar concern raised questions about European society in the minds of many of the forerunners of modern social sciences such as Marx, Maine, Weber, Simmel, and Durkheim. In order to understand how such people drew the distinctions and conclusions they did, one has to understand what was going on in the world around them and their own position in relation to these happenings.

If we are to try to link our own situations in our own times and places with those of these thinkers, one productive approach is this: later nineteenth and early twentieth century theorists were experiencing a group of closely related transforming moments in the increasing dominance of capitalism and in the development of forms of the modern state which were part of that dominance. In Canada we are also experiencing transforming moments in this process, but they

---

* The technical language of kinship studies is a field for critical study in itself, as this paper demonstrates. I have therefore provided the reader with a list of the more frequently used concepts in this field, along with their conventional meanings, in a Glossary at the end of the paper. I recommend that the reader consult this before tackling the text itself.

are more advanced moments, in another place, and at a much later period of time. Fortunately for us, there are several Canadian scholars who are working intensively to formulate a conception of "where we are." Most of them are not anthropologists. They are people identified with fields such as sociology, political science, history, and economics. What they have in common is an interest in "political economy." Not only are these scholars investigating things "economic" and "political" in the narrow sense (e.g., the nature of, and changes in, patterns of production and circulation, work, ownership, inequality, decision making, control); at the same time many of them are looking at those aspects of ideology, belief or culture which are part of these patterns. In English Canada, the most comprehensive recent statement is Marchak's *Ideological Perspectives on Canada* (Marchak 1975). Marchak talks about the ideological picture drawn of the individual, free enterprise, society, classes, voting, and a number of other important categories, and she points to the social, political, and economic conditions to which such important categories relate. [2]

Scholars are also presenting analyses of how men and women are imaged as human beings in relation to their position under corporate capitalism in general, and under Canadian conditions in particular (see, e.g., Guettel 1974; Smith 1975; Stephenson, ed., 1973). We also have research conducted in particular communities and regions which deals with the political economy of Canada's regions in relation to the broader picture, and which includes material on the kind of world which people think they are living in.

Here the place of the study of kinship as part of the study of the relation of ideology to political economy is the clearest: in order to understand what is going on in families and to understand how that ties in with other things, one has to understand the concepts and realities of *work*. In order to understand the work options that exist for people in different regions of Canada, one has to understand why the labour force, agricultural forms, industries, and other businesses that exist in particular places do exist in those places and not in others. In order to understand the latter, one has to know about the modes of capital investment; patterns of ownership and control (including foreign ownership and control); federal land, immigration, and taxation policies; provincial property and inheritance laws, and so forth. There is a very large "and so forth," but there we are.

When people in Western countries recognize "family" as a reality, we should query why "family" is regarded as an entity at all. We must understand how and why people can act in relation to "it" and "outside it." We should focus our attention on the definitions and images of "it," and consider them in relation to those of its characteristics which are aspects of a larger social whole. We can tentatively see such a whole, for the purposes of asking questions about kinship, as being constituted first by our nationally and historically specific organization of capitalism; second by certain other forms of organization which are not fully capitalistic in nature but which are themselves dominated by capitalist-related institutions (e.g., parts of the agricultural sector); and third by the organizations which are contesting the dominating institutions. The most productive point of departure for the understanding of western "families" or kinship units, then, is not whether they are nuclear or extended, unilateral or bilateral, corporate or non-corporate. It is the extent of both their subservience and resistance to the interests of a system of production relations (see Zaretsky n.d.).

This raises two very intimately related questions on the link between kinship, ideology, and political economy. Firstly, what is the relation between kinship institutions and the ideological-political-economic forms which shape our lives? Secondly, what is the relation between the ways we look at kinship institutions as anthropologists, and the forms which shape our lives? One of the reasons why these two questions are intimately related is that many of the categories which are tied to (at least) anglophone kinship are the same categories which anglophone anthropologists use to describe kinship and social organization among radically different peoples. Rather than looking at this fact as a coincidence, or even as an inevitability, we should look at it as a *problem*. Let us inquire into this matter a little more closely, and very informally.

ON CATEGORIES

In teaching introductory anthropology courses in London, Ontario, and in Vancouver, British Columbia, I presented students with a classroom exercise informed by questions raised in Schneider's *American Kinship* (Schneider 1968), a study which owes as much to French and British varieties of anthropology as to American varieties, and some of the conclusions of which seem to tap into a certain set of understandings of the world which one will probably find in sectors of many Western liberal democracies.

I presented students with the question: "What is 'a family' "? I was asking students to give definitions of family according to their own understanding of it; or somewhat more loosely, to say what they think "a family" means. They answered the question in terms of other categories with which they were familiar. Their answers were of the order of: a family is a group of people related by blood and marriage; a family is composed of mother, father, and children, who are their offspring; a family is a group of people linked by common understanding and interest; a family is an institution through which society communicates its values. A "family" could apply to The Family of God; a "family" could apply to a family of plants. We pursued these answers to uncover other categories. For example: what is "blood"? What is "society"? What is "marriage"? In answer to the latter, people said things such as "a sexual bond" and "a bond between people living together, sanctioned by society."

Soon a further point emerged: a "family" included mother, father, and children, but in order to understand what "mother" and "father" meant one had to understand what "women" and "men" meant. "Women" and "men" were two kinds of "individuals" and the distinction between them had to do with the procreation of children and the roles each had in relation to children. Men, women, mother, father, husband, wife, children, family, society, individual all appeared as part of a charmed circle, or system of categories, closing in upon itself. These categories are used by both anthropologists and by the people in his or her own society. The categories not only refer to one another (as above) but also often appear to refer to things which are real, natural, and necessary and are tied up with other sectors of social life (e.g., kinship, politics, economy, religion).

Further analysis revealed certain properties common to most of the above categories. First, there is the biological aspect—the individual, the family, men, and women are defined in terms we consider "physical." Second is the double aspect to being and relation—both are given in nature and both are the product of human activity. Third is the primacy given to "the individual"—collective categories are "reduced" to individuals, while individuals are seen as outside collectivities. Fourth is a particular kind of abstractness—the individual is conceived as being apart from social relations; society is apart from specific individuals and specific social relations (society as a system of "norms" or rules); the family is an entity unto itself. Fifth is a peculiarly "liberal" paradox—individuals are seen as being on the one hand unique and different, and on the other hand similar and even substitutable.

These properties are of more immediate interest to us than many of the categories themselves as they seem closely linked to the political economy of Western societies. In fact in their present form, these meanings and, indeed, the categories themselves have only recently appeared in Western history. In other words, what many people now regard as having always been, is probably not more than four hundred years old (on the individual, see Dumont 1965, 1971).

According to Williams (1961) a shift in meaning of the terms "individual" and "society" occured in the late sixteenth and early seventeenth centuries. In medieval thought "individual" connoted inseparability. It was elaborated in theological discussions of the Holy Trinity as a way of explaining ". . . how a being could be thought of as existing in his own nature yet existing by this nature as part of an indivisible whole" (1961:73). It was then applied to a member of a group or species in such a manner that membership was an integral part of the concept. The shift was toward thinking of "individual" as more of a separated entity, without reference to a group or class. "Individual" was imaged as being outside a network of relations rather than an aspect of them. "Individual" was abstracted out of the relations of which it was part. Similarly, "society" had referred primarily to people—actual social relations and contacts. It now began to appear more as a thing in itself, abstracted from the real relations of real people.

"Family" as a term appeared in English in the late fourteenth and early fifteenth centuries, from the Latin for "household," which itself came from the Latin for "servant." According to Williams (1961), "family" moved from describing a household to describing a kin group, usually a unit of codescendants. Its meanings widened to include ". . . a people or group of peoples, again with a sense of specific descent from an ancestor; also to a particular religious sense, itself associated with previous social meanings, as in 'the Father of our Lord Jesus Christ, of whom the whole family in heaven and earth is named' (Ephesians, 1:10)" (Williams 1976:109). Even in the eighteenth century, there were rural usages which suggest the Latin derivation, as "family" could include servants living in the household. The ". . . later distinction between family and *servants* was in this instance much resented" (ibid.: 110).

Here is a useful if lengthy quote from Williams. (Note that in the text quoted below, Williams uses a few abbreviations. C: followed by a numeral, is century; eC: first period (third) of a century; mC: middle period (third) of a century; lC: last period (third) of a century. Capitalized words are those which appear in bold-faced type in the original.)

> The specialization of FAMILY to the small kin-group in a single house can be related to the rise of what is now called the BOUR-GEOIS FAMILY. But this, with its senses of household and property, relates more properly, at least until C19, to the older sense. From eC19 (James Mill) we find this definition: "the group which consists of a Father, Mother and Children is called a Family"; yet the fact that the conscious definition is necessary is in itself significant. Several lC17 and C18 uses of FAMILY in a small kin-group sense often refer specifically to children: "but duly sent his family and wife" (Pope, Bathurst) where the sense of household, however, may still be present. FAMILY-WAY, common since eC18, referred first to the sense of FAMILIAR but then, through the specific sense of children, to pregnancy. There was thus considerable overlap, between mC17 and lC18, of these varying senses of lineage, household, large kin-group and small kin-group.
>
> The dominance of the sense of small kin-group was probably not established before eC19. The now predominant pressure of the word, and the definition of many kinds of feeling in relation to it, came in mC19 and later. This can be represented as the apotheosis of the BOURGEOIS FAMILY, and the sense of the isolated family as a working economic unit is clearly stressed in the development of capitalism. But it has even stronger links to early capitalist production, and the C19 development represents, in one sense, a distinction between a man's work and his FAMILY: he works to support a FAMILY; the FAMILY is supported by his work. It is more probable, in fact, that the small kin-group definition, supported by the development of smaller separate houses and therefore households, relates to the new working class and lower-mid-

> dle class who were defined by wage-labour; not FAMILY as
> lineage or property or as including these, and not family as
> household in the older established sense which included ser-
> vants, but the near kin-group which can define its social relation-
> ships, in any positive sense, only in this way. FAMILY or FAM-
> ILY AND FRIENDS can represent the only immediately positive
> attachments in a large-scale and complex wage-earning society.
> And it is significant that class-feeling, the other major response
> to the new society, used brother and sister to express class affi-
> liation, as in trade union membership, though there is also in this
> a clear religious precedent in certain related religious sects. It is
> significant also that this use of brother and sister came to seem
> artificial or comic in middle-class eyes. FAMILY, there, combined
> the strong sense of immediate and positive blood-group relation-
> ships and the strong implicit sense of property (Williams
> 1976:110-111; see also Arriès 1962).

I do not think that it is unreasonable to suggest that we should take
pause when we find that certain notions which began taking form
during the time of the development of commercial capitalism, and
which were consolidated under industrial capitalism, can be found
both in Western ideology and in Western anthropology, which are
not supposed to be exactly the same.

Of course our approaches to kinship are not mechanical emana-
tions from that ideology which is most closely tied to the political
economy of capitalism. There is more involved than that. I will try to
indicate some ways of thinking about the relationship.

The historical matrix. The intellectual origins of modern Western anthropology are to be found in the Renaissance, the Reformation, and
the Enlightenment, which were themselves moments in the development of the political economy of the West. Goldmann has observed
for the Enlightenment:

> In the perspective of social history the Enlightenment is a histor-
> ically important stage in the development of western bourgeois
> thought, which, as a whole, constitutes a unique and vital part of
> human intellectual history. To understand the essential ideas of
> the Enlightenment, one must accordingly start by analysing the
> activity that was most important to the bourgeoisie and most in-
> fluenced its economic and social evolution. This was the develop-
> ment of the economy, and above all its essential element, ex-
> change (Goldmann 1973:17).

Such a statement may appear strange in the current anthropological context, in which "exchange" can be taken as a metaphor for social life in general, and for what is going on in kinship systems in particular. Marriage, for example, can be seen as "the exchange of
women between groups." Or people can speak of the exchange of
women for goods and services. The fact that we can generalize the
idea of exchange to the point that we generalize it is, indeed, part of
the problem.

But exchange in the sense in which Goldmann means it is not just the apparent movement of persons or things between points A and B. What he is referring to is a socioeconomic order based on "the market," on production for exchange value: what is dominant is the production of commodities produced for sale. In the fully developed market economy most people cannot consume what they produce because they do not own the means of production; most people have only one commodity to sell, their labour-power, which they must sell to the owners of the means of production. As this mode of production develops, the idea also develops that the "individual" (who appears as *the* actor in the market), particularly the individual consciousness, is the true subject of action. Social processes are seen as a kind of product of the actions of individuals reacting to each other as they rationally pursue their individual interests. By what might seem to amount to a paradox, a complement of this assumption is "universality" (Goldmann 1973). As buyer and seller confront each other in the market it is not their personal characteristics that regulate their exchange, but rather general rules operating independently of their personal qualities.

If social life is regarded as the product of individual actions (in relation to one another), the question still arises of ". . . how to obtain at least the minimum of agreement needed to make society as a whole function tolerably smoothly, if not perfectly" (Goldmann 1973:32). Or, once we make the break between the "individual" and "society," and once we concede the possibility of the former as the locus of reality but the latter as having the property of orderliness, we have to account for that orderliness. Some thinkers of the Enlightenment used ideas of God to account for this; anthropologists use culture, normative systems, technology, biology, adaptation.

Rules. Other ideas emerged during the Enlightenment which drew on the scientific conceptions of the seventeenth century, i.e., an earlier phase in the development of capitalism. We have from the seventeenth century,

> The idea that nature is a book written in mathematical language, that the entire universe is governed by general laws that know no exception, the elimination of all that is mysterious or strange or unusual, and the virtual elimination (although many scientists cautiously refrained from making this part of their theory explicit) of the miraculous; the assumption of constant, unchanging natural laws conforming to reason (Malebranche, who was a priest as well as a philosopher, held that God worked only through general laws); the assertion that these laws required confirmation by experience . . . (Goldmann 1973:24-25).

Kinship studies are nothing if not rules. Anthropologists have rules (or the closely allied "principles") about terminological classification, rules about inclusion in groups, descent rules, residence rules, marriage rules, prescriptive rules, preferred rules, optional rules, rules for negotiation, decision-making rules, transformational rules, rules about rules and hierarchies of rules. Futhermore, we have legalistic conceptions of rules, linguistic conceptions of rules, operational conceptions of rules. There are rules *for* the people we study *by* the people we study (we assume); there are rules invented by anthropologists (analysts' constructs) to explain these rules and the behaviour governed by these rules.

This obsession for rules in anthropology not only has its origins in the view of science and rationality developed during the Enlightenment, but also mirrors a more contemporary obsession in liberal democratic societies. And this relates to particular forms of domination historically developing in these societies. Weber pointed out some time ago that there were basically three ways of legitimizing domination, namely, tradition, charisma, and the law. Legal legitimation exists ". . . where a system of rules that is applied judicially and administratively in accordance with ascertainable principles is valid for all members of the corporate group" (Bendix 1962:294; cf. Goldmann 1973). Western liberal democracies have developed legal domination to a high point and our image of societies everywhere as rule governed may use its qualities as a point of reference.

Part and Whole. The distinction "part and whole" is closely related both historically and structurally to the distinction individual and society. On the one hand we pose the "individual" as the "individual" in the modern liberal sense, the individual as a separate unit unconnected to a larger whole. On the other hand, we pose the individual (perhaps as a "social person") as part of a larger whole. (These notions were not born with capitalism, but they were closely connected with its development.) In similar fashion we pose domains of analysis which we regard as autonomous, such as "kinship," while recognizing that they are really part of a larger whole (see Barnett and Silverman 1977). That is, while we can talk about "kinship" as a subject matter, we recognize that in life as it is lived, it is very difficult to point to something actually happening and say, "that is kinship, not politics" (or not economics, religion etc.). Thus we create for ourselves the problem of the relation between kinship and other things by posing some kind of break between kinship and other things in the first place.

In part at least, this fragmentary way of thinking about kinship, or any other domain, developed in response to the continuities and discontinuities of our own past historical development. Our predecessors had to find a way of describing the massive social dislocations they were experiencing and observing. Words such as "family," "custom," "religion," and "tradition" helped them make sense out of their situation, in the sense that these things were being singled out as of declining importance. Words such as "science," "freedom," "rationality," and "individualism" were helpful in identifying things that were being singled out as of increasing importance. Several writers saw the movement as one in which family-like relations, or concrete relations between persons, were being pushed aside by relations which had the appearance of relations of "contract." The individual was now to make his way in the world unencumbered by the weight of previously important social ties, and free labour was now to enter the labour market and make specific arrangements with employers rather than remain tied to feudal lords or landowners in relations which were more personalized, permanent and involved most aspects of life.

It was this kind of thinking which has helped us distort our picture of the nature of social relations in non-Western societies and in Western societies.

WHAT, THEN, IS "KINSHIP"?

The boundaries or points of departure for the analysis of kinship vary between frameworks that are constructed in advance by the analyst (e.g., kinship as, pre-eminently, genealogical relations), and those that are constructed by the peoples we study (i.e., reflected in their indigenous concepts and categories). Once we focus attention on boundaries or points of departure constructed by peoples themselves we may find our thinking on the other plane seriously challenged.

Kinship from the Outside. The identification of kinship as something we *already* know about is, in fact, but a short step from the dominating ideology of our own society. Looking at kinship as "systems of consaguinity and affinity" is close to the English-speaking folk definition of family ties as ties of "blood and marriage." The development of our understanding of "descent systems" (e.g., lineage systems) was an important step especially when it revealed the importance of marriage as an institution and as a continuing relationship between "groups" (see, e.g., Lévi-Strauss 1966). This contrasts with the situation in the West, where marriage is something between "individuals," or at least is conceived as such for a significant proportion of the population. But constituting these societies in terms of "groups" raises certain questions.

"The group" is also an important popular conception in the West, in addition to being an anthropological concept. "The group" is thought of in ways similar to "society," that is, as an enduring entity of which individuals are a part, yet which transcends them. A good deal of concern with "the group" has been concern with "corporateness," or with some kind of estate principle having to do with property—and domination. But one of the problems with this concept as a universal category is that many social arrangements, including "kinship" arrangements, are not very group-like. A recent paper is, indeed, entitled "Are there social groups in the New Guinea Highlands?" (Wagner 1974). We might therefore think of the concept "network" as a category intermediate between individual and group; we might think of "hereditary alliance" as a category intermediate between blood and marriage. The latter concept tries to describe marriage alliances (often as "groups exchanging women") which persist

67

over several generations. In other words, people are born into given categories or groups whose members should marry those of other categories or groups.

In kinship studies we have taken such familiar terms as these, turned them into typologies (e.g., unilineal and bilateral descent, uxorilocal and virilocal residence, parallel and cross cousin marriage), and then fit them to categories, forms of behaviour, and relations found in some other society because of some superficial correspondence between them. The Cree Indians, for example, are classed as a "bilateral" descent system, like ourselves, merely because they recognize minimally, genealogical ties through both the father and mother. To accommodate the awkwardness of such impositions we then modify the original "English" meanings of the original terms in a language which only becomes understandable to other people studying "kinship." The explicit or implicit point of reference for these typologies, then, derives from an ideological representation of what "our system" is like (eg., as based on the "nuclear" family) or of what our system is *not* like, but "not like" only in opposition to familiar terms (e.g., another system as featuring "prescribed marriage rules").

In sum, these emphases and typologies are basically constrained by a combination of the terms: individual/group and blood/marriage. Group + marriage = marriage as building and continuing alliances. Group + blood = corporate descent groups. Individual + marriage = marriage as an affair primarily involving individuals. Individual + blood is an anomaly as it practically denies kinship—perhaps its referent is the genuinely contracting individual.

Kinship from the Inside. Approaches to empirical research (also part of our bourgeois heritage) have recently begun to make some inroads into the "outside" way of categorizing things. "Consanguinity and affinity" has a nice familiar ring to it and the distinction seems obvious, but many anthropologists are now encountering or rediscovering findings which challenge even the simple biological idea of "blood relation." This notion has not only been behind conventional anthropological ideas of kinship, it has also been a popularly held belief. The reports of lack of knowledge of physiological paternity among some people such as the Australian Aborigines and Trobriand Islanders became something of an anthropological sensation when first published. Whether or not those peoples recognize physiological paternity is, in a sense, not the point: the point is that it should be such an interesting issue to us. If we could accept the fact that some people did not recognize physiological paternity, at least we could continue to assume, as some of the nineteenth century evolutionists assumed, that everyone knew who a person's mother was. A recent paper by Tonkinson (1975) however, challenges this point: among a group of Australian Aborigines in the Western desert, it is *not* automatically clear that a woman who bears a child is the true mother of the child.

Other challenges to a simple genealogical model of kinship are several and overlapping. For example: (1) some relations which we take to be relations by birth are not so believed by other peoples; some of them are regarded as relations by marriage (e.g., my "father" is really my "mother's husband"), or can be so constructed by anthropologists; (2) some relations which somehow really ought to be on the consanguinity side are *not* relations by birth, but involve mixes of the sharing of a common locality, access to common resources, eating food together, producing together. These are not relations by marriage and they are more than "friendship." They may even involve people becoming members of "descent groups," which makes one wonder about calling some descent groups *descent* groups; (3) some relations which really ought to be on the consanguinity side appear as relations into which people *decide* to enter, rather than relations they are born into.[3]

When physiological paternity or maternity is denied, we have to wonder about assuming a "natural" basis for kinship and about the unity of the domain of kinship. When the same kind of relationship involves not only genealogy, but also locality and property; when we add the possibility that people who produce together or eat together can be thus regarded as kin, not to mention clansmen, we call into question talking about "the functions of kinship." One can propose that both the very wide occurrence of genealogical representations as part of kin relations, *and* the fact that these relations are not exclusively genealogical but can also involve things such as land and co-production, are both aspects of another question: the kinds of separations people make in their life activity. Where people are not alienated from social relations and the material things involved in those relations as they are in a fully developed market society (and perhaps also in slave society; Bloch 1975), it should come as no surprise that people can ground relationships in things having to do with their bodies, their property, their actions.

Approached from the inside through the indigenous notions of the people we study, a whole new set of possibilities and sensitivities arises, not only for kinship studies but also for the way we construct and act on the world. Consider these remarks by an aboriginal Canadian, George Manuel:

> . . . when I met with the Maori people, on my first trip beyond the shores of North America, if I had said, "Our culture is every inch of our land," the meaning would have been obvious to them. Wherever I have travelled in the Aboriginal World, there has been a common attachment to the land.
>
> This is not the land that can be speculated, bought, sold, mortgaged, claimed by one state, surrendered or counter-claimed by another. Those are things that men do only on the land claimed by a king who rules by the grace of God, and through whose grace and favour men must make their fortunes on this earth.
>
> The land from which our culture springs is like the water and the air, one and indivisible. The land is our Mother Earth. The an-

> *imals who grow on that land are our spiritual brothers. We are a part of that Creation that the Mother Earth brought forth. More complicated, more sophisticated than the other creatures, but no nearer to the Creator who infused us with life.*
>
> *The struggle of the past four centuries has been between these two ideas of land. Lurking behind this struggle for land was a conflict over the nature of man himself. Aboriginal people were not born with the debit balance of original sin to work off in this world to assure their place in the next. We did not think of the individual existing prior to his being a part of the tribe or clan. If a task was incomplete at the time of his departure, it was an inheritance of the nation to carry on, not a judgement against man (Manuel and Posluns 1974:6).*

The four centuries of struggle Manuel speaks about is the period during which, from the European side, capitalism developed and flourished and during which indigenous people were exploited as a consequence. It was also the era in which many of the categories we use today in anthropology and in our everyday life in general, took form. Statements such as this, by integrating what we separate, become more than ethnographic; they become political. Manuel goes on:

> The Fourth World is a vision of the future history of North America and of the Indian peoples. The two histories are inseparable. It has been the insistence on the separation of the people from the land that has characterized much of recent history. It is this same insistence that has prevented European North Americans from developing their own identity in terms of the land so that they can be happy and secure in the knowledge of that identity *(Manuel and Posluns 1974: 12; emphasis in the original).*

Manuel and Posluns' discussion relates not only to questions of theory (e.g., "giving" is spoken of instead of "exchange"), but also of practice (e.g., land claims). The eventual clarification of theoretical issues in the "kinship" field may well occur through attention to the whole practical debate over land claims, in other words, the debate over the kinds of control people have or do not have over their own lives.

Not only do we have to listen to what other people in other societies are saying about the nature of social life as it is lived; we must also listen to those who are challenging established views of social relations within Western capitalist societies. These challenges may be "in principle" or of the "we should not" or "here are other alternative ways of living" variety, or they may be "in practice" from people who live a different reality or see a different reality within the dominant one. Within kinship studies this latter kind of critique and rethinking is largely coming from women anthropologists and from the women's movement in general (see Leacock 1973; Rosaldo and Lamphere, eds. 1974: Weiner 1976). For example, the image of clans, lineages, or localized lineages "exchanging women" raises certain difficulties, even when it is recognized that it is usually men who are directing the exchanges. The active role of women in these arrangements may have been grossly underrated for a variety of societies, and one wonders what it means to say that even chauvinist men "exchange" women.

The reference model here is probably that of fully-developed commodity exchange, in which something is bought and sold with a fair degree of finality, a thing which has no rights of its own, and in which the direct producer has no rights. It is even small comfort to suggest that in marriage and kinship, ". . . women constitute the most valuable and productive currency of all" (Lewis 1976:10). I am suggesting that while anthropologists do not treat the "exchange of women" as if it were fully-developed commodity exchange there seems to be something profoundly wrong with the metaphor and the thinking behind it.

It also becomes rather bizarre to speak, as the pre-eminent ideology does, of a segment of our own form of society as having no fixed residence rule, or as able to exercise "choice," in that area, when in that segment the wife is, more often than not, expected to follow the husband to the area where he finds employment; and when the choice of the place of residence in that area is often severely restricted by rents. Focussing on "the couple" ("the family") itself, can be taken as a way of avoiding the discussion of the relative positions of men and women. Focussing on residence in terms of whether or not the couple live with kin of this side or of that can also be taken as a way of avoiding that discussion, as well as the discussion of the relations "between" the family and the rest.

When men monopolize certain activities which matter dearly to them, and women do not seem to mind, or even regard what men are doing with less than utter seriousness (see Murphy and Murphy 1974), who, if anyone, is the object of a ruse?

In connection with this discussion of critiques of our own categories from within capitalist society we should examine a paper by Needham which challenges the unity of the field of kinship studies, and the unity of some of its categories (e.g., "the incest tabu"). After an interesting register of many of the difficulties in using terms such as "matrilineal" and "patrilineal" descent, and even "matrilineal" and "patrilineal" "societies," Needham observes: "Given two sexes, and transmission of rights by these, we may distinguish six elementary modes of descent" (Needham 1971b:10.) Needham goes on to discuss kinship terminologies and suggests that we abandon typologizing them. He proposes a different kind of distinction be made:

> Relationship terminologies can be divided formally into (a) lineal and (b) non-lineal. By the former term (lineal) I refer to classifications in which the typical feature, in the medial three genealogical

levels at least, is the distinction of statuses according to whether relationship is traced through persons of the same sex or not (1971b:19).

Needham also adopts the position that "Incest prohibitions do not in fact compose a definite class, and if this is so there cannot be a general theory that applies to all of them" (1971b:25). He documents the differences between cultures in concepts of incest. He goes on to develop a line of argument about incest theory, one of the important observations of which is that we are dealing with "rules" which ". . . by definition, have to do with access to women" (1971b:28). Women are "social valuables." "Access to socially recognized valuables is always socially regulated; the regulation expresses the evaluation" (1971b:29).

In a paper in the same volume Rivière observes:

> *The constituent units of marriage are men and women, and this seems to be marriage's single, universal feature. Thus the study of marriage must in the first place concentrate on the categories of male and female and the relationship between them (Rivière 1971:63).*

While Needham seems to be suggesting that the categories he talks about (descent, kinship terminology, etc.) are rather miscellaneous, in each case they involve a statement about the relations between men and women. This may be stating the obvious, but it must be realized even if "men" and "women" do not mean or imply exactly the same things everywhere.

The issue of "gender" (as some now call it, rather than "sex," "sex-roles," etc.) can thus appropriate many of the issues which we conventionally think of under the heading of kinship. At this point we can see how kinship studies can make a productive contact with Marxist studies, but the encounter is still fraught with difficulties.

Marx and Engels quite early wrote of the ". . . production of life, both in one's own labour and of fresh life in procreation . . ." (Marx and Engels 1845-1846 [1970]:50). Engels later wrote:

> *According to the materialist conception, the determining factor in history is, in the last resort, the production and reproduction of immediate life. But this itself is of a twofold character. On the one hand, the production of the means of subsistence, of food, clothing, shelter, and the tools requisite therefore; on the other, the production of human beings themselves, the propagation of the species. The social institutions under which men of a definite country live are conditioned by both kinds of production: by the stage of development of labour, on the one hand, and of the family, on the other* (Engels 1884 [1970]:449; see discussion in Leacock 1973, also Godelier 1972).

We need not proclaim *ex cathedra* that it is universally appropriate to speak of production as production of the means of subsistence and of production as procreation as one and the same process. It is possible both to generalize the idea of "production" to such a point that it has little content, and to narrow it dogmatically in a way that reproduces those forms of alienation characteristic of capitalist society by focussing on only the production of *things*. Nevertheless, interested scholars see good reason to bring into question the use of what have become standard Marxist categories such as mode of production, infrastructure, superstructure, and while not wishing to abandon them, have certainly been willing to entertain modifications.[4] Many years ago, Gluckman pointed to some of these connections, but his observations did not penetrate into the heart of kinship studies as much as they should (see Gluckman 1965).

We know now that in many (but not all; see Bloch 1975) noncapitalist societies, what appear in terms of our own ideology as relations between people and things—property relations—appear as aspects of relations between people. For some rather speculative ethnography of my own about a Central Pacific people, the Banabans, I have suggested that the alternatives of representing relations as either "relations between persons" or as "relations between persons and things" are themselves two alternatives too close to our ideology (Silverman 1977). We can better think of relationships as being composed of aspects of persons, things (such as land) and behaviours which are continuous with one another and which partially define one another. One can call these relationships just "relationships"; the word "kinship" does not add much.

At least in many Oceanic societies, property does not appear to be external to relationships. Neither does productive activity. People do not work with one another as "labour." Their work (or activity) and its nature is tied to the kinds of relationships they are in with other people. At the same time, we know that what is often called the "sexual division of labour" is rather widespread. How and what and with whom men and women produce is represented as being closely tied to their nature and education as men and women.

We have known for a long time that, among many peoples, "religion," "ritual" and "mythology" feature such interrelated themes as productivity, gender, fertility, and growth. These observations and those in the preceding few paragraphs should be combined with insistence that we look to various cultures and to our own descriptive practices to be able to answer questions about gender domination. Recently, French Marxist anthropologists have opened a debate about looking at the domination of younger men by elder men in respect of marriage, and about marriage as usually tied to things which can be described as procreation, fertility, the reproduction of labour, access to resources, property.[5]

We have seen how the issues of "domination" and "gender" can appropriate many of the things we conventionally think of under the heading of kinship, at least for some societies. The two issues are very intimately related. It seems at this point that what can most effectively appropriate things under the heading is the question of the nature of social wholes, which we can begin to grasp most immediately through asking about the organization of gender, production, reproduction, and domination, including the local categories which are part of those wholes. Terms such as gender, production, reproduction, and domination are here seen not as different things, but as different ways of beginning to ask about the same set of relations. As Lévi-Strauss (1966:21) remarked, anticipating this development, findings by anthropologists like Firth in Polynesia, Fortes in Africa, Goodenough in Oceania, Cuisenier in the Arab world and Dumont in India had "split the seams of the fabric that held our traditional categories together." He went on,

> Even though we should evade the results of over-bold theoretical speculation, the very facts would compel us to a more flexible outlook, and to devise new methods of research, thus keeping ourselves in readiness for the tasks that lie ahead. May I predict that in so doing we will find ourselves more and more in agreement with native theories, either expressedly formulated or still hidden in symbolic representations, ritual, and mythologies.

In this respect it is instructive to look at our own "native conceptions" of our own "kinship system." For example, the hypothesized Indo-European root from which the English "kin" descends meant "to produce" (and in Greek the derived word meant "race, kind, sex, genus"; Onions 1966:505). And according to another authority, the Latin word from which "produce" descends meant "to lean forward, bring forward, bring forth, beget, produce, draw out, lengthen" (Klein 1966:1248).

Raising such questions may pose dilemmas, but, even so, approaching the problem in this way seems much more interesting than worrying about the classification of terminologies and descent systems, or whether bilateral kin groups are the same order of phenomenon as uni-lineal kin groups. And these questions place the understanding of "kinship" within the orbit of the questions we ask as we try to understand the relation of ideology to political economy.

In conclusion, we should point to another very important consideration as we ponder the nature and future of kinship studies, this time in relation to the political economy of academic anthropology itself: if the boundaries of kinship study are—and correctly so—quite nebulous, what is not nebulous is that kinship is defined as a field of study. People are specialists in it, give and take courses in it, write and read books and chapters about it, construct and sit for examinations in it—if only to indicate why there should have ever been the appearance of it as a subject matter at all. Kinship thus is, among other things, a way of "making a living" for some, of increasing capital for others. Whether it can long survive as such if one of its major points becomes its own negation as a subject matter is (alas) the subject of another essay, but is an aspect of the larger question to which this chapter has been addressed. A certain variety of Marxist might summarize part of the current (or already passing?) position as a contradiction between the relations of production (involved in university appointments and requirements, the administration of grants, etc.) and the level of development of the forces of production (our knowledge about "kinship" and what it is not). Situations of this kind are, at the very least, interesting.

NOTES:

1. *For comments, references, and encouragements on matters associated with this chapter I would like to thank M. Ames, C. Farber, D. Schneider and D. Turner. I should note that for the Glossary I consulted Keesing 1975 and Fox 1967.*
2. *Many items are included in the bibliography to Marchak 1975. See also papers and references in Gold and Tremblay 1973. The continuing publications of the Institute for Social and Economic Research, Memorial University of Newfoundland should be noted. Recent approaches dealing with these problems are also discussed in Hedley, this volume.*
3. *See for example, Leach 1961; Strathern 1973; Rappaport 1967; Turner 1977.*
4. *See, for example, Bloch 1975, Labby 1976, Turner 1978.*
5. *See, for example, Meillassoux 1972, Terray 1972; a number of papers have appeared more recently addressing the question for African societies.*

GLOSSARY OF CONVENTIONAL KINSHIP CONCEPTS

Affinity	A relation through one or more marriage links; usually contrasted with consanguinity.
Alliance	A condition in which kin collectivities continue relationships with one another for several generations, which relations include (but are not restricted to) relations of affinity
Bilateral descent	Descent traced through both male and female links
Clan	A unilineal descent group in which many of the remoter links to the common ancestor are not precisely known; usually contrasted with lineage, lineage being both smaller and with more precisely known links
Classificatory kinship	In anthropological discussions of kinship, "classificatory" is sometimes used to indicate that terms for certain relatives who are, in the English sense, inside the nuclear family, are also used for relatives who are outside the nuclear family. One also encounters expressions such as: "Ms. Y is Mr. X's classificatory mother." This is a kind of short-

75

	hand. It means that Ms. Y is not Mr. X's mother in our presumed sense, but that the term used for her is the same term that would be applied to Mr. X's mother.
Consanguinity	A relationship based on the recognition of descent from a common ancestor, the sharing of a common substance (e.g., blood, genes), etc.; usually contrasted with affinity
Corporate kinship group	A kin collectivity the members of which form a unity in relation to something and/or to outsiders
Cross-cousins	The children of brother and sister, or of more distantly related opposite-sex members of the same generation; usually contrasted with parallel cousins
Cross-cousin marriage	Marriage with people who fall into a category which includes cross-cousins; interesting where alliance involved
Descent	A recognition of continuity through the generations from an ancestor; the constitution of a category or collectivity through the inclusion of descendants of a common ancestor
Descent group	A collectivity the members of which recognize a common ancestor
Extended family	A concept used to indicate a situation in which people are living together and some of their links are more distant than nuclear family links
Genealogical	In the sense of thinking about kinship in a genealogical way: thinking about kinship in a way which makes kin relations appear as if they were the relations between persons on a family tree
Incest tabu	Prohibition on sexual intercourse (and some related practices) between kin who stand in certain relations to one another
Kinship terminology	The terms people use to identify kinds of kin
Lineage	A unilineal descent group in which the links to the common ancestor are assumed to be precisely known; usually contrasted with clan
Localized lineage	A lineage with a core membership which resides in one area

Network	In the context of kinship studies, the network concept can be used to deal with situations in which individuals and/or families interact with others using their consanguineal and affinal connections, but there is no real group constituted by all of them, together
Nuclear family	Parents and children
Parallel cousins	The children of same-sex siblings, or of more distantly related same-sex members of the same generation
Parallel cousin marriage	Marriage with people who fall into a category which includes parallel cousins
Preferred rules	Rules stating a preference, but not a requirement, for marrying people in a certain kin category, which might locate them as members of kin collectivities with which one's own collectivity is in an alliance relation
Prescriptive rules	Rules requiring one to marry people in a certain kin category, which might locate them as members of kin collectivities with which one's own collectivity is in an alliance relation; rules stating who is and who is not an eligible spouse in terms of the kin category or kin group memberships of both parties
Unilateral kinship group	A kin collectivity with a core membership composed of people related through same-sex links
Unilineal descent	Descent traced through same-sex links
Uxorilocal residence	Residence after marriage by a married couple with the wife's kin
Virilocal residence	Residence after marriage by a married couple with the husband's kin

BIBLIOGRAPHY

Ariès, Philippe 1962. *Centuries of Childhood*. New York: Knopf.

Barnett, Steve and Martin G. Silverman 1977. *Persons, Units and Relations: Anthropology, Neomarxist Thought, and the Problem of Ideology and the Social Whole*. Forthcoming.

Bendix, Reinhard 1962. Max Weber: *An Intellectual Portrait*. New York: Doubleday (Anchor).

Bloch, Maurice 1975. Property and the end of affinity. In *Marxist Analyses and Social Anthropology* (ASA Studies 2), edited by M. Bloch. London: Malaby.

Dumont, Louis 1965. The modern conception of the individual. *Contributions to Indian Sociology* 8:7-69.

Dumont, Louis 1971. Religion, society and politics in the individualistic universe. In *Proceedings of the Royal Anthropological Institute for 1970*.

Engels, Frederick 1884 [1970]. The Origin of the Family, Private Property and the State. In *Selected Works*, by Karl Marx and Frederick Engels. Moscow: Progress Publishers.

Fox, Robin 1967. *Kinship and Marriage*. Harmondsworth: Penguin.

Gluckman, Max 1965. *Politics, Law and Ritual in Tribal Society*. Chicago: Aldine.

Godelier, Maurice 1972. *Rationality and Irrationality in Economics*. London: NLB.

Gold, Gerald and Marc-Adelard Tremblay 1973. *Communities and Culture in French Canada*. Montreal: Holt, Rinehart and Winston.

Goldmann, Lucien 1973. *The Philosophy of the Enlightenment*. Cambridge, Mass.: MIT Press.

Guettel, Charnie 1974. *Marxism and Feminism*. Toronto: Women's Press.

Keesing, Roger M. 1975. *Kin Groups and Social Structure*. New York: Holt, Rinehart and Winston.

Klein, Ernest 1966. *A Comprehensive Etymological Dictionary of the English Language*. Amsterdam: Elsevier.

Kontos, Alkis, ed. 1975. *Domination*. Toronto: University of Toronto Press.

Leach, Edmund R. 1961. Rethinking anthropology. In *Rethinking Anthropology*, by E. R. Leach. London: Athlone.

Leacock, Eleanor B. 1973. Introduction. In *The Origin of the Family, Private Property and the State*, by Frederick Engels. New York: International Publishers.

Lévi-Strauss, Claude 1966. The future of kinship studies. In *Proceedings of the Royal Anthropological Institute for 1965*.

Lewis, I.M. 1976. *Social Anthropology in Perspective*. Harmondsworth: Penguin.

Manuel, George and Michael Posluns 1974. *The Fourth World*. Don Mills, Ont.: Collier Macmillan Canada.

Marchak, M. Patricia 1975. *Ideological Perspectives on Canada*. Toronto: McGraw-Hill Ryerson.

Marx, Karl and Frederick Engels
1845-1846. [1970] *The German Ideology*. New York: International Publishers.
1848 [1970]. Manifesto of the Communist Party. In *Selected Works*, by Karl Marx and Frederick Engels. Moscow: Progress Publishers.

Meillassoux, Claude 1972. From reproduction to production. *Economy and Society* 1:93-105.

Murphy, Yolanda and Robert F. Murphy 1974. *Women of the Forest*. New York: Columbia University Press.

Needham, Rodney 1971a. Introduction. In *Rethinking Kinship and Marriage*, edited by R. Needham. Association of Social Anthropologists, Monograph 11. London: Tavistock.

Needham, Rodney 1971b. Remarks on the analysis of kinship and marriage. In *Rethinking Kinship and Marriage*, edited by R. Needham. Association of Social Anthropologists, Monograph 11. London: Tavistock.

Onions, C.T., ed. 1966. *The Oxford Dictionary of English Etymology*. Oxford: Clarendon Press.

Rappaport, Roy A. 1967. *Pigs for the Ancestors*. New Haven: Yale University Press.

Rivière, Peter 1971. "Marriage: A reassessment." In *Rethinking Kinship and Marriage*. edited by R. Needham. Association of Social Anthropologists, Monograph 11. London: Tavistock.

Rosaldo, Michelle Zimbalist and Louise Lamphere, eds. 1974. *Woman, Culture and Society*. Stanford: Stanford University Press.

Schneider, David M. 1968. *American Kinship*. Englewood Cliffs, N.J.: Prentice-Hall.

Schneider, David M. 1972. 'What is kinship all about?' In *Kinship Studies in the Morgan Centennial Year*, edited by P. Reining. Washington, D.C.: Anthropological Society of Washington.

Silverman, Martin G. 1977. Some problems in the understanding of Oceanic kinship. In *The Changing Pacific*, edited by N. Gunson. Melbourne: Oxford University Press. In press.

Smith, Dorothy 1975. An analysis of ideological structures and how women are excluded. *Canadian Review of Sociology and Anthropology* 12:353-369.

Stephenson, Marylee, ed. 1973. *Women in Canada*. Toronto: New Press.

Terray, Emmanuel 1972. "Historical materialism and segmentary lineage-based societies." In *Marxism and "Primitive" Societies*, by J. Terray. New York: Monthly Review Press.

Tonkinson, Robert 1975. Semen versus spirit-child in a Western desert culture. Forthcoming.

Turner, David H. 1977. "The concept of kinship: Some qualifications based on a re-examination of the Australian data." *Bijdragen tot de Taal-Land-en Volkenkunde* 133:23-43.

Turner, David H. 1978. Structuralism, social organization and ecology. *L'Homme*.

Wagner, Roy 1974. Are there social groups in the New Guinea Highlands? In *Frontiers of Anthropology*, edited by M. J. Leaf. New York: Van Nostrand.

Weiner, Annette B. 1976. *Women of Value, Men of Renown: New Perspectives in Trobriand Exchange*. Austin: University of Texas Press.

Williams, Raymond 1961. *The Long Revolution*. London: Chatto and Windus.

Williams, Raymond 1976. *Keywords*. London: Coume Helm.

Zaretsky, Eli n.d. *Capitalism, the Family, and Personal Life*. A *Canadian Dimension* Pamphlet, reprinted from *Socialist Revolution*.

CHAPTER 3

THE ECOLOGICAL-EVOLUTIONARY MODEL AND THE CONCEPT OF MODE OF PRODUCTION

Two Approaches to Material Reproduction

MICHAEL I. ASCH
University of Alberta

INTRODUCTION

The subject of this essay is how anthropologists study the process by which human societies produce and circulate the material goods needed for continued existence and how changes in this process might arise.

I would like to compare two very different models used by many anthropologists who study processes of "material production." One, often called "cultural ecology" and/or "cultural evolution" (and which I will call "ecological-evolutionary") sees these processes analogous to those of genetic-evolutionary biology.[1] The other sees the processes as uniquely human and reducible to a complex set of technical and social factors called a "mode of production."

The primary objective of this essay is to introduce the mode of production model and explain some of the reasons for its superiority as an explanation of the general processes of material reproduction. In order to do this, I will first lay out what I consider to be the main principles and methods of the ecological-evolutionary model. Then, after providing some of the fundamental shortcomings which make it unacceptable as a general model of material reproduction and change, I will turn to a more detailed discussion of the mode of production model as an alternative. In my conclusions, I will address a few remarks to the limitation of the mode of production approach for "explaining" change.

THE ECOLOGICAL-EVOLUTIONARY APPROACH

The ecological-evolutionary position rests on an analogy between human societies and biological populations. On the one hand, it asserts that human societies and biological populations are similar in that 1) they both evolve specific adaptions to particular environments, and 2) when examined chronologically both exhibit a development through time from simpler forms with lower energy capturing potentials to more complex ones with higher capacities (Sahlins & Service 1960:12f).

On the other hand, it equally recognizes that human societies differ markedly from biological species in that the transmission of specific characteristics—and thus the potential to "evolve" and "adapt"—is not controlled genetically, but is rather the result of "culture" (or knowledge acquired through learning and transmitted symbolically (as through language)). However, the difference between the two forms of transmission is generally argued to be one of quantity, not quality, for it is asserted that transmission through culture merely represents the logical development of genetic transmission into a more efficient and adaptable form. Indeed, as a definition of culture, the members of this school suggest, "culture is man's means of adaptation."

In short, the ecological-evolutionary model asserts that human societies can be seen as behaving very much like biological species. And it follows from this thesis that proponents of the model consider that concepts such as "adaptation" and "evolution" developed in genetic-evolutionary biology can be extended properly to the study of material reproduction in human society, provided of course that "cultural" transmission is substituted for "genetic."

For the purpose of analysis, the ecological-evolutionary model divides the study of material reproduction in human society into three phases: *Production*, which is seen as a consequence of "adaptation" and an aspect of "cultural ecology"; *Distribution*, or the allocation of goods and services, a topic which is discussed under the rubric "substantive economics"; and *Change*, which is conceived of as an aspect of variability in adaptation and hence an aspect of "cultural evolution." Finally, the model makes certain assertions regarding causality in the relationship between material reproduction of society and the formation of certain social institutions.

*   *   *

In the ecological-evolutionary approach, *production* is considered a by-product of a society's "adaptation." That is, it is one outcome of the interrelationship between the specific environment in which a society exists and its "culture core" (or the particular constellation of features developed by that society to exploit its environment). Of these features, most crucial both to adaptation and production is subsistence technology. Four main kinds of subsistence technology are recognized. These include:

82

1. *Hunting-gathering:* in which naturally raised foodstuffs (i.e., animals, vegetables, and fruits) are captured by hunting, fishing, and gathering techniques, using tools such as clubs, spears, knives, bow-and-arrow, traps, and snares.
2. *Animal husbandry:* in which animals, such as sheep and goats, are domesticated and held captive by means of corrals, surrounds, and/or the use of other domesticated animals such as dogs.
3. *Slash-and-burn agriculture:* in which crops are raised by techniques such as burning the bush in order to fertilize the soil, and thus require the shifting of fields at regular intervals.
4. *Irrigation agriculture:* or the raising of crops using techniques such as irrigation that allow for permanent use of fields.

The level of production available to a society is said to be controlled by three factors. The first and by far the most important is the "techno-environment" or the relationship between the society's environmental context and its means of adaptation (or subsistence technology). Furthermore, except in rare instances such as enormous environmental richness, the productive potential of the "techno-environment" is conceived to be almost exclusively a function of the productive potential of the kind of subsistence technology adopted. That is, in a given environment, the productive potential of a society will depend upon which subsistence technology it uses to exploit it.

The second factor said to control the amount of production is the "ecological function" of specific institutions within a society. One example of this phenomenon is the Kaiko ritual of the Tsembaga which Rappaport claims is a mechanism which directly controls pig populations and, since pigs eat yams, indirectly acts as a means of maximizing production in that staple food (Rappaport 1967).

The third factor controlling production is said to be labour in the technical sense of its organization efficiency and the intensity of effort expended in production. The incorporation of this factor is based on recent studies of people like the !Kung Bushmen (Lee 1969) which hold that "underproduction," or production below maximum sustainable yields, is due in some degree to the limited time and effort expended in the productive process.

Furthermore, it is claimed that the culture core as a whole and especially the techno-environment of a society will affect the development of other social institutions in two ways. Firstly, it is asserted that the productive potential of a particular techno-environmental adaptation will determine the general level of institutional complexity attainable by a particular society. That is, for example, a society such as the !Kung that depends on a hunting-gathering subsistence technology in an environment of "average productivity" is thought unable to produce a permanent enough surplus to support a large class of non-producers required as in a complex society.

Secondly, it is often argued that a society's techno-environmental adaptation will determine the shape of other social institutions that are closely tied to the productive process. Thus, for example, Julien Steward, one of the fathers of modern Cultural Ecology stated that

> *the occurrence of patrilineal bands among certain hunting peoples and of fragmented families among the Western Shoshoni is closely determined by their subsistence activities (1955:41).*

Although this claim has lost some favour among some prominent exponents of the ecological-evolutionary model, others, like the Cultural Materialist Marvin Harris, still adhere to it rigorously. Harris states (1968:4):

> *This principle [of techno-economic determinism] holds that similar environments tend to produce similar arrangements of labour in production and distribution and that these in turn call forth similar kinds of social groupings. . . .*

On the other hand, even those who, today, take a much less determinist view of the techno-environment still seem to see it as determining at least the general form of other closely related social institutions. Thus, for example, Netting, after repudiating the specific claims made by Steward above, still takes the position (1977:14) that "the fluidity of local group composition among hunters-gatherers is obviously correlated with environment and the size of the human group utilizing it."

The distribution or allocation of goods and services is said to be based on principles of "exchange." Three fundamental kinds of exchange systems are recognized. These are:

1. *Reciprocity:* or the direct exchanges of goods and services between symmetrical groups such as individuals, kinship groups or local bands.
2. *Redistribution:* or the movement of goods and services to an administrative centre and their return to local groups by the Central Authorities.
3. *Market exchange:* or the exchange of goods and services on the basis of supply and demand and through the use of all-purpose money.

While it is accepted that societies with market exchange economies will have institutions with specific economic functions, it is argued that in societies with reciprocal or redistributive economies, the distribution or exchange function is embedded in other institutions such as religious festivals, village feasts, and/or kinship obligations. As well, there is a clear implication that the form of exchange dominant in a society is dependent to some extent on the productive surpluses generated by the techno-environmental adaptation. Thus for example, it is argued that societies which depend primarily on hunting and gathering do not, except in unusual cases of environmental richness, produce enough surplus to allow a redistribution exchange system to become dominant (Otterbein 1972:32).

Finally, it is suggested that in some instances a specific system of distribution may result from a particular techno-environmental adaptation. This is exemplified by an interpretation of the potlatch among the Northwest Coast Indians which suggests that the peculiar techno-environment of that region provided great variability in levels of surplus and thus necessitated a redistributive exchange system such as is found in the potlatch (Vayda 1961, Harris 1975:292-5).

In the ecological-evolutionary model *change* is conceived of as an aspect of a society's techno-environmental adaptation and can be described as the creation of a new equilibrium in the interrelationship between the "culture core" and the environment. New equilibria occur because there is continual variation both in the "culture core" and the environment. This variation in the case of the culture core arises through faulty transmission, recombinations, borrowings from adjacent cultures, or independent invention (Sahlins and Service 1960:24). In the case of environment, it can result from such natural phenomena as shifts in climate or size or composition of animal and plant populations.

Given the above, change can be said to occur either when a society recombines, borrows, poorly transmits or invents new culture traits in order to readapt to new environmental conditions, or when through recombinations, borrowings, mis-transmissions or new inventions, a society fundamentally alters the manner in which it adapts to its environment (Sahlins and Service 1960:57).

As in biological populations, change can be described as occuring in two evolutionary progressions. The first, called *specific evolution,* refers to the process whereby human societies evolve, through time, more productive ways of adapting to their particular environments. The second, or *general evolution,* concerns the process whereby human society has, through time, evolved more productive means of exploiting the environment from less productive ones (Sahlins and Service 1960:12f).

The process of general evolution is said to be "incremental." Yet a number of distinct "stages" of development can be recognized. As these are distinguishable primarily on the basis of their inherent energy-capturing potential, they are said to correspond, broadly speaking, to the forms of "techno-environmental" adaptation, and specifically the kinds of subsistence technologies described above.

CRITIQUE OF THE ECOLOGICAL-EVOLUTIONARY MODEL

Recent years have witnessed a growing dissatisfaction with ecological-evolutionary models (see, for example, Alland 1972, Friedman 1974, Godelier 1972, Murphy 1971). Indeed, it has been abandoned by at least one of its earliest proponents (Sahlins 1972). Yet this dissatisfaction has not been clearly expressed in texts intended for introductory students. Rather, as is the case of Harris (1975), Netting (1977) and Otterbein (1972)—all authors of recent introductory texts—the adequacy of this approach remains unquestioned.

Below, then, I will undertake this exercise and outline three of the main criticisms that have led me to conclude that the ecological-evolutionary model is unsatisfactory and that an alternative which better explains material reproduction and change in human society should be developed.

1. The first criticism is that while the model is able to describe and classify *forms* of "adaptation" and "evolution," it cannot account for the *process* by which "adaptation" and "evolution" are realized. To put it in concrete terms, the model can describe the form of a particular techno-enviromental adaptation and it can even classify specific "stages" of evolution, but it cannot explain the process by which a techno-environmental adaptation or a transformation from one evolutionary stage to another took place.

Yet, the power of the evolutionary model in biology (and hence presumably its reason for being extended to society and culture) does not arise primarily because of its ability to classify and describe forms, but rather because it provides a scientific theory (which has only recently been "proven" empirically) to account for *process*. The nub of this theory is the hypothesis that "adaptation" and "evolution" result from the mutual operation of two autonomous dynamic variables: the genetic-reproductive system of a biological species and the environmental system within which that species exists.

By contrast, in the ecological-evolutionary model, while much attention is paid to the analysis of the systemic operation of the "environmental context" within which a human society exists, no scientific hypothesis has been generated to account for the systemic operation of the internal dynamic of human adaptation. That is, there is no thesis comparable to the genetic reproductive hypothesis of evolutionary biology to account for how culture traits are structured and recombined.

Without such a thesis, it is of course not possible to assert with any degree of certainty that human societies "behave" like biological populations, except, perhaps, in the most superficial ways. Nor, of course, can one develop a model parallel to that found in evolutionary biology to explain the process by which "adaptation" and "evolution" take place. Indeed, ultimately all the model can do is describe and classify the *apparent* results of the *presumed* operation of an undefined *process*.

2. The second criticism concerns *causality* and refers specifically to the claim that the techno-environment determines both the *level of* complexity which a society can develop and (at least in the opinion of some exponents) the *shape* of social institutions intimately connected with the productive process.

At the outset I will agree that the first part of this claim is valid, but hasten to add that, at least at the very general level at which it is advanced, it is hardly significant. By contrast, the second part of the claim would prove of great significance if it could be validated empirically. Unfortunately, this is not the case.

One of the most elegant refutations of this assertion is provided in the following comparison by Godelier (1974:46f). Both white and Montagnais-Naskapi trappers exploit fur bearers in the Labrador peninsula. Both groups exploit precisely the same environment, use precisely the same technology and pursue precisely the same resources. That is, each group has the same techno-environmental adaptation. Nonetheless, each group developed a unique and different way of institutionalizing all aspects of their social life, even those which dealt explicitly with the way in which fur bearers would be exploited. Clearly, then, the same techno-environmental adaptation had produced different social results and hence the claim that it determines the shape of certain social institutions intimately ties to subsistence is refuted.

A similar fate awaits the claim that hunting-gathering adaptations are "flexible." Flexibility is usually defined as "that (which) may be adapted or accommodated"; or as "adjustable to change" (McKechnie 1957:701). As such it clearly does not depend on techno-environmental adaptation, but is rather a characteristic universal to human society (and indeed to biological populations as well). Nor does techno-environmental adaptation even play a significant role if "flexibility" is defined in the more restricted sense of "the ability to move people to resources." All societies have this ability and, indeed, constantly circulate both people and resources. The mix as well as the "ease" with which this occurs appears to depend much more on patterns of trade, methods of transportation and ideological factors, than upon subsistence technology (Turner 1978).

Admittedly, there is one condition under which I believe the claim might be substantiated. It is the techno-environmental adaptation that could result given the use of certain subsistence technologies under extreme *environmental* conditions. But, of course, such cases would be a rarity.

In short, then, with the possible exception cited above, the evidence indicates that techno-environmental adaptation plays little significant role in the formation of social institutions. One is forced to conclude, therefore that, except in the most trivial ways, the shape of social institutions and the level of social complexity appears to arise independently of technical aspects of production.

3. My third criticism of ecological-evolutionary anthropology is philosophical and specifically concerns the conception of human existence implied by the model. To me, extending the evolutionary biological model to the analysis of human societies implies that we, like biological populations, reproduce our material existence and change through processes which are largely outside our control. Now such a fatalistic view of the human condition may well reflect the perceptions and experience of some anthropologists, and, indeed, it may also accurately mirror the apparent realities of both anthropologists and their subjects of study during the late colonial period.

However, such a perspective does not reflect the emerging reality of the post-colonial world as recently decolonized peoples begin to reshape societies deeply warped by the colonial experience. Nor, closer to home, does it mirror the perceptions of many Native American peoples—such as the Dene of the Canadian Northwest Territories—who are struggling hard against long odds for the right to determine for themselves how they will shape their own existence. For them, to paraphrase a famous title of an article on evolutionary theory, the question is not, *does* man control his own civilization (White 1968), but rather, *which* men control it?

Thus, recent evidence would seem to indicate that the conception of man's relationship to the processes of material reproduction and change is not correct. Men do control them. Hence, any model which posits to the contrary—that the processes are remote and removed from our consciousness—must be considered "inaccurate."

In short, then, ecological-evolutionary anthropology classifies forms but does not show the processes by which these forms maintain themselves (that is adapt) and change (that is evolve). Its claim to demonstrate that social institutions are structured on the basis of techno-environmental factors is not sustained by empirical evidence. Also contrary to recent evidence, it posits that the process of change operates completely outside the consciousness of human beings. It is primarily for these reasons that I believe the model is untenable and that an alternative method of explaining the processes of material reproduction and change therein, must be developed.

To my mind, the approach that offers the most promise focuses on the mode of production and I will now turn to a brief exposition of its main features.

THE CONCEPT OF MODE OF PRODUCTION

The concept of a mode of production rests ultimately on a presumed logical consequence of two fundamental assumptions about the nature of human beings. The first is that humans possess "consciousness" or the ability to think rationally. The second is that a person can never alone fulfill all his material needs throughout his lifetime. Thus, it is argued, people must enter into social relationships with others in order to reproduce their material conditions and, because people possess the ability to think rationally, it follows that these relationships are conscious and thus will play a formative role in structuring the process of material reproduction.

As a consequence, it is asserted that the process of material reproduction in human society cannot be understood merely by analyzing the "technical" aspects of production. Rather, it is argued, the framework of analysis must include at the most fundamental level both the "physics" of production and the social relationships human beings enter into in order to motivate (or operate) the technical dimension of production.

This key concept—that the structure of material reproduction in-

88

corporates both technical and social components—can be illustrated by the following concrete example. Take a look at the book you are now reading. It is a material good and as such is a product that contains certain raw materials which have been transformed by the use of certain instruments and a certain amount of labour power into a useful product—a book. But this analysis is only partially complete. Because human labour is involved, the process of material reproduction involves many social relationships, all of which you, as the purchaser of the book, are party to. These include not only your relationship with me as the author, but also your relation to all the labourers who produced this book from the salesperson who sold it to you to the lumberer who cut down the tree which provided the paper for the book. As well, because we live in a capitalist society, by purchasing this book you have provided income for the publisher who owns the printing press, the business person who owns the logging mill, the trucking firm that transported the book, the store owner where you bought the book and, lastly, the corporation that owns the timber rights to the land from which the paper for this book came. In other words, by purchasing the book you have not only participated in a technical process, you have also helped to reproduce a set of social relationships in which some people (entrepreneurs or capitalists) received income because they "own" or "control" raw materials or technology, while others (workers) received income by providing labour power for these "owners."

From a formal point of view, a mode of production can be defined as a structure which results from the mutual and simultaneous operation of two sets of components: the technical and the social. In order to understand the operation of this structure, the analysis begins by examining each of the components separately.

The technical sphere is defined as consisting of three primary elements, known collectively as the *"forces of production."* The first is called "land" or "natural resources." It is equivalent to "environment" in the ecological-evolutionary model and refers specifically to the raw materials used in production. The second, often called "technology," incorporates into a single aspect both the "subsistence technology" and the infrastructure through which goods are produced and circulated. The final factor is "labour" or "labour power." It deals with labour expenditure and its organization in the process of production. As in the ecological-evolutionary model, the physical potential of a system to produce materials is said to be determined by the interaction of these three factors.

The social component is known as *"the social relations of production."* It is somewhat analogous to "social structure" but it takes as its point of departure, not abstract principles such as "descent" or "kinship" or questions of biological reproduction, but rather focuses on the relationships that obtain in the production process. It includes concepts, such as "ownership" and "control" over the means of production that are intimately tied to this process. The amount of material production necessary to continue an economic system beyond the mere replacement of the means of production is determined by the social relations of production. That is, unlike the ecological-evolutionary model, which sees the social relations of production as determined by the technical capabilities of a system to produce surpluses, the concept of a mode of production implies that the existing social relations of production will—within limitations imposed by the technical potentials of a system—determine the quantity and type of material goods that will be produced.

Thus all systems of material reproduction are structured on the basis of two imperatives: one is the possibilities inherent in a particular set of productive forces, the other the necessities required to reproduce the social relations that motivate the system. At times the two are in harmony and in such situations the society is marked by stability. This is illustrated by the example of the Slavey Indians of the Canadian Northwest Territories in the late precontact period.

THE EXAMPLE OF THE SLAVEY INDIANS

The primary unit of production was the "local production group" (or local band). It consisted of perhaps twenty or thirty individuals who were collectively responsible, under normal conditions, for their own material survival. The primary "raw materials" used by this group consisted of large game animals such as moose and caribou, small game animals such as beaver and muskrat, and fish, berries and timber. The game animals were dispersed so that moose and caribou ran freely throughout the region, but small game and fish were found in abundance in microenvironments close to the lakes which dominate the area. The primary dynamic of the raw materials was the cycles that created variation in animal population sizes and distributions in different years.

The subsistence technology at this time was dominated by techniques associated with snaring and entrapment. Thus, for example, all animals, even some big game such as moose, were captured by building snares along habitual trails through the forest and muskeg. Fish were taken by netting. As well, tools such as the bow-and-arrow and spear were used to capture big game, especially when crossing open water. Finally, fires may have been set in spring time to open up potential grazing areas for certain big game such as moose which like to feed on secondary growths (Lewis 1977).

In winter, transportation depended exclusively on labour power and was accomplished on foot. In summer, however, waterways transecting the region were the main transport routes.

Production was then a labour intensive activity. Labour was divided along age and sex lines with the adult men responsible primarily for the capture of big game animals which required much mobility. The old men, women and children were responsible for the production of small game and fish associated with the lake environments. Thus, groups encamped most frequently around the shores of lakes and it was from these bases that the men would roam the countryside. However, due to the problems of winter transport, whenever large game was captured at any distance from the encampment, people would move the camp to its place of capture.

The evidence indicates, contrary to popular belief, that there were sufficient raw materials that the entire Slavey population could easily be sustained given their traditional subsistence technology. However, due to the variability of the resource base, there were occasions when an area exploited by a local production group could not maintain its material requirements. The "problem," then, was how to get surpluses to people in need. Obviously, given the limitations of the transportation system, it would be virtually impossible to shift goods to people. The alternative, adopted by the Slavey, was to move people to areas of potential surplus, even when these were inhabited by other local production groups.

The social dimension of this mode of production was characterized by collective control of "land" and "raw materials." This was not just by the local production group, but rather by the Slaveys as a whole. As a result, no one group could deny access to land as a means of production to members of any other local group. On the other hand, subsistence technology and labour power were controlled by individuals, while transportation routes, being an aspect of "land," were communally held.

The actual production harvested was mutually shared by all members of the local group. That is, generally speaking all participated equally in the good fortune of the hunters and all suffered equally when their luck turned bad. Although the distribution system was basically informal, there was apparently some formality concerning the way in which certain animals were shared in that specific parts were reserved for the hunter and closely related persons. In this way, individual ability could be recognized, but not at the expense of the collective good.

These relations of production were expressed *juridically* by a kinship system that, through the use of lateral extensions, incorporated the rights of local production group membership to all Slaveys (and indeed all Dene); an inheritance system that forbade the transmission of land, raw materials, technology and, indeed, "special" hunting knowledge from one generation to another; and a marriage system that required for its operation the continual outmovement of members of each local production group. It was expressed as well in an *ideology* that did not allow "sacred" knowledge to be transmitted from one human being to another.

THE QUESTION OF CHANGE

The above example illustrates how a mode of production can create stability and how it can extend its influence beyond the system of material reproduction to incorporate social and ideological aspects of a society. Now I would like to turn my attention to a brief examination of how the concept can be used to analyze the process of change in general and specifically the process by which a transformation in the structure of a mode of production arises.

Obviously, structured change can be imposed by external forces as has happened, for example, during the recent colonial period. How this takes place and the forms of resistance to it are of utmost historical importance. Elsewhere (Asch 1977) I have dealt in detail with this issue as it relates specifically to the Dene of the Canadian Northwest Territories. Here, however, I will not again cover that ground. Rather, I will limit my discussion to another and theoretically more difficult question: how a transformation can arise within the existing mode of production itself.

To begin with, although modes of production have "flexible" structures and thus are able to accommodate many variations and improvements without changing their fundamental form, they are not infinitely malleable. Indeed, the very direction of their "flexibility" would appear to depend on their structure. The introduction of certain "innovations," both technical and social, even those considered to be "advances," will be greatly resisted simply because their use could undermine this structure. Thus, for example, in the feudal period it proved virtually impossible to introduce new and more efficient scythes. Although these would have lightened the labour of serfs, the latter strongly resisted their use. The reason was the scythe's very efficiency "for, by cutting crops close to the ground, less would be left for gleanage which was a widely established right of serfs" (Kay 1976:23). Another example, from our own society, is the great resistance on the part of corporations to the introduction of pollution controls, a development all would agree would greatly improve our quality of life. This resistance is not caused primarily by the "perniciousness" of individual entrepreneurs, but rather by the underlying logical structure of our mode of production which requires a company to produce as cheaply as possible or be driven out of business.

Thus, given that these structures only have a limited elasticity, there are, theoretically, situations that might arise which would require changes that transcended the logical structure of the system. These might be caused by some external factors, such as in the Slavey case, a severe depletion of raw materials throughout their entire region or the forced introduction of new social relations of production engendered by individual trapline registration. But what is most crucial to our argument here, is that it is possible to envisage such situations arising directly out of the operation of a system of material reproduction itself. Thus, hypothetically, there could be a case in which the social relations of production on the one hand demand ever-increasing production while, on the other, the forces of production fix a finite limit on the potential productive capabilities of that society. Under such circumstances, although the disparity between the two dynamics might not be apparent at the early stages of their development, eventually the antagonism between the two could become so great that the entire mode of material reproduction faces collapse.

Clearly, the development of such conditions sets the stage for a structural transformation, but it does not ensure it. The transcending of a mode of production requires the introduction of new factors, of which at least the following three are essential.

The first, and by far the most important, is conscious knowledge of an alternative method of material reproduction that includes, at minimum, a clear concept of alternate relations of production. Our model asserts that man has the ability to think rationally and, at minimum, "rational thought" must include the ability to conceptualize the negation of a revealed reality. Out of this "dialectical" process, then, alternative conceptions can arise through, at minimum, the recombination of existing elements and their negations. This can be exemplified by our ability to conceptualize the alternative of a system in which producers would control the means of production, although we now live within a mode of production characterized by its negation. This was demonstrated in the work of Karl Marx which laid out the process by which the capitalist mode of production would create conditions in which such a transformation could take place.

The second condition is that the productive forces in existence must be developed sufficiently to sustain the new relations of production. In other words, it places a minimum limit on the kinds of alternatives that can be instituted.

The third factor is political power. By this I mean the ability to mobilize collective action on the part of many people to ensure the realization of a particular transformation. While at times this may involve a military component, at minimum all that is required is the general acceptance that the new relations of production provide a better solution to the problem of material reproduction than do the ones presently dominant.

Thus, in sum, the "mode of production" position asserts that internally generated transformation can take place, even under "pristine" conditions (Fried 1967). The normal operation of a mode of production will, on the one hand, present, through the intrinsic limitations to its flexibility, the context within which structural change occurs. On the other hand, it will create, from the existing social relations of production, the materials out of which people can construct new forms. Yet, structural change is not "automatic" and the potential for its realization remains dormant until people, apprehending new possibilities arising from old elements, mobilize collectively and act to transform it.

THE KATCHIN

An example which neatly illustrates the operation of all these dynamics is provided in Johnathon Friedman's analysis of the mode of production of the Katchin of highland Burma (1974, 1975). Among the

Katchin, the forces of production are such that for optimum operation, the system of farming requires twelve fallow years for each year
planted. Beyond this point, fertility and productivity of labour decrease greatly. Thus, the system requires thirteen times the land used
in a single season in order to operate at an optimum. The primary
unit of appropriation and exchange is the local lineage. Several local
lineages form a hamlet which usually clears a single field.

Relations of production are organized so that land is communally
held by all Katchin. However, surpluses accumulated by each local
lineage are considered to be its own property. Nonetheless, the property must be shared in that it must be distributed to all during religious feasts.

The fact that surpluses are not controlled by the whole community
leads to the possibility of social differentiation. This potential is reinforced by a marriage system based on generalized exchange in which
marriage partners cannot be exchanged directly but must be circulated indirectly. That is, if local lineage A gives a "woman" to lineage
B, B cannot give one back directly. Rather, A receives its women from
another lineage which is linked to it by a circular chain. This process
can be diagrammed as follows:

$$\text{A} \longrightarrow \text{B} \longrightarrow \text{C} \longrightarrow \text{D} \longrightarrow \text{E}$$

One aspect of the marriage exchange system is the existence of
"bride price" and thus material goods circulate in the opposite direction. All things being equal, this would have no effect on the operation of the system. However, the mere existence of bride price as an
aspect of the system creates the potential to undermine its egalitarian
nature for it allows for the material expression of status differentiation.

This potential for social differentiation is further reinforced and ultimately "operationalized" by an ideology that considers surpluses to
be the result of "god's will" rather than man's work. Hence, those
lineages that can provide the largest feasts are considered to be favoured by the gods. As a result, they obtain increased prestige and so
can command higher prices for their daughters. And, with this additional "currency" they can "purchase" more women so that, ultimately, they create for themselves a still larger labour force and so can
potentially increase production still further.

The process by which differentiation develops ultimately creates a
ranked hierarchy (gumsa) out of a series of equal lineages (gumlao).
This consists of chiefly lineages which control entire domains; aristocratic lineages which, under the direction of the chiefs, control a cluster of villages; and commoner lineages which operate within a single
village. The social relations are held together by the continued maintenance of the generalized exchange marriage rule. Only now it takes
a slightly different form.

Chiefly lineages from a number of domains now marry in an egalitarian circle with goods flowing in one direction and women in the

other. Within each domain, aristocratic lineages also marry in a circle as, ultimately, do local lineages within a single village. The link which unites these "ranks" into a single unit is provided by marriage exchanges between a chiefly lineage and one of its aristocratic lineages and, again, between the aristocratic lineage and one of the commoner lineages within a village. This link is realized through hypogamy, that is, women marrying down. Due to the difference in rank, the bride price, in such cases, is set extremely high. These prices continue to rise for two reasons. First, chiefly surpluses, and hence prestige, grow, and second, in order to maintain rank differences in prestige, debts must be incurred by aristocrats. Thus, prices are set at levels that cannot be sustained even under optimum conditions.

Thus, according to Friedman's analysis, the most fundamental flaw in this mode of production is the antagonism between a set of productive relations that require ever-expanding surpluses matched with a set of productive forces that only provide finite ones.

Initially at the egalitarian (or *gumlao*) stages, this flaw is not realized, for the system has a great capability for expansion. However, as the limits of extension of production are reached, the flaw in the system becomes manifest, for, although first rates of return and then absolute surpluses begin to decline, this has no effect on the "inflation" rate in bride prices. The initial response on the part of the aristocratic lineages tied to the chiefly ones is to intensify production. But this eventually produces diminished returns and, thus, in the end, these lineages pile up such debts that they are reduced to a de facto workforce and thus to the status of commoners.

According to Friedman's analysis, by this point the chiefly lineages will attempt to "transform" the mode of production by introducing new relations of production. In the actual case, they borrow the system of the neighbouring Shan states and introduce true class relations characteristic of the "archaic state." Here society is divided into two endogamous classes: the non-producers, or chiefly lineages; and the direct producers, or an amalgamation of aristocratic and commoner lineages.

On the other side are the aristocratic and "commoner" lineages which, apparently, see the developing contradictions as growing from a "perversion" of the proper operation of the existing social relations of production and, hence, do not develop an alternative conceptualization of the social relations of production.

This whole process could develop naturally in Katchin society. The existing relations of production do, in fact, operate to create greater antagonisms between the chiefs who control more and more surpluses but directly produce less and less, and the aristocrats who control less and less production activity but must participate ever increasingly in the productive process. This antagonism drives the aristocrats closer and closer to the commoners and thus produces the incipient class formation of the archaic state. However, as long as there still exist marriage links between the chiefs and the now "de facto" commoners (the aristocrats), this class relationship has no *juridical* expression. Yet, as the system continues, a point will come in which the aristocrats are so indebted that they can no longer pay the bride price and, as intermarriage would then stop, the juridical impediment to true class relations would be removed and the classical archaic state could emerge. Thus, hypothetically, this conceptualization would not need to be borrowed but could emerge directly from the operation of the Katchin's mode of production itself.

In either case it becomes apparent that the productive forces are not developed enough for the chiefly lineages to maintain the existing social relations of production in face of the collective opposition of aristocrats and commoners. As a result, a rebellion against the chiefs led by the aristocratic lineages will be successful. Yet, because the victors do not have an alternative conceptualization of their system, their victory merely reforms the surface inequities in the system and leaves untouched the underlying conditions which could eventually lead once again to the same antagonistic contradiction.

CONCLUSION

As the foregoing discussion indicates, the concept of "mode of production" is superior to the ecological-evolutionary approach, in that it demonstrates that the technical and social aspects of material reproduction in human society are really two dimensions of the same structure, and it enables us to see the process by which material reproduction both operates and creates conditions which demand structural change. Furthermore, by positing that human beings are "conscious" at least with respect to understanding the relationship between the two dimensions, it adds a motivating force both to the process of material reproduction and its transformations.

However, this is not to say that the model—at least the one posited here—has "solved" satisfactorily the problem posed at the beginning of this essay: "the process by which human societies produce and circulate material goods needed for continued existence and how changes in the mode of this process might arise." Further work must be done, particularly on the issues of "dialectics" and consciousness, which will enable us to see how change arises and is accomplished. For now I can merely underline my belief that it is human actions— and not matter itself—that in the end determine the direction of change. However, I would also hold that new directions can only be perceived through the immanent possibilities developed through the operation of the system itself.

NOTES

1. *Students should be aware that there are many strains of thought among cultural ecologists and cultural evolutionists and that this essay is not intended as a survey of them all. Nor is it intended as a summary of recent developments in the field.*

Rather, my aim is to provide a concise critique of what I consider to be dominant trends in the thinking of those who have adopted ecological and evolutionary models. Nonetheless, the field is rather heterodox, and I am sure that some of the concepts I lay out here as characteristic of the approach—or at least my formulations of them—will not be shared by all anthropologists who label themselves either cultural ecologists and/or cultural evolutionists.

2. *Although Friedman's analysis offers an explanation of the operation of Katchin society that differs from that of Leach (1961, 1965) and Levi-Strauss (1969), it does not contradict them. Rather, it provides a material basis for their analyses. For the intellectually ambitious student, a useful exercise would be to read each scholar's explanations, beginning, perhaps, with Leach (1965) which is based primarily on cultural features, then moving on to Levi-Strauss (1969: chapts. 15 and 16) and Leach (1961) all of which are based on "structural logic," and then finally to Friedman's (1974, 1975) which provides a material dynamic that unites these other forms of explanation.*

BIBLIOGRAPHY

Alland, A. 1972. *The Human Imperative* New York: Columbia University Press.

Asch, M. 1977. The Dene Economy in M. Watkins (Ed.) *Dene Nation: The Colony Within.* Toronto: University of Toronto Press.

Fried, M. 1967. *The Evolution of Political Society.* New York: Random House.

Friedman, J. 1974. Marxism, Structuralism and Vulgar Materialism. *Man* Vol. 9, No. 3.

Friedman, J. 1975. Tribes, States and Transformations in M. Bloch (Ed.) *Marxist Analyses in Social Anthropology.* London: Malaby Press.

Godelier, M. 1972. *Rationality and Irrationality in Economics.* London: New Left Review Editions.

Godelier, M. 1974. Considerations Theoretique et Critique sur le Problem des Rapports entre L'Homme et Son Environment. *Social Science Information* XII: 31-60.

Godelier, M. 1972. Comments on the Concepts of Structure and Contradiction. And Reply to Seve. *International Journal of Sociology* Vol. II, No. 2-3.

Harris, M. 1968. *The Rise of Anthropological Theory.* New York: Crowell.

Harris, M. 1975. *Culture, People, Nature: An Introduction to General Anthropology.* 2nd Edition. New York: Crowell.

Kay, G. 1976. *Development and Underdevelopment: A Marxist Analysis.* London: Macmillan.

Leach, E. 1961. The Structural Implication of Matrilineal Cross-Cousin Marriage. in E. Leach *Rethinking Anthropology.* London: London School of Economics Monographs on Social Anthropology.

Leach, E. 1965. *Political Systems of Highland Burma.* Boston: Beacon Press.

Lee, R. 1969. !Kung Bushman Subsistence: an Input-Output Analysis in A. Vayda (Ed.) *Environment and Cultural Behavior.* Garden City, New York: Natural History Press.

Lévi-Strauss, C. 1969. *The Elementary Structures of Kinship.* Chaps. 15 & 16. London: Eyre and Spottiswoode.

Lewis, H. 1977. Muskuta: The Ecology of Indian Fires in Northern Alberta. *Western Canadian Journal of Anthropology* 7: 15-32.

McKechnie, J. 1957. *Webster's New Twentieth Century Dictionary of the English Language* (unabridged second edition). New York and Toronto: Library Guild, inc.

Murphy, R. 1971. *The Dialectics of Social Life.* New York: Basic Books.

Netting, R. 1977. *Cultural Ecology.* Menlo Park, Cal: Cummings Publishing Company.

Otterbein, K. 1972. *Comparative Cultural Analysis: An Introduction to Anthropology*. New York: Holt, Rinehart & Winston.

Rappaport, R. 1967. Ritual Regulation of Environmental Relations among a New Guinea People. *Ethnology* 6: 17-30.

Sahlins, M. 1972. *Stone Age Economics*. Chicago: Aldine Publishing Company.

Sahlins, M. and E. Service, 1960. Evolution and Culture. Ann Arbor: University of Michigan Press. 572 S131 Ev

Seve, L. 1972. The Structural Method and the Dialectical Method. And Reply to Godelier. *International Journal of Sociology*, Vol. II, No. 2-3.

Steward, J. 1955. *Theory of Cultural Change: The Methodology of Multilinear Evolution*. Urbana: University of Illinois Press.

Turner, D. 1978. Structuralism, Social Organization and Ecology. *L'Homme*, Spring. 572 H753

Vayda, A. 1961. A Re-Examination of Northwest Coast Economic Systems *Transactions of the New York Academy of Sciences*, Section 2. Volume 23, Number 7: 618-624.

White, L. 1968. Man's Control over Civilization: An Anthropocentric Illusion in M. Fried (Ed.) *Readings in Anthropology*, Vol. II.

CHAPTER 4
ANTHROPOLOGY
AND THE
STUDY OF RELIGION

R. McDONNELL
University of Toronto

It is not unreasonable to ask anthropologists what they mean when they use the general word "religion" in reference to such otherwise diverse phenomena as Indonesian eating habits, African cattle terms or some fine point of Buddhist theology (cf. Cohn, 1967). What, after all, could such things be said to have in common since, on the face of it, they are so utterly different? Current opinion would tend to answer this sort of question in the negative—at least on the empirical level. Religion is not so much a thing or entity as a process and, specifically, an ordering process. It is known by what it does rather than how it appears and it is of secondary importance whether this ordering function is maintained or is seen to be manifest in the context of metaphysics, eating habits, or ethical injunctions. Consequently, current definitions of religion do not markedly deal with attributes such as kinds of concepts, ideas or activities. Rather, they point in the direction of order and understanding and are thus concerned with symbolic systems and achieved meaning (Geertz 1965), comprehensive folk explanations and ordering principles (Douglas 1975:76) or, in sweeping fashion, all that "underlies and pervades" a way of life (Burridge 1973:169).

It would take many pages to trace the numerous, opposed, tangential, and parallel considerations that have culminated in the above stance on the subject of religion. My intention here is simply to make accessible the nature of certain broad shifts in emphasis and to outline the general character of some thinking on the subject. To this end it is useful to bear in mind from the beginning that part of the problem in understanding the subject matter involves the existence of different and, in certain respects, competing perspectives. This point is important, so allow me to underscore it by effecting an analogy between the following example and some general problems of collecting and classifying ethnographic material.

100

A few years ago a friend of mine who had an interest in perception made some tests with both his introductory class and some Inuit friends of his on Baffin Island. The tests involved playing a recording and then having members from each group interpret and describe the noises they heard. The recording began with deep rhythmic and breathing punctuated by a few gasps and moans. After some minutes the breathing speeded and became less rhythmic, and the moans grew louder and there was an occasional infantile peep and muffled cry. Eventually it ended in a crescendo of hoarse breathing, cries, and moans. Not a word was spoken throughout. Although both groups agreed that the sounds were made by humans their reactions were otherwise quite different. Soon after the recording started the students began to snigger and titter. Eventually they were laughing without reservation. To them the sounds indicated a couple copulating. By contrast, when the Inuit heard the recording they remained silent throughout. When asked what it was they had heard they were not immediately certain. Eventually they agreed that it had to be one of two things; either it was two men trying to run down a caribou over rough ground, or it was a single man straining with all his might on a harpoon line attached to a large seal under the ice.

If we bear in mind that the noises heard in our example are meant to represent any empirical event we may draw from this specific case a number of general considerations. Firstly, whether as noises or visual images the facts do not, in important respects speak for themselves. Properly speaking they are not heard or seen at all—they are recognized. Such recognition rests on specific means of discriminating and relating and it is these, secondly, that the anthropologist cannot presuppose in a given ethnographic investigation. Thirdly, in ordering his ethnographic evidence, the anthropologist is also obliged to discriminate and relate as he recognizes various activities and ideas as manifestations of this or that type of custom. It is on this level that there exists for the anthropologist important differences of perspective which stem, like the earliest means of identifying and classifying ethnographic material, from the broader cultural tradition out of which anthropology emerged.

In this last respect it is instructive to review some of the problems that beset those who initially tried to catalogue the cultural fragments that had been gathered by explorers, commercial travellers and missionaries who had visited non-European communities. For those who had an interest in such things during the sixteenth and seventeenth centuries, there existed a basic problem of classification, since many of the customs they wished to catalogue were odd and in obvious ways unlike anything from their own tradition. As Hogden points out (1964:167-8), but rather too objectively, these early ethnologists had two options to pursue; they could emphasize either differences or similarities between these new customs and their own. As it turned out they opted for the latter course and in doing so brought to bear a set of adjectives, images, and distinctions which, as a broad formula for classifying customs, seem entirely familiar today. By 1650, for example, travellers to strange lands were being urged to record on such matters as religion, trade, technology, eating habits, forms of marriage, myth, and methods of government.

As one might expect, the word "religion" became increasingly vague and capacious when used in this manner. The ethnographic materials which it encompassed were soon so diverse and varied in content that there was no question that religious phenomena could be identified by such specific criteria as a notion of God, church services in any of their particulars, church functionaries in any of theirs, or dogmas and doctrines derived from Biblical teachings. There was no question of it precisely because early observers could often find *no* evidence of such things. And what they did find and describe in many cases were rough similarities to some aspects of religion as they understood it. Thus, if there was no notion of God then they might find evidence of some notion of a spiritual being or power and include *that* in their description. If there was no church then some temple or shrine could be found and if no Bible, then some stories about how the world began could be located and so on (Hogden 1964:194-5).

This procedure contributed to a rather fragmented form of ethnographic documentation which lasted well into the twentieth century. Activities, stories, ideas, and beliefs identified as religious were not presented with an emphasis on their internal coherence and interrelatedness. More often than not they were presented as assemblages which simply itemized various beliefs or ritual activities in a series, frequently lumping at the end what appeared least coherent of all— the myths.

Examples of this rather unfocussed approach are to be found in the studies Rasmussen made of the Inuit during the 1920s. His work, which was based on sustained field experience and a knowledge of the language, provides a rich ethnographic document. I intend to draw on portions of it to illustrate particular points in this essay. It should be mentioned, however, that by the 1920s tutored ethnographers like Rasmussen were fully aware of the troublesome vagueness of ethnographic rubrics like "religion." They had, furthermore, a heightened sensitivity to "the natives' own view of life and its problems, their own ideas expressed in their own fashion" (Thule v. III, 1929:11). By allowing for the associations, ideas and considerations emphasized by the "natives," the ethnographer, in his turn, was allowing for the inclusion of material that was both more and other than anything he might intuitively recognize as religious in nature. It may be assumed that it was partly for this reason that Rasmussen was prompted to use the phrase "intellectual culture" in the titles of his various Inuit studies and consider things religious to be a subdivision of intellectual activity and a special branch of knowledge.

In addition, and quite explicitly (Thule v. III, 1929:10), Rasmussen also viewed "intellectual culture" (and hence religion) as derivative from material concerns and methods of maintaining life. In this regard he displays agreement with a position that received full and articulate expression at least as early as the seventeenth century and which, both before and since Rasmussen's work, has been espoused in various ways by anthropologists such as Tylor, Frazer, and Malinowski.

The stance all these men assumed on religion was retrospective in nature. Essentially it asked of religious phenomena "what would the conditions or considerations have had to have been in order for anyone to believe that idea or perform that rite?" Tylor, who published a major work in 1871, asked just this sort of question after he had quite arbitrarily defined religion as a belief in spiritual beings. The perspective employed in this enormous two volume study is evolutionary in character and, with regard to religious phenomena, Tylor saw it as a "mental history" of some sort (1958, v. 11:532). His concern, furthermore, was to demonstrate that religion, from its most rudimentary to most advanced forms, is based not on divine revelation but on human reason. His problem, however, was to discover how anyone could ever arrive at the idea that there were spiritual beings. In other words how is the idea of such a belief possible? He resolves his difficulties here by inventing an original first moment in which a reasonable but "primitive philosopher" reflects on such matters as the images of deceased or absent people that appear in dreams. How can such images appear when, in a material sense, the people either no longer exist or are not present? Tylor, playing primitive philosopher, answers by surmising that the evidence of dream images indicates a spiritual side to the material. From this utterly contrived beginning Tylor goes on to develop what he calls "the doctrine of human and other souls" and the whole business of believing in spiritual beings. Such beliefs are thus, so he argues, based on reasons not revelations. They are also based on utter ignorance of the true nature of images appearing in the mind and, in this sense, religion, for Tylor, is rooted in illusion (1958:11-13).

A century later anthropology is still entirely sympathetic to Tylor's inclination to show primitive beliefs to be rational and coherent given the premises proper to such beliefs. Indeed, some cultures, or rather some individuals in some cultures, have actually justified their beliefs in a manner similar to Tyler's argument from dream images. It is not, however, possible to go much further with Tylor since, firstly, not all people justify their beliefs in this way; secondly, not all people believe in anything that could be called spiritual beings; and, thirdly, not everyone can justify or give reasons for their beliefs whatever they may be. In this last respect Rasmussen's experience with the Iglulik is familiar to every ethnographer. After providing him with detailed information on ritual practices, rules of conduct in special situations, and descriptions of the nature of various powerful beings, the Iglulik were eventually stumped with Rasmussen's incessant use of "why." For most, the only answer to the "why" of a belief or ritual was "because it is the custom." But eventually after much thought, one old man came up with the kind of comprehensive answer for which Rasmussen seemed to be looking. In this case the justification was fear (Thule v. VIII:54). The reason, in other words, involved a sentiment and in this sense the Inuit answer points in the direction of what J. G. Frazer, and after him Malinowski, referred to as magic.

In his influential multi-volume study *The Golden Bough* (1890/1915), Frazer develped his ideas on magic and religion. Like Tylor he cast his argument in a general evolutionary design and, indeed, many of his ideas on magic found their first formulation in Tylor's work. Unlike his predecessor, however, Frazer postulated that magic preceded religion in man's development and it resulted not so much from reflection and reason as from a concerned and anxious appreciation of those events that are recognized as important but over which man has little control. It does not necessarily entail a spiritual being or agency and does have the distinctive character of being concerned with influencing events in the material world. The spells and activities of magic are thus identified, interpreted and judged in terms of a stated or implied desire to cause some definite effect.

The impetus for magic is thus anxiety and the logic behind it is, in principle, comprehensible because it is, in intent, causal. This logic, however, was judged by Frazer to be a recurring and patterned misconception of causal relationships. One main form of this pattern is illustrated by what he termed "the doctrine of lunar sympathy" (1907:369-77) for which he found evidence in the beliefs of a number of different cultures. These beliefs, in broad outline, hold that it is propitious to initiate certain activities such as, say, gardening or a business venture when the moon is waxing. When the moon is waning the reverse is believed to hold and hence such activities are avoided. Often, on the basis of less evidence than this, Frazer would then insert the notion of causality. The belief that one's vegetables or one's fortunes would grow or diminish in sympathetic accord with the natural lunar cycle was thus interpreted as a belief that the lunar cycle caused such events.

There is no doubt that some people do explain beliefs of the above kind in terms of cause and effect and ethnographers have described in detail how a people can sustain and defend such arguments in the face of failure and counter-evidence (cf. Evans-Pritchard 1937). In many cases, however, the notion of cause is not engaged by the people at all. Hence, to judge their "rain dance" as an activity believed to cause rain, the waxing moon as an agent believed to cause growth, and so on, is to distort these beliefs in important ways and render them as so much quaint mumbo jumbo. In principle it is causal and rational, in practice, ignorant absurdity.

According to Frazer, the fallacy of magic was eventually realized by certain thoughtful primitives reflecting on the inadequacy of their causal understanding. This prompted some, so his conjecture runs, to imagine a hidden more comprehensive power at work, and it was in this conscious, reflective, and sequential manner that Frazer envisioned the emergence of religion (Frazer 1907:3-4).

Malinowski (1954:85-90) rejected outright the evolutionary perspective of his predecessors, although in general design his views on magic and religion were very similar to those we have just considered. He accepted, for instance, that beliefs and rites were predicated on a mixture of sentiment and an intuited but misguided understanding of causality. In this respect his views involved no real advance. His contribution consists primarily in his emphasis on what was achieved by or followed from such beliefs and activities once they were in place. He asked, in short, of their function and argued that they helped instill a "mental attitude" which, in the case of religion, enhanced the individual's capacity to remain balanced and confident in the inevitable event of such dangers and catastrophes as birth and death. Magic, that "specific art for specific ends" as he called it, functions as the means whereby the individual can bridge with poise and optimism the gulf between his primitive ignorance and his anxious appreciation that it is necessary to try and promote certain results (e.g., the presence of adequate food and clothing) and effect the absence of certain others (e.g., starvation or exposure.)

Rasmussen's Inuit material illustrates, or can be seen to illustrate, the general position that has been advanced by Frazer and Malinowski. Caribou hunting, for instance, was extremely important as a source of food and clothing for most Inuit groups. Before the introduction of firearms, these migrating animals were intercepted in large numbers while swimming lakes and fording rivers in the later summer and fall. In general accord with Frazer's expectation, the entire period of the hunt was circumscribed with rules on how men and women were to conduct themselves. These rules pertained to such diverse considerations as eating habits, the sewing of clothing, menstruation, and the use of sealskin. An infraction of any was thought to be both wrong and dangerous. Frequently but not inevitably the danger was directly associated with the success or failure of the hunt (Thule v. VIII 1929-190-95).

In similar vein there were a variety of observances surrounding birth which involved the solitary seclusion of the mother during delivery. After delivery the child was wiped clean with the skin of a snipe and then mother and infant moved to a larger abode where they spent some weeks. During this period they were allowed female visitors but were not permitted to visit. Throughout confinement the mother was considered unclean and it was believed she emitted a smoky vapour that was invisible to humans but visible and offensive to game and certain spirit powers. She had special eating utensils used by no one outside the hut and drank only warm water. When this period ended the event was marked by the mother visiting every abode in the community and receiving from each a small piece of meat. She returned with these to the hut she usually shared with her spouse. Not until the meat had been boiled could she resume drinking cold water (Thule:169-76).

In some way these various ideas and observances would function, according to Malinowski, to buttress the solitary mother during child-birth. Since we all know about, and perhaps have had experience with, a rabbit's foot, a special pen for writing exams, or the advantages of being in a buoyant "frame of mind" in athletic competition, there is reason to take seriously his rather vague assertions in this regard. Malinowski, however, does not take the matter much further. The position as presented here would advance on the above information by recognizing the possibility that a material consideration such as hygiene may at one time have been involved in the mother's confinement. This was subsequently obscured by the inclusion of ideas and activities influenced and brought into association not by a logic of causality but by the anxieties and desires attending the inevitable dangers of childbirth. These ideas and activities, being predicated on sentiment, have in themselves no rational interconnection, since a logic of material concerns cannot connect birth, snipe skins, vapours, and warm water it is assumed they constitute a haphazard assemblage.

It is arguable whether the approach that Tylor, Frazer, and Malinowski took to religious and cognate phenomena was to any large extent derivative of the ethnographic material they examined. There seems in the overall contour of their thought, something that is slightly more than just reminiscent of the position advanced by Hobbes in 1651 and, for this reason, it is instructive to consider briefly the work of this earlier writer. Firstly, Hobbes was an outright materialist. Human knowledge, as manifest in ideas, words, beliefs, and images of all kinds is a more or less dissipated or distorted version of what is initially realized as sense impression. From initial poise, texture, visual impression, etc., we retain an image which gradually "decays" the longer we are removed from the source of sensation (1958:27). Secondly, humans intuitively grasp the notion of causation and are naturally inquisitive into causes of events around them. This natural bent is especially evident regarding those events which influence their fortunes for better or worse. Since humans do not always know the causes of events important to their fortunes, they become anxious, insecure, and fearful. This fear, thirdly, prompts them to invent an agent, and since the cause of the event is not visible, then, Hobbes argues (1958:93-4), it is presumed to be invisible. The source, fourthly, of such invisible causes derives from an original and ignorant state in which people were unable "to distinguish dreams and other strong fancies from vision and sense" and from this "did arise the greater part of the religion of (heathens) . . . and nowadays the opinion that rude people have of fairies, ghosts, and goblins and of the power of witches" (1958:31).

In drawing your attention to this similarity between the thoughts of a seventeenth century social philosopher and later anthropology, our purpose is more broadly ethnographic than narrowly historical. What it shows is that a specific means of discriminating and relating classes of ideas and activities was part of a broader tradition and not in any

106

large measure derived from the evidence. As documented, the ethnographic evidence did not require this interpretation at all and there were contemporaries of the anthropologists considered above who, in examining much the same sort of material, recognized other relations and developed quite different kinds of arguments regarding the subject of religion. Among these were Robertson Smith, Durkheim, and Lévy-Bruhl and we will consider some of their ideas below. But in doing so we should bear in mind that they too, for all their inventiveness, were also informing the evidence from the vantage of a broad intellectual tradition which had already explored such ideas as morality as a social phenomenon (Hume), and sentiments as functionally related to specific social institutions (Montesquieu). In this we have clear indication of an approach which does not take an anxious and ignorant individual as point of departure.

The publication of W. Robertson Smith's *Lectures on the Religion of the Semites* in 1889 (1972) provides some important differences to the position already reviewed. In this work Smith makes a number of points of lasting significance. Firstly, he is not concerned with creating a "primitive philosopher" who reacts and reasons in a rudimentary circumstance. Religion, for Smith, is not something selected and framed by the individual at all; it comes "as part of the general scheme of social obligations and ordinances laid upon him, as a matter of course, by his (social) position" (1972:28). Secondly, in that religion consists of both beliefs and ritual acts, it is the latter which are more important. Smith argued this on the basis that ritual observances (for the Semites) were fixed and obligatory, whereas faith in the various beliefs associated with such rites was a matter of individual discretion. He continues this important emphasis by asserting that "in . . . religion the reason was not first formulated as a doctrine and then expressed in practice, but conversely, practice preceded doctrinal theory. Men form general rules of conduct before they begin to express general principles in words; . . . religious institutions are older than religious theories" (Smith 1972:20). Thirdly, given that the core of primitive religion consisted of instutionalized ritual acts, these were subject to interpretation. In other words the ritual acts themselves expressed ideas and it was Smith's contention that such ideas were transposed from the domain of human interaction and placed a value on those aspects of social life that bound person to person, promoted social order and stressed moral obligation (Smith:53). Thus religion in its early form existed "for the preservation and welfare of society and in all that was necessary to this end every man had to take part" (Smith 1972:29).

In advancing these ideas, Smith retained the distinction between religion and magic and reserved for the latter many of those individualistic considerations already examined. Emile Durkheim, although acknowledging the inspiration of Smith's social explanation of religion, was not so accommodating. In 1912 Durkheim published *The Elementary Forms of Religious Life* (1965) in which, by way of presenting his own views, he launched a concerted and explicit attack on those attempts which based religion on individual reason, ignorance, intuited causality, and so on. In the main, his objection was that these explanations were an attempt to account for the whole in terms of the part and the constant in terms of the variable (1965:28). There is, so Durkheim would argue, no grounds for accepting the explanation that Inuit caribou hunting in the fall is circumscribed by sundry rules and given special consideration because Inuit feel insecure in their control over this important resource. Other cultures, for instance, treat with similar circumspection specific kinds of animals that are not valued as a material resource in any way. In such cases apprehension may exist but it must be taken as a part of the ritual activity and not a basis or reason for it. Similarly, important material resources may receive relatively little ritual attention or none at all. In this regard the relative lack of attention attending the individual pursuit of caribou on the open tundra is a case in point.

It is in terms of the above sorts of considerations that Durkheim asks how it is that certain places, activities, and things become "sacred"—a word he used for that which is set apart and forbidden and which he considered a necessary feature of religion. Given our case material, the question becomes "what prompts the Inuit to set apart the fall caribou hunt as a special activity?" If the answer is not within the individual and the reasons s/he might give for his/her conduct, and if it is not within nature and some intrinsically significant attribute of, say, caribou, then what explains Inuit conduct in this case? In tailoring an answer here some rather impressive liberties must be taken with Durkheim's thought. This is unavoidable but should be kept in mind.

The fall caribou hunt regularly required cooperation and the coordination of activity. Women and children drove caribou along cairn fences to places by a lake or river where men waited in kayaks ready to shoot or spear them as they swam. It is by such common action, so Durkheim would argue, that the group becomes conscious of itself and each individual senses that s/he is part of a more encompassing totality. "Caribou hunting" in consequence represents a concentrated expression of collective life and a moral experience; people cooperating with each other in harmony and social unity. It is thus the common experience of cooperation that is signified, and not the caribou, the crossing place, nor any individual's reasons for participating in the hunt. Reference to the hunt and its ritual circumscription, therefore, function as a concise representation of a kind of social experience which renders each individual as part of a larger whole.

It is roughly in these terms that Durkheim asserts that "action dominates the religious life" and it is through collectively meaningful representations of such action that an assemblage of interacting individuals gets an idea of itself as a group or society. Thus the central notion contained in religious beliefs and activities, or what Durkheim called "collective representations," is the idea of society (1965:262-3, 465-70).

108

In a more comprehensive manner Durkheim also argues that the form of social life is the basis for all "collective representations." In other words the social means of discriminating and relating constitute for an individual the basic mode that allows for the recognition and classification of order in nonsocial domains. This includes such apparently objective notions as time and space which, as first conceived, were varieties of social time and social space. Even the idea of causality was, for Durkheim, derivative of social action (1968:405-13).

Few anthropologists today would be tempted to argue such a strictly sociological line either with respect to human knowledge or religious phenomena. There is, for instance, the principal difficulty of using the form of social life as a point of departure in generating or developing conceptual order in other areas. This difficulty centres on constituting the means for recognizing a particular social form. In other words, with what does man discriminate and relate socially? Durkheim is not at all clear on this and to the extent it does concern us we will return to it briefly in reference to the work of Lévy-Bruhl. What is clear, conversely, is that it is largely due to the emphasis Durkheim helped develop that anthropology has been prompted to research certain areas. For example, in postulating the social order as a basic model, Durkheim was carried into an investigation on the structural agreement between conceptual orders in quite different domains. Latterly, anthropology has pursued this tactic to advantage and produced a number of studies which, although not granting a privileged position to social form, have shown similar arrangements of categories in various schemes of classification within the same culture. In addition, by developing the notion "collective representation," Durkheim drew attention to the social and communicative dimension of the elements of religion. He did not, as did others, challenge religious beliefs by invoking a specific rationality and then show those beliefs to be false and illusory. He accepted them as representations of a reality—although that reality was social rather than religious in nature.

A number of central concerns of Durkheim were also taken up by Lévy-Bruhl who was especially interested in different ways of thinking as these were evident in the use, content and form of "collective representations." The general direction and development of Lévy-Bruhl's thought has been given generous minded treatment by Evans-Pritchard (1965) and more recently Cazeneuve (1972). It will not concern us here except to point out that Lévy-Bruhl began his studies with the intention of demonstrating the existence of a "primitive mentality" that was distinct from "civilized mentality." For him this was not simply a matter of discovering different premises but rather of describing a different way of thinking. In later years he came to recognize that his two main types of mentality were in some respects common to all people.

Lévy-Bruhl was not directly concerned with the institutional correspondence and social implications of different "mental habits." It is partly because of this, perhaps, that he appreciated "collective representations" in a challenging and interesting manner which was unemphasized but not entirely unanticipated by Durkheim (1953:1-34). He did not, for instance, treat in direct opposition the notions of experience and representation. He was no idealist, but in a very important sense "representations" were unequivocally the means whereby a person had an experience (cf. Lévy-Bruhl 1923:12-13, 60-61). As was evident in the Inuit/student example given earlier, the experience of the noise heard was strikingly different for the various parties listening. To Lévy-Bruhl this would be a function of the different "representations" of those who heard the noise. Sociologically, of course, the implications of collapsing this opposition are very serious, and for Durkheim and many others it leaves up in the air how anyone could have an experience of social relationship or apprehend the form of social life without first having in place "collective representations."

In addition, and in a manner similar to Durkheim, the notion of "representation" included, for Lévy-Bruhl, categories, ideas, sentiments, and activities. In thought, so Lévy-Bruhl observed, representations seem to be somehow "preconnected." His ideas on what such preconnection involved are not of great interest, but his observations in this regard are important in that they point to the fact that "representations" occur together in the thought and custom of all people. The linkage is not a matter of inference. Representations rise in the mind simultaneously, not sequentially, and people are often very clear about what does and does not occur together, e.g., black dress for widows not brides, sitting straight not slouching at the dinner table, solemnity at funerals not weddings, planting vegetables when the moon is waxing not waning, drinking warm not cold water after childbirth, and so on.

As I mentioned earlier, reflection and conscious thought about why certain representations go together is not required and indeed is rather rare. Jean Cocteau, in describing his attempts to recapture some memories from his childhood, nicely illustrates the sort of spontaneity that is often involved here. In visiting the neighbourhood of his youth he found that much had changed and nothing brought to mind his early life in the area. Not dissuaded, he decided to reenact a habit of his childhood in the hope that this would trigger some memories. Consequently, he ran down the street trailing his hand against the railings and lamp posts as he used to do on his way home from school and "it all came back: my cloak, the leather of my satchel, . . . , certain things I then said, the tone of my grandfather's voice, the smell of his beard and even the material of which my sister and mother's frocks were made" (Cocteau 1956:131).

Cocteau recognized that he might trigger something from the context of his youth by reconstructing a single element and, to the extent that other things from that context came to mind, he was right. In itself this suggests the existence of certain ordering principles or logical operations of the human mind; not a rationality unfolding from a

110

given premise, but a largely unconscious faculty of thought. The guise is different but one can see here a move which again grants the individual a privileged position. A move, furthermore, which emerges from precisely that vigourous sociology that Durkheim advanced to rout the kind of individualism adopted by Tylor and Frazer in their explanation of religous phenomena.

In some respects the ideas of Van Gennep anticipate a bridge and partial synthesis of these opposed perspectives. Party to neither and energetic critic of both, his work falls somewhere in between and it is perhaps for this reason that his most notable contribution, *The Rites of Passage* (1909), was separated from the main intellectual currents of the time and failed to have an early influence; a fact Van Gennep could well have found deeply ironic.

In *The Rites of Passage* Van Gennep argued that a person's life can be viewed as a succession of positions and the concern of his book is to describe the formal features of those rituals "whose essential purpose is to enable the individual to pass from one defined position to another which is equally well defined" (1960:3). He considers various broad classes of position such as social status, occupation, and territory, and implicit in all his illustrations is the idea that movement or passage occurs between positions that are in some respects members of the same class. In such movement a special situation arises in which a person wavers on the boundary or margin between two positions. In other words, there is an imaginary point on the threshold in which a person is in neither one position nor the other. S/he may be viewed as being either out of position entirely or in both positions simultaneously. It is the crossing of this threshold or liminal point that is the concern of Van Gennep and he outlines three broad phases of a ritual sequence that frequently attends the passage. These are nicely illustrated in the Inuit observances surrounding birth.

The first phase involves rites of separation in which a person is symbolically isolated from others. In this regard you will remember the Inuit woman effecting her own delivery in solitary seclusion. The second phase, which involves liminal or threshold rites, marks the social passage between positions. The weeks of restricted movement and change in eating habits of the Inuit mother illustrate that normal activity is placed in abeyance during this phase. Finally, there are rites of incorporation as the person is socially reintroduced in the new position. This is partly signified in the Inuit case by the new mother and child visiting all members of the community and receiving a portion of food from them.

In making his argument, Van Gennep insists that the positions as well as the passage between positions are entirely a social phenomena. In the present case, of course, it may be argued that in the event of one person becoming two in the act of birth there is a natural rather than a social basis for the rite. This is true, but there is nothing in the act itself which requires weeks to complete. Similarly, puberty rites are a social recognition of an event which may or may not coincide with the physiological event. And passage from one territory to another is significant not because of some natural topographical feature but because some imaginary line is socially recognized as a border.

The point here is that the ambiguous transitional phase is a function of the cultural means of discriminating between positions. These means vary and what is stressed by one culture may be unemphasized or ignored by another. The stress in Van Gennep's study is placed on ritual sequence and the ambiguity created by a person voluntarily or involuntarily moving between positions. It is made quite explicit, however, that movement and the problem of movement varies with the mode of classifying positions. For example, the gradual passage from infancy to physical maturity is common to all, but only some cultures punctuate this continuous process with a ceremony marking the passage from child to adult. Similarly, many cultures recognize that there are broad classes of activity associated with land and water but few practise the strict separation that Inuit observed between such activities.

In certain respects Van Gennep's work initiates the investigation of the obverse side of Durkheim's emphasis. It was not for over half a century, however, that anthropology began to seriously investigate the business of disorder and ambiguity from the vantage of culturally distinct modes of classification. Douglas (1966) for instance, has explored the general ethnographic problem of why and how people react to disorder and muddle. She, along with others (e.g., Leach 1964), has shown how it is possible to gain insight into the largely implicit ordering principles contained in a specific cultural mode of classification by focussing on those activities, events, and objects which a people symbolically isolate and consider dangerous or filthy. In general terms her argument is that when important cultural boundaries are in doubt people react by circumscribing the object or event in some way. Frequently this involves the use of such pejorative labels as "dirty" which, for Douglas, "is a kind of compendium category for all events which blur, smudge, contradict, or otherwise confuse accepted classifications. The underlying feeling is that a system of values which is habitually expressed in a given arrangement of things has been violated" (1975:51).

Since Inuit judged new mothers and menstruating women to be "unclean" there is clear suggestion in Douglas' work on how to approach this evidence. One is led to suppose that this judgment follows from an Inuit experience of something being out of place. The "thing" in this case is blood released from their own bodies. If any were to get on their clothes it was not cleaned off; the offending spot was actually cut away with a knife. Conversely, blood from animals killed is not "matter out of place" at all; it is food.

It is also possible to reexamine the ritual circumscription of the fall caribou hunt from this general perspective. This prompts the search not for utilitarian significance, not for direct social significance, but for some sort of category muddle in which something is experienced

112

as out of place or ambiguously astride two places at once. To appreciate the event in this light we have only to set it off against the clear
and insistent separation Inuit observed between activities of the land
and those associated with the water. The fall caribou hunt clearly in-
vokes these two major domains simultaneously in that it involves a
land animal being hunted in the water.

Parenthetically, but not insignificantly, many of the elements that
constitute the Inuit ritual of birth reflect a structural concordance with
the culturally ascribed marginality of the event itself. Different in substance and causally unconnected, there is yet agreement between the
various elements in the sense that they are marginal themselves. This
relates back to why, without reason or definite insight into form, a
people will participate in a custom and often without reflection or
hesitation know what element goes with what circumstance. In the
present case we can simply observe the series; skin of snipe, a shore
bird, and hence both of the land and the water; warm drinking water,
neither cold nor hot being allowed; the imagery of smoky vapour
evokes the idea of something blurred and indistinct. Finally, if it is absolutely required, there is one category of person who may assist in a
difficult delivery. This is a shaman and s/he is deemed by Inuit to be
half living and half dead.

There is no suggestion here that all rituals evidence this particular
structural agreement and it is only drawn out to indicate how "unob-
vious" it may be in any particular instance. To the extent, however,
that these mediating categories each imply a set of opposed and contrasting terms, we have here a regular expression of certain comprehensive and persuasive discriminations whereby Inuit achieve their
experience of events. In this regard, a number of general considerations must be emphasized. First, no element can be considered in isolation; neither caribou, nor snipe skins, nor smoky vapours, nor the
judgment that something is "unclean" can be granted any significance whatever without reference to other elements within the same
cultural field. This raises the question of how and in what manner
each element in a cultural field achieves significance and how all the
elements can be viewed as systematically interrelated and productive
of order, ambiguity, and contradiction.

The prevailing drift of an answer to this question is strongly in the
direction of investigating logical operations of the human mind insofar as these may be evident in the manipulation and use of cultural
signs and symbols (Lévi-Strauss 1966, Leach 1976). An important
consequence of making such a move is that it provides a framework
in which there no longer exists the fateful opposition between ideas
and activities that found expression in the distinction between belief
and ritual in the various works considered. Both ideas and acts, and
for that matter sentiments, colours, textures, techniques, and whatever else may signify in a given cultural field are subsumed by a general system of signification which is the culture itself. As Lévi-Strauss
observed some time ago, however, this procedure precludes "reli-

gious phenomena" from having any distinct character (1963:104). Its reality is to be found not in an institutional mode but in a certain mode of thought which may find expression in Indonesian eating habits or African cattle terms or even aspects of those institutions in this culture which we recognize as religious in nature.

BIBLIOGRAPHY

Beidelman, T.O. 1974. *W. Robertson Smith and the Sociological Study of Religion.* Chicago: The University of Chicago Press.

Burridge, K. 1973. *Encountering Aborigines.* New York: Pergamon Press.

Cazeneuve, J. 1972. *Lucien Lévy-Bruhl.* London: Basil Blackwell and Mott Ltd.

Cohen, W. 1967. Religion in Non-Western Culture. *American Anthropologist,* vol. 69 pp. 73-76.

Cocteau, J. 1956. *The Hand of a Stranger.* Elek Books.

Douglas, M. 1966. *Purity and Danger.* New York: Frederick A. Praeger.

Durkheim, E. 1912/1965. *The Elementary Forms of the Religious Life.* Glencoe: The Free Press.

Durkheim, E. 1953. *Sociology and Philosophy.* Glencoe: The Free Press.

Evans-Pritchard, E.E. 1937. *Witchcraft, Oracles and Magic Among the Azande.* London: Oxford University Press.

Evans-Pritchard, E.E. 1956. *Nuer Religion.* London: Oxford University Press.

Evans-Pritchard, E.E. 1965. *Theories of Primitive Religion.* London: Oxford University Press.

Frazer, J.G. 1907. *Adonis, Attis, Osiris.* (later published as Vol. 1V of *The Golden Bough*) London: MacMillan.

Geertz, C. 1966. Religion as a Cultural System, in M. Banton (ed.), *Anthropological Approaches to the Study of Religion* (A.S.A. Monograph 3). London: Tavistock.

Hobbes, Th. 1958. *Leviathan.* London: the Liberal Arts Press (1651).

Hogden, M.T. 1964. *Early Anthropology in the Sixteenth and Seventeenth Centuries.* Philadelphia: University of Pennsylvania Press.

Leach, E. 1964. Anthropological Aspects of Language: animal categories and verbal abuse, *In* E. H. Lenneberg ed., *new Directions in the Study of Language,* Boston: MIT Press.

Leach, E. 1976. *Culture and Communication: the logic by which symbols are connected.* Cambridge: Cambridge University Press.

Lévi-Strauss, C. 1963. *Totemism,* London: Merlin Press.

Lévi-Strauss, C. 1966. *The Savage Mind.* Chicago: University of Chicago Press.

Lévy -Bruhl, L. 1923/66. *Primitive Mentality.* Boston: Beacon Press.

Malinowski, B. 1954. *Magic, Science and Religion.* New York: Doubleday Anchor.

Rasmussen, K. 1929. Intellectual Culture of the Iglulik Eskimo. In *Report of the Fifth Thule Expedition,* Vol. VIII. Copenhagen.

Robertson Smith, W. 1889/1972. *The Religion of the Semites: the Fundamental Institutions.* New York: Schocken Books.

Tylor, E.B. 1871/1958. *Primitive Culture*, Vol. II. New York: Harper Torchbooks.

Van Gennep, A. 1960. *The Rites of Passage.* London: Routledge and Kegan Paul.

CHAPTER 5

BEHIND THE MYTHS

*An Introduction to the Structural Study of Myth and Folklore**

DAVID H. TURNER
University of Toronto

INTRODUCTION

The contribution of the Structuralist School to the study of myths and their "miniature" counterparts, folktales, has been to demonstrate logical organization within material where none was thought previously to exist. The logic discovered is binary or oppositional, and derives from an interplay between the mind and concrete reality. The predominant figure in this endeavour has been the French anthropologist Claude Lévi-Strauss and it is primarily to his work that I would like to address myself here.

It is characteristic of Lévi-Strauss' approach that analysis proceeds from the specific to the universal. However, in dealing with his work I will invert this procedure and begin with some of the more general aspects before progressing in a logical fashion down to the specifics. By starting with the universals he claims to have discovered (or rediscovered) and ending with the data from which these universals were presumably derived, it is possible to gain a clearer, if more simplified, understanding of his work and that of the Structuralist School in general than were we to begin with his analysis of specific societies and cultures.

GENERAL PRINCIPLES

An assumption behind practically all Lévi-Strauss' work is that human cognitive processes are universal—that is, all members of the

* This is a revised and extended version of a paper published in Anthropological Forum, Vol. 4, No. 1: 3:18.

sub-species Homo Sapiens Sapiens share the same potential for logical and rational thought. Differences between "ourselves" and "others" in this regard are quantitative, not qualitative. As he says in *The Savage Mind* (1966:268):

> The false antinomy between logical and prelogical mentality was surmounted at the same time. The savage mind is logical in the same sense and the same fashion as ours, though as our own is only when it is applied to knowledge of a universe in which it recognizes physical and semantic properties simultaneously.

As the Berndts point out in *The World of the First Australians:*

> . . . it does seem, from the results of many investigations, that the potential ability of all peoples is identical: that all make use of the same mental processes, the same principles of thought, in conceptualizing their environment, although they start off from different premises (1964:11).

Having stated this principle in general terms it remains for me to define some of the more particular characteristics of mental processes as set down by Lévi-Strauss. The foremost capability of the mind, he says, is its ability to grasp order in the chaos which is presented to it as "datum of experience" (Lévi-Strauss 1966:253). It is not so much that these data are not ordered in the real world as that the relations between them are not directly perceivable. The mind, therefore, does not *impose* order on that world; rather, it interacts with the order there so as to render it intelligible. Imposition *may* occur when a fixed idea of what that order is becomes institutionalized and persists despite significant changes in that order. Even so, the dialectics of thought operate such that a tension will be established between the old "ideology," the new reality and the order that develops in that reality, to produce a pressure for ideological change. Both the development of the ideology and the tension with the new reality and order are founded, says Lévi-Strauss, on thought processes which demand order (Lévi-Strauss 1966:10). Thought, then, seeks to locate the order present in relations between phenomena whether these be natural, cultural, or social.

In summary, what we have, according to Lévi-Strauss, is a universal cognitive process at work which both locates order in experience and imposes order on that experience. This process is carried out unconsciously, although on certain occasions it may be raised to consciousness (e.g., through philosophical introspection).

What makes it possible for thought to operate so as to discover order in the world and to question its discovery as that world changes is its ability to comprehend oppositions or incompatibilities and correlations or analogies in reality. When oppositions are brought into relation by reality (e.g., profits and wages in the economic system), we have a contradiction; when equivalences are brought into relation by reality (e.g., the hierarchial structure of religion and the hierarchial structure of society) we have an analogy. Oppositions (e.g., maximum wages/maximum profits) mutually exclude one another; correlations support one another. The thought that grasps the incompatibility of related things Lévi-Strauss calls dialectical reasoning; the thought that sees the similarity of related things he calls analogical reasoning (see Lévi-Strauss 1966, Chapter 9). Mythical thinking, as we shall see, involves both types of reasoning.

Myths, according to Lévi-Strauss, function basically to resolve real contradictions, but on a logical level. Myths are intellectual solutions to puzzles arising from our mental operations on "cooked" data. To explain what this means I must resort to a rather lengthy passage from *The Savage Mind*:

> *Nature is not in itself contradictory. It can become so only in terms of some specific human activity which takes part in it; and the characteristics of the environment take on a different meaning according to the particular historical and technical form assumed in it by this or that type of activity. On the other hand, even when raised to that human level which alone can make them intelligible, man's relations with his natural environment remain objects of thought: man never perceives them passively; having reduced them to concepts, he compounds them in order to arrive at a system which is never determined in advance . . . The mistake of Mannhardt and the Naturalist School was to think that natural phenomena are* what *myths seek to explain, when they are rather the* medium through which *myths try to explain the facts which are themselves not of a natural but a logical order* (Lévi-Strauss 1966:95).

Mythological thought is a theoretical exercise in which the mind encounters data at one level—the "raw"—orders or "cooks" it, then in the process of thinking about relations between the data and between these data as a whole and other data (e.g., between natural classifications and social classifications), sees parallels and inconsistencies. The contradictions myths deal with, then, stem from an already constructed and meaningful reality. In trying to resolve the inconsistencies located, thought must rework the events, data, and classifications surrounding the oppositions within the contradictions. Mythical thought is neither entirely concrete, nor entirely symbolic. Rather, it operates at a level somewhere between "percepts and concepts" (Lévi-Strauss 1966:18). It takes to pieces and reconstructs events which are significant within the culture—images which are already imbued with meaning. The task of the anthropologist is to examine these "sets of meaningful events" and concepts (or "mythemes," as Lévi-Strauss calls them) which constitute a particular myth in order to discover the oppositions they embody and the contradictions in the society to which these, in turn, relate.

STEPS IN THE ANALYSIS

What, according to Lévi-Strauss, are the basic procedures to be followed in myth analysis? Unfortunately, beyond some initial instructions, Lévi-Strauss is somewhat vague as to just how he gains the insights he does into the meaning of any myth. It will clarify matters if we divide his analysis into two main categories; the first dealing with the study of particular myths within the same culture, and the second dealing with different myths, or of variations of the same myth, in different cultures. The latter type of analysis is an attempt to discover, among what appear to be widely disparate texts, similarities of a highly abstract nature which would allow these tales to be classified into the same type (e.g., myths concerned with the nature/culture opposition, the autochthony problem and so on). As Lévi-Strauss (1963:208) remarks in this connection, the apparent arbitrariness of myths collected in different regions in terms of the events and sequences they embody, is belied by their astounding similarity on this more abstract level.

In this paper we are more concerned with the structural study of myths within a culture, although some remarks will be made about the analysis of myths in different cultures, particularly as relates to the question of the transmission of myths from one culture to another. In his treatment of myth, Lévi-Strauss makes one thing clear— a myth cannot be studied apart from its cultural context. As he states in *The Savage Mind*, "it is not possible to interpret myths and rites correctly, even if the interpretation is a structural one (not to be confused with just a formal analysis) without an exact identification of the plants and animals which are referred to . . ." (1966:46). He goes on later to say that "Even this is not however enough. It is also necessary to know the role which each culture gives them within its own system of significances" (1966:54).

Method

Specific instructions as to how to go about analyzing a myth after all the relevant data are in are as follows: first, break down the story of the myth into its component sentences. Then write each sentence down on an index card bearing a number corresponding to the unfolding of the story. Each card should now show a given subject performing a certain function. This is called a RELATION. Similar kinds of relations are termed BUNDLES OF RELATIONS. Relations within the same bundle will appear diachronically at remote intervals throughout the myth, but when we group them together into their respective bundles we find we have reorganized the myth on a synchronic level. Each relation within the same bundle is given the same number so that the myth can be read as follows:

1-2-3-4-5-2-3-4-6-7-1-4-5-7-8-1-2-5-7-3-4-5-6-8-

Here the myth reads from left to right through twenty-four sentences with similar relations occuring in sentences two and six, three and seven, and so on. We now reorganize the myth along two dimensions:

```
1   2   3   4   5
    2   3   4       6   7
1           4   5       7   8
1   2           5       7
        3   4   5   6       8
```

To *recount* the myth disregard the columns and read the rows from left to right, top to bottom. To *understand* the myth also read left to right but column by column.

What Lévi-Strauss finds is that each bundle focusses on a series of oppositions relating to a single theme—that is, involved in a particular contradiction—usually sociological, theological, economic, or political. As the myth proceeds he also finds there is progression from a statement about oppositions in each bundle to a statement about their resolution but that this resolution is always more apparent than real. What happens is that two opposites with no intermediary relating to a particular contradiction come to be replaced by two "equivalent" terms (or so the myth would have us believe) which admit of a third one as a mediator. From analyzing many myths in these terms, Lévi-Strauss concludes that the purpose of myth is to provide a logical model capable of overcoming a contradiction—an impossible achievement if the contradiction is real. The "solution" is usually effected by substituting weaker terms for the oppositions involved in the contradictions dealt with in the myth so as to make the contradictions appear less serious than they really are (i.e., "resolution" through analogical reasoning). The problem is to deduce the contradictions behind the myth whose oppositions are being weakened in this fashion. To do this one must examine the oppositions in reality to see if they are in a relation of contradiction within the culture.

The critical aspect of all this is whether Lévi-Strauss has, indeed, discovered these principles in myth, or whether he has simply assumed them from the outset. Lévi-Strauss may be instructing us not to examine the data and discover its order, but to look for his kind of order in the data. As Burridge (1967:113) suggests, "Lévi-Strauss's method seems to impose a spurious uniformity on the material, spurious because order springs not from the encounter between investigator and data but from the categories of a closed system which cannot admit further possibilities." This critique is echoed in these remarks by Leach (1965:778):

> Lévi-Strauss' own extremely ingenious mind is able to detect and recognize similarities of structure embedded in the most unlikely contrasted materials. Once he has demonstrated the existence of these structures, it is undeniable that the structures are there. But is it equally certain that the structures are significant?

But, as Einstein (1938:291) says,

> It is easy to find a superficial analogy which really expresses nothing [e.g., society as an organism]. But to discover some essential feature hidden beneath the surface of external differences

> *to form on this basis a new successful theory is a typical example of the achievement of a successful theory by means of a deep and fortunate analogy [e.g., social relations as homologous to cultural relations; mythological relations as homologous to relations between categories of thought].*

ASDIWAL

Lévi-Strauss' approach can best be seen by examining his treatment of the story of Asdiwal (Lévi-Strauss, 1967). First the setting. The myth comes from the Tsimshian Indians of the Northwest Coast of Canada. The Tsimshian are a hunting, gathering, and fishing people who live along the lower reaches of the Skeena River. They move according to the seasons between their winter villages in the coastal region and their fishing places on the Nass and Skeena Rivers (Figure 1). Food is stored during the summer in preparation for the winter famine and in the spring the Tsimshian migrate from their villages to the Nass River for the arrival of the candlefish. Following this they return to the Skeena for the salmon fishing season. Sociologically, the Tsimshian are divided into four exogamous phratries subdivided into clans which are in turn subdivided into lineages or houses. Each village or tribe is usually composed of members of all four phratries. The head of the dominant clan in each village is the head of the tribe. Residence is patrilocal and descent and inheritance matrilineal. Children are born in their father's house among his lineage mates but belong to the mother's lineage and inherit titles and privileges through the mother's brother. To effect this inheritance children must move to the mother's brother's house among their own lineage mates as they are growing up. Ideally, a man marries his mother's brother's daughter, a woman her father's sister's son. But while a "commoner" usually marries within his own village, members of the chiefly lineage usually marry into a different village (Rosman and Rubel 1971:10-22).

I will not attempt to deal with the Asdiwal myth in such detail that all relations, bundles, and oppositions are located. Rather, I have distinguished three dominant bundles within the myth and have listed only sentences relating to these bundles. The first bundle deals with residence patterns which are closely related to the general movement of action in the myth (#1), the second with hunting patterns (#2) and the third with the cosmological or supernatural (#3). Now the story.

The myth begins with a mother and her married daughter living in separate villages (indicating they are of chiefly lineages) following the patrilocal residence rule (#1) (M and D Figure 1). With the deaths of their husbands through famine (2) they each leave their villages of residence, the mother travelling from west to east, the daughter from east to west, meeting midway between them (at A) (1). Here a stranger (bird of good omen) visits them and marries the daughter (1) who gives birth to a son, Asdiwal, who is given magical objects by his father (3). After he is born the stranger leaves (1), the daughter's

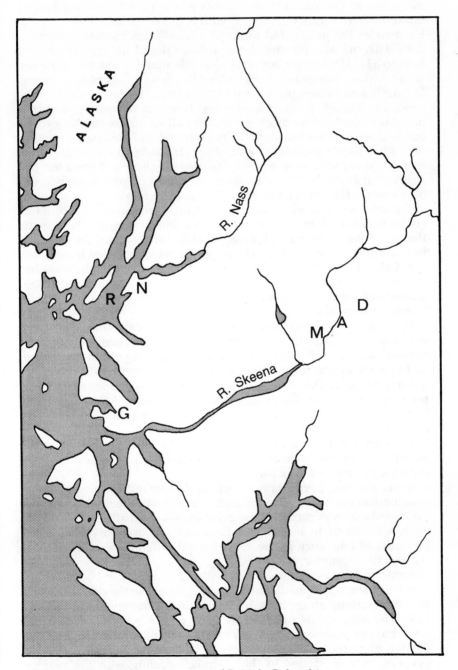

Figure 1. The North-west coast of British Columbia.

mother dies, and the daughter and son set off westward to live in her *native* village (1). Asdiwal then hunts a bear (2) which leads him to heaven where it turns into a girl who is the daughter of the sun (3). He marries the girl (1) but longs to return to his mother, which he does with his wife (1). But, he is unfaithful and his wife returns to heaven (1). He follows her and she kills him (1) but the sun, his father-in-law, brings him back to life (3). He again longs to return to his mother and does, but his wife leaves him (1). Finding his mother dead, he sets off downstream (to G) (1) where he marries a chief's daughter who has four brothers (1). They all set out for the Nass River but Asdiwal shames the brothers in a hunt (2) and they part company with him, taking their sister with them (1). Asdiwal encounters four more brothers with a sister (at N), marries the sister and has a son (1). Asdiwal also shames these brothers on a hunt (2) and is abandoned on a reef (R) (1). He is taken from here to a sea lion's den by a mouse and cures a sea lion which he had previously wounded on a hunt (2). He then sails back to the coast in the sea lion's stomach where, with the aid of his wife (1) and his magic (3) he brings about the death of her brothers. Asdiwal then returns to the Skeena Valley leaving his wife behind (1). Later he is joined by his son (1) to whom he gives his magical bow and arrows (3). On a hunting trip (2) Asdiwal forgets his snowshoes and is stranded halfway up a mountain where he is turned to stone (3).

In the discussion that follows, I have merged Lévi-Strauss' analysis with my own. Such differences in interpretation as arise do not alter Lévi-Strauss' overall conclusion about the meaning of the myth, and so I leave it to the reader to compare this treatment with the Lévi-Strauss original. The account that follows is also simplified to illustrate the main principles of analysis and argument. Many questions will remain unanswered and many gaps will appear in the logic of enquiry. However, despite these, I am sure the reader will be convinced that the approach is a promising one that could lead to gaining genuine insight into the logic of another culture and, by implication, into the logic of aspects of our own.

In his analysis, Lévi-Strauss proceeds to trace out sociological, geographical, economic, and cosmological bundles in the myth and to locate oppositions in each of these bundles. As we shall see, it is, however, difficult to treat each bundle as an autonomous series since elements of one, such as the cosmological, often appear in another, such as the economic.

According to Lévi-Strauss, Asdiwal's adventures can be viewed as a series of attempted mediations which fail because the contradictions they are working on are irresolvable within the framework of the culture. The oppositions involved in these contradictions are manipulated but not transformed; weaker terms are substituted to give the illusion of resolution. This process of weakening and mediation is, perhaps, best illustrated in the "bundle" dealing with the patrilocal/matrilocal residence opposition, clearly the dominant opposition and bundle in the myth. The opposition is "resolved" by substituting weaker terms for both extremes which allow of a mediator.

At the beginning of the myth, patrilocal residence is negated by death and substituted with a neolocal/matrilocal form (mother and daughter in a neutral area). In this neutral area there is a short-term matrilocal experiment (stranger and daughter) which fails. The locale then moves to Asdiwal's mother's *native* village (associated with her father's matriclan) which is neither patrilocal (it is not her husband's village) nor matrilocal (her husband is not with her). In this neutral area there occur two short-term matrilocal experiments (in both, Asdiwal is with the sun's daughter) around a short-term patrilocal one (sun's daughter with Asdiwal). All fail and are followed by a quasi-bilocal situation with Asdiwal and the sun's daughter moving to separate villages, although Asdiwal does not go to his *native* village as he should in a truly bilocal arrangement. Once more the locale shifts to neutral ground, with Asdiwal moving by himself to an apparently unrelated village. Here a matrilocal experiment is tried but fails (Asdiwal with the sister of the four brothers) and generates a series of oppositions involving Asdiwal and the group, land hunting/sea hunting, land and water. Another matrilocal solution is tried in yet another neutral area (Asdiwal with sister of second four brothers) but ends in matrilocal residence in principle (Asdiwal is residing in his wife's village) and bilocal residence in practice (Asdiwal is stranded on a reef and prevented from returning to his wife). Then follows a neolocal/patrilocal situation with the wife joining Asdiwal in neutral territory and helping him to slay her brothers. This, in turn, is followed by bilocal residence with the wife in her village and Asdiwal in the Skeena Valley (though not in his *native* village). In this concluding arrangement we find Asdiwal's son first in the mother's village then in the father's, the actual mobility pattern in Tsimshian society except that the sequence is reversed (he should be with the father and then with the mother's brother). Thus, even the final "resolution" fails to mesh with reality.

By implication, then, the only solution that does mesh is *the one actually practised in the society*—matrilineal descent, patrilocal residence and marriage outside the phratry, house group, and village (at least for members of chiefly lineages). In summary, the patrilocal/matrilocal opposition is first weakened in the myth by adding a neolocal qualifier to either extreme, which in turn is mediated by bilocality. Neutral areas are not covered by existing rules and allow new forms to be established, even if they prove unsuccessful.

The geographical oppositions involved in these actions remain unmediated, as action involving Asdiwal proceeds from east to west, south to north, east to west, west to east, north to south, and west to east. Lévi-Strauss interprets this constant oscillation as a form of resolution. However, it could equally be said that the oppositions remain unresolved, perhaps reflecting Tsimshian awareness that some aspects of nature (such as the seasons) are beyond human control.

Cosmologically, the oppositions heaven (sun) and subterranean (sea lion's den) are replaced by sky (high) and earth (low) which in turn are substituted by peak and valley. Asdiwal who is himself sky (through his father) and earth (through his mother) cannot overcome this duality until it is reduced to peak and valley. He is then transformed into stone on a mountainside which mediates the two weakened poles.

Economically, the analysis becomes somewhat more complex because of the role magical skills (a cosmological factor) play in mediating relations between Asdiwal and the group, land hunting and sea hunting. Indeed, an opposition between magical skills and human skills is also apparent throughout the myth, perhaps deserving designation as a separate bundle. However, I will discuss these together as "economic" here. What I have termed human skills/magical skills is, in fact, an already weakened version of an implicit opposition between human technology and supernatural technology. These are introduced when Asdiwal receives magical objects from his father in the form of duplicate human objects (bows and arrows, snow shoes etc.). The weakening is effected by placing both forms of technology at man's disposal—that is, at the mercy of his imperfect human qualities and institutions. Following receipt of these objects, there follows a series of successes and failures within the framework "supernatural techniques in supernatural hands are superior to supernatural techniques in human hands are superior to human techniques in human hands are superior to human hands alone."

Man's natural skills seem to have failed at the outset as there is winter famine. Then Asdiwal's magical skills apparently fail while land hunting (he fails to kill the bear), but then succeed (he wins the girl who is the bear transformed). Again his magical skills appear to fail (he is killed by his wife), but the sun's magic succeeds in bringing him back to life. Then Asdiwal's magical skills are successful in land hunting whereas the human skills of the first four brothers fail sea hunting. The second four brothers' skills fail sea hunting and again Asdiwal is successful. Asdiwal then travels to the sea lion's den where he saves (life) a sea lion he has tried to kill (death). His magical skills are thus at the same time unsuccessful (they failed to kill the sea lion) and successful (they cure his wound.) Asdiwal and his magic are then successful as he kills his wife's brothers, but then so are his wife's human skills as her help is required. Finally, Asdiwal's magic is *potentially* successful land hunting, but he gives his bow and arrows to his son and forgets his snowshoes. His human technology is also *potentially* successful but he does not carry it with him. Asdiwal (man) himself, then, is responsible for his shortcomings as a hunter and his destiny as a mortal being. Magical objects are unavailable through an inappropriate act of succession (father to son) and a bad memory;

126

human objects are not there through lack of foresight. Both forms of technology are therefore absolved from blame in Asdiwal's (man's) final defeat. Left unresolved, then, is the ultimate superiority of one over the other—an intelligent appreciation of the relation between magic and science in a developing human society.

Finally, the opposition between Asdiwal and the other—the individual and the group—is weakened insofar as magical objects are substituted for human ones in Asdiwal's case (making him somewhat more than an individual) and insofar as the "others" he opposes are never of his own matrilineage or village (making them a particular class of "others"). Conflict between Asdiwal and the group is thereby attributable to supernatural intervention and alien human influences. This weakened opposition is finally mediated by Asdiwal forming his own domestic group with his son who comes from the mother's village, a mediation made possible by the magical "weakener" which allows him to kill his wife's brothers who have a claim on his son through their sister (they are his mother's brothers) and by the alien-other weakener which allows Asdiwal reaccess to his own group's territory to establish a household. This final mediation is, however, unsuccessful as the partnership leads to Asdiwal's death. The message here is clear—conflict and danger result from an alien presence in one's own village; exogamy is both necessary and an impediment to the survival of the corporate group.

How is all this to be interpreted? Lévi-Strauss agrees that the main bundle of relations is the one dealing with residential patterns and sees the oppositions therein as relating to a real contradiction in the society between the rules of residence and the rules of inheritance. Since a man must bequeath his inheritance to his sister's son, his own son and his children in general are excluded from the process. To try to establish inheritance links with his own offspring, the argument is that a man (EGO Fig. 2) will seek to marry his own daughter to his sister's son, the person to whom he will pass on his inheritance. This is accomplished through the rule of matrilateral cross cousin marriage (where a man marries his mother's brother's daughter). Even this, however, only partly solves the problem as his own son inherits from his wife's brother and must reside in the mother's brother's house or village (if he is of a chiefly lineage) in order to fulfill this requirement. Patrilocal residence and cognatic ties pull him toward his father; succession realities pull him to the mother's brother. Furthermore, the father cannot substitute the "lost" son with a sister's son, as the latter is subject to the same opposing forces. The Asdiwal myth, then, can be seen as an attempt to resolve a conflict between residence rules and inheritance rules which is unsuccessfully resolved in the society by matrilateral cross cousin marriage. The myth attempts new forms of residence to see if better solutions can be effected. But the myth is unsuccessful in this attempt as Asdiwal discovers the disastrous effects of matrilocal residence (or at least a form thereof), then finds that

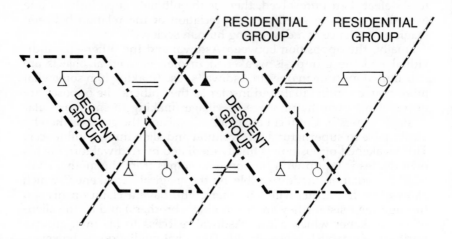

Figure 2. Tsimshian Descent and Inheritance Relations.

patrilocal residence (again, in an impure form) is no more successful. It is disastrous theologically, economically, politically, and organizationally.

> *All the paradoxes conceived by the native mind, on the most diverse planes: geographic, economic, sociological and even cosmological, are, when all is said and done, assimilated to that less obvious yet so real paradox which marriage with the matrilateral cross cousin attempts but fails to resolve. But the failure is admitted in our myths, and there precisely lies their function (Lévi-Strauss 1967:27-28).*

Granting this interpretation, it is still possible to incorporate the residence/inheritance problem into a more general one dealing with endogamy and exogamy. In fact, the residence/inheritance problem in Tsimshian society only arises if there is a rule of exogamy, which forces villagers to seek spouses outside their own phratry and household, and if, at another level, members of chiefly lineages marry outside the village. Following such marriages, no matter what residence rules are followed, there results an alien presence in the phratry, household, or village of either or both parties to the alliance. The Asdiwal myth attempts to remove this alien presence at the village level by creating bilocal residence, thereby excluding the wife from Asdiwal's phratry and village, but this leaves his son caught between two phratries and villages, as he actually would be in the society if he were of a chiefly lineage. In the bilocal arrangement he is necessarily born of the mother's village and must move away if he is to be with the father, an eventuality which culminates in disaster for the latter. Bilocality merely postpones the inevitability of undesirable alien influence for one generation.

Perhaps a better actual solution to the problem in Tsimshian society would be for members of chiefly lineages to marry always within the phratry and village such that husband and wife would be of the same descent group and locality. The alien spouse problem would now not exist and the son would be able to remain in the same village with both parents even if he were required to move between households within it (at a lower level, a solution would be to marry within the housegroup and lineage). However, the Tsimshian do not even entertain this as a possibility in the myth—obviously there is a powerful force at work within chiefly lineages or within the village as such that dictates the former marry out and form alliances with other phratries and villages (and within the village that marriages be between different households and lineages). It is likely that this is a political or economic necessity within Northwest Coast society (Rosman and Rubel suggest a "feudal tendency" as chiefly lineages realize their class over their village or phratral interest). However, exploration of this possibility is beyond the scope of this paper—we are already well beyond the "facts" of the case.

If we can generalize from the results of this analysis, it seems evident that in creating and practising a social system, people become aware that existing solutions to their problems are imperfect and require improvement, but that in enacting changes new problems will be thereby created—a perpetual problem so long as the system as a whole is not altered. Until it becomes necessary to alter tried and relatively successful solutions, those in effect must be justified lest they be altered prematurely. Myths of this type confirm the status quo by showing the disastrous consequences of changing only a part of the system. On this level two anthropological theories of myth converge—the Structural and Functional. Myths may be charters for action (Malinowski 1948:78-9) even though they do not carry the society's rules directly to the audience. In the context of the Asdiwal myth, Lévi-Strauss (1967:30) concludes,

> Mythical speculation about types of residence which are exclusively patrilocal or matrilocal do not therefore have anything to do with the reality of the structure of Tsimshian society, but rather with its inherent possibilities and its latent potentialities. Such speculations, in the last analysis, do not seek to depict what is real, but to justify the shortcomings of reality, since the extreme positions are only imagined in order to show that they are untenable. This step, which is fitting for mythical thought, implies an admission (but in the veiled language of the myth) that the social facts when thus examined are marred by an insurmountable contradiction.

. . . in abandoning the search for a constantly accurate picture of ethnographic reality in the myth, we gain, on occasions, a means of reaching unconscious categories.

MYTH TRANSMISSION

What happens to the Asdiwal myth when it is transmitted to a neighbouring people? Lévi-Strauss finds that there is a general weakening of opposition in the myth and a reversal in the structural correlations as the myth passes to another group. This group is the Nisqua Indians to the north who live a settled and more secure existence than the Tsimshian and who differ in certain features of social organization. From his analysis of the versions in both cultures Lévi-Strauss (1967: 42) concludes,

Thus we arrive at a fundamental property of mythical thought . . . When a mythical schema is transmitted from one population to another, and there exists differences of language, social organization or way of life which makes the myth difficult to communicate, it begins to become impoverished and confused. But one can find a limiting situation in which instead of being finally obliterated by losing all its outlines, the myth is inverted and regains part of its precision.

Thus, if a myth is passed from one group to another who differ in certain aspects of culture and social organization, then certain opposed elements within the myth will become less extreme (e.g., Heaven versus Hell might become high versus low), and parallel sequences will become reversed (e.g., west-east action in the first version will become east-west in the second). I found similar processes at work in the eastern Arnhem Land region of Australia (Turner 1974: 94-8) and it is this example I would like to discuss here as it points out the general nature of Lévi-Strauss' theory.

The eastern Arnhem Land people of Groote Eylandt, Bickerton Island, and the adjacent mainland (Figure 3) have a myth that rationalizes a moiety division of the patrilineal local groups in the region. The culture hero Blaur is believed to have travelled from Groote Eylandt to the mainland via Bickerton Island passing through the countries of a number of patri-groups in the course of his journey. He eventually reached the land of the Ridarngu people further inland where he died and was buried. All people in the patri-groups so linked are prohibited from intermarrying and all take part in the same ceremony celebrating Blaur's journey. Blaur's exploits border on the supernatural in the same sense as the totemic creatures who roamed the region in the Dreamtime. The travels of these totemic, half human, half animal beings, link all patri-groups in eastern Arnhem Land into four separate phratries through the same process as Blaur effects linkages on a moiety level.

My guess was that the Blaur track was recently introduced from the mainland interior and had the effect of combining all patri-groups in

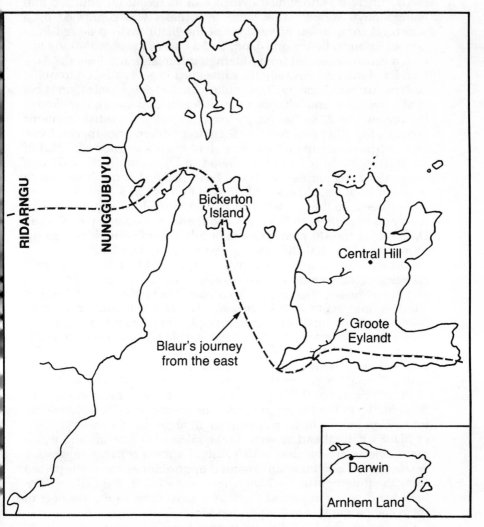

Figure 3. The Eastern Arnhem Land Region.

two of the indigenous phratries (the phratry linked by the Rainbow Snake and the one linked by the East Wind) into one moiety. The fact that the songs which celebrated Blaur's expoits were sung in the adjacent mainland Nunggubuyu language and not in the Groote Eylandt language seemed evidence of its recent introduction to that island, though there was no similar evidence of its recent introduction into Nunggubuyu society. This latter hypothesis was confirmed by a structural comparison of versions of the Blaur myth collected from Groote Eylandt, Bickerton Island, and adjacent mainland informants with a version collected from Ridarngu informants and from the Arnhem Land interior. Basically the same version was gathered from the eastern Arnhem Landers. Their culture and social organization is basically the same, and, although two different languages are spoken in the region, the Bickerton people are bilingual and mediate relations between the other two peoples. Significant differences appear, however, when we compare their version of Blaur's journey with that of the Ridarngu. Blaur's name is altered to Djadjabul in the Ridarngu version and his journey is said to have proceeded not from east to west but from west to east. It begins at Rarrawa in Ridarngu country and proceeds to the Arnhem Land Coast through Nunggubuyu territory, and from there to Bickerton and thence to Groote Eylandt. Here Djadjabul is transformed into a high hill, identified by Ridarngu informants as "Central Hill" the highest point on the island.

Furthermore, Ridarngu informants regarded Blaur as a mythological being in the same sense as the totemic creatures mentioned above, and not as *human*, the category he is placed in by the eastern Arnhem Landers (informants called him *amamalya*, real or natural, not *alawudawarra*, supernatural—the appropriate label for totemic beings).

In short, the eastern Arnhem Land people possess a version of the Blaur myth which is partly inverted insofar as the direction of travel is reversed, and partly weakened insofar as it contains the neutral mediator "burial" between the opposites natural/supernatural implicit in Blaur's existence (his exploits are superhuman if his being is not). By contrast, in the Ridarngu version the mediator is "transformation into a high hill," which, in Aboriginal thought, would preserve some of Blaur's natural and supernatural qualities (all animate and inanimate objects are imbued with spiritual substance).This suggests a weakening of a natural/supernatural opposition as the myth passed from the Ridarngu to the Nunggubuyu. As I said, the eastern Arnhem Land people regarded Blaur as a man, some of the younger of them comparing him to the prophet Moses.

Consistent with Lévi-Strauss' theory, the Ridarngu organize themselves differently to the Nunggubuyu, Bickerton, and Groote Eylandt people. For example, they prefer marriage with the mother's patrigroup, do not exchange women directly and emphasize the moiety division of the phratry, in contrast to the eastern Arnhem Landers (see Warner 1964:36; Turner 1974). They also speak a different language.

Now, if the myth was transmitted from one society to another in the sequence, Ridarngu, Nunggubuyu, Bickerton Islanders, Groote Eylandters, and if journeys like this are necessary to rationalize linkage between patri-groups, then it is reasonable to suppose that the moiety division of patri-groups was recently introduced into the eastern Arnhem Land region. Certainly it serves no important function as far as marriages are concerned (in the preferrred arrangement here marriage is between the same two patri-groups in alternate generations which would, by definition, preclude marriage with the mother-in-law's patri-group and all others in that phratry) and no indigenous mythological beings link any pair of phratries into one division. Only Blaur does this.

Used in this way as a deductive model, Lévi-Strauss' theory may prove useful to prehistorians who wish to make inferences about the past but who have no concrete data about the direction of cultural influences.

OTHER APPLICATIONS

There is no reason, in principle, why the techniques of Structuralist analysis cannot be applied to the "folklore" of modern "Western" society. Although a written tradition poses special problems by virtue of the "permanency" of its texts, these are not insurmountable (see Leach 1969). To illustrate how structural analysis of cultural products yields interesting insights into our own society I would like to disect the American film *Jaws*.

The plot is well known. The inhabitants of a small New England resort town are plagued by a great white shark at the beginning of the tourist season. The first attack is made on a woman swimming alone at night after making love on the beach. After an investigation by the local two-man police force, the chief, Brody, decides to close the beaches until the danger passes. But local businessmen put pressure on the mayor and newspaper editor to keep them open as they fear the publicity will keep people away during the Fourth of July national holiday period. Persuasion gives way to threats and the chief yields to the pressure. The shark, however, strikes again, killing a young boy and an old man the same day. Brody now closes the beaches and sends a fisherman out to hunt the shark. His boat is later found abandoned with gaping holes in its sides—evidence of a shark attack. A young technocrat now arrives on the scene from the Oceanographic Institute to investigate the shark incident and offer his services to the community. With no further attacks and under pressure once more from business, the beaches are once again opened for the Fourth of July holiday, this time patrolled by the police and the Oceanographer, Hooper. Hooper is not able to spot the shark in his technologically advanced boat and it, in fact, tracks with him to reach a swimmer but does not attack. Brody is now convinced the shark must be killed and hires Quint, a local and very traditionally-oriented charter fisherman, to do the job. He and Hooper go along as crew, the shark is eventually encountered and the battle is on. After a number of skirmishes and failures, Hooper is killed in his shark cage when he neglects his weapon in favour of his camera. The shark attacks the boat and begins to dismantle it, killing Quint in the process. Armed with only a rifle and a few rounds of ammunition, Brody is reduced to occupying the end of the mast as the boat sinks beneath him. As the shark makes its final attack he takes one last, futile shot at the fish and by chance hits an oxygen tank which had become lodged in its jaws when it was demolishing the boat. The shark is blown to bits and Brody survives.

This tale can be organized into a series of oppositions with each expressing a separate but related theme. First is the major opposition between land animals (people) and sea animals (shark) which is mediated by swimming land animals. This "anomaly" is at once removed by a sea animal through the process of incorporation (eating). But this reverses the relationship of man to animals within the Judeo-Christian tradition. It has been ordained that man will dominate (incorporate) animals (here, fish). What follows in *Jaws* after this initial reversal has been established is really an attempt at re-reversal to re-establish people's domination over nature. The first step in the process is to deny the original opposition and its mediation altogether. An attempt is made to prevent land animals from swimming, but it fails because it is opposed to the business interest—the tourists will not come to spend their money in the area if swimming is prohibited. A new opposition is thus raised in the story, namely the private versus the public interest. The next attempt involves trying to prevent the sea animal's existence, but this also fails because of poor technology (a conventional fisherman with conventional equipment). Ultimately this "solution" cannot succeed within the framework of the tale because the original major opposition is misphrased—people (species) are opposed to shark (individual). No matter what happens to *this* shark there is the possibility that others will take its place.

With these initial failures, four factors are introduced to solve the problem, paired into two opposition-couples; first is folk knowledge versus scientific knowledge, and second, an older experienced sea captain versus a young college graduate. Scientific knowledge and youth at first fail to locate the shark and kill it, while folk knowledge and experience find the shark but cannot kill it—in fact the shark kills the sea captain, removing the alternative he represents as an ultimate solution to the problem of the tale. Scientific knowledge, but in a traditional form (rifle and bullet) and in the hands of a nonscientist (a middle-aged policeman), then reappears to kill the shark, but does so by chance—chance consequent on the prior destruction of modern technology (shark cage, scuba equipment) by the shark. Left unresolved, then, is the ultimate status of folk versus scientific knowledge, youth versus experience, the public versus the private interest (the policeman is at the same time responsible for the deaths of the tourists as well as for their eventual protection by killing the shark), and man versus nature (people have achieved dominance over the individual not the species).

Other oppositions can be located within the extended plot and developed further, such as man/woman, natural/supernatural, but they seem to fall within the major themes outlined above. The significant thing about these themes together with their constituent oppositions, mediations and attempted solutions is that they all remain within the frame of reference of mainstream American capitalist society. In *Jaws* there is nothing which transcends already thought solutions to already experienced contradictions. And perhaps this is the point of all "soap opera." It is intrinsically entertaining precisely because it locates problems that can be grasped by most people and offers and rationalizes those solutions already in practice in the society. In short, *Jaws* is a-critical, being neither educative nor illuminating. Like the Asdiwal myth, it reassures the audience that the present system, while imperfect, works well enough. The conservative-liberal, capitalist-competitive system balances stability with progress and deals adequately with problems as they arise even if the odd disaster must be tolerated. Unlike Asdiwal, however, its solutions do not realize the limits of the system within which its problems are conceived. Existing elements and relations within society are not transformed into their opposites in the text. Perhaps it would be instructive to imagine what a Canadian *Jaws* would look like given the added "social democratic" and "Red Tory" dimension of mainstream Canadian political life.

Here we may have begun to distinguish between various levels of thought and various qualitatively distinct products of human thought, which do not rest on a priori ethnocentric division of the world's peoples into civilized-complex/primitive-simple. Some of the myths of so-called primitive people may be of the same stature, objectively, as texts as the great literature of Western civilization, and some of the texts of our society may be of lesser stature than many of the myths and legends of these "primitives" (see Turner 1978).

BIBLIOGRAPHY

Berndt, R.M. and C.H. 1964. *The World of the First Australians*. Sydney: Ure Smith.

Burridge, K.O. 1967. Lévi-Strauss and Myth. *In* E. Leach, *ed. The Structural Study of Myth and Totemism.*

Einstein, A. 1938. *The Evolution of Physics*. New York: Simon and Schuster.

Leach, E. 1965 (Review of) Mythologiques: Le cru et le cruit, *American Anthropologist*, Vol. 64, No. 3.

Leach, E. ed. 1967. *The Structural Study of Myth and Totemism*. London: Tavistock.

Leach, E. ed. 1969. *Genesis as Myth and Other Essays*. London: Cape.

Lévi-Strauss, C. 1963. *Structural Anthropology*. London: The Penguin Press.

Lévi-Strauss, C. 1966. *The Savage Mind*. London: Weidenfeld and Nicholson.

Lévi-Strauss, C. 1967. The Story of Asdiwal. *In* E. Leach, *ed. The Structural Study of Myth and Totemism.*

Malinowski, B. 1948. *Magic, Science and Religion and Other Essays*. Glencoe: The Free Press.

Rosman, A., and P. G. Rubel 1971. *Feasting with Mine Enemy*. New York: Columbia University Press.

Turner, D.H. 1974. *Tradition and Transformation*. Canberra: Australian Institute of Aboriginal Studies.

Turner, D.H. 1978. Dialectics in Tradition: myth and social structure in two hunter-gatherer societies. *Occasional Papers of the Royal Anthropological Institute*. 36.

Warner, W.L. 1964. *The Murngin*. New York: Harper Torchbook.

ADDITIONAL REFERENCES

Barthes, R. 1975. *Mythologies*. New York: Hill and Wang.

Frye, N. 1971. *The Critical Path*. Bloomington: University of Indiana Press.

Leach, E. 1969. *Genesis as Myth and Other Essays*. London: Cape

Leach, E. 1970. *Lévi-Strauss*. London: Fontana.

Lévi-Strauss, C. 1966. *The Savage Mind*. London: Weiden Feld and Nicholson.

Maranda, P. ed. 1972. *Mythology*. London: Penguin.

Maranda, P. ed. 1977. Symbolic Production Symbolique. *Anthropologica*, N.S., 19, 1.

CHAPTER 6

THE USE OF CLASS ANALYSIS IN SOCIAL ANTHROPOLOGY

GAVIN A. SMITH
University of Toronto

In this article I am going to discuss how a class analysis can help in the examination of those kinds of societies which usually concern social anthropologists. Although anthropologists have recently begun to study peoples living in metropolitan and industrial societies, such studies can draw upon the abundant literature attempting class analyses of these kinds of societies.[1] For those anthropologists who continue to be interested in peoples who live on the periphery of contemporary metropolitan societies, the task of a class analysis is more problematic, however, and I think, for this very reason, more important. This article is concerned only with the latter kinds of peoples.

The whole reason for stressing the importance of undertaking a class analysis of any society, of course, rests on the assumption that class praxis—the purposive action of the significant groupings of people in a society—is a crucial force in the transformation of societies. Nevertheless, the student who wishes to undertake a class analysis of a particular society must recognize two stages in the task: the revealing of the objective classes which exist in a particular social formation, and the examination of how these classes actually express themselves historically—their praxis. Since space is limited, I shall aim for a clear exposition of the first step in this exercise. This is because I think that you will often find, in your reading and in your discussions, that the two steps are muddled.

This said, however, it is imperative to bear in mind throughout what follows, what the essential purpose is for undertaking a class analysis in the first place: to locate those elements in the society where people's intentional actions will serve to transform the existing social structure.[2]

The discussion will progress as follows. I shall begin by locating class analysis within the more general examination of a social struc-

137

ture, or social formation. Then I shall state the basic elements of class and anticipate some of the possible elaborations which will be necessary when applying the elementary concept to nonindustrial social formations. The concept thus formed can then be tested by seeing what it might reveal when applied to certain types of nonindustrial groups. Finally I shall make my own assessment of the validity of a class analysis of these kinds of peoples and leave you, the reader, to take your own position in the matter.

SECTION ONE

Transmission

Class analysis is less concerned with breaking down society into discrete groupings of people with bundles of common characteristics than with trying to examine the whole social structure as a system of classes. So the problem of slotting particular individuals into certain categories called "classes" is a second order concern. What is of primary importance is to assess how the working of a particular social structure acts to push people toward one another in one direction, and against others in another direction. So the kinds of classes existing in a society are essentially linked to the kind of social structure the society has. It follows from this that the first task of a class analysis is to ascertain the nature of the social structure being examined.

So before saying anything about *class*, I must say something about what I mean by social structure. In fact, I prefer the expression *social formation*, because it helps to remind us that societies are engaged in an endless dynamic of forming and re-forming the essential relationships which give them a particular character. This view of society needs clarifying before we can go on.

Let us suppose that societies can be seen as factories which are in the business of producing social relations. Let us go further and suggest that, while this is their ultimate task, in order to undertake it successfully they have to produce many other things besides social relations. In fact, they have to produce people, and goods to satisfy the desires of those people. In a sense then, societies are the mirror image of our common-sense view of a factory: a car factory serves to maintain and reproduce a certain set of social relationships—between shareholders, managers, workers, and salespeople—in order to produce its end product: a car. A society has to reproduce goods and people in order to produce its end product: a particular set of social relationships.

If this analogy seems a little far-fetched, let me re-examine what I have just said about the car factory. It is at least possible that the car factory exists not so much to produce cars, but to provide dividends to its shareholders and a wage for its managers and workers; should the production of cars become unprofitable, shareholders, managers, and employees may all be agreeable to changing the end product to something else. The product changes in order to maintain the factory (strictly speaking, the set of social relationships which we have called a "factory"). Whether or not you find this second view of the factory acceptable, you will, I hope, agree that, as *social* scientists, it might be useful to look at factories in this light.

Anyway, whether we are talking about factories or social formations, the key concept is that of *producing*. In looking at a particular social formation, the question that matters is, "How does this social formation produce and reproduce through history the social relations contained within it?"

Social anthropologists answer this question by suggesting that it is done through the interaction of people, mediated through things. There are in fact two processes involved here, which are so closely intertwined that it is impossible to think of one without holding in our minds at the same time our concept of the other. Nevertheless, for the purpose of analysis we have to try to separate them out. On the one hand, people act upon the material of the world in order to produce the goods which society deems necessary for its survival (in its present form). On the other hand, it is impossible to conceive of people doing this without entering into relationships with one another. In fact, I have already suggested that, in the *social* world we live in, it is the needs of these social relations which call forth and then give form to the former activity of work.

The reason why there is this reversal, in society, of what appears to our common sense (i.e., work leads to social relations) is that the act of appropriating goods from nature (i.e., work) involves not only the input of labour, but also access to essential things: tools and raw materials. And in any given society access to these things is laid out by the social relations of the society: men have axes, women baskets; the tiger clan have the river bank, the leopards the forest, and so on. In order to emphasize my interest in society as a system of production, I shall refer to these relationships as the *social relations of production*.

The actual work of putting out energy in order to appropriate good from nature, I shall refer to as the *forces of production*, and besides the combination of labour with tools and raw materials, I shall also include under this rubric the actual *way* in which these are combined as a function of the skills of the producers and the technical development of tools which prevails in the society. This will give us the technological division of labour for producing a certain good in the society: a loaf of bread, a suit of clothes or whatever. (It is important to note, at this point however, that this easily visible set of technical relations arising during the production of a particular good must not be confused with the often far less discernible *social relations of production*).

In any particular social formation being studied, it is possible to examine the way in which the *forces* and *social relations* of production are intertwined, the one determining and constraining the development of the other. For example, the introduction of the production line in the U.S., (i.e., an instrument in the *forces* of production) had a significant influence in modifying the social relations of North American society. This was so because of the impetus it gave to economies of scale, thus allowing a very few, very large, firms to control production, (an element in the *social relations* of production). On the other hand, existing social relations of production in contemporary North America mitigate against the development of efficient public transport systems, partly because of the threat they would be to existing social relations of production and partly because the social relations of production in a capitalist society make it difficult to develop a communications network within the framework of "free enterprise."[3] From this latter point of view then, social relations influence the development or not of the forces of production. I shall refer to this two-fold process as *reciprocal causality*.

To say that these two elements are intertwined, however, is not to say that their interrelationship is complementary. In many social formations the relationship between forces and relations of production is one of endless tension and contradiction. This becomes clearer if you reflect that the control over the resources of a society (social relations of production) is of little use to those who have control unless the resources can be given value by being put to work (by the forces of production). Your control over a tractor, for example, may not be especially advantageous to you, if nobody is willing or able to drive it for you. By the same token, it makes no odds if you are the straightest ploughman in the neighbourhood; if you have neither plough, nor oxen, nor tractor you will go without work unless you can gain access to these necessary instruments. Here I am stressing the ties between those who offer labour and skill and those who control resources; it can be referred to as a relationship of dependency.

But where the control over resources is separated from the input of the human energy that makes them work (as in the example I have just given), there is likely to be latent tension in the society, and this I shall call a relationship of conflict.

It is here that we move from a discussion of the general characteristics of a social formation to the question of *class*. What gives class interaction its dynamic quality is the coexistence of these two relationships: dependency and conflict. As a political strategist, you would have to reflect hard on what the implications would be for political tactics if you found a relationship of conflict but no crucial dependency, or one of dependency but no conflict. In neither case would you be looking at relations between two *classes*.

If the social anthropologist can locate the points in the social formation where this kind of structural tension is inherent to the way the society is put together and made to work, then he or she can begin to discover the social forces behind the development of that society. This is because, where the elements of a system are not perfectly compatible, they are subject to constant reformulation. Their total destruction and replacement by new relations between the elements will, in the last analysis, take the form of a conflict between classes: interests representing preservation versus interests representing

140

structural change. It is for this reason that class analysis of a society is important.

SECTION TWO

We can now look at the essential features of class. I shall do this by basing the discussion on a statement made by Lenin in 1919, when the understanding of the important classes in Russia was crucial for the direction of a revolution.[4]

> Classes are large groups of people differing from each other by the place they occupy in a historically determined system of social production, by their relation (in most cases fixed and formulated by law) to the means of production [i.e., tools and raw materials], by their role in the social organization of labour, and consequently by the dimensions of the share of social wealth of which they dispose and the mode of acquiring it. Classes are groups of people one of which can appropriate the labour of another owing to the different places they occupy in a definite system of social economy [in our terms: social formation] (1971:486).

class definition

According to this formulation, classes are determined by both the social relations of production and the forces of production. In terms of the social relations of production, we are talking about people who can either control the important resources of the society (the means of production) or not. And in terms of the forces of production, the organization of labour is such that either the controllers themselves work the tools and raw materials (you drive your own tractor), or people separated from control do it (somebody else drives your tractor).

Two points arise at this stage. Firstly, it is impossible to understand what a class is without placing it in the context of the working of the whole society. And secondly, a class arises out of a relationship and must therefore be understood by reference to other classes which act to define and confine it. As the angle of a triangle cannot be thought of without reference to its position vis-à-vis the other two angles, so too with classes in society.

Emmanuel Terray has suggested that we can formulate four types of essential classes:

1. Producers controlling the means of production.
2. Producers separated from the means of production.
3. Nonproducers controlling the means of production.
4. Nonproducers separated from the means of production.

At a very schematic level what we have is as follows. In the first case you have a hypothetical society with only one class: those who produce also control. There may be a few people, such as old people and children, who fall into the fourth kind of class in such a society, but these people hardly constitute a class since they are not related to the means of production in any way (according to Terray's break-

141

down). In essence then, this would be a classless society: the producers may put aside some surplus in order to maintain the nonproducers in the fourth kind of class, but it is they (the producers) who can decide what this should be, since they also control the means of production.

In the case of (2) and (3), we are talking about a conventional class society of some kind, consisting of producers and controllers. The controllers' command of the means of production puts them in a position to be able to demand some surplus from the producers. Because the producers, in this kind of society, must rely on the controllers in order to get the necessary tools and raw materials in order to produce at all, they are obliged to relinquish some of what they produce over and above what they require for their own sakes alone. Conversely, by dint of having control over the valued resources of the society, the controllers do not themselves have to work productively in appropriating good from nature (after Terray, 1975:87-88).

This gives us the essential configuration of what is involved in a class analysis, while at the same time raising a number of problems. The most important of these are: "How is control over the means of production by a particular class exercised in any given society, i.e., what form does it take?" "What other elements in the social formation such as ideology, and politics are brought into play as part of this control?" "How is this control used as a means for extracting surplus from the direct producers?" "How does the controlling class reallocate this surplus in such a way as to ensure its own continued survival?" and finally, "What are the varying roles of the fourth type of class which Terray suggests, in the differing kinds of societies we study?"

We can best answer these questions by turning the spotlight onto some of the different kinds of societies which interest social anthropologists.

SECTION THREE

Limitations of space make it impossible to dwell at any length on a class analysis of "tribal" social formations. What I can do is suggest the kinds of questions which would be relevant for establishing the power of class relationships as a social force in any such society.

Despite the fact that very little class analysis of the kind I have been discussing has been undertaken for "tribal" societies, two things immediately become obvious when attempting such an examination of these societies. Firstly, it is impossible to come up with any universally valid criteria of what establishes class relationships in all societies; and secondly, since class has to do with access to valued resources, so many other elements in the social formation may be brought into play—such as the ideology of kinship, or the use of physical might (power)—that it would be misleading to restrict class analysis to an examination solely of the forces and relations of production. Such an analysis may give you the beginnings of class relationships without allowing you to see how those relationships were expressed in the specific society you were looking at.

Let us imagine a society in which both agricultural and animal husbandry takes place. Agricultural land is divided into two categories: there is land which is farmed by the group as a whole supposedly for the benefit of the community and its gods; and there are smaller plots farmed by each household unit. Labour on communal land and the distribution of the small plots to households are supervised by the elders of the group. Livestock are held by individual households; pasture is held by the community, but the location of flocks on the land is again supervised by the elders.[5]

The questions which concern us are whether or not there is a group in this society with a capacity to exclude and hence control certain important resources, what these resources are, and, if such control does exist, from what does it derive?

In our rather abbreviated example, it is clear that the elders do appear to have some control. In some cases, they may only have discretionary control over the distribution of the final product: their authority may simply be limited to distributing the products of labour on community land. If this is so, then the actual power to retain some of this surplus for themselves will be severely restricted. If, however, the elders control this *distribution of the social product* as a function of their *prior control over some of the essential means of production,* as is the case in the example given here (they not only supervise the labour on the communal fields and the distribution of the harvest thereafter, but they also *control* the distribution of individual household plots and pasture), then the possibilities for them to retain surplus for themselves are clearly much greater.

So it is necessary, then, to distinguish between *control over the distribution of the social product* (in this case the harvest on communal land) from *control over the distribution of the means of production.* The first is essentially functional for social production; when this includes some supervision of the labour process itself, as in our case, we may refer to it as *the management function.* The second is at least potentially exploitative, by which I mean that control over the means of production may allow the elders to hold back some of the surplus in order to use it for the continued reproduction of their position of power.

Nevertheless, this may not be the only way by which elders can retain surplus. Where control over the distribution of the social product does not derive quite so overtly from control over such obvious means of production as the land, domination may be retained through the use of ideology: the maintenance of myths about reciprocity, for example (Godelier, 1977b and c) and the control of important symbols. This, however, is likely to lead to the allocation of certain surpluses into the ideological apparatus—shrines, priests, etc.—and insofar as this apparatus is used for the maintenance of dependency relationships, it is not true to say that the surplus used to

143

cover such "costs" is being redistributed entirely for the benefit of the direct producers.

All I have done here is raise the questions relevant for a class analysis of "tribal" societies. It seems, to me at least, that while we have avoided the danger "of presenting producers in classless societies as all equal controllers of the means of production," (Godelier, 1977a:32), we are not necessarily referring to class relationships in quite the nice way suggested by the scheme laid out in Section Two. To begin with, the elders are not recruited on the basis of their relationship to the means of production, but rather on the basis of their position in the system of kinship, and possibly other criteria more ascribed than achieved. Secondly, while what Rey refers to as "the power of function" (management) may be turned to "the power of exploitation" (1975:29), it remains the case that at least *some* surplus must be disbursed outside the dominant class, in what Sahlins (1966) refers to as "the politics of generosity." This would seem to mitigate against the possibility of any real class-like formation among one group. Thirdly, we must be careful to distinguish between "managers" and "controllers," between a *technical* process and a *social* relation. It would seem that the two kinds of class, (2) and (3) in my earlier schema, do not quite work here, because elders may in fact not necessarily be either real controllers (in the sense of exclusive possessors) nor entirely nonproducers, insofar as they are performing an essential management function on behalf of the direct producers (Hindess & Hirst, 1977a:54; 1977b:67-72).

One final point should be made. These remarks about prestate social formations seem to call into question just what can be referred to as *means of production*. It would seem that particular symbols in some societies are vital for the process of production—certain totemic emblems for example. Does control over these constitute a form of control over the means of production? If this is so, then class analysis must concern itself with far more than the purely "economic," narrowly conceived.

The question of the role of "class" interaction in the historical development of "tribal" societies must remain unanswered, as long as ethnography continues to concentrate on the effect of status relationships on the functioning of "tribal" societies, rather than on the way in which differential control over valued resources and variations in position in the process of social production gives a class-like characteristic to such social formations. Until class analysis is undertaken, the question of transition from classless to class societies will likewise remain a matter of conjecture.[6]

SECTION FOUR

Because the study of peasants has become so much a part of the discipline of anthropology, it behoves me to turn the spotlight on them.

But it is difficult to discuss the class analysis of peasantries because the term itself—"peasant"—is such a vague one:

> *In its general and untheoretical usage the vagueness, the reso-*
> *nances and multiple meanings are an essential part of the term*
> *"peasant" and can be lived with. The notion will, indeed, stretch*
> *from the man good King Wenceslas fed, after some difficulty, to*
> *the Frenchmen who sometimes block the road with tractors*
> *(Ennew, Hirst & Tribe 1977:295).*

Social anthropologists, faced with this vague term, have long argued among themselves about what the defining criteria should be for a "peasant." Rather like zoologists arguing among themselves about the defining difference between a sheep and a goat, the denouement comes when the student is told, "Don't worry, you'll recognize one when you see one."

For our part we can dispense with all this by stating, without much controversy, that whatever else it is, the term "peasant" is not a class term of the same order as "the working class" or "the rentier class." So let me simplify matters by saying that the ensuing discussion is concerned with how we should go about a class analysis of small-scale farmers who do not own their land (in the sense of being able to buy and sell it freely) and who rely predominantly on the labour of their own household. For convenience, let us also say that, although the social relations of production prevailing in the social formation in which they are found (feudal, capitalist, etc.) may demand a rent or service from the farmer (see below), his first priority is to provide the livelihood needs of his own household.

In the first section of this paper I emphasized a relationship of dependence within the concept of class: the need of controllers and workers for one another, which derives from the separation of the latter from the tools and materials which they need to be productive. But in the case of these small farmers, the farmer is generally actually living on or near the land which is his primary means of production. In many cases, moreover, the household makes the crucial decisions about what to produce and how. On this basis, "peasants" would appear to conform to class-type (3) in our schema. On the other hand, the household also constitutes the labour force necessary to make the farm produce, i.e., (2) in the schema.

The relationship of dependence which I initially set forward as a characteristic of class, therefore, would seem to disqualify the view of peasants as constituting a class:

> *While the labour of the peasant may (or may not) be necessary for*
> *the existence of society as a whole, it is not to the same extent nec-*
> *essary for the existence of the peasant (Galeski, 1972:112).*

This situation does indeed have a profound effect on the political behaviour of peasants and some writers have suggested that it goes some way to explaining the attraction of anarchism to peasants (Hobsbawm, 1959). But the fact remains that peasants do exist within the confines of the nation state and do interact with other sectors of society: the confusions arise because the social relations of production of which they are part vary from one time and place to another.

Let us begin by saying something about the interaction of peasants *within the same community* before turning attention to their interaction with other sectors of the society. Despite the fact that many small-scale farmers rely on the labour of their household, there are often times during the year when extra labour is needed. Moreover, even in the ideal peasant community there are likely to be households with a labour deficit and others with a land deficit. There are a number of different ways in which these imbalances can be met. It is useful to begin our discussion by suggesting that all these possible arrangements are guided by a spirit of equivalence, or reciprocity.

In many peasant communities this direct relationship of mutual indebtedness between individual households is accompanied by a further indebtedness to the community as a whole, which is "paid off" through the exercise of certain community responsibilities. The household cannot survive without the existence of the community, and this is acknowledged by the amount of time and thought which is put aside for community matters. These may in fact involve work on community projects, such as road building or work in the community fields.

For such a peasant then, there are three kinds of work. There is work on his own plot for his own household, and there is work which he does for his neighbour on an exchange basis. But since this latter is done on the basis of direct reciprocity, in principle at least, it neither expands nor contracts the total amount of labour he must undertake. The third form of labour is that which he puts aside for the community as a whole and this is subtracted from the time he has available for his own farm, but presumably he receives a return in terms of what he gets out of being a member of the community. There are usually elected members of the village or especially trusted household heads, or simply the older men, whose job it is to assure that such a balance is indeed maintained.

What I have described here of course, is a pristine peasant community existing in a vacuum. What becomes obvious, once we look at the myriad of different small-scale farmers throughout the world—from Mexico to France and from India to China—is that the real social formations of which they are part have quite different characteristics. Since classes are a function of the workings of the social formations in which they are found, it follows that the class relationships of the peasants in this pristine village will vary according to the nature of the larger society in which the village is found.

Even if, for example, all that concerns the state which controls these peasants is that they should pay their taxes each year, then this in itself will effect the social relations of production within the community itself. In many cases states have found that the most efficient way of extracting such taxes is to leave the apparent workings of the village intact, while relying on its leaders to collect the necessary taxes: a form of indirect rule practised alike by colonists as different as the Incas and the British. Under such circumstances, where previously the householder had put aside some of his labour (or produce) for the benefit of the community as a whole, now the village authority holds some of this for payment to the state.

What concerns us in this situation is the effect it will have on class relationships, and in this respect we can note that where village leadership arose as a function of village production, it has now become functional to the state. In order to preserve this function, the state must offer certain benefits and protections to leaders, and this in turn at least provides the opportunity to alter the balance between village authorities and villagers. While in our pristine example, the leaders had some control, they had few sanctions which would allow them to retain surpluses for their own benefit. But with the advent of state intervention of even such distance as this, the seed of class relationships may be planted in the village.

I have already remarked that a system such as this for extraction by the state of surpluses from small-scale producers has in its favour that it is relatively cheap to maintain, requiring a minimal amount of bureaucratic expenses while minor policing functions can be left to local leadership. It must be noted, however, that such a system is dependent upon the maintenance of the village ideology of how social relationships work because it is on this basis that the village leaders gain access to household labour. In other words, the nature of control, so vital for the extraction of surplus, lies in this instance very largely in the realm of ideology of mystification and disguise.

This then gives some idea of how a community of small farmers can be effected by their location in a particular social formation. Now let us look at a situation where the most significant surplus extraction takes the form of the payment of rent to a large and powerful local landlord. When this rent is extracted from peasants by virtue of the fact that landlords as a class have monopoly control over land it is sometimes referred to as "feudal" rent, reflecting the period of its apogee in Western Europe. By "monopoly" I mean that it is difficult for peasants to find any immediately productive land which is not in the hands of a landlord. Since the peasant is not actually separated from his land, the lord must rely on the actual or potential use of power, in order to extract rents from him.[7] Where this power takes the form of a private army, the lord may actually perform the function of protecting the sedentary peasant from the ravages of plunderers from without, but since this is only to allow the lord to continue to plunder the peasant from within, it is a protection of doubtful value to the peasant. The power of such a lord is likely to be somewhat more covert than this, however, relying over time, on the support of the state laws, and police in order to reinforce his position.

Rent can take two forms: labour rent, where the peasant is given a small plot of land for his own subsistence and then pays a rent to the lord by doing a certain number of days' labour on his demesne land; or rent in kind, where much of the land of the estate is carved up into small plots, and the lord simply extracts rent in the form of a fixed amount of goods. In either case, however, the amount of rent is not established by reference to any economic criterion. It does not, for example, follow the shifts in the prevailing price of land, or the swings in the market price of agricultural goods. It stands to be established between the wide area bordered on the one hand by the power of the lord to extract it, and on the other by the ability of the peasant to produce it and yet still survive.

It is not hard to see why conspicuous expenditure on the extravagant display of wealth and on anything which serves to show that the lord is something quite qualitatively different from the peasant, plays such an important part in this kind of relationship. Nor is it hard to see how the lord's role as a patron for his peasant clients acts as a suitable *modus vivendi* for both, saving the former from the expense of ever having to exercise his might, and giving the latter at least some recourse to personal relationships.

Such an ideology of patronage establishes a superficial set of status differences, along testamental lines, throughout the social formation. This means that social differences are rigidly defined in relation to proximity to the source of power; patron-client relations are thus a superficial reflection of the fact that the relationship between lord and peasant rests on power—both actual and symbolic.

This underlying fundamental class relationship between lord and peasant in turn generates a particular form of social relations within the village itself. Insofar as the lord has ultimate control over valued resources, the ability of one group of villagers to extract surplus from others by virtue of their control over certain means of production will derive from their proximity to the power of the lord. In other words, while these dominant villagers may not actually own the resources they manipulate to exploit their fellows, they do gain sufficient control, through the lord's patronage, to place their feet on the shoulders of others.

Such an arrangement may appear to be beneficial to the "middle peasantry": insofar as it fragments the peasantry as a whole it is certainly beneficial to the lord. But it must be remembered that the position of "middle peasants" cannot attain a proper class formation while their control of certain means of production is dependent upon his favour. While the lord's position *as a lord* remains unchallenged, class formation within the peasantry is restricted since the total amount of resources within the village is limited by his presence. It is this which lies beneath the graded-hierarchy appearance of such societies, where "each man knows his station," and also this which provides its latent class conflict: the "middle peasant" is at once dependent on the lord and constrained by him.

The spread of commodity markets often serves to make manifest this tension. [8] This is so because their presence makes the production of a surplus by the peasant, over and above that needed to pay his rent, a worthwhile undertaking insofar as it gives him access—through the market—to commodities which he cannot himself produce. Needless to say, it is the "middle peasant" who is best placed to produce such a "super surplus." The ensuing tension is further promoted by the fact that the spread of commodities breaks the lords' monopoly over the one really valuable resource (land) by introducing other valued productive resources controlled now by merchants.[9] The seeds are thus planted for new class formations to occur.

In these circumstances the "peasant" can be more strictly referred to as a simple commodity producer. He is a commodity producer now, because he is producing some items specifically in order to sell them (i.e., commodities), and this is "simple" in the sense that his production is not primarily for accumulation of profits (though this may also occur), but rather in order to sell something he can produce in order to buy something he cannot.

The reason why this term—simple commodity producer—is more suitable to us than the vaguer term "peasant" is that it points up yet another possible class relationship which may embrace the small farmer: one in which his surplus is extracted not by the lord, so much as the merchant, who uses the mechanism of the market place to do it. For while the farmer is prepared to go to market with a pig he doesn't need and return with three clay pots he does need which are of the same value as the pig, the merchant goes to the market with money and is not likely to be satisfied to return from the market with different coins having the same value. In short, to act as a trader the merchant charges a fee, and the existence of this fee means that neither the farmer nor the potter carry home with them quite the values they took to the market.

Simple commodity production of this kind is unlikely to be a very permanent arrangement, as either the merchant seeks to increase the division of labour and thus turn the farmer's partial reliance on the market to a total one, or the landlord steps in to adjust the system of production in his own favour.

Thus, even where the monopoly of landlords has been broken, the phenomenon of the tenant farmer continues to be one of the most significant variables locating small farmers in the class structure of Third World social formations. Its most common form is that of sharetenancy.

In this form of rent—share rent—the controller of land allows another to farm it. Either the controller or the labourer may have to provide the seed, and tools, depending on the details of the arrangement. The two parties then split the proceeds of the harvest between them on a share basis. Two points are of interest here. Firstly, at least nominally, the labourer shares with the controller of the land the risks of production. In fact, however, in many cases we are talking about a situation where the peasant is operating very close to subsistence. His consumption needs remain the same whatever the quality of the harvest. This means that, in order to maintain his household in a bad year, he may be unable to pay to the landlord his share of the rent. The landlord may gain from this by taking control of even larger amounts of the surplus in subsequent years.

The second point to note is that, for the owner of a piece of land, share cropping is merely one form of getting somebody to work it. Share tenants are, in effect, a particular kind of piece worker, being paid for the amount they produce. Since share cropping is especially well suited to the extraction of surplus with only minimal investments in equipment on the part of the owner (since the tenant shares or often incurs these costs in their entirety) it is often found in situations where land ownership is by no means the most profitable form of investment: it has the effect of releasing capital for investment elsewhere.

I have suggested above that, while "feudal rent" (that is, rent whose amount is not set by market conditions, but is extracted through power) does have a distinct effect on the internal social relations of the peasant village, the lord's control over the most vital means of production does tend to limit the formation of actual classes within the community of small farmers. What then can be said about this rather different farming community? Here, in the case of share-rent, it is frequent that a combination of factors allows a number of tenants to accumulate plots in excess of the amount of farm labour available within the household (or through reciprocal arrrangements with others). There are two alternatives open to such a farmer: he can seek out those households who have insufficient land for their own needs (possibly as a direct result of his own expansion); he can then either sublet some of his own land to them, or he can employ them to work as his labourers.

Communities in which this process is occurring, or has occurred, are often broadly referred to by anthropologists as "peasant communities," and there is no reason why the term should not serve such a broad purpose. But if the lumping together of all the villagers under the one term stops there, we risk missing the underlying forces which are at work. From the point of view of a class analysis, what is occurring here is that, on one side of the peasant's small farm household there are springing up petty-capitalist producers, and on the other side people who—in one form or another—labour for better-off farmers. Neither of these two extremes—the better-off and the impoverished—are any longer the kind of small farmers I described earlier. The rich "peasant" is now either partially a landlord with tenants and/or capitalist with employees; the poor "peasant" is either partially a rural labourer supplementing his inadequate farm income by selling his labour to others, or totally so, having entirely abandoned his land.

In any case it is likely that these incipient class relationships are buried deep within the idiom of the customary social relationships which exist in the village. Share-rent or rent paid in the form of labour-service can well be disguised behind the mask of the old forms of reciprocal labour exchanges; the employment of extra-household labour can take the form of the temporary adoption of the young sons of impoverished households.

It seems to me that political economists on the one hand and social anthropologists on the other are frequently misled by their own conceptualizations at this point. The anthropologist, wedded to the amorphous term "peasant" frequently becomes enmeshed in the appearances they find by emphasizing the peasant *community* over class relationships. The political economist, on the other hand, is often too impatient with the "primordial customs" of small farmers and thus runs the risk of undervaluing the effects of preexisting social relations and ideologies on contemporary class praxis.

Let me take as an illustration the idea of the "community." It may be defined and confined by a group of people who are able and willing to use the idiom of *communitas* (Turner, 1969) (the village, the neighbours, kin) to express social relationships of identity. This would be a kind of moral community demanding something more than simply an uncommitted statement of membership, in the form of performances which demonstrated one's commitment. Those outside the community are those who do not and cannot so express themselves (this may or may not have anything to do with the physical boundaries of the village-community). In such a situation landlords and merchants are landlords and merchants because they talk and behave like landlords and merchants. Villagers remain villagers no matter how much land they control nor how much mercantile activity they engage in, so long as they speak and behave as members of the community.

All we have done here is describe how people conduct themselves. We have not delved deeper to discover why they do so. While a class analysis which was insensitive to this moral community would be incomplete, a community analysis which was unaware of the forces disguised by the use of "community feeling" would be equally incomplete. The idiom of *communitas* is used by all the actors on the scene, big people and underdogs alike, but it is not enough to restrict analysis to this kind of usage, unless we can also be aware of the tensions which are being brought to bear on *communitas* by the incipient class forces which are being worked out through the contemporaneous social relations of production of the entire social formation.

The complexities of these class relations as we have so far encountered them, moreover, are multiplied still further by the fact that many small farmers are unable to subsist on the land available to them and therefore become a pool of surplus labour in the larger society outside the village. The existence of a labour market, of course, both within the village (as I have discussed above) and outside it, has significant consequences for class analysis. But even with this release of labour from the land, we are unlikely to find a class of people totally committed to the sale of their labour, as we see in the West. The fact that there are a minimal number of jobs available in Third World countries (and, for these impoverished rural people, in the industrialized West as well), and the fact that few jobs that can be got, provide a wage sufficient for the total livelihood of the worker, often lead such people to continue the maintenance of a plot of land (however small); this fact gives a special quality to the labour pool as a class.

On the other hand, the fact that it is often not the poorest peasants who migrate (and certainly not they who migrate with the greatest success), but the better off, has significant effects on the social relations of the peasant community. I have already suggested that sharecropping is especially pervasive where agriculture is no longer the most profitable way of investimg time or money. This can be as true for the rich peasant as for the large landowner. Under circumstances such as this, share-renting within the village need not take place only when the farm is too big for the labour of the immediate family. It may in fact occur when members of the household have found it preferable to work elsewhere while still maintaining their farms. [10]

To sum up: those small farmers who are frequently referred to as peasants are in fact found in quite different kinds of social formations. So we are likely to find small farmers who, despite their similarities over time and space, do in fact exist within quite different social relations of production. Ideally these may be historically clear and specific—feudalism, capitalism, etc.—but what is more frequent is that the social relations of production in Third World social formations are not entirely consistent; more "traditional" customs coexist alongside capitalist social relations and the articulation between them acts to modify all the relationships involved. Class analysis must try to sort these out and assess the tendencies in the system being studied and the implications for class activity. The fieldworker faces this problem by attempting to provide herself or himself with a comprehensive set of those questions which I set forth at the end of Section Two.

SECTION FIVE

Confusion among students about just what is meant by the term "class" results from the fact that the term has come to be used by schools of thought having quite incompatible views of how societies work. Although the concept of class is usually associated with Marxism, none of the great figures of postwar Marxism have concerned themselves much with class analysis—neither Adorno, Goldmann, Marcuse, Lefebvre, Sartre, Althusser nor Coletti (the possible exception would be Lukacs, although his concern was more with the question of consciousness than a thorough-going class analysis). [11] By contrast, virtually all studies of "social class" published during this period have been undertaken by members of the functionalist tradition of academic social science. English-speaking students have therefore felt obliged to relate their work on "social class," not to the writings of Marx, but to the more recent studies of "social class" undertaken by Lloyd Warner (1936), Davis & Moore (1945), *et al*, whose views were derived from the work of Max Weber. It is far beyond the scope of this paper to undertake a critique of these studies or of the view of social structure from which they emerge.[12] It is important only to note that none of them is based on the principle that the task of sociology is to reveal the forces for structural change which are imminent in class conflict. For this reason class analysis is by no means the cornerstone of this conventional social science. Since class relationships are not seen as the underlying forces beneath a whole range of surface categories, class *analysis* is replaced by *descriptive* studies of a whole bundle of groupings (such as occupation, ethnic group, status, and so on) of which "social-class" is just one. What the goal was for such studies—i.e., a more or less complicated description of social categories—should be the *problem* which lies at the beginning of a proper class analysis: to reveal the underlying forces which manifest themselves in those social categories.

To avoid adding further to this confusion, I have restricted myself to setting forth the outlines of the task which would have to be undertaken in order to reach such a goal in social anthropology. Even this highly schematic outline has, of necessity, been limited in scope. The most regrettable limits are twofold. While I do not regret being unable to discuss the class analysis of modern metropolitan societies (there are, after all plenty of such studies available in sociology), I do regret having no space to refer to the kind of task involved in attempting to locate Canadian Indians and Inuit in the class structure of our own society. It is a task imperative for their future.

Secondly, by concentrating on what I have called the first of two steps in class analysis—assessing objective class—I may have given the very wrong impression of structural determinism. The second step—an analysis of class praxis—would reveal how definite class forces act on all elements of society—economic, legislative, political, etc.—to change its form.

What I have tried to do here is to start from the followine premise:

> The specific economic form, in which unpaid labour is pumped out of direct producers, determines the relationship of rulers and ruled . . . It is always the direct relationship of the owners of the conditions of production to the direct producers . . . which reveals the innermost secret, the hidden basis of the entire social structure . . ." (Marx, 1971:791).

This has led me to suggest that class relationships must be defined quite differently for different social formations; one set of criteria does not suffice for all the variety of conditions in which humans live. This calls for the empirical analysis of each specific group that the anthropologist is studying. Marx makes this emphatically clear:

> This does not prevent the same economic basis . . . from showing infinite variations and gradations of appearance, which can be ascertained only by the analysis of the empirically given circumstances (1971:792).

153

It is not, therefore, an ivory tower task nor, for that matter, a task of participant observation; rather it is a matter of observant participation.

In this paper I have attempted to raise the kinds of questions which would be relevant in a number of different situations: the sort of things which I think one should look out for on fieldwork or when reading an ethnographic monograph. In the case of "tribal" formations this means paying due attention to the dominance of other elements besides the economic. But even after that is said, I have suggested that the first task, when faced with such formations, is not to seek out the significant classes but to begin by assessing the extent to which *any form* of class analysis can be of value in understanding the underlying social forces which lead to transformations in the social structure.

In the case of "peasantries," so varied are the conditions in which they live that the crucial task is not to lay out a formula for their universal definition, but to express clearly the nature of the underlying ties which condition their relations, to each other and to the larger social formation of which they are part.

The complexity of the task should not deter us from undertaking it. Failure to do so on the part of social anthropologists may be of no significance one way or the other; political practitioners failing to do so tend to pay a higher price.[13]

NOTES:

1. *For recent examples, see Poulantzas 1972, 1974; and Westergaard & Resler 1975.*
2. *This reason for taking an interest in classes contrasts with a purely academic concern with differences in wealth (economic stratification) or the hierarchical way in which informants choose to view their fellows (status).*
3. *Bernier's article in this book gives a far more extensive outline of the way this process works out in urban society.*
4. *I make this point about the historical circumstances of Lenin's analysis, in order to stress that class analysis is by no means a purely academic matter. See note 13.*
5. *There is no space for the discussion of all the possible relationships which would be revealed by the thorough analysis of a real ethnographic example, but this schematic summary could be applied to Pre-Incaic Peru (Wachtel 1977: 61 ff).*
6. *I have not of course referred to the relationship between "tribal" societies and other sectors of the modern nation state. Recent work in Africa has been addressed to this issue (Meillassoux 1972).*
7. *In fact, the lord may control access to some important tools for production, such as the mill. The important point, however, is that his position as lord derives from his access to instruments of power.*
8. *Commodity markets arise out of the workings of feudal production. It is not, therefore, their "advent" as an independent variable, which matters, but the growing dominance of a new class: the merchants. For a difference between analyses which stress the significance for change of merchant capital versus those stressing the importance of markets, see Kay, 1975 versus Polanyi 1958, Dalton 1971.*

9. Lords, of course, can and do use any means at their disposal to hinder this process.
10. Such people need not necessarily be involved in wage labour. They may, for example, become small merchants, or invest their time in the acquisition of a remunerative skill.
11. Although the entire method of Marx's work leads to the need for a class analysis, he only made explicit statements about class in the Communist Manifesto and in the unfinished final chapter of the third volume of Capital.
12. A brief comparison is made in Ossowski (1969).
13. Lenin (1971) and Mao (Schram ed., 1969) both made such analyses of peasantry; Che and General Westmoreland did not—Q.E.D.

BIBLIOGRAPHY

Dalton, George 1971. Economic theory and primitive society. *Economic Anthropology and Development*. New York City: Basic Books.

Davis, Kingsley and Wilbert E. Moore 1945. Some principles of social stratification. *American Sociological Review* 10. 2.

Ennew, Judith Paul Hirst and Keith Tribe 1977. 'Peasantry' as an economic category. *Journal of Peasant Studies*. 4.4.

Galeski, Boguslaw 1972. *Basic concepts in rural sociology*. Manchester: The University Press.

Godelier, Maurice 1977b. The concept of 'social and economic formation': The Inca example. Godelier, *op cit*. Also in *Critique of Anthropology*, No. 1 Spr 1974.

Godelier, Maurice 1977c. The non-correspondence between form and content in social relations. Godelier, *op. cit.*

Hindess, B., and P. Hirst 1977a. Mode of production and social formation. *Pre-capitalist modes of production:* a reply to John Taylor. *Critique of Anthropology* No. 8 Vol. 2 Spr.

Hindess, B., and P. Hirst, 1977b. *Mode of production and social formation: an auto-critique of 'Pre-capitalist modes of production!* London; MacMillan.

Hobsbawn, Eric 1959. *Primitive rebels*. New York: Norton & Co.

Kay, Geoffrey 1975. *Development and underdevelopment: a marxist perspective*. London: MacMillan.

Lenin, V.I. 1971. *Selected Works*. One Vol. Moscow: Progress.

Marx, Karl 1971. *Capital* Vol. III Moscow: Progress.

Ossowski, S. 1969. Old notions and new problems: interpretations of social structure in modern society. *Social Inequality*. (ed) Andre Beteille Harmondsworth, Penguin, Reprinted from *Transactions of the Third World Congress of Sociology* International Sociological Association. London. (1956).

Polanyi, Karl 1958. The economy as instituted process in *Trade and Markets in the early empires*. (eds) Polanyi, C. Arensberg and H. W. Pearson. New York. Free Press.

Poulantzas, Nicos 1972. *Political power and social classes*. London: New Left Books.

Poulantzas, Nicos 1975. *Classes in contemporary capitalism*. London: New Left Books.

Rey, P.P. 1975. The lineage mode of production. *Critique of Anthropology*. No. 3. Spr.

Sahlins, Marshall 1966. *Tribesmen*. Englewood Cliffs: Prentice-Hall.

Schram, Stuart 1969 (ed). *The political thought of Mao Tse-Tung*. Harmondsworth. Penguin.

Terray, Emanuel 1975. Classes and Class consciousness in the Abron

Kingdom of Gyaman in *Marxist analyses and social anthropology.* (ed) Maurice Bloch. London: Malaby Press.

Turner, Victor 1969. *The ritual process.* Harmondsworth: Penguin.

Wachtel, Nathan 1977. *The Vision of the Vanquished.* Hassocks, Sussex: The Harvester Press.

Warner, W. Lloyd 1936. American caste and class. *American Journal of Sociology.* 42.

Westergaard, J. and H. Resler 1975. *Class in a Capitalist Society.* London: Heinemann.

CHAPTER 7

LANGUAGE AND SOCIETY

LOUIS-JACQUES DORAIS
Université Laval

INTRODUCTION

The study of languages has for a long time been undertaken in a vacuum. Linguists generally pursued purely formal analyses, without considering the social aspects of the phenomena they studied. Following De Saussure, they thought that "language is an entity unto itself and a principle of classification" (De Saussure 1932:25). Today, despite input from anthropology, sociology, and other social sciences, many researchers study language as an abstract entity functioning outside of history and the environment.

This form of linguistics, whether it be structural, generative, or transformational, is perhaps necessary but it is far from being sufficient. If it enables us to understand the mechanisms by which messages are transmitted (by means of a system of articulated sounds), it provides us with little information as to the content of these messages and informs us even less about the conditions which give rise to them. A true science of language, if it is to be complete and useful, must take account of the social context in which communication occurs. It must explain how discourse arises, how these messages are transmitted and the ends they serve.

In the following pages, we will describe certain salient features of this social linguistics. After demonstrating the ways in which the Structuralist, Whorfian, and Ethnosemantic approaches are inadequate, we will sketch a model of the articulation of the relationships between language and social structure. In the second part we will analyze the relationships that exist among language, social classes, and ideology, so that a concrete example of the role of language in society may be presented—the linguistic policies of the Québecois government since the end of the 1960s.

LANGUAGE AND SOCIAL STRUCTURE: THE STRUCTURALIST APPROACH

Despite its sometimes introverted appearance, "pure" linguistic research, especially that inspired by De Saussure, has influenced many anthropologists. The structuralists, for example, have attempted to discover models in phonology and morpho-syntax that enable them to understand better the functioning of societies. Some anthropologists are much inspired by the work of Roman Jakobson. According to this linguist each phoneme must stand in opposition to all other phonemes in the language by at least one trait (an alternative element with differential value). In English, for example, the words *nark* and *dark* or *mark* and *bark* are different because their first phoneme is sometimes nasalized; at other times it is not:

nark/dark = mark/bark = nasalised/not nasalised

But *bark* and *park* are opposed because the first phoneme of one is voiced, while the other is voiceless. In fact, whenever someone hears any phrase, the listener must constantly make an unconscious choice between the two terms with reference to many kinds of oppositions.

The totality of distinctive traits and their combination into phonemes as well as the rules governing the linkage of these phonemes constitutes a code to which all speakers (users) of a language refer. The elements of this code form a structure which organizes oral communication. It is because this code is shared by all members of a given linguistic community that communication is possible for the members.

The system of language is acquired during infancy within one's group of origin and upbringing. Beyond a certain age, however, such acquisition becomes impossible. ("Wolf-children" who have matured outside human society cannot learn to speak when they rejoin it.)

The phonological approach has greatly influenced the French anthropologist Claude Lévi-Strauss and, later, the entire structuralist school. For Lévi-Strauss (1958) there is an analogy between the notion of structure as defined by the linguists (such as Jakobson) and anthropological models. Each kinship term, each narrative unit of a myth plays the role of an element within a structured code carrying a message (alliance norms, world view, etc.). One cannot directly apply the linguistic approach to the analysis of social facts but, by analogy, one can speak of "structure" in both cases.

For example, the phonological method comprises four fundamental steps which bear on the social sciences:

a. it permits the passage from the study of conscious phenomena (sounds) to the phenomena's unconscious infra-structure;

b. it uses the relations between terms as its analytical base (rather than the terms themselves);

c. it reveals systems and their structures;

d. it encourages the discovery of general laws, by induction or deduction.

By proceeding in analogical fashion, certain social phenomena—for example kinship—can be analyzed since:
a. kinship terms are elements of signification, like phonemes;
b. they are integrated into unconscious systems;
c. kinship phenomena are the result of general laws, since similar phenomena occur in widely separated areas.

Myths form structures in the same way. The diverse elements of a group of variations of the same myth are integrated into a system where each element is opposed to every other element.

In fact, for Lévi-Strauss, language and sociocultural phenomena constitute two parallel modalities of one basic activity, that of the human mind. Correlations between the formalized expressions (organized into systems) of linguistic structure and social structure must be sought. There is thus no point in comparing the superficial manifestations (cultural attitudes, common expressions) of these structures. There exist certain correlations between language and society, between certain aspects and at certain levels. Both, however, proceed from the same fundamental structure, the human mind.

THE SAPIR-WHORF HYPOTHESIS

By concentrating on the structural aspects of linguistic-social correlations, Lévi-Strauss contradicts (rightly so, it would seem) a hypothesis formulated in the 1930s by the American linguist Benjamin Lee Whorf (1957). This hypothesis is known as the Sapir-Whorf hypothesis since it owes much to the work of another linguist, Edward Sapir. It can be stated as follows: the cultural behaviour of the members of a society is determined by the language they speak.

Especially for Whorf, the social habits of individuals are determined by the manner in which they judge and analyze the situations they encounter. This analysis rests on linguistic categories since, when somebody reflects on any problem, he uses words and phrases that are part of a given language. It is thus grammar and vocabulary which in the final analysis determine thought and behaviour.

Whorf uses the example of Hopi (an American Indian language found in the Southwestern United States). In this language, time is not objectified. There are no morphemes expressing the time period of any action—unlike European languages. Rather, it is the names of people or objects which change their form, and, accordingly, the listener conceptualizes their referents as either presently existing or in the process of becoming. Contrary to the European languages, which conceive of time as lineal, Hopi appears to contain a series of possible modifications bearing on situations or objects basically immutable by nature.

To Whorf, this manner of conceptualizing the world determines Hopi behaviour (as expressed in religious rituals, for instance), behaviour which is based on the anticipation of what is yet to be actualized. In the Occident, on the other hand, the conception that time has an objective existence would explain the importance attached to preciseness and punctuality.

These interpretations, although alluring, are not satisfying since they do not explain the origin of the language pattern in question. If, in fact, linguistic categories determine behaviour, what is the origin of these categories? On what are they based? Would it not be more logical to reverse the Sapir-Whorf hypothesis and consider language to be the expression of the socio-cultural experience of a human group? In fact, the correlations observed by Whorf between linguistic categories and behaviour remain at a very superficial level (a reproach which could have been made by Lévi-Strauss). Language influences thought, but not directly. Discourse is at the same time generated and mediated by the context in which it occurs and by the social relations which structure this context (see below). Thus the relations are logically prior to language. Further, it is of primary importance that we explain how language interprets socio-cultural experience, rather than viewing language as the primary source of all thought.

ETHNOSEMANTICS

Before going further on this path we will say a few words on a relatively recent development of American socio-linguistics, largely inspired by Whorf's ideas. This is ethnosemantics, or the anthropology of knowledge (see Tyler 1969).

The basic postulate of ethnosemantics is that each people have their own system of perception and way of organizing material phenomena. The human mind continually classifies the reality perceived by the senses in order to transform it into models of behaviour. It is the totality of cognitive models found in a given society which, for ethnosemanticists, constitutes its culture.

In order to have access to these cognitive models, the vocabulary used by the members of the society under study must be analyzed. The natural phenomena perceived through the senses are grouped into classes—into hierarchically-arranged categories—which for the most part are labelled. The nature and organization of these classes vary from one culture to another. For example, the visible spectrum is a physical continuum which can be subdivided into arbitrary categories (the colours). For Canadian francophones, there are ten such categories given the following names: *noir* (black), *blanc* (white), *rouge* (red), *vert* (green), *bleu* (blue), *jaune* (yellow), *brun* (brown), *violet* (violet), *gris* (grey), and *rose* (pink). For the Inuit of the Quebec Arctic, on the other hand, their language distinguishes only seven colours: *qirnitaq* (black), *qakuqtaq* (white), *qupaqtuq* (red and pink), *tungujuqtaq* (green, blue, violet), *quqsutaq* (yellow), *kajug* (brown) and *isuqtaq* (grey).

These classes are often grouped into taxonomies, such that the larger categories (genera) include more specific ones (species). In Canadian French, the genera *"jaune"* (yellow) includes the species *"jaune orange"* (orange-yellow), *"jaune citron"* (lemon-yellow), *"beige"* (beige), etc. The names designating each of the classes are called lexemes.

All the elements that are part of the same taxonomy must have at least one common trait. These signifying traits serve to define each of the classes of the taxonomy. Thus the colour called *"jaune orange"* (orange-yellow) has two principal traits: it belongs to the category *"jaune"* (yellow), while implying a hint of red. It can thus be distinguished from *"jaune citron"* (lemon-yellow) which, although part of the same category *"jaune,"* has the signifying trait "bright."

For ethnosemanticists, each culture is constituted by several semantic domains organized around numerous signifying traits. Domains and traits vary from one culture to another. The researcher's task is to discover the ideological order imposed on the environment by the members of a society.

How can this be done? Informants must be asked questions in their native tongue concerning the domain under study: what is this called? is this called by the same name? how many different types of these are there?, etc. This is called the method of *controlled elicitation.* The responses must be interpreted while in the field so that the questionnaire can be changed if need be. Then follows a formal analysis of the bulk of the data, locating the semantic traits which characterize these elements and the relations which order these traits. A coherent view of the cultural domain studied is thus obtained.

The cultural representations elicited by ethnosemantics nonetheless do not satisfactorily explain the link that exists between language and society. If these representations allow us to describe the manner in which a given population conceives of reality, they do not inform us about the causes of this perception nor about the reasons why the classification of reality differs from one society to another.

We are thus still faced with the search for a general model which enables us to understand the manner in which language and society articulate. The deficiencies of the Sapir-Whorf hypothesis have been examined above. Its idealist tendency (the domination of underlying reality by ideas), which makes social behaviour dependent on preexisting linguistic categories, cannot deal with a fundamental question: why does this or that category exist in a given society at a precise moment in history?

Does structuralism provide a more satisfactory answer? While it explains in a sophisticated manner how some correlations can exist among different systems of interlinked elements (kinship, mythological and linguistic structures, etc.), it fails to explain the manner by which these systems appear and transform themselves. Even if it constitutes a sound synchronic method of analysis of language and society, it must not be considered as an explanatory theory, since it leaves several fundamental questions unanswered.

LANGUAGE AND MODE OF PRODUCTION

The basic components of a mode of production have been defined in Chapter 3 of this book (see also Harnecker 1974), and there is no need to repeat them here. But what exactly is the role of language in a mode of production? It would appear that it forms a dual relation comprising, on the one hand, semantic categories and, on the other, grammatical and lexical elements. The semantic categories (which roughly correspond to the genera and species of the anthropology of knowledge) define the content of language. The grammatical and lexical elements (called lexemes by ethnosemanticists) translate this content into discourse in such a fashion that it can be thought and communicated.

Semantic categories do not exist in a vacuum. They are the mental representation of a very concrete reality: the physical and social environment, economic relations, political institutions and the ideologies characteristic of a given social formation. Since this reality is determined by the requirements of a given type of production, which is usually undertaken for the benefit of the dominant class, language, because of the bias of its semantic component, is thus linked in a specific way to the internal structure of the particular mode of production in question.

Language is, nonetheless, not totally included in the mode of production, since the grammatical and lexical units which translate its meaning have an autonomous history (of an etymological order). Thus, when a mode of production transforms itself (in the change from feudalism to capitalism, for example), language is only partially affected. If the semantic categories representing certain social relations are then subjected to change, this does not automatically change the words which translate these categories. For example, consider the term "democracy." While for the Soviets it represents "dictatorship of the proletariat," in the West, it retains the meaning, "representative parliamentary regime." The same lexeme, therefore, translates two different semantic categories, thus reflecting the transformation of social relations.

Discourses produced by language form one of the components of the social environment, acting as raw material for the elaboration of political and ideological superstructures. Because of this tendency, language has a certain influence on the social structure which, in turn, determines its content. It is thus in a dialectical relationship to social structure.

In the following pages we will see how diverse social classes attempt to use this instrument of communication to their advantage.

TOWARDS AN ANTHROPOLOGY OF LANGUAGE

Up to this point we have leaned towards the theoretical aspects of the relation between language and society by defining language as a relationship between semantic categories and lexico-grammatical forms, the first ideologically reflecting a mode of production, the second translating representations in order to communicate them. It is an epistemological construction which allows us, despite appearances, to grasp the true functioning of society.

As has already been mentioned, what exists concretely are social formations, that is, entities composed of relationships, institutions and beliefs which interact and, often, contradict each other. Thus, for example, Canada constitutes, at one level, a social formation in the sense that its economic and political institutions are, at least partially, autonomous and form an integrated whole.

Within social formations, language plays a very important role. Like all other components of societies, it interacts with and contradicts the diverse parts of the social-economic system. Like these parts, it is used to reinforce and reproduce the social relationships which dominate the formation. In this section, we will study these more concrete aspects of the relation between language and society.

CLASS LANGUAGES

Every modern social formation includes a certain number of antagonistic classes. Indeed, because of the very nature of the dominant social relationships, certain groups control the production and distribution of goods at the expense of others. Since the position of each class is unique within the social formation in which it is found, there necessarily must be class ideologies which reflect this position. It is obvious that in Canada, the world view of the majority of manual laborers is different from that of the bourgeois intellectual or professional (despite the fact that some workers attempt to imitate this world view in order to climb the social ladder). While professionals and intellectuals support the status quo, where higher education, the law and, traditionally, the church play an important role, workers' priorities are concerned with bettering their living conditions by any possible means. This lies at the source of the accusation (levelled by the bourgeoisie) which holds that the lower classes are amoral and have no respect for established institutions.

Since semantic categories and, indirectly, the lexico-grammatical units which translate them, are linked to ideologies, it can be concluded that there exist class languages or dialects. These are more or less distinct manners of expression linked to a certain class or given social group. In Québecois French, for example, the frequency of blasphemy (swear-words with a religious content) is linked to class membership. Among intellectuals, professionals, and business people this trait is generally not so common, while its incidence rises sharply among employees and workers. The phenomenon denotes, ideologically, that the latter group is in revolt against traditional religious values while the former is not. This revolt, in turn, reflects the dominant role held until recently by the Catholic Church, allied to the bourgeoisie.

When the members of a given ethnic group are all largely members of the same social class, it is often that their language plays the role of class language. This is the case with Canadian Indians and Inuit who, for the most part, are members of the lowest strata in society, and whose language was the object of scorn for a long time. Until the end of the 1960s, the education policies of the federal and provincial governments were more or less consciously aimed at the eradication of native languages. It is only recently that, with a change in the economic and political climate, the Indians and Inuit have been accorded some linguistic rights. The development of the North has underlined the strategic role that northern inhabitants can play as a reserve labour force.

On the methodological level, two conclusions emerge from our considerations. On the one hand, an anthropology of language must be defined in such a way that it takes account of the dynamic quality of social relationships. On the other hand, a "differential linguistics" must be practised and capable of reflecting those variations in language which are tied to class membership.

As far as the anthropology of language is concerned, it is essential that it reveal the relation which exists between the usage of a particular mode of expression and the position of any given class within the social relations of production. The dominant class generally considers its manner of speaking to be the best. In order to gain access to directorial positions, for instance, an aspirant must master the language of the controllers of these positions, whether this language be a variation of the national language or a particular idiom. In Quebec, for example, the federal census of 1961 and 1971 revealed that monolingual French-speakers had a low average income, while monolingual English-speakers held the highest rung in the wage scale, with bilingual speakers in an intermediate position. This signifies that access to economic power (which, in Quebec, is largely in the hands of English-speakers), is subject to control of a linguistic nature.

Language also constitutes a factor in the social classification, or labelling, of an individual. It contributes to maintaining and consolidating class relationships: the capitalist holds onto his privileged position while the labourer, who cannot express himself properly (according to the bourgeoisie), continues in his subordinate role.

Reciprocally, language can become an instrument for the liberation of the lower classes. Many Québecois writers and intellectuals (such as the dramatist Michel Tremblay, author of *Belles-soeurs*) are working for the establishment of a *"joual"* (French with a high English content) literature in order to create a culture which truly reflects the values and aspirations of the people.

Later we will see how the class which controls power in the economic and political spheres also controls language use. But at present we will explain the concept of "differential linguistics."

Classical linguistics has almost always idealized grammatical and lexical variations linked to social differences. Structuralist and transformational descriptions of a given language are based on the idea that everyone speaks in the same manner. This way of proceeding is far from a true reflection of reality, as we have just seen. There are class dialects and they play a very important role. They must thus be taken into account when a language is described. Linguistics will only be a true social science when it takes this type of variation into consideration.

A few researchers have attempted to work from this viewpoint. In the United States William Labov has studied the English spoken in New York (Labov 1966). For Labov, the linguistic system cannot solely account for the origin of phonological and grammatical variations observed among the speakers. The explanation of this origin lies in observing the interaction between social groups, an interaction that is influenced by the respective position of each group within the larger society. However, even if nonlinguistic factors are called upon, the specificity of the observed variations is nonetheless determined by the evaluation of the structure of the language. The relationship between social and linguistic variables thus remains arbitrary.

Despite the absence of an explanation of social dynamism based on class antagonisms in Labov's work (and even of an adequate theory of social relations), his study remains a very good example of what "differential linguistics" can accomplish. This is also true of the research of Canadian sociolinguists Gillian Sankoff and Henrietta Cedergren. Accomplished in the beginning of this decade, this research attempted to measure linguistic variation among French-speakers in the Montreal region. Their conclusions are instructive. The variations studied formed a continuum stretching from "international" French to "joual." Each speaker can be located somewhere along this continuum, his position determined by his sex, age, profession, and social standing. This situation is largely the result of the interplay of ideological factors, as we shall now see.

LANGUAGE AND IDEOLOGY

In many social formations the language of the dominant class has a tendency to overshadow the language of the dominated class. This domination by language contributes to reinforcing the preponderance of the dominators. It is not, however, the principal problem, which lies in the economic sphere. Indeed, as long as workers have no control over the enterprises which allow them to live, it will be the owners of these enterprises who will have the last word, in language as in other matters, due to the pressure they can exert on the state because of their financial power.

Linguistic domination is thus rendered possible by the control the dominant class exerts on the governmental apparatus. The state generally develops policies aimed at ensuring the hegemony of one particular type of language. These policies may be manifested directly or through the intermediary of ideologies.

The majority of governments directly intervene in linguistic matters by favouring a language or particular dialect (geographical or social) at the expense of others. In many countries there is only one official language that everyone must learn regardless of language of origin. In France, for example, there are at least nine different types of speech: French, Occitan (language of Languedoc), Provencal-French, Catalon, Basque, Breton, Flemish, Corsican, and Alsatian. Only French is taught in the schools. This situation results in the weakening of other linguistic forms, which tend to disappear. Thus members of minority groups are disadvantaged. To accede to education and the realm of power and thus find better paying work they must abandon their maternal tongue.

The same situation exists in Canada. In the majority of provinces English is the only official language. Natives as well as Slavic, Italian, and French groups thus have an inferior position in the social hierarchy. Their economic advancement depends on a knowledge of English. The statistics on the rate of anglicization in Canada are self-evident.

Linguistic hegemony is manifested even within the majority group. We have seen above that there are class dialects. A worker or labourer does not speak in the same fashion as a lawyer, doctor, or company president. The official language, found in government documents, education and literature, is always a bourgeois language. In our social system it would be unthinkable, for example, to teach common French or English in the schools. Workers are thus disadvantaged; their language is undermined. They are obliged to learn the dominant class' speech. Economic exploitation is thus paralleled by a linguistic inequality which reinforces the former.

The unwarranted meddling of the dominant class in linguistic matters is not always so direct. It is more common for control to be exercised through the intermediaries of political institutions and ideological representations, since each of those elements of the social structure enjoys a certain autonomy. If, as we have seen, the existence of these elements cannot be explained without reference to the economic infrastructure, their function is nonetheless not completely dominated by the forces and relations of production. These institutions may even exercise a certain influence on the latter. This is known as overdetermination.

It is due to overdetermination that ideology plays a role in the reproduction of social relations from one generation to the next. Indeed, the systematization and justification of certain values or attitudes favour the lengthy maintenance of domination by certain classes. Christian ideology, for example, which teaches "the poor will always be among us," has for a long time contributed and still contributes to maintaining a fatalist attitude among the disadvantaged, an attitude which prevents them from realizing the true nature of the social relations to which they are subject.

Since a language constitutes one of the main vehicles for ideology (we have seen that discourse is part of the social environment structured by the relations of production), it has a very important function within the process of overdetermination. As has been noted, linguistic relations unite lexico-grammatical forms with semantic categories which reflect a certain form of social relations. The language we speak thus represents a determined system of thought. But in capitalist societies it is the language of the bourgeoisie which is the most favoured. This situation thus contributes to disseminating the world view of the dominant class through all social strata. An attempt is therefore made to justify and reproduce the exploitation of the majority by a minority.

Schooling plays a primary role in this process, since it is largely here that the younger generation first encounters the values and dominant beliefs of society. Even if education sometimes transmits elements which favour the development of popular culture, the general orientation of the educational system tends to reproduce existing inequalities. In the spring of 1975, for example, a group of unionized teachers in Quebec prepared a document entitled: "Towards a school day in the service of the working class." Their goal was to take advantage of the first of May, the workers' day of celebration, so that students could be made aware, through lessons and exercises adapted to their level, of the true nature of capitalist relationships in our society. The reaction of the authorities was extremely negative. The Ministry of Education, supported by many school boards, vigorously condemned this initiative as "subversive and immoral." In fact, the Québecois state did not wish the *status quo* to be questioned.

School thus plays a direct role in the reproduction of the social structure. It does this not only by diffusing the dominant ideology, but also by using a particular type of language as an instrument of transmission. The role played by the language of schooling has been revealed in a very subtle way by the English sociolinguist Basil Bernstein (1971). According to him, children from the lower classes use a restricted linguistic code (especially favouring the expression of emotions), while members of the higher classes have both the more limited code and an elaborated one, facilitating rational statements. As the school only teaches the elaborated code, lower-class students are disadvantaged. They are obliged to use instruments of communication with which they are unfamiliar. This leads to a disinterest in school work and a lag in scholastic achievement which contribute to maintaining their social inferiority.

School language thus influences social relations. For example, among the Canadian Inuit of the Western Arctic, English is the sole language of instruction for economic and political reasons—a desire to integrate the northern populations into the larger Canadian society. The direct consequence of this practice is that many students' competency in their mother tongue is reduced. An inquiry we conducted at Igloolik (Northwest Territories) in 1975 revealed that young educated speakers were ignorant of or malinformed about nearly twenty percent of the words used by their parents (who never went to school). Socially, this has made communication between the generations very difficult. When elders discuss hunting, sewing, or other traditional activities, young people have difficulty understanding and lose interest in conversation. The parents' reaction is to conclude that their children belong to an entirely different world than theirs. They hesitate to teach them the techniques and other areas of knowledge native to Inuit culture, even if some of the younger people wish to be initiated into that culture.

The young are thus alienated, cut off from the social and natural environment which imbues life in the Arctic with significance. For the most part, unable to hunt or fish as a principal occupation, they are obliged to seek wage labour. But the education they have received does not even perform this function for "average Canadians," let alone the underprivileged Inuit. Their knowledge of English is usually deficient. Few of them have the desire or means to go away for higher education. They are thus often limited to menial labour, while schooling has turned them into disadvantaged labourers who are incapable of taking control of their own economic destiny.

LINGUISTIC POLICIES IN QUEBEC: BILL 63

We will now provide an example of the real workings of the linguistic policies actualized by a predominantly capitalist state by reviewing Quebec legislation in the area of language since the end of the 1960s. (On this subject, see Mallea 1977.)

In the fall of 1968, trouble arose in St. Léonard, a Montreal suburb. The non-French-speakers of this area, largely of Italian origin, demanded the maintenance and total anglicization of the bilingual schools which had served them up to this point. Some people of French origin protested. They rapidly gained the support of many nationalist francophone associations. Tension between the two groups increased.

Faced with this situation, the provincial government (Union Nationale) was forced to react. It prepared a Bill (Bill 85) which made certain concessions to the proponents of anglicization. Faced with widespread opposition from French-speaking groups who found the text of the law too ambiguous and compromising, the Premier, J. J. Bertrand, rescinded the proposed Bill in February 1969.

The situation in St. Léonard continued. In the fall of 1969, protests organized by diverse nationalist movements degenerated into violent confrontations. The Bertrand government then decided to propose a new law (Bill 63) dealing specifically with the language of instruction. To prevent protests, the text of the law was not subjected to public hearings. Despite protestation from many of the French-speaking pressure groups, the National Assembly adopted the law in November 1969.

Bill 63 had three principal aspects:

169

a. Every parent could freely choose the school where s/he would send his/her children (French or English);
b. Immigrants would be urged (it was not made clear how) to learn French:
c. An inquiry (Gendron commission) would study the Quebec linguistic situation.

Non-francophones were, on the whole, in agreement with the law. In accordance with their position it guaranteed every individual the right to choose the language s/he desired his/her children to speak. For French-speaking nationalists, on the other hand, these individuals' rights should be subordinated to the collective rights of the majority. In a province where roughly ninety percent of immigrants assimilate into the Anglophone community, the French-speaking majority felt it had to oblige the greatest number possible to send their children to French schools so that it would ensure its survival.

In fact, two principles are in contradiction here. The first, inspired by liberal bourgeois ideology, insists on the rights of individuals: each individual is free to educate, entertain or enrich him/herself as s/he desires (the domination of workers by a small number of owners is justified in this way). The second, more socialist in inspiration, upholds the right of the majority to develop collectively, even if this goes against the privileges of a few. Those that defend this position, the nationalist French-speakers, also belong to the bourgeoisie, but to a segment of this class whose development is within the context of larger-scale capitalism. They hope through an ideological alliance with the majority to re-align the socio-economic situation to their ends.

If the Union National government, despite its traditional nationalist allegiances, tended towards the liberal ideology, it was due to strictly political considerations. Elections (held in April 1970) were looming and if the government wished to survive, it had to cater to some of the demands of the Anglophone electorate. To do this, it had to abandon its nationalist appearance, especially in the light of the reaction to the De Gaulle affair of 1967 (General De Gaulle, a guest of the Quebec government had publically declared: "Vive le Québec libre!") and to the declarations of ex-premier Daniel Johnson ("Equality or independence").

The politio-linguistic strategies of J. J. Bertrand served him to no good end and in the spring of 1970 general elections brought the liberal premier Robert Bourassa to power.

LINGUISTIC POLICIES IN QUEBEC: BILL 22

Starting in 1970, the political situation changed rapidly in Quebec. In the April elections, the Parti Québecois obtained twenty-three percent of the vote (in 1966, its forerunner, the "Rassemblement pour l'indépendance nationale" had only obtained six percent). In 1973 this percentage rose to thirty.

In the social sphere, the October crisis in 1970 (kidnapping and murder of cabinet minister Pierre Laporte) and the events of the spring of 1972 (general strike of the civil service) forced the Liberal government to seek a means of restoring order.

Realizing that language was an important issue for a large segment of the French-speaking population, Premier Bourassa decided to enact laws in this area. In the spring of 1974 he presented a proposed piece of legislation (Bill 22) which attempted to provide some guarantees for the French language while leaving the anglophones' social and economic privileges unchanged. Bourassa had hoped to decrease the agitation which was fomenting throughout the province.

In fact, the government also attempted to resolve the linguistic contradiction which made English, the minority language in Quebec (it is used by twenty percent of the population), the principal means of communication for many French-speaking workers and the main language of the majority of immigrants. The Liberals hoped, consciously or otherwise, to mask the principal contradiction by means of this biased legislation—the economic contradiction which deprived Quebec workers of the real value of what they produced.

Despite opposition from a majority of pressure groups, francophone as much as anglophone, the law was passed July 31, 1974. It had five main components:

a. French was to be the official language of Quebec (this is purely a moral stand not backed by anything else in the law);

b. civil government was to use primarily French, but every English-speaking citizen or group of citizens could participate in government in their own language;

c. private enterprise would be urged to increase its use of French; after a date to be determined later, a certificate of French competency would be required in order to obtain a government contract;

d. a student must be fluent in English before registering in an English school; otherwise all students would be placed in French schools; tests may be used to evaluate each student's linguistic competence;

e. the government was to set up a French-language Commission to enforce the new legislation.

The law caused general controversy right from the start. French-speakers thought that it did not go far enough in ensuring the francification of Quebec (through incentives rather than coercive measures), while anglophones, on the other hand, protested that the law abrogated individual rights by taking the choice of language of education out of the hands of parents.

This opposition is inherent in the very nature of the law. By attempting to calm francophones' nationalist sentiments without panicking English-speaking business people, it satisfied no one with its half-measures.

Following the passing of the law, government spokespeople tried to mollify the business community, thus proving that the Liberals' main objective was to maintain the economic status quo. The Minister of Education, Francois Cloutier, emphasized the moderate and practical aspects of the legislation. The first two presidents of the French-Language Commission were neither linguists nor educators but representatives of the upper bourgeoisie.

This preoccupation with the maintenance of the economic *status quo* was explicitly expressed in a speech made September 9, 1975 by Guy Saint-Pierre, Minister of Industry and Commerce given to New York business people (Saint-Pierre 1975). He affirmed that the economic policies of the Quebec government had not changed, ("We are against all discriminatory policies as regards foreign capital for the development of Quebec"). The difference between Quebec and the United States is strictly cultural in nature (and not socio-economic). This difference, according to Saint-Pierre, is a positive trait:

> [*the American capitalist located in Quebec*] *could, after a few months, sit down in a charming continental restaurant in Old Montreal or Old Quebec and reflect: "Business is good and I have another culture at my doorstep"—a double value.*

Despite these reassuring views, the Liberal government was not able to convince the electorate of the soundness of its policies. In November 1976 the Parti Québecois was swept to power, auguring future changes in Quebec linguistic legislation.

CONCLUSION

We have seen that language, semantic reflections, and lexico-syntactical correspondences with the social relations in a society can all be used for ideological and political ends.The example used was Quebec, where the manipulation of linguistic phenomena has been particularly apparent especially in the last few years. With the rise to power of the Parti Québecois, new policies have been elaborated. Bill 101, for example, limits access to English schools to students whose parents have already studied English in Quebec. However, nothing has been settled on the economic level. By continuing to legislate in the cultural domain without attempting to resolve the fundamental contradiction, the Levesque government is encouraging the maintenance of Quebec's capitalist structure. Representing the petty-bourgeoisie, its basic positions are the same as the previous government's. Some extracts from its platform (removing the allusions to independence) could have been uttered by a Liberal minister:

> The first order of business, obviously, will be maintaining and adjusting the economic regime which a sovereign Quebec will inherit . . . we are not the only ones who desire this. All of Canada, and especially Ontario, has a direct interest that the separation takes place in an orderly fashion and without upsetting economic relationships which are so useful that no one wishes to renounce them (Parti Québecois 1970: 17).

Despite everything, this transfer of power from one segment of the bourgeoisie to another can have unexpected results because it relies strongly on nationalist ideology. If the Parti Québecois government succeeds in attenuating the effects of Quebec's unique linguistic contradiction, it is possible that Quebec workers, largely francophones, will be able to concentrate all their efforts on resolving the basic economic contradiction. The greater importance attached to French as the language of work will thus contribute to raising the workers' class consciousness.

BIBLIOGRAPHY

Bernstein, Basil 1971. *Class, Codes and Control, Vol. I.* Routledge and Kegan Paul, London.

DeSaussure, Ferdinand 1962. *Cours de linguistique générale.* Payot, Paris.

Harnecker, Marta 1974. *Les concepts élémentaires du matérialisme historique.* Contradictions, Bruxelles.

Labov, William 1966. *The Social Stratification of English in New York City.* Center for Applied Linguistics, Washington.

Lévi-Strauss, Claude 1958. *"L'analyse structurale en linguistique et en anthropologie".* Anthropologie structurale (C. Lévi-Strauss), Plon, Paris: 37-62.

Mallea, John R., ed. 1977. *Quebec's Language Policies: Background and Response.* Les Presses de l'Université Laval, Québec.

Parti Quebecois 1970. *La solution. Le programme du Parti québecois.* Editions du Jour, Montréal.

Saint-Pierre, Guy 1975. "Le Québec face aux investissements étrangers. *Le Soleil,* 10 septembre: A5.

Tyler, S.A., ed. 1969. *Cognitive Anthropology.* Holt, Rinehart and Winston, New York.

Whorf, Benjamin Lee 1957. *Language, Thought and Reality.* Wiley, New York.

CHAPTER 8

LANGUAGE AND SOCIETY IN PAPUA NEW GUINEA

GILLIAN SANKOFF
Université de Montréal

Linguistic diversity is one of the most striking facts about Papua New Guinea. In this newly independent nation of some two and a half million people, more than 700 distinct languages are spoken. This chapter will attempt to explain the social significance of this fact; to understand what it has meant in the lives of Papua New Guineans. We will start by reconstructing the role of language in precolonial Papua New Guinea, and then consider the changes that have occurred since the beginning of the colonial period approximately a hundred years ago.

In the past, most Papua New Guineans were born into fairly small local communities, living in hamlets or villages of about 100 to 400 people. They made a living by growing their own food in gardens which were efficiently and lovingly cultivated with horticultural techniques—that is, without benefit of the plough or draught animals, each plant receiving more or less individual attention from its gardener. Known as long-fallow, swidden, or slash-and-burn, this method of producing food involves cutting down the secondary jungle growth, leaving this to dry out for a period of weeks, and then clearing and firing the remaining bush. The planted field lasts for about a year and a half, after which it is left to fallow for a period of perhaps only two or three years if soil conditions are good, or as many as ten, twelve, or fifteen years, in less fertile terrain. Most people also raised pigs and, in coastal areas, the diet was supplemented by fishing.

In each local community everyone could somehow or other be related by family ties, but the particular kinds of groupings people formed were quite varied. In some cases there were moieties, that is, two exogamous kinship groups, usually described (from a male point of view) as "exchanging women." In other places there were local

175

groups including three or more kin groups, usually but not always exogamous. One's affiliation with a particular group was sometimes determined by the father, sometimes by the mother. But often the ties of both parents were significant, and a person could claim affiliation with several groups through various relatives. Belonging to such a group was important, especially as a means of inheriting land, the most precious resource.

Political groupings were small and also somewhat evanescent. Leadership was generally not hereditary, and men acquired personal, local followings, becoming "big men" through a combination of good connections and clever politicking, wheeling and dealing in the financial affairs involved in ceremonial exchanges, principally marriages.

For present purposes, what is important to note about these political and social arrangements is that there was no recognized political dominance of any particular locally-based group over other such groups. Hostilities sometimes resulted in one group losing some part of its territory and having to flee for shelter with allies. But though such events may sometimes have led to a sharp diminution in the numbers of speakers of a particular language, they did not lead to a recognition of the hegemony of any one language group. The situation, then, was one of extreme linguistic diversity, but with little or no inequality among language groups. Language boundaries did not coincide with or correspond to political boundaries, and thus could not come to symbolize them.

LANGUAGE IN PRECOLONIAL PAPUA NEW GUINEA

The languages of Papua New Guinea belong to two large language families: the Austronesian languages which are distributed throughout the Pacific; and the non-Austronesian or Papuan languages, specific to Papua New Guinea and adjacent islands of Melanesia. The largest language groups are mainly Papuan, found predominantly in the centre of the Papua New Guinea mainland as well as in the centre of many of the smaller islands. Though not all languages in the coastal areas are Austronesian, this is where they are concentrated, and only a few Austronesian groups lie inland. Many Austronesian groups are very small pockets on the coast, surrounded by Papuan speakers. This distribution tends to support the theory that Austronesian-speaking peoples arrived in Melanesia after the Papuan speakers, occupying many of the coastal areas and forcing Papuan speakers inland. The large size of many of the interior Papuan-speaking groups in the Highlands would also suggest a relatively recent and rapid expansion.

In most areas other than the wide valleys of the Highlands, then, linguistic groups tend to be relatively small, and even within the Highlands, dialect differentiation is such that neighbouring groups often speak perceptibly different dialects. Thus most New Guineans living before the colonial period probably had personal experience of linguistic diversity, without having ventured very far from their home villages. We may well ask, however, what this linguistic diversity implied in social terms, i.e., what were the social parameters which made for a considerable degree of linguistic diversity, and what degree of knowledge did people have of other varieties. The kind of contacts between neighbouring groups were those of trade, warfare, and marriage. Clearly women who married into "other-language" or "other-dialect" villages would gain competence in the second language or dialect, as might their children, particularly if the visiting of affines were kept up. It is likely that a sizeable minority of Papua New Guinean women have had the experience of being at least to some degree linguistic "foreigners" in the village into which they have married.

Given this general situation, we might well ask why such contacts did not lead to a *lessening* of linguistic differences, through dialect or language levelling. Here we may find that the explanation lies at least in part in cultural attitudes and behaviour with respect to language. R. F. Salisbury, for example, has described the importance which the Siane (Eastern Highlands Province) attach to the distinctiveness of their own language from neighbouring languages. Many Siane are bilingual in Dene, and use code switching between Siane and Dene as a creative rhetorical device in speechmaking. It appears that for the Siane, contacts with and awareness of other languages have led not to levelling but to heightened consciousness of, and pride in, difference.

This type of situation also prevails among speakers of Buang, a total population of approximately 8000-9000 whose traditional home is along the slopes of the Snake River Valley in Morobe Province southwest of Lae. Twenty-three villages are strung out over a distance of approximately fifteen miles, and they are divided into three major dialects recognized by all: the eight headwaters villages speaking a dialect we shall refer to as "headwaters," the ten central villages speaking the "central" dialect, and the five lower villages speaking the "downriver" dialect, a "dialect" (according to the folk view) which is sufficiently different to rank as a separate language. Within each of the three, speakers recognize still further subdivisions. Thus a resident of a village in the headwaters area is likely to state that there are three main subdivisions of headwaters Buang itself, and cite lexical and phonological differences among them; that there is another, "central" dialect, which is somewhat more difficult to understand, again citing lexical and phonological differences, but not explaining that there are any subdivisions within this dialect; and that there is a third, "downriver" dialect which is quite difficult to understand, and citing probably only one or two lexical differences.

Knowledge of these related language varieties fades out with distance, but within such a system of recognizably related varieties, speakers will insist that their own variety is the best, that it is the easiest to understand, that it is in fact understood by people from miles around, that it is the easiest to learn, and so on. Other varieties are judged to be some kind of corruption or aberration from the speaker's own, and imitations occasion much mirth on the part of any local audience. Each village feels its own dialect to be the best, and accentuates its particular features especially in contrast with those other varieties it is most familiar with, i.e., the closest ones, geographically and usually also in terms of degree of similarity.

In precolonial Papua New Guinea as a whole, then, language diversity was at least as marked as in Europe, for example, but lacking stratified societies, far-reaching empires, and nationalist consciousness, this horizontal diversity was not accompanied by any linguistic stratification. Everyone was ethnocentric about his or her own variety, but since the groups which supported this view were all very small, since people knew that other people thought their own were the best, and since within a region there was no consensus that a particular variety was the best, the situation was very much an egalitarian one.

The question of whether in precolonial times there existed any non-egalitarian situations with respect to language use and attitudes brings forth three possible affirmative answers, all of which revolve around the idea of language as a resource. Malinowski's *Coral Gardens and their Magic* is the most detailed treatment of the language of ritual, sorcery, and spells for any Papua New Guinean language. His analysis of the language of Trobriand magic stresses the importance of what he calls "weirdness" in giving language its power. He notes that,

> a great deal of the vocabulary of magic, its grammar and its prosody, falls into line with the deeply ingrained belief that magical speech must be cast in another mould, because it is derived from other sources and produces different effects from ordinary speech (p. 218).

Nevertheless, Malinowski shows that magical language is based on ordinary language, but involves lexical, phonological and grammatical elaboration, including literary devices such as "use of metaphor, opposition, repetition, negative comparison, imperative, and question with answer" (p. 222). Other authors furnish little detail, simply alluding, for example, to "esoteric formulae" or "nonsense syllables" when discussing spells; the language used may be supposed to be that of the gods or ghosts, but not that of other groups. Fortune, in *Sorcerers of Dobu*, states that:

> The words of Dobuan magic are not words of ordinary speech.
> They form a secret esoteric language of power (1963:130).

Differential access to magical language and the power it brings may be determined by sex, as well as by social position and personality, attributes which have to do with whether or not an individual is taught this language by local experts. In any case, this language does

178

not appear to constitute an entirely separate code, but is either limited in scope (a set of nonsense syllables) or is some sort of elaboration or alteration of normal speech as in the Trobriand case.

The second case of a nonegalitarian situation with respect to language concerns the linguistic skills of leaders in precolonial Papua New Guinea. It appears that many such men have possessed extraordinary linguistic resources, both in terms of rhetorical skills and in terms of bilingualism. Salisbury mentions bilingualism as a high-status characteristic among Siane, and biographical material on some current leaders in New Guinea also gives supporting evidence. Stoi Umut, Rai Coast Open Member of the House of Assembly during the mid sixties, was trilingual in Komba, Selepet, and Timbe, and this was an important aspect of the ethnic base of his popularity. The multilingualism of current politicians in local languages offers some indication that the traditional leaders of the past also outstripped their fellows in such skills. The Gakuku leader Makis (Read 1965) would appear to be one example.

Bilingualism was useful to traditional big men in at least two ways: most obviously as a means of communicating when away from home, and second as one in a battery of rhetorical skills used in speechmaking in their own village areas. Skill in oratory is characteristic of Melanesian big men, who must know when to speak in public (optimally after consensus has been reached so as not to lose face by taking an unpopular position), how to convince an audience, how to hold the floor without being interrupted, and so on.

A third situation of linguistic inequality occurred in the realm of commerce. Knowledge of the lingua franca of the traders in the coastal areas where long distance trading circuits were in operation was obviously an advantage. (This was probably the only clear case where a particular language could be seen as having higher status than others.) Trading visits were often of fairly long duration, and of considerable economic and social importance. To be able to communicate with the traders was advantageous, but learning "their" language (generally a pidginized version thereof) did not carry the added connotation that "their" language was in any way inherently better—simply, more useful. Even magical language could be seen in this light and probably was, since spells had commercial value in many areas of Papua New Guinea, and were a means or resource to be applied to a particular end.

In summary, it would appear that in the precolonial era the basic relationship of languages and dialects was a socially symmetric one. Language was viewed as being essentially pragmatic, a means to communicate with natural or supernatural beings, whether local or foreign, and people learned and used languages as a function of their personal exposure and interest. Differential size of the various language groups can thus be seen not as a result of the general prestige or economic utility of these languages, but rather as a result of the differential rate of expansion of the populations speaking them and of their success in competing with other populations for material resources such as land.

In the few situations where linguistic differences within a community displayed a nascent correlation with power differentials, it is clear that the language disparities must be considered to be the dependent variable. Individuals would learn ritual languages, *lingue franche*, neighbouring languages, etc., as just one aspect of their economic and political striving. The oratorical behaviour of leaders was in part a result of the deliberate development of rhetorical skills by aspirants to leadership positions, and in part a reflection of the self-confidence of leaders and of the respect they enjoyed within their communities as a result of their political or economic position.

LANGUAGE AS A SYMBOL OF INEQUALITY

We have seen how language can serve not only as a resource but also as a symbol of identity. The question we now wish to ask is under what circumstances can the identity function become inverted such that a particular group becomes alienated from its own language or language variety and begins to regard it as inferior to some other language or language variety?

A phenomenon which regularly coincides with class-based differentiation of speech is an attitude of linguistic insecurity and linguistic alienation on the part of those who speak nonprestige varieties. The well-known hypercorrection of the "middle" class and of people who have undergone rapid social mobility without adequate opportunity to learn the linguistic behaviour appropriate to their new station is evidence of such insecurity. People recognize that they have stigmatized features in their speech, but in lamenting this state of affairs, they *accept* a standard external to their own behaviour; that is, they acquiesce in another group's definition of features in their speech or of the whole code itself as being inherently inferior. This is a type of "mystification" in which a symbol (here language, or particular features of language) takes on *in its own right* the negative evaluation of the object (in this case a group of people) with which it has become associated. Acceptance of such mystification is self-defeating, since other symbols can always be found if and when the group in question alters the present set of offending behaviours.

There are two mutually reinforcing phenomena here: first, the extent to which lack of knowledge of a particular language or language variety blocks access to other resources or goods within a society—education, jobs, wealth, political positions, and so on; and second, the extent to which the inferior political and economic position of a particular group results in a devaluing of its language or language variety, and in feelings of inferiority on the part of its speakers. In its extreme form, this set of attitudes is similar to the "complexe de colonisé" described by Fanon (1961).

It seems clear that the latter phenomenon, the devaluation of a

180

speech variety to reflect the socioeconomic position of its speakers, is primary, and that the converse, the negative consequences of speaking a given variety, is but a derivative effect. Historically, the changing political and economic fortunes of countries or nations have been followed, with a certain lag, by a reevaluation of their languages. However, it would be difficult to find a clear case where the change in status of a language variety led to a change in the socioeconomic status of its speakers. This is equally true within a society, when the language of a particular class or region has been promoted to the status of national standard, as that class or region has become nationally dominant, its language henceforward receiving the support and blessing of the society's institutions.

It is also the case that when differential linguistic knowledge becomes important in providing access to other goods and resources, society also determines differential access to the resource of language itself. Language can become a symbol of an individual's place in the society, since it represents the opportunities s/he has had for learning language varieties, the people s/he has been in contact with, and so on.

SOCIAL CHANGES

In order to understand to what extent language has come to symbolize social inequality in present-day Papua New Guinea, then, we must examine how this social inequality has come about. The social, economic, and political changes which have occured since the begining of the colonial period are massive. In this section I will discuss the impact of some of the changes, with particular attention to the way they have been experienced by the Buang people.

In traditional Buang society, probably the most important resources powerful men could draw on were land and labour. Yam growing was the prestigious activity, and large and well-tended yam gardens required both. Land was managed by the kin group, but individual inheritance of particular garden sites or portions thereof meant that some people found themselves with more and better land than others. The labour supply depended not only upon the demographic vagaries of one's close family, but even more upon clever manipulation of available kin, trade, and friendship ties. The man of substance who had successfully managed his marriage(s) and his inherited resources could always count on finding a ready work force when he needed a roof thatched or a large garden cleared. He could entertain such work parties in style, with pork from his own herd or hunted in the forest—and he could also entertain distant trade friends, having the time and resources to cultivate such contacts.

Thus in any community there were influential and powerful men with large and well-tended gardens, possibly more than one wife, many pigs, the authority to direct community activities and command a large labour force. They likely had a better command of foreign languages than their fellows as well as a larger collection of trade goods, particularly the highly visible clay pots from the coast. Big men could, through a combination of seniority and astute political behaviour, become managers of the garden and forest land of their descent group. There were also, of course, the ordinary men, who more often found themselves clearing other people's gardens than vice versa.

The coming of colonialism immediately began to transform the configuration of power. The localized and unstable community influence wielded by individual big men was dwarfed by the power of the colonial authority. How did this affect the big man system? Since colonial authority, including missionary influence and the power brought to bear by commercial interests, was exercised only in connection with certain matters, such as warfare, taxation, religion, paid labour, and relations with non-New Guineans, and was only sporadically viable except in town and government stations, the big man tradition was able to continue, albeit in a somewhat modified fashion. Indeed, the cessation of warfare permitted a certain expansion of the influence of particular big men from the local to the regional level.

Nevertheless, power with respect to all matters of a nonlocal nature was clearly vested in the colonial trio of government, mission, and business. This was understood by all concerned from the earliest stages of colonization. It was most apparent and most significant in towns, government stations, missionary outposts, and commercial enterprises such as plantations and mines.

Despite the clear stratification between Europeans and New Guineans—correlated with exaggerated power disparities—there were some possibilites for vertical movement for New Guineans within the colonial power structure. Foremen, in the work context, police sergeants in government service, and evangelists within the mission hierarchy are examples of positions whose incumbents often had considerable influence and control over other New Guineans through colonial institutions. Such people gained prestige and authority through their closer association with the true power holders, not only within town and station communities, but also on return to their own villages.

Today, skills such as literacy, accounting, the ability to drive a truck and knowledge of the language(s) of the wider arena(s) can be of immense benefit to those who possess them, and can lead to much larger differences among villagers than could possibly have existed in the precolonial society. These differences may even be measurable in traditional resources such as land, as when a local entrepreneur gains permanent control of large tracts of good gardening land for cash crop production. Young Buang men in their twenties who cultivate the traditional virtues and take pride in their yam gardens find that they are less knowledgeable about "outside" matters that have become important to everyone than their peers who have decided to go away to work and earn money. The sophistication of the retired policeman, for example, in the workings of modern society, his well-educated children who return home only for brief visits on vacation from "good" jobs in town, have not failed to impress those who stayed at home. Indeed, political astuteness became synonymous with the ability to further big man status locally using achievements and associations within the colonial world, while simultaneously improving one's situation within the urban or station community by using the economic resources and political support of the people from one's local area.

Fundamental alterations have occurred in village level politics, though a number of formal aspects have remained the same. In some Buang villages the men's house has fallen into disuse, but there are still "big men," influential leaders whose opinions carry weight in meetings, who can recommend courses of political or economic action which others will follow, and who can organize a large labour force for community work of various sorts. But both political issues and the resources used in deciding them have undergone changes. Firstly, the scope of decision-making at the village level has expanded to take in issues concerning wider arenas—the regional and national levels and the questions which their agents raise. These include questions like the support of local Lutheran religious officials and of Buang Lutheran evangelists in other areas of New Guinea, preparation for a visit by the health inspection team of the Local Government Council, participation in the agricultural cooperative, work on roads or airstrip, and so on.

Secondly, decisions emanating from these wider arenas can effect the lives of village people in ways which completely surpass any possible input from the local level. Geography alone has had a huge effect on access to markets for local producers, as well as access to schools, jobs, and the like. Economic decisions made internationally (e.g., the World Coffee Agreement) or in another country (e.g., Australian decisions regarding imports of sugar) or even at other levels or in other areas of New Guinea (e.g., the decision about where to put a road or a bridge or a factory) can have effects whose magnitude at the local level is greater than that of any decision taken locally.

LANGUAGE CHANGES

Tok Pisin, otherwise known as New Guinea, or Melanesian, Pidgin, is the modern language which developed out of the nineteenth century Pacific trading pidgin, becoming firmly established in German New Guinea (beginning with the plantations of the Gazelle Peninsula of New Britain) in the 1880s. From its base as the common language of plantation workers, it has always been spoken principally in what is referred to as the "New Guinea side," i.e., the ex-German territory (current island provinces of Manus, New Ireland, East and West New Britain, and Bougainville, and mainland provinces of East and West Sepik, Madang, Morobe, Chimbu, Eastern and Western Highlands, and Enga).

In 1971, of the approximately 1 600 000 Papuans and New Guineans age ten and over, 44.5 percent spoke Tok Pisin (Papua and New Guinea Population Census 1971 Bulletin No. 1, Table 8). Table 1 shows the number and proportion of current Tok Pisin speakers by District, comparing the 1966 and 1971 Census figures.

The first Buang men to learn Tok Pisin acquired it in the classic tradition—as indentured labourers on a plantation. The plantations at this stage, just before World War I, were German, and the men were taken by ship to New Britain where they reported having worked for seven years before being returned home. Buang men also worked as carriers on "patrols" of various sorts—including trips of exploration for minerals and police patrols. The impetus for learning Tok Pisin was provided by the Bulolo gold rush in the early 1930s. Because of its relative proximity to Buang territory, it attracted dozens of Buang

Table 1
PAPUA NEW GUINEAN TOK PISIN SPEAKERS BY DISTRICT*

District	No. of Tok Pisin speakers age ten and over		Percentage of the population age ten and over speaking Tok Pisin	
	1966	1971	1966	1971
New Ireland	32 550	37 443	94.2	93.1
Manus	11 784	14 232	89.2	93.1
East Sepik	79 680	91 031	76.6	82.1
West New Britain	21 026	34 090	75.7	89.4
East New Britain	48 464	54 208	69.5	73.4
Bougainville	31 843	45 575	68.0	76.1
West Sepik	45 208	39 223	67.4	63.8
Madang	62 426	74 950	61.5	68.9
Morobe	65 634	93 175	47.1	59.3
Central	25 630	41 772	28.2	35.9
Eastern Highlands	35 237	50 863	26.3	33.4
Northern	7 267	11 991	19.1	28.6
Chimbu	20 706	27 604	17.4	26.4
Western Highlands	26 385	56 228	13.0	24.2
Gulf	2 873	4 446	8.0	12.5
Southern Highlands	9 592	20 356	7.7	15.9
Milne Bay	3 547	5 742	5.2	8.1
Western	1 844	4 198	4.5	9.7

* Current provinces were known as districts until 1975.

men to their first opportunity to earn money and the things it could buy.

In retrospect, men who had worked for Europeans in the early days had almost nothing good to say about the experience. They complained of long hours, hard masters whose whims were difficult to understand or comply with, and low pay. Some of them escaped and came home; others stayed to earn more money, or out of fear of reprisals, and learned more about how colonial society worked.

We can only extrapolate as to the effects on village politics of these early returnees, with their goods and their knowledge. Men of this group say that they gave many of their goods away; like more recent returnees in areas where the first return of indentured labourers has occurred when an anthropologist was there to observe it, probably they found their goods rapidly integrated into the distribution system controlled by older men who had not been away. But knowledge was another matter, and especially valuable was the knowlege of Tok Pisin, referred to in Buang as *bubum ayez*, ("the white men's language"), the language which permitted access to the colonial society. Indeed, knowledge of Tok Pisin was originally the criterion for appointment as a *tultul* (one of the village officials given military caps and expected to translate for visiting government officials, to assemble the population for censuses and tax collection—in other words, to be the official brokers between the village and the secular colonial society).

The regimented character of contacts between villages and visiting whites in the early colonial period, added to the highly disciplinary tone of contacts between master and "boy" (as black workers were universally called), made for a strong association between Tok Pisin and authoritarian behaviour. Tok Pisin was demonstrably a language for giving orders and being obeyed, even if the persons to whom the orders were given displayed little comprehension (as was the case for most workers during the early phases of their indenture). Though Tok Pisin has now become a common denominator, even a language of equality among urban New Guineans from diverse linguistic groups, it has retained its connotations of power and authority at the village level, learned by each new generation in the context of giving orders and shouting at people, as well as in playful imitation of such contexts.

The extent to which returned Buang labourers used Tok Pisin during this early period remains unknown, but it is likely that they at least repeated common expressions of the *kiap* (patrol officer) or other visiting dignitary, explaining to the others what they meant. Certainly the high degree of comprehension of Tok Pisin among people under fifty in Buang villages today (including women and people who have not been away or to school) would attest to the early use of Tok Pisin locally. There is some sex difference in comprehension of Tok Pisin (men showing a higher level of use and understanding), however education makes very little difference in competence in Tok

Pisin. Tok Pisin is definitely not a school language, but a language introduced in the sphere of outside work which has been integrated to some extent into village life. It is common to hear a father instructing his daughter who can barely toddle, *Yu kam!* ("come on!"), and children's games include epithets such as *bladi* ("bloody") and *yupela klia* ("you guys get out of the way").

Village meetings are, however, the most common context for the use of Tok Pisin, particularly the *lain* morning meetings where people (particulary women) are supposed to line up and receive orders about daily work; and the "special events" meetings often called to discuss economic (cash economy) matters. The forced regimentation of the *lain* borrows the symbolism of "lining up" as well as the language of the prototype—village visits or "patrols" by government officers. Men will get up and harangue the crowd alternately in Tok Pisin and Tok Ples (in this case Buang) regarding issues like absenteeism at the *lain,* work not properly done, orders not followed, and so forth.

The rhetorical devices used in speechmaking at this and other kinds of village meetings are many. Synonymy through borrowing is particularly frequent. One device is code switching, where whole passages are spoken in Buang, the point being stressed by repetition, with minor changes, in Tok Pisin.

Though people being shouted or sworn at in Tok Pisin do not necessarily take this behaviour very seriously on all occasions, neither can it be completely disregarded, since its use reflects the village power structure. In eight village meetings for which I recorded language use by all participants, the two most influential men in the village used Tok Pisin more frequently than all the others combined, and they frequently switched codes during a speech. "Special events" meetings sometimes use a device clearly borrowed from the "patrol" situation, i.e., the formal use of an interpreter. Formal interpreters may even be used when the "visiting dignitary" is himself a Buang. In such a case the "visiting dignitary" speaks Tok Pisin throughout the meeting, the translator repeating at short intervals in Buang.

For the past thirty years or so, Buang parents have seen the acquisition of Tok Pisin as a very important stage in gaining their children access to the riches of the colonial society, and have been anxious that they learn it. Its obvious usefulness and the relative ease with which it could be learned, however, made it the type of practical resource which was readily within the grasp of almost anyone. In the past ten years, there has been a growing awareness that, on the contrary, Tok Pisin is insufficient for getting ahead in modern society, that it is not the white man's language after all. It is English that must be known.

The introduction of English has put the position of Tok Pisin into clearer relief. For though Tok Pisin has indeed been the language of colonization, it has been far more. From earliest days, it has been the *lingua franca* of New Guineans of diverse ethnic backgrounds. It is the language of much everyday life in towns such as Lae, Rabaul, Madang, Goroka, Wewak and Mt. Hagen, in most of which a majority of people speak it (see Table 2). Though from the village perspective Tok Pisin may have been considered the white man's language, its integrating and solidarity functions in the activities of multi-ethnic New Guinean urban and commercial life have been increasing.

The dramatic introduction of English over the past ten or fifteen years has again symbolized, perhaps even fostered, the changing social structure of Papua New Guinea. It is a scarce resource—to have your children learn it, you must send them to school early and pay for them to stay there for many years.

Though in the past, villagers thought of Tok Pisin as an important resource for getting on in the colonial society, its accessibility made its integration into village life relatively undisruptive. Big men used it as an added resource in rhetoric; signs were posted on competitive festive occasions stating the cost of the food being distributed; its understanding by virtually everyone within a fairly short time span meant that it could be more useful than symbolic.

Permanent or relatively permanent urban living is also a novel phenomenon in Papua New Guinea. It is chiefly in urban centres that learning English has become possible. But accompanying the spread of English as an elite language is the spread of Tok Pisin as a general language of solidarity among the urban population. It is the language in which a growing minority of urban children and adolescents are most fluent and it has become the first language of many. Many well-educated New Guineans who are perfectly fluent in English use Tok Pisin in relaxed, informal situations with friends. Urban New Guineans I talked to about it in 1971 waxed very enthusiastic about its communicative usefulness, and the ease and naturalness of speaking it.

The current situation is one in which English is reinforcing and clarifying urban social stratification, as indicated by the figures presented in Table 2. Already in 1966, over 30% of the Papua New Guinean population of most major towns spoke English, and in 1971, the percentage of urbanites speaking English had risen considerably in almost every case. This reflects the much greater possibilities for higher education in the towns than in the countryside. In 1971, the seven largest towns contained less than 6% of the country's population, but more than 16% of its English speakers. Comparing Port Moresby with the total population of the Central District, for example, we find that the percentage of English speakers in the nation's capital is 64.6%, as opposed to 45.4% for the District as a whole. Subtracting Port Moresby's population (which accounts for almost half of the total), we find that only 34.9% of the *rural* population of the Central District speaks English.

Perhaps the biggest social factor that differentiates speakers of English and Tok Pisin from those who do not speak these languages is that of sex. Table 3 indicates that the number of men who spoke English and Tok Pisin in 1966 was more than double the number of

Table 2
LANGUAGE DISTRIBUTION IN THE SEVEN LARGEST TOWNS OF PAPUA NEW GUINEA
(EXPATRIATES EXCLUDED)

Major towns of Papua New Guinea	% of Tok Pisin Speakers 1966	1971	% of English Speakers 1966	1971	Total Papua New Guinean Population 1966	Total Papua New Guinean Population 1971
Port Moresby (Central)	54.9	60.9	64.4	64.6	31 983	59 563
Lae (Morobe)	94.2	95.1	36.1	43.8	13 341	32 076
Rabaul (E. New Britain)	97.1	94.0	37.4	51.3	6 925	22 292
Madang (Madang)	96.2	97.4	30.8	47.3	7 398	14 696
Wewak (E. Sepik)	96.2	97.0	27.8	52.7	7 967	13 837
Goroka (E. Highlands)	89.6	85.9	31.6	42.7	3 890	10 509
Mount Hagen (W. Highlands)	82.7	77.5	27.0	37.3	2 764	9 257
TOTAL					74 268	141 973

women, and the difference was only slightly less exaggerated in 1971.

Currently, in every town, there is a constant flow of new migrants and transients (e.g., market vendors or village people visiting urban relatives) who speak only Tok Ples, with little or halting Tok Pisin or none at all. These are the *bus kanaka* ("bush natives"), the country bumpkins, who are increasingly ashamed of their inability to communicate in anything but Tok Ples. Next is the bulk of the urban proletariat—mostly Tok Pisin speaking, and working at service jobs or as manual labourers. They may resent being spoken to in Tok Pisin by a white person or a Chinese, or sometimes even by a Papuan, regarding it as an insult even if they do not speak English. Then there are the English speakers, who tend to be fairly young (no statistics are so far available giving language ability by age groups) and who work in stores or offices, or in technically skilled jobs, or as teachers. Among these people, it is recognized that there are many degrees of fluency in speaking English, and that speaking it "well" is a difficult but worthwhile task. But as English instruction spreads, Standard 6 educated speakers will increasingly find that having limited competence in English is not a very useful resource. Speaking English "well" (i.e. having the amount of schooling that fluency in English can symbolize) will increasingly come to mark the elite.

Table 3
SEX DIFFERENCES IN SPEAKING ENGLISH AND TOK PISIN

		Males	Females	Total	Percentage of the population age ten and over
1966	English	130 429	62 908	193 337	13.3%
	Tok Pisin	369 855	161 835	531 690	36.5%
1971	English	211 651	112 115	323 766	21.0%
	Tok Pisin	469 770	237 355	707 125	44.5%

Though the distinction between Tok Pisin and English is still very clear, there are some signs that the urban New Guinea linguistic situation is moving toward what David De Camp has characterized as a "post-creole continuum" in other colonial and excolonial situations. As educated Papua New Guineans replace Europeans in high government posts, as agressive rural migrants succeed in setting up profitable businesses, as school leavers enter the public service, Standard English, English spoken as a second language with varying degrees of fluency, highly anglicized Tok Pisin, of migrants, and the creolized Tok Pisin of the urban born coexist and loosely reflect the emerging social stratification of urban New Guineans.

It is likely that the correlation between education, speaking English, and office holding at every level will increase. Villagers as well as urbanites readily admit that the person most equipped to deal with "outside" is the person with the most education, who can speak the language of the educated and sophisticated people with whom he will have to deal.

Prolonged exposure to a situation where a knowledge of English is a clear advantage will probably not lead to the loss of many local languages, since there is every indication that most people will continue to use Tok Ples or Tok Pisin among family and friends. But the symmetrically egalitarian relationship which existed among local languages—Tok Ples—has already been irrevocably altered by the spread of Tok Pisin and of English. That some speakers are manifestly "more equal than others" may lead Papua New Guineans to the conclusion that some languages, and particularly some language varieties ("good" English) are more equal than others. From here it is but a short step to inverting the equation, that is, to the belief it is this unfortunate "linguistic inferiority" (symbolizing, for some, even *cognitive* inferiority) which is the *cause* of poverty and powerlessness.

NOTES

1. *This chapter is based on an article entitled "Political power and linguistic inequality in Papua New Guinea," published in* Language *and* Politics, *W. and J. O'Barr, editors, 1971. It has been revised and updated considerably, with data included from the 1971 Papua New Guinea census.*

2. *The range in size of language groups is very great, and relatively few languages approximate the national average, i.e., one language for about 3 000 people. In fact, the 100 largest languages are spoken by about a million people (an average of 10 000 speakers), with some languages claiming as many as 60 000 (Chimbu) or even 100 000 (Enga dialects). Many of the remaining 600 languages have very few speakers indeed, often only a few hundred.*

3. *New Guinea was a former German colony which came under Australian rule in 1914; Papua was a former British colony which passed to Australian rule in 1906. They were jointly administered by Australia from 1946-1975 under United Nations supervision. I do not specifically discuss the postindependence period in this chapter, since the latest census figures available at time of writing late in 1977 were those of 1971.*

BIBLIOGRAPHY

Fortune, R.F. 1963. *Sorcerers of Dobu*. Paperback edition, New York: Dutton & Co.

Fanon, F. 1961. *Les damnés de la terre*. Paris: François Maspero.

Malinowski, B. 1935. *Coral gardens and their magic*. London: Allen & Unwin.

Read, K.E. 1965. *The high valley*. New York: Charles Scribner's Sons.

PART III
WAYS OF LIFE

CHAPTER 9

HUNTING AND GATHERING: CREE AND AUSTRALIAN

DAVID H. TURNER
University of Toronto

For all but the last 10 000 years, people have lived on this earth as hunters, gatherers, and fishermen without the benefit of cultivated crops, domesticated animals, or machine technology. Yet less is known of the hunting and gathering way of life than of any other in our history. By the time an interest had developed in recording and studying hunter-gatherer ways of life, much of the foraging world had been overtaken by developments in agriculture and husbandry, and the foraging mode had been relegated to the world's marginal areas like Australia, the Kalahari Desert, and the Arctic. And even in these areas the hunter-gatherers studied by anthropologists were not without contact with more economically developed peoples, principally those of European origin who had come upon them during the colonial era. In fact, it was only in regions where this contact did not lead to immediate destruction and collapse that peoples survived to be recorded in the annals of anthropology.

The result has been that virtually no anthropological account of hunter-gatherers exists which does not have to be qualified by the contact factor. But where the nature and duration of the contacts are known, their influences, to some extent, can be controlled and inferences made about the nature of the contacted society prior to contact. In this paper I will write about two hunter and gatherer ways of life as they *probably* existed prior to modification by Europeans. This is not to say that there were only two ways of life prior to the development of herding and horticulture or even that these two ways were necessarily predominant in the hunting and gathering period. It is to say, however, that two extremely different, yet structurally related, ways of life did exist prior to these developments and that the principles they embody seem to characterize a large number of hunter-gatherers about whom we now have ethnographic information.

On the one hand I will deal with the Australian Aborigines, particularly the Aranda, and on the other the Cree of Northern Canada, particularly the Shamattawa Band.

THE AUSTRALIAN ALTERNATIVE

The first inhabitants of Australia probably reached that continent from Southeast Asia or New Guinea some 30 000 years ago and thereafter remained more or less isolated from developments elsewhere in the world until the arrival of Europeans in the latter half of the eighteenth century. Apart from the dog, there were no domesticable animals and no cereals or grains to be cultivated in Australia so that internal economic development was extremely difficult. Prior to the coming of the European, what outside contacts there were, were confined to northern coastal areas where Macassan traders from Celebes came in search of trepang (used in soups), pearlshell, tortoiseshell, and timber. But their visits were intermittent and they did not settle.

At the time Australia was "discovered" in 1770 the native populaton was some 300 000, a number which declined rapidly with subsequent contact and which is only now recovering to its former level. This population lived in small clusters of intermarrying patrilineal land-owning groups whose sizes and territorial jurisdictions varied with ecological and demographic conditions. In the Western Desert, for instance, where resources were relatively scarce and rainfall particularly low (12" or less per year) the population density was about one person for 14 square miles and each land-owning group held sway over some 1 000 square miles. Membership of these groups varied from 50 to 100 people. By contrast, in Eastern Arnhem Land, a coastal area with relatively abundant resources and high rainfall (94" per year), the population density was about one person for three square miles and each territorial jurisdiction about 100 square miles.

In general the Australians subsisted on small game, fish in coastal and river areas (for the most part provided by the men) and roots, plants, and fruit (provided by the women). Vegetable foods formed the bulk of the diet, in some cases upwards of 70 or 80% of it (Meggitt 1957: 143). Technology was simple and consisted in the main of stone axes, chisels and wedges, spears and spearthrowers, throwing sticks and clubs, baskets and bags, nets and harpoons, and rafts and bark and dugout canoes in coastal and river areas.

Success in the food quest here as in all hunter-gatherer societies meant knowing when, where and what to look for, and over the millenia each Australian clan and grouping of intermarrying clans (connubium) built up a fund of knowledge of the location and variety of edible plants and of the habits of the various species of animals, birds, and fish in their region which was passed on from generation to generation. But in addition to acquiring these basic knowledges and skills—something common to all hunter-gatherers—the Australians developed a system of organizing social relations which ensured success even under crisis conditions. This system basically involved spacing people over the landscape and establishing rules of conduct between them such that cooperation was ensured despite the likes, dislikes, and personal preferences of individuals.

An Australian was at once an individual and a member of a social/territorial group and the rules which bound his or her group to others transcended his or her individual preferences. It follows that if Aborigines recognize descent from their "parents," their "parents' parents" in turn and so on (within their definition of paternity and maternity) then they are "related" in kinship terms; but they are not only related to each other as individuals but as members of ownership groups. This means that they are also "related" (but not necessarily in kinship terms) to other people in those groups on other generations. Given the small number of groups in any region and the fact that marriages were contracted between different groups, it would soon come to follow that any given individual would soon be "related" to most groups in his or her universe. That is, his mother would be from one group, his mother's mother from another, his father's mother from another and so on, depending on the rule of marriage alliance.

In fact, in Australia, attached to these kinship/ownership group relations, are rights and obligations which permit the movement of people across clan boundaries. These rights of access may have had their origin in a spacing process which ensured that no one clan could be self-sufficient in economically necessary resources (see Turner 1978b). In other words, the system may have been designed in such a way that people must move between territories in association with the owners who, first of all, possess some of the resources they need but don't have and, second, know how to effectively exploit their own clan area.

The two basic ways people are moved through different territories are by marriage and by ritual association. On the latter side, people sharing the same totem(s) or clan symbol(s), gather together each year to perform ceremonies associated with the totem(s). Totems like kangaroo, parrot, and shark symbolize, simultaneously, natural species and clan, and express the common creative, spiritual force at the source of both. Whatever the origins of the pattern, by the time they were studied by anthropologists, these totemic ties linked peoples widely scattered over vast areas of the continent and served as the rationale for their sporadic association. But for this these peoples would have had little or nothing to do with one another over the course of a hunting season, or even a number of seasons. In fact, all Australian land-owning groups are part of the same network of totemic brotherhoods dividing the universe into one, two or four groupings. The Kunapipi track, associated with one set of totems, for instance, links clans in Central Australia to others at the northeast tip of Arnhem land in northern Australia and to still others in the Kimberley region of northwest Australia. Another track associated with a different set of totems, in turn, links the clans excluded from the Kunapipi brotherhood (see Berndt 1951).

All such tracks are rationalized by the belief that the same creative beings have been at work in the territories of the clans concerned. The celebration of the exploits of these beings takes the form of annual ceremonies held at various points along the track in question with the consequence that over the years visitations are made by local clans to more remote areas representing a wider range of resources and ties than are found within their own respective connubia. This gives them the opportunity to trade for the goods and resources they cannot obtain locally. People within totemic brotherhoods normally do not intermarry (except in the one brotherhood Western Desert area; see Turner 1978b). Marriages, in contrast to brotherhood ties, are a means of establishing close ties to nearby people so that hunting and gathering activities can be carried out fairly close to home. Marriage brings together at least two people from two different land-owning groups—the husband's and the wife's—each of them equipped to exploit effectively his or her own respective estate. Thus each partner will gravitate to his or her own estate after marriage, but in association with the other party. Over time this means that the people in one's own clan will interact with and come to know more about certain clan areas than others—the areas of the clans one's own ancestors have married into in the past. It is these clan territories one tends to frequent more than others.

Australian societies, in fact, differ from each other to the extent their clans prefer more ties of marriage to more ties of brotherhood. A clan may wish to maintain marriage ties to two or three other clans by alternating its exchanges over a certain number of generations; another may wish to maintain ties through marriage to only one other clan; and yet another may wish not to renew a tie at all once it has been formed. On the other dimension, a clan may be in a brotherhood extending to all clans in the universe, to half of them or only to a quarter. Generally, ties of brotherhood are balanced against ties of marriage in any given society so that a clan having more ties of one kind will have less of the other. The Kariera of the West Australian coast, for instance, had two totemic brotherhoods and preferred a spouse exchange between the same two clans in consecutive generations. The Aranda of Central Australia, on the other hand, had four totemic brotherhoods and spouse exchange between the same two clans in alternate generations. Any given Kariera clan, therefore, would have a wide trading network and more distant ties to more distant people than any given Aranda clan, but would have a more restricted foraging range (primarily own and mother's estates) than an Aranda (primarily own, mother's and father's mother's). However, the Aranda would have trading links only to one in four clans outside their own complex of intermarrying clans instead of one in two as in the Kariera case.

ARANDA

The Aranda-speaking peoples of Central Australia traditionally occupied the region about what is now the town of Alice Springs. The environment in which they lived was tropical/dry continental, semi-desert with an annual rainfall of some 16" a year. The population density of the region at the time of prolonged contact was about one person for 12.5 square miles. On linguistic and sociological grounds anthropologists have distinguished the northern, western, eastern, and southern Aranda, the latter group being the most distinct, due to influence from the people of the Western Desert. Each of these Aranda sectors is really a cluster of intermarrying clans which, through prolonged interaction over time, has come to constitute a linguistic and social unit.

One of these sectors, the Western Aranda, is divided into ten patrilineal clans, each centred on a *pmara kutata* or "everlasting home" where the spirits of the most important totemic ancestors of the clan are located. The clan territory within which the *pmara kutata* is situated is called the *"Nyinanga* section area." Clans belonging to estates or "section areas" with *pmara kutata* on the track of the same ancestral beings regard one another as "brothers" and perform the same ceremonies. In all there are four such brotherhoods among the Aranda.

Nyinanga sections, as distinct from section areas, are generation divisions within the clan and brotherhood and combine alternate generations into one category. That is, a man belongs to a different division than his children but the same division as his father's father and his son's son. His children and his father are in the same division. Since there are four brotherhoods it follows there must be four *Nyinanga* sections each comprising father-son couples of categories. These couples are,

Panangka-Bangata
Kngurarea-Paltara
Purula-Kamara
Ngala-Mbityana

As I mentioned earlier, the Aranda preference in marriage is for exchange between the same two clans in alternate generations. This means that father and son will marry different clans but that father will marry the same clan as his father's father and son's son, and son will marry the same clan as *his* father's father and son's son. Thus, father and son are similar insofar as they are in the same clan but are different insofar as they each marry a different clan. People in alternate generations in the same clan are similar insofar as they marry the same clan. *Nyinanga* section names are merely a means of keeping track, across linguistic boundaries, of the composition of one's brotherhood and people who marry the same clans as oneself. This is an easy way of establishing your relationship to the people you occasionally encounter who are unrelated by actual kinship and marriage, but who possess the same section system. People in the same *Nyin-*

anga section or brotherhood do not intermarry and gather together each year to perform the same ceremonies.

It is not so much that people in the same brotherhood or *Nyinanga* section were originally one people who separated and moved to different territories (although this may have been true in some cases); rather totemic ties and common descent ideology are used to justify current clan relationships. In fact, clans may over time change from one brotherhood to another and conveniently "forget" their previous associations adopting instead the totemic ideology of the clan they join (Turner 1978a). This changeover is effected by "finding" new signs in the environment of the presence of the totemic beings in question. Once in the brotherhood, friendship and hospitality are assured across linguistic and connubium boundaries and over great distances.

The Honey Ant track, for instance, links *pmara kutata* in clans of the Western and Northern Aranda speaking peoples and the non-Aranda Pintubi, Kukatja, Unmatjera, and Iliaura. The people sharing the same totemic centres in each of these areas all belong to the same *Nyinanga* section (father/son couple of alternate generation categories), and when they convene it is the occasion for the performance of ceremonies and for the exchange of food, tools and symbolic objects such as the *tjurunga* (see Strehlow 1947: 153-163).

In the Aranda alliance arrangement it takes at least four clans to make a system—two to marry and one to marry the one you do not marry in any generation. This means, of course, that there will always be one clan you theoretically never marry but who marries one of the clans you marry. In practice the Aranda have institutionalized this arrangement and unite the two clans which do not intermarry and the two complexes of brother clans attached to them into an exogamous moiety basing the association on travels of still other totemic beings.

Both marriage and brotherhood or *Nyinanga* section ties are utilized to provide access to resources and people outside one's own clan estate. As Strehlow (1965: 142) found, when Aranda move outside their own clan estates or *Nyinanga* section areas they go only a short distance into the territory of a neighbour with whom they have exogamic marriage, or ceremonial ties.

Compared with the Desert peoples to the west of them, the Aranda prefer strong ties to a few clans (the Western Desert people prohibit an exchange with the same clan every one or two generations); compared with the Kariers on the western coast, by contrast, the Aranda prefer weak ties to many clans (the Kariera prefer a renewal of exchange ties every generation). While the number of clans one exchanges with would thus appear to increase as environmental conditions become more extreme as we proceed from the Kariera to Aranda to Western Desert areas, we must not forget that as marriage ties increase, trade or brotherhood ties generally decrease, so that one clan is not necessarily better off if it increases its ties by marriage over the generations.

THE CREE ALTERNATIVE

Like the Australians, the Cree and all North American Indians are Asian migrants, having come to North America via the Bering Sea land bridge some 30 000 years ago. By 5 000 B.C. the ancestors of the present Cree had reached the northeastern boreal forests of Canada where they were when Europeans began to arrive in the sixteenth century. In contrast to the Australians who were more or less economically irrelevant to the Europeans (whose main interest lay in ranching and farming), the Cree found their traditional skills well suited to the European fur trade. Lacking the strong proprietary, religious, and emotional attachment to small areas of land of the Australians, the Cree were more willing to move away from intensive involvement with Europeans when necessary and act as a vanguard for the fur trade on the edges of European westward expansion. This, of course, meant encroaching on the domains of other bands and language groups. Their subsequent history was one of continual conflict with other native groups as they attempted to retain their position as middlemen in the fur trade (see Ray 1974: 51-71). As we shall see, however, this kind of situation was probably not unknown in the traditional situation.

Although it is difficult to know for certain how the Cree lived prior to contact, a number of studies have shown which contemporary features are most likely to have been fur-trade induced (see Bishop 1974, Hickerson 1967, Ray 1974). This allows us to delete them from contemporary accounts, particularly of groups remote from intensive contact, and gain some insight into traditional patterns and relations.

In general, the Cree seem to have lived in bands of from 100 to 200 people ranging over an area of from 10 to 20 000 square miles. Cree population densities were considerably lower than Australian. Among the Mistassini Cree in Quebec, for instance, the 1829 ratio was one person for 200 square miles and in 1815 among the Shamattawa Cree of northern Manitoba it was one person for 167 square miles. One of the lowest densities recorded in Australia is the Walbiri's: one person for 35 square miles.

A band's range was that region habitually exploited by the same people and their "descendants" over time. In some cases, such as at Shamattawa, boundaries were well established and recognized by adjacent bands. In other cases, such as at Mistassini, the collective sense of territory was much weaker and boundaries at the band level much harder to define. There seem to have been no smaller territorial jurisdictions within a band prior to the introduction of the fur trade and people seem to have moved freely across a general range in varying associations each hunting season. Every summer the members of the band would convene at a central meeting place to plan production activities for the following season, exchange ideas and information, arrange marriages and perform ceremonies such as the "shaking

201

tent" and the "goose dance." The first was an attempt to control events and forces in nature and society through contact with the spirit world; the second to propitiate the spirits of the geese to ensure a successful hunt (see Meyer 1975; Preston 1975). Following these activities the band would disperse into small hunting groups for the winter season.

Like the Australians, the Cree subsisted on small game, birds, fish, plants, roots, berries, and fruits (rabbit and squirrel, grouse and ducks, whitefish and pickerel, roots and gooseberries). But in contrast to the Australians, the Cree supplemented this food with large game such as caribou and moose. Technology was simple and very similiar to that of the Australians except that the bow and arrow was used instead of the spear and spearthrower.

In terms of organized social relations, the Cree seem to have established themselves over a territorial range of sufficient size and variability that a high degree of self-sufficiency could be achieved within that range. Outsiders could be incorporated into the band through residence and work association, and required no prior kinship, marriage or symbolic ties to be acceptable as in Australia. Within the band associations were formed directly out of productive and reproductive ties (within the Cree's definition of paternity and maternity) without the mediation of proprietary groups at the local level.

As people grew up and worked together they established within the domestic group (all the people living in one house), relationships which continued even after they married and formed domestic groups of their own. Working relations at one stage simply overlapped and merged with those at another. This pattern pivoted around the relations between same sex generation mates within the domestic group. A male learned to hunt with his father in association with his unmarried brothers often accompanied by the father's brother(s) who had established a similar tie with the father the previous generation.

Similarly, a female learned collecting and preparation techniques from her mother in association with her sisters, often accompanied by a mother's sister or the wife of her husband's brother. And when the father's brother and mother's sister came to renew the working relationship, they were accompanied by the unmarried children they had produced through their own marriages. Thus, father and his brother, their wives and their children, mother and her sisters, their husbands and their children formed a loose grouping which convened from time to time for production purposes and general sociability. These primary ties of production and reproduction were expressed culturally by the application of the same "kinship" terms to all people in the network. Older males within this set of relations were called *Nistes* and older females *nimis*, while younger males and females were called *Nisim*.

Similarly, when same sex siblings renewed their working relationships after marriage they brought with them their spouses and spouses' same sex siblings, and if these latter people were married they brought with them, in turn, their spouses and their same sex siblings. This set of relations was literally an extension of the first, and with the exception of spouse's same sex siblings who were called by the same term as spouse, all those within the set were called *Nistes* etc., as above. Secondary brotherhood ties such as these were also designated by the general term *Niciwam* (used by males in relation to males) and *niciwamiskwem* (used by females in relation to females). Marriage was generally prohibited between people in the brotherhood and was prescribed with someone without, who, within the logic outlined above, was a person with whom one did not have a production or reproductive tie. Such people were called *Nítim* (applied to people of the opposite sex), *Nístáw* (same sex, male speaking) and *nicáhkos* (same sex, female speaking). Basically a marriage could be negotiated with anyone who was not *Nistes*, etc.

The incorporative logic noted at the band level, then, was duplicated at the brotherhood level and was based on the principle of the unity of people who lived and worked together. The basic reproductive unit of man and wife, in the absence of ties to larger descent or proprietary groups, provided the initial point of association for people as they grew up within the society.

SHAMATTAWA

The Shamattawa Cree are part of the York Factory band and traditionally occupied a hunting range of some 20 000 square miles near the Ontario-Manitoba border as it approaches Hudson Bay. The focus of this territory was the convergence *(shamataw)* of the God's and Echoing rivers before they joined the Hayes. It was here the band convened during the summer months. With the establishment of the York Factory depot by the Hudson's Bay Company at the mouth of the Hayes River, just within the band's range, in 1714, the band, in effect, became bifocal with a portion in more or less permanent contact with the post, and a portion more or less confined to the bush. This arrangement eventually became institutionalized so that the band came to have a "traditional" and a "modern" sector. With the closing of York Factory in 1955, the modern sector chose to settle near Gillem and Split Lake, close to sources of wage labour, while the traditional sector formed a community at Shamattawa. The reasons they give for going there are very much traditional—a plentiful supply of game, fish, and timber, and a long standing continuity with the area (see Turner and Wertman 1977). The present population of the Shamattawa Band is about 480, more than double what it was in 1947. The York Factory Band as a whole has experienced an increase in population from 278 in 1910 to 1 097 in 1974, and both trends can be attributed to improved medical services brought about by increased contact with the wider Canadian society. In the opposite direction, the band's range has been pared down from its traditional size to a legal range of only twenty-two square miles, the Shamattawa Band's treaty entitlement. The other two sectors of the York Factory Band now reside outside the traditional hunting range and have slightly smaller entitlements.

Shamattawa hunters and trappers, however, do not restrict their activities to such a small area as their government allotment. Rather, they utilize the entire traditional area and allow unrestricted access by band members to any part of the range. This appears to have been the traditional pattern. In contrast to other Cree groups such as the Mistassini Band, the Shamattawa people did not develop "family" hunting territories which tied down small groups to small areas within the range from season to season (see Hickerson 1967: 313-343). Such a system was devised by Europeans in the interests of administration, control of output and capitalization of the fur trade industry and tended to individualize production and distribution.

The Shamattawa system still today, however, stresses group over individual relations in respect of hunting and trapping. First, the Shamattawa people distinguish between "hunting partners" (*Nwiciwagan* or *Niscas*) and people who merely "come along" as part of the domestic groups of any of the people involved. Hunting partners are most likely to be chosen from among married brothers, father or his brothers, the offspring of these brothers or men in domestic groups which have recently intermarried with one's own. Partners, then, are chosen from amongst people with whom one has had some prior contact while growing up within the domestic group of origin, or people with whom one has come to have some contact after marriage. Within this range, associations are formed on pragmatic grounds and depend on who is available at a particular time, who one gets along with and whose skills complement one's own.

After marriage a person will alternate between the residence of his own domestic group of origin and that of his spouse, thereby maintaining familiarity or becoming familiar with the people who gravitate there. Eventually the couple will probably settle near the man's father which was certainly the tendency in the fur trade era when the husband had access to the means of production (guns, ammunition, traps, fish nets, snares, etc.) of the people who gravitated there, such as his father and older married brothers. Older informants say that, in the past, residence shifted more frequently from husband's to wife's camp than it does today. Shifting residence would also allow the wife to maintain ties to her sisters and the women who gravitated to her parent's camp.

All this is reflected in the relationship terminology of the Shamattawa Cree. The offspring of men in the domestic groups of origin of males who married one's mother's domestic group of origin in her generation and the offspring of women of the domestic groups of origin of females who married members of one's father's domestic group of origin in his generation, are called *Nistes*, etc. Also designated by the same terms are people in other domestic groups of origin whose same sex domestic group mates have married into the same domestic groups of origin as same sex members of one's own domestic group of origin. To a Shamattawa Cree these terms imply communality, sharing, cooperation, marital and, to some extent, sexual inaccessibility. By contrast, the offspring of males of the domestic groups of origin of females who married members of one's father's domestic group of origin the previous generation and the offspring of females of the domestic groups of origin of males who married into one's mother's domestic groups of origin the previous generation, are called Nītim and are ideal marriage partners. Over seventy-five percent of all marriages at Shamattawa over the past three generations were with people called Nītim and of the other twenty-five percent only five percent were between brotherhood mates.

While this all sounds complicated in English, in Cree it is merely "common sense" and is the formal expression of the working and nonworking relations outlined above with respect to the Cree in general.

On average, each Shamattawa person has about the same number of brotherhood mates as potential affinal alliance partners—twenty-five. This generally establishes the limits within which hunting partnerships and marriage choices are made. The actual choices themselves are based on an evaluation of performance and compatibility. As one informant put it,

> For the parents of man, a woman (his potential wife) has to be a good worker; for a woman's parents a man has to be a good hunter.

As this quote also implies, the parents of the couple are very much involved in the marriage process. This contrasts with the Australian situation where the interested parties are the patrilineal relatives of both partners (i.e., the man's and the woman's respective fathers and their clan brothers and sisters). But while in Australia the parents retain their clan identities and remain opposed as members of spouse-giving and spouse-taking clans throughout their lives, in Shamattawa the man and woman are seen to merge into one person after they marry. As the Shamattawa people put it, "they become one body." In other words, the domestic unit formed on marriage is as much an incorporating unit as the brotherhood and band.

PRODUCTION GROUP UNITY AND PRODUCTION GROUP DIVERSITY

The Cree are primarily interested in forming structurally undifferentiated, unified production or work groups; the Australians, structurally differentiated, diverse, production groups. Formation of such groups in the Australian case is effected through the operation of a lineal, exclusive principle of group formation, and in the Cree case, through an incorporative, inclusive principle.

When people marry and form production groups in Australia they will always be divided in terms of the allegiances and identities of their members. The husband and wife will belong to different land-owning groups with different totemic affiliations and each will gravitate toward his or her own clan estate and fellow clanspeople. In this system the children will naturally gravitate to their father's clan. This situation sets up a movement of people across wide areas after they marry and this means access to a wider range of resources than one's own estate possesses. Flexibility is here achieved by a set of rules which formally interrelates the clans into a system of periodically recurring alliances. And if marriage ties do not achieve access to a wide enough range of resources and people in themselves, then brotherhood ties will. For these ties are, in effect, pan-Australian, linking peoples unrelated in linguistic, kinship, and residential terms into basically two or four categories—two where marriage exchange is with the same two clans in consecutive generations, four where it is between the same two clans in alternate or every three generations. From the point of view of any one clan in each system, a person has trading links with half or a quarter of the clans in the Australian universe.

When people marry and form production groups among the Cree, however, they are seen to merge into a single unit. Their offspring are regarded as the children of one parent (two as one). These children are successively incorporated into an ever-expanding network of working relations as they grow up, mature and marry. Here quasi-proprietary rights of land use are at the band rather than local level and the band is defined in terms of those with whom brotherhood and spousehood ties exist. Ties outside this network are minimized, ties inside maximized. Flexibility is achieved by maintaining a mobile labour force over a range at least as large as the Australian connubium of intermarrying clans and by leaving choice of spouse and hunting partner more open to pragmatic considerations. In short, the Australian alternative of internal territorial divisions of proprietary jurisdiction is rejected in favour of forming a cohesive labour force.

PROBLEMS OF HUNTER-GATHERERS

Common to all hunter-gatherers are the problems of, firstly, how to maintain a regular relation to the land when you are constantly on the move in the food quest, secondly, how to achieve continuity of knowledge of an area over the generations under the same conditions and, thirdly, how to form groupings which can be reasonably self-sufficient and autonomous yet retain positive ties to other people which can be utilized in time of crisis. These problems must all be solved within the limits of a stone technology, limited geographical mobility, and seasonal resource variation.

As we have seen, the Australian solution to these dilemmas was to establish an abstract, proprietary relation between people and land thereby ensuring that the land would retain a continuity in space and through time regardless of the movements of people, and that future owners would stand in a predictable relationship to present owners. This permitted the planning of production relations to proceed both in the present and for the future. Marriages between land-owning groups ensured access to other estates than one's own and brotherhood ties to still other groups ensured access to an even wider range of resources through trade and occasional visits. A brotherhood tie rationalized by a common creative force also meant that legitimate owners of clan land would exist were the present owners to die out or even move as a group. The land would merely merge with that of a nearby "brother" clan.

The Cree solution was to establish a concrete (labour) relation between people and land and literally blanket an area with a mobile labour force. A sufficiently large range was established containing a small enough population that subsistence requirements could be met even in time of crisis, thereby minimizing the band's dependence on other peoples and territories. Cree continuity was based more on residential and production principles of group formation than on abstract, symbolic ones. The aim was to contain people within a range and maintain them there. The brotherhood system of the Cree did not as a rule extend beyond the limits of the band, a unit roughly comparable to the Australian connubium of intermarrying clans. Incorporative, inclusive principles of group formation pulled the Cree band inward, not outward as was the case with the Australian brotherhood.

Once these two alternative solutions were effected, however, they would have generated problems specific to their own respective traditions. In the Australian case the dominant problem would become how to maintain ownership of land and continuity of clan in the face of production necessities which took people away from their own estates for long periods of time in association with the owners of other estates. With the Cree the problem was how to maintain residence on the land and continuity of people as a band without a cultural principle of ownership and inheritance. The Australians with their production group diversity system have the problem of retaining ownership of land they do not occupy; the Cree with their production group unity system have the problem of retaining occupancy of land they do not "own."

Since the Cree maintain use of the land through residence, they must prevent others from establishing themselves on the land and thereby asserting a legitimate rival claim. To do this they must maintain powers of physical coercion once they have settled on a range. Since the Australians maintain their ownership through abstract cultural principles of ownership and descent, they must ensure that nonowners share the same "rules" as themselves. They must therefore maintain universally recognized symbols of ownership and open channels of communication with clans outside their own connubium. This may, to some extent, explain the infrequency of organized warfare, particularly for the purposes of acquiring territory, among the Australians (Berndt 1968:299-305), but its prevalence among the Cree, the influence of the European notwithstanding (Parkman 1885, Introduction).

CULTURAL EXPRESSION OF PRODUCTION PRINCIPLES

The two kinds of production systems outlined above and the problems they generate are not merely the invention of this anthropologist; they are articulated by the people who live them and are expressed within their myths and legends. In fact, in the same way as the two kinds of production systems are in opposition to one another, so the myths and legends of people who practise one system are unintelligible to those who practise the other. For example, while cannibal myths are characteristic of the Cree and Algonkians, they are rare in Australia, and while the Cree always seem to be getting lost in their myths, the Australians always seem to know where to find each other.

In terms of our model of these two systems, eating is a superb symbol for incorporation—something external is internalized or made a part of oneself. Getting lost and not knowing the whereabouts of particular people is more likely to occur when you have 200 people or so scattered over a 20 000 square mile range opportunistically searching for food and furs than where you have the same number over a 2 000 square mile range divided into clans and estates all linked by prescriptive marriage and brotherhood ties. As we have seen, as a rule the Australians space larger numbers of people over smaller areas than the Cree.

To take one example of how these problems are expressed, in a Cree myth recorded by Stevens and Ray (1971:74-75) a family frequents a certain place every hunting season because of the abundance of game available there. One year they find they have much more meat than they themselves can consume and they cannot decide what to do with the surplus. If they leave it behind it will rot; if they take it back to the summer encampment place they will not have room in their sled for their children—two sons and a daughter. So the parents decide to take the meat first, then return for their children later. After they have been gone a few days, the daughter disappears from camp and the two boys search unsuccessfully for her. They are afraid to wander too far afield because of the wolves they hear in the woods. As they lament the loss of their sister they are transformed into two birds and fly off into the woods, returning to the camp for food. When their father returns he cannot find his children and, after a long search, concludes they have been eaten by wolves or bears. As he laments their death his transformed sons come to him and tell him of their lost sister. Crying, they fly off into the forest leaving their father alone.

In the language of production group unity-band systems, disaster follows the establishment of, firstly, permanent ties between a domestic group and a hunting territory, secondly, the hoarding of food, and thirdly, the separation of parents from children within the domestic group of their origin. An overabundance of meat causes the parents to place accumulation over the welfare of their children and the domestic group as a whole. Abandoned in the bush the children are left in a potentially incestuous situation—two brothers with their sister—which could lead to an even greater degree of domestic autonomy and closer ties to the local area. This prospect is, however, prevented with the disappearance of their sister. Attempts to regroup fail and the brothers find themselves in danger of being incorporated (eaten) by an alien "band" (wolves). To overcome their immobility and fear, the boys are transformed into birds, resolving one problem but creating another: reunion with sister is now impossible as she is human and they are now birds. Father is now also unable to reunite with his children and re-form the domestic group. Fragmentation is complete—brothers without sister, parents without children, father without mother, domestic groups without locality.

Rather than suggesting a solution, then, the myth explores potential problems. It asks, "What would happen if people behaved in an un-Cree fashion and adopted a more sedentary and individualized existence," and it answers, "The consequences for current institutional arrangements would be disastrous."

In an Australian myth, to take a different example (in Turner 1974: 18-24), we find at the outset an island inhabited by four patrilineal clans. The members of three of these clans are living in their respective estates; the fourth is not. Two men then set out from their own estates in the southeast and northwest respectively toward the unoccupied lands. But before they arrive there, another man descends from the sky to the estate they are headed for, claiming to be a member of the owning clan. In discussions with the other two men when they arrive, an attempt is made to establish the legitimacy of the stranger's claim. Residence in itself is not sufficient for his claim to be recognized, nor is a simple statement of affiliation. But the stranger speaks the island's language and knows how he should be related to people in the clans of the other two—one as father's mother's clansman, the other as mother's mother's. To resolve the ambiguities, his mother's mother's clansman suggests that if he really is who he claims to be he should go and join his fellow clanspeople on the other side of the island where they are staying with the people of their mother's clan. But the stranger says, no, it would be best to bring them back to their own country to meet him. So one man goes to fetch his clan and the other to bring back his own from the opposite side of the island. On their return the local owners agree to accept his claim—he speaks the language and knows the relationship system—but not without some reservations. The "stranger" then marries, has a son, and dies.

What we have at the outset, then, are two potential claims to land through residence mediated by a third claim by residence on the part of someone claiming prior ownership on more abstract, cultural, grounds. The two other clansmen are immediately forced into a defence of the status quo (which does not recognize residence as a criterion of ownership) in order to explore the claim of the third party. This defence is so complete that they actually bring the legitimate owners back to their own territory. The problem of the initial situation is then resolved in favour of the original owners by their acceptance of the stranger's claim. His objective position as an unrelated resident is now submerged under the rubric of a common code. He is accepted along the same lines as a remote brotherhood mate. The myth explores a potential problem—the legitimacy of a residential claim to land ownership—and resolves it in favour of the status quo, but not without some ambiguity (significantly, in this myth, no one is lost—everyone knows where everyone is and should be.)

SUMMARY

It has been taken as axiomatic for some time in anthropology that all hunter-gatherers face a common problem of population size in relation to available resources and that their systems are ways of solving this problem (Harris 1975:248-250). Perhaps in the remote past, many millenia ago, such a problem led to the formation of the production group unity and production group diversity alternatives—the one spacing large numbers of people over small areas in proprietary groups and relying on alliance rules to achieve mobility over a region, the other spacing small numbers over large areas in production groups and relying on shifting associations and pragmatic considerations to achieve mobility and access to resources.

But once instituted, it is difficult to see how the population/resource problem would be an experienced, lived, seasonal issue structuring relations between people. As we have seen, the two systems are capable of handling a very wide range of demographic and ecological conditions—from extreme desert to tropics, from woodlands to prairie and from very high to very low population densities. Only in times of extreme variation in population and resources, then, would this so-called "classic problem" of hunter-gatherers be a problem at all. Once instituted, the production group unity and diversity systems submerge the population-resource problem and develop new ones dealing with how to maintain the system one has in the face of "dissenters," "strangers," deviation from the rules of life, and so on.

Once established, each system also alters the conditions under which the population/resource problem arises; and when it does arise, each system handles it in a very different way. A production group diversity system, in effect, creates an "artificial" *shortage* of resources on a local level, but within a framework of alliances which allows the possessory group access to a wide range of resources and people through ritual and marriage ties. When populations *must* move, there is, already established, a mechanism for entry into other groups' territories as "co-owners"—the preexisting ties of common totemic brotherhood. A production group diversity system, on the other hand, creates an "artificial" *surplus* of resources by establishing much smaller numbers of people over much larger and more diverse areas. When crisis conditions do require a population to move, movement depends on successful negotiations with neighbours, and failing in this, on waging successful campaigns of warfare. If we have characteristically "affluent" hunter-gatherers (e.g., the Bushmen; see Chapter 18), they have likely *made themselves* affluent by application of production group unity, band, logic. Conversely, characteristically "impoverished" hunter-gatherers (e.g., the Birhor; see Williams 1974) have likely put themselves under pressure through application of production group diversity, connubium/brotherhood, logic.

Both the production group unity and production group diversity systems are two alternatives, indeed opposed, ways of living as hunter-gatherers. Most such peoples of which we have ethnographic knowledge would seem to fit into one or the other mould. Toward the Cree end would be the !Kung San of Southern Africa (The "Bushmen") the Inuit and the Malaysian Negrito. Toward the Australian end would be Birhor of Northern India and the Vedda of Ceylon. Utilizing aspects of one system at one level of organization and aspects of the other at another would be the North West Coast Indians of British Columbia and the Ojibwa of Northern Ontario (Cree principles at the village or production level, Australian at the level of alliance symbolism).

The idea of hunters and gatherers as a uniform type or stage of development common to all mankind must therefore be rethought and the possibility of qualitatively different, parallel streams of historical development, entertained.

BIBLIOGRAPHY

Berndt, R. 1951. *Kunapipi.* Melbourne: Cheshire.

Berndt, R.M., and C.H. 1968. *The World of the First Australians.* Sydney: Ure Smith.

Bishop, Charles 1974. *The Northern Ojibwa and the Fur Trade.* Toronto: Holt, Rinehart and Winston.

Harris, Marvin 1975. *Culture, People Nature.* New York: Thomas Y. Crowell.

Hickerson, Harold 1967. Some Implications of the Theory of the Particularity, or "Atomism" of Northern Algonkians, *Current Anthropology,* 8:313-343.

Meggitt, M.J. 1957. Notes on the Vegetable Foods of the Walibiri of Central Australia, *Oceania,* Vol. 28, No. 2.

Meyer, David 1975. Waterfowl in Cree Ritual—the Goose Dance. *In Proceedings of the Second Congress, Canadian Ethnological Society.* Vol. II. eds. Jim Freedman and J. H. Barkow. Canadian Ethnology Source Paper No. 28. Ottawa: National Museums of Man, Mercury Series.

Parkman, Francis 1885. *The Jesuits of North America.* 20th edition Macmillan: London.

Preston, R.J. 1975. *Cree Narrative—expressing the personal meaning of events.* Canadian Ethnology Series No. 30:25-170. Ottawa: National Museums of Man Mercury Series.

Ray, Arthur 1974. *Indians in the Fur Trade.* Toronto: University of Toronto Press.

Rogers, Edward 1969. Band Organization Among the Indians of Eastern Subarctic Canada. In *Contributions to Anthropology: Band Societies.* ed. D. Damas. National Museums of Canada Bulletin 230. Ottawa: National Museums of Man.

Stevens, James and Carl Ray 1971. *Sacred Legends of the Sandy Lake Cree.* Toronto: McClelland and Stewart.

Strehlow, T.G.H. 1947. *Aranda Traditions.* Melbourne: Melbourne University Press.

Turner, D.H. 1974. *Tradition and Transformation.* Canberra: Australian Institute of Aboriginal Studies.

Turner, D.H. 1978a. *Australian Aboriginal Social Organization.* Canberra: Australian Institute of Aboriginal Studies.

Turner, D.H. 1978b. Structuralism, Social Organization and Ecology. *L'Homme,* Fall.

Turner, D.H. and P. Wertman 1977. *Shamattawa: the structure of social relations in a northern Algonkian band.* Ottawa: National Museums of Man Mercury Series.

Williams, B.J. 1974. A Model of Band Society, *American Antiquity,* 39, no. 4, pt. 2, memoir 29.

ADDITIONAL REFERENCES

Australian Aborigines

Elkin, A.P. 1964. *The Australian Aborigines.* Sydney: Angus and Robertson.

Falkenberg, Johannes 1962. *Kin and Totem.* Oslow: Oslow University Press.

Lévi-Strauss, Claude 1969. *The Elementary Structures of Kinship.* Part 1. ed. R. Needham. London: Eyre and Spottiswoode.

Maddock, Kenneth 1972. *The Australian Aborigines: a portrait of their society.* London Allen Lane, The Penguin Press.

Cree

Knight, Rolf 1968. *Ecological Factors in Changing Economy and Social Organization among the Rupert House Cree.* Anthropology Papers No. 15. Ottawa: National Museums of Canada.

Mandelbaum, David 1940. *The Plains Cree* American Museum of Natural History Anthropological Papers, 37(2):155-316.

Manuel, George and Michael Posluns 1974. *The Fourth World: an Indian Reality.* Toronto: Collier Macmillan.

Rogers, Edward 1963. *The Hunting Group-Hunting Territory Complex among the Mistassini Indians.* National Museums of Canada, Bulletin 195. Ottawa: National Museums of Canada.

Tanner, Adrien 1978. *Bringing Home the Animals: the hunting rites of the Cree Indian of Mistassini.* London: Hurst.

CHAPTER 10

THE CUIVA BAND

BERNARD ARCAND
Université Laval

INTRODUCTION

We should never forget that one of the most obvious limitations of any anthropological report is the length of the actual fieldwork on which it is based. We should keep in mind that researchers often spend only a few months in the field, during which time they try as best they can to find some regularity in the life of the society around them. This regularity is then presented as a set of rules or principles of social organization which allow the ethnographer to relate in a simple and ordered fashion what has been observed in the field. Although the anthropologist has caught only a glimpse of the life of a people, this image is presented as the fixed and permanent code of its social organization; and this image may even become a standard against which other societies are measured. Much of the following description of a particular band society should be taken as a note of warning against the ethnographer's habit of rapidly jumping to conclusions.

Anthropology tells us that the band is the typical form of social organization for hunting and gathering societies, and that it represents the dominant type of social grouping over all of human history prior to the neolithic. The band is usually defined as a group of roughly 40 to 200 individuals who occupy a specific territory, which is shared freely among all members of the band and over which they have exclusive rights. Because they think there is an adaptive advantage to male solidarity in such societies, some authors have suggested that most bands follow the principle of patrilineal descent, or at least the rule of patrilocal residence, so that sons can better learn and cooperate in hunting with their fathers (Steward 1955; Service 1966). All in all, the anthropological literature often leaves us the impression that bands are always of a certain size, that they occupy a well-defined territory and that their organization follows precise and strict rules.

On the other hand, it seems that Western anthropology has always been concerned with discovering the structure of political authority within the band. Although everyone now recognizes the egalitarian nature of these societies and the fact that bands have neither formal government nor legal institutions, many authors seemed determined to show that the band as a social unit holds at least some form of power over the lives of its members. Under such titles as "Law and Order" (Harris 1975) or "Polity" (Service 1966), textbooks tell us how political power within the band rests with influential individuals, usually charismatic older men. It is these old men, much respected for their experience and knowledge, who are in the best position to influence and affect the lives of all members.

This view is probably correct. At any moment in the life of a band there will probably be a few respected older members whose advice on most matters is generally followed by others. It is, however, far less certain that this kind of influence rests exclusively, or even most frequently, with men. It is also doubtful that, by focussing on what happens at any moment in the life of a band, ignoring its development over a longer period of time, these authors can truly reflect its political situation.

By insisting on the power of the band over the individual, however weak it may be, the same authors succeed in placing band society in a neoevolutionist perspective: the band is seen as somewhat of an underdeveloped form of political organization. It is the maximal unit of political power in society and as such is similar to the more organized "tribe" and "nation" in other societies. From this perspective, the band is simply a more amorphous and less developed form of political authority, but its structure is not essentially different from that of other more institutionalized systems of power.

My first aim in the following description of the Cuiva band is to qualify some of the impressions left by this anthropological literature. I want to show how band membership is not always defined by precise and strict rules and how the band has often very little relevance for the social and political life of a hunting and gathering people. In fact, its importance may well be for reasons opposite to those suggested by most textbooks. But before considering the band itself, we must first look at the general situation of the Cuiva and describe the smaller social groups within Cuiva society.

THE CUIVA

I should, first of all, point out that the term "Cuiva" refers to people to whom this name is quite meaningless. As we shall see later, they simply call themselves "We, the people" and the word "Cuiva" is nothing but a name found in the literature on the area and one now commonly accepted in Colombia. The people themselves have often no idea that others call them "Cuiva" and consider them to be part of a country called Colombia.

The term refers to three groups of people living mostly along the banks of the rivers Casanare, Ariporo, and Agua Clara in the part of Colombia called the Eastern Plains (Llanos Orientales). At the time I was visiting them, between 1968 and 1970, the three groups had on average 179, 211 and 149 members respectively.

The Cuiva were then hunters and gatherers in the fullest sense of the expression. All the food produced was the result of hunting and gathering. They did not even work the soil marginally like other local foragers by cultivating tobacco, drugs, fish poison, or cane for making arrows. They had no permanent villages, and built only temporary shelters on camping sites which they changed every few days. Their technology was relatively simple and included only the most basic elements of a material culture found over most of lowland South America: they made and used bows and arrows, canoes, lean-to shelters, bark cloth, baskets, string, and a few other minor tools. Any adult in Cuiva society could normally make any of these objects, and their preparation, except for string and canoes, required but little time and energy.

As with practically all other hunters and gatherers, anthropologists of an earlier generation would have described the Cuiva as a rather desolate bunch of people, barely surviving in a poor and harsh environment, and would have placed them near the bottom of any evolutionary scale. My own observations lead me to conclude that the Cuiva are relatively affluent, since they consume large quantities of food which they obtain through spending less time and energy than any other society known to me. The quest for food is a daily activity, but the milieu and the hunting and gathering techniques are so reliable that one needs to "work" only a few hours in order to secure a more than sufficient diet. I calculated that the Cuiva eat a daily average of about 525 grams of meat and 375 grams of vegetables and fruits, while the men spend roughly between fifteen and twenty hours every week hunting and the women spend ten to fifteen hours every week gathering vegetables or fruit (Arcand 1976). This, of course, leaves long hours every day for rest and leisure, and I also estimated that men spend an average of sixteen hours per day lying in their hammocks, which is roughly three hours more than the average for women.

The description of the migration pattern of these people poses to the ethnographer the kind of problem I mentioned at the beginning. After twelve months of fieldwork, I had noted a clear and complete cycle of migration and was prepared to describe how the Cuiva change camps hundreds of times during the year, always in search of specific and well-localized food sources. Only during the second year did I discover how arbitrary this pattern really was: those who had been North last year and eating vegetables were now South and fishing, those who had been East were now West, and so on and so forth.

216

Almost no one was repeating the migration of the previous year. Apart from the widest tendencies of moving to the larger rivers during the dry season and upstream during the earlier part of the rainy season, Cuiva migrations cannot be predicted. At any time, there are always four to five possible sources of food and it is very much a matter of personal and collective choice which one will be exploited.

The recent history of the Cuiva, like that of so many other Indian groups in South America, is essentially a history of increasing pressure forced on them by external powers. During the last twenty-five years, the Colombian invasion of Cuiva territories comes close to being a showcase for genocide. On the whole, the Cuiva have reacted with fear and have consistently tried to avoid contact with the invaders by retreating into the refuge of the smaller rivers, away from the main waterways which have been the routes of the European invasion since the sixteenth century. But nowadays, the Cuiva can no longer escape, as they have reached the physical limits of their traditional territory. After 1970 two of the groups have progressively adopted the cultivation of manioc, established themselves in more or less permanent villages, and have become less and less dependent on hunting and gathering.

ELEMENTS OF SOCIAL ORGANIZATION

In order to understand how the band operates in Cuiva society we must first grasp how the life of the individual is shaped and determined by such other aspects of social organization as kinship, the rules of marriage and residence, the constitution and authority structure of the family and the local groups.

Cuiva kinship seems almost as straightforward and uncomplicated as their technology but nothing is more difficult than to summarize another people's kinship terminology. Let me try by saying simply that Cuiva terminology is classificatory in the widest sense, since every person in the world is given a kinship label. There are only six basic kinship terms (each one subdivided by sex) which cover all human beings known to any given person (Ego) whether they are from the same group or from distant bands. Within Ego's generation, there are two categories of relatives: one includes Ego's brothers and sisters, the other includes Ego's cross-cousins. In Ego's parents generation, again only two categories: one includes Ego's parents, the other includes Ego's mother's brothers and father's sisters. Again two categories in the generation of Ego's children: one including these children, the other the children of Ego's cross-cousins. The mention of these genealogical relatives should not be misleading and we should keep in mind that the terminology is classificatory and that these relatives represent only a fraction of those included under any one kinship term. Since the terminology extends to all, any of the six basic terms covers roughly one-sixth of all members of the band.

This means the individual is born into a vast network of kin and is told from birth how s/he relates to every single other person in the social universe. But if Ego is related to everyone else in the band, the Cuiva also distinguish between what they call "close" and "distant" relatives. The distinction is not always rigorous but generally the "close" relatives include all people who can trace a real and usually short genealogical link to Ego (parents and their siblings, siblings and their children, children and their spouses, spouses and their parents). Another way to be considered a "close" relative is to have been for some time, and for reasons that have nothing to do with blood or genealogy, Ego's friend and associate. People choose these friends on the basis of amenity and they become one's intimates, one's "close" relatives, together with one's immediate family.

To a large extent, the kinship system matters for the individual Cuiva because it imposes particular rules of behaviour toward each category of kin: one must pay respect to those designated by the kinship terms of one's parents' generation, one must joke with those in the same category as one's brothers, exchange food with those in the same category as cross-cousins, and so on. Thus, at the same time as the individual learns his or her kinship relation to all other members of the band, s/he also knows the proper way to behave towards each one of them. Perhaps the most important of these rules of behaviour is the one specifying that marriage should always be with someone from the category which includes Ego's cross-cousins.

The Cuiva also say that everyone should marry as soon as the proper age has been reached; this means roughly sixteen years old for boys, whereas girls should marry before puberty. This leads to a situation where the isolated individual, bachelor, divorced or widowed, is very much a rarity and where almost every adult has a spouse. Together they form the minimal social group, which the Cuiva call "those who sleep in the same hammock."

Children are brought up in the shelter of the parents and upon reaching marriage age it is the boys who leave this home to go and live with their new wife and her parents. In other words, residence after marriage follows the rule of uxorilocality. Daughters remain with the parents and are joined there by their husbands.

THOSE WHO SLEEP UNDER THE SAME SHELTER

Besides the couple, the two persons who share the same hammock, the second and larger group distinguished by the Cuiva is created by "those who sleep under the same shelter." Sharing a shelter literally means sleeping under the same palm-roof, using the same fire, cooking and eating together. Following the rule of uxorilocal residence, a shelter is normally composed of a man, his wife, their daughter, her husband, and the unmarried children of both couples. These people always live together, producing and sharing food as a unit. While a woman enters the group at birth and leaves it only at death, a man can also move in or out of the group at marriage or divorce.

Before marriage, one lives in the shelter in which one was born, together with one's brothers, sisters, and parents, and the Cuiva say the atmosphere of the family should be joyful and that relations between parents and children are always friendly. This changes somewhat as the children grow up and brothers leave to marry women in other shelters, while some cousins move in and marry the sisters. When a man comes to live in the shelter of his new wife, he often does not know well all the other members of the group, and since the rules of behaviour based on kinship prescribe extreme formality toward his wife's parents, he will normally remain very polite, if not even avoid, his parents-in-law; and thus bring to the shelter an air of formality which was not there before.

In fact, if it were not for the way they share the same food and shelter, it might seem that a man and his father-in-law have little to do with each other. They hardly ever talk and do not even hunt together; a man normally hunts much more with his wife, his sons, or friends from other shelters, than with his son-in-law. Each man is involved in a marital relationship which is said to be of no concern to the other. Nevertheless, all recognize that the father-in-law, who is usually the oldest man of the group, normally takes the responsibility of making some of the few decisions involving all members of the shelter (mostly about where and when to move next). I have seen cases where father-in-law and son-in-law obviously wanted to move camp in very different directions, and in each case the younger man simply gave in, but not without first trying to influence his father-in-law's decision through his own wife and through her influence with her mother.

But if the relation between father-in-law and son-in-law is assumed to be very formal, it is not devoid of mutual esteem and in any case is never supposed to be tense. For a man who married for the first time at an early age, a father-in-law is someone who takes the place of his father in completing his education; through his wife, or simply by listening to his father-in-law talking to his children, a man often learns a great deal. The amount of Cuiva knowledge, from geology to philosophy, is vast and it is practically impossible that a man should already have learnt everything from his own father; and, of course, his own father may have had very different interests and capabilities than his father-in-law. From the other man's point of view, a son-in-law is seen as a young hunter coming to help him produce the food for his family and coming to support him and other members of the shelter group in his old age. It is not surprising then to find that most people speak with respect and esteem of the roles played by these relatives, while also expressing publicly and privately admiration for their own father-in-law and son-in-law.

Over the years, the relations between members of the shelter will change as the parents grow old. More and more, the decisions as to where to move and what to hunt, activities which are no longer carried out with ease by the older man, will fall on the son-in-law. Increasingly, the younger couple becomes central in the shelter and it is as if the parents are in fact becoming dependent on their daughter and son-in-law who will care for them in their old age. At the same time also, this younger couple has now turned into a middle-aged man and woman, who have raised their own children and are now entering the first stage of a similar relationship with the men who come to live in the shelter and marry their daughters.

The group of "those who sleep under the same shelter" is in fact a kind of extended family and one of its major responsibilities is to ensure the socialization of children. While the hammock is the proper place for sexuality, the shelter is where the child is born, cared for and educated. All aspects of this education, as well as all matters of relations between members of the same shelter are the sole concern of the group and no outsider would normally interfere. The group has complete authority over these and they are of considerable importance in the life of any Cuiva: most of the long hours of leisure are spent eating, sleeping or chatting with members of one's shelter.

But the group is never autonomous in at least two crucial aspects. It seems more than doubtful that a shelter could ever live isolated from the rest of society and consistently succeed in producing enough food for all its members; some shelters have only two adults and should one of them fall ill, production would be seriously impaired. Secondly, the shelter is an exogamous unit, as one must necessarily look outside to find a marriageable relative. These two reasons seem enough to explain why "those who sleep under the same shelter" hardly ever live in isolation and are always part of a larger social unit, which I call "the local group."

THE LOCAL GROUP

The Cuiva themselves have no name for this group. They speak vaguely of "shelters living close to one another," but they have no formal category corresponding to these intermediate groups between the shelter and the band.

What I call the local group is simply the lasting association of a few shelters. In any of the three bands visited, there were about ten such local groups, formed by the constant association, over two years, of the members of anywhere between two to six shelters. The largest local group I saw had thirty-eight members, the smallest had only ten, and the average group had seventeen members. Since shelters very rarely live on their own, this means the members of the same local group are in fact the people who live, travel, and hunt together.

There are no clear-cut jurally defined modes of affiliation to a local group, but it appears from observation that there are in practice some definite tendencies in the composition of the various groups, as well as specific modes of affiliation which seem valid in all cases. Firstly, every member of a local group is related to at least one other member of the group by what could be called a "primary kin link": by this I mean that the person is either a husband or a wife, a father or a mother, a brother or a sister, a son or a daughter, of at least one other member of the group; and these relations are taken here to mean, as in English, "real" biological relatives. Secondly, each of the local groups included at least one pair of siblings of different sex: the shelter of a woman associated with the shelter of her brother.

This second characteristic of the local group has immediate importance for patterns of marriage, since children of brother and sister are cross-cousin to each other and thus fall into the marriageable category of kin. Even more so if we consider a further dimension which the Cuiva add to their rule on marriage: they say that Ego should not only marry someone from the kinship category which includes cross-cousins, but also the "closest" relative possible. If we keep in mind that a "close" relative is an immediate genealogical relative or someone with whom Ego has associated for some time, it becomes obvious that Ego's ideal marriage partners are likely to be found within the local group. The Cuiva say that whenever there is such a partner available within the group, Ego will be left with no choice but to marry that person. The marriages I have witnessed over two years were not enough to guarantee the relevance of my observations, but all tended to confirm a strong endogamous tendency within the local group.

The relations between members of the same local group are to a large extent guided by the rules of behaviour dictated by the kinship system. Besides these rules, there is also a structure of authority, based essentially on the relative ages of the members. The Cuiva hold that knowledge is cumulative and that those "who know" are really the adults over the age of about forty. These people are said to be the only ones who really know all parts of the territory, who understand the habits of every animal, who have memorized many songs and myths, and who have met members of distant bands, all matters about which they can talk for days. However, when a person finally becomes very old, he or she will still be much respected but at the same time no longer considered vigourous enough to have much influence on decisions about such daily matters as where to move camp and what to hunt next.

In fact, the activities over which the older members of the local group can exercise any form of authority are rather limited. First, anything that involves "those who sleep in the same hammock" (husband and wife) and their children are strictly their own private concern and no one else in the group can interfere. The same is also true of all matters internal to the group of "those who sleep under the same shelter" (matters such as how to cook the food, when to repair the roof, etc.). The most common situations, involving equally all members of the same local group, are when decisions must be taken on where the group should travel, when to build canoes, or how to solve a quarrel between members. This is when the advice of older members will often be decisive. They are the ones making the most suggestions and they will often discuss these matters among themselves.

This authority of the elders seems most efficient when settling a dispute between younger members of different shelters within the same local group: the older members of the group will quickly form an opinion on the matter and settle it by using their authority over their own children, within their own shelter. But should there be a serious quarrel between the older members themselves, it appears that there can be no other solution than the breaking up of the group; the various shelters would leave and associate themselves with other local groups. However, I have never seen a local group being dismembered following such a dispute and they seem to be very rare. In fact, the relations between members of the same local group could be said to be friendly by definition. If we remember that the Cuiva do not have any formal category for this social unit and do not draw strict rules concerning its membership, the best definition of the local group probably is: a group of about ten friendly relatives and their children, who enjoy each other's company and who always travel, work, and live together. In the absence of any clear definition and of any formal leadership, it is essential to maintain a certain consensus of opinion, at least among the adults of the group. Thus, even if I have not been able to observe the evolution of local groups over a long enough period of time, it is possible to forecast that as the group increases in size, consensus will be more difficult to maintain, common decisions will be more difficult to reach, and the local group will ultimately divide. The state of cohesion of the group depends on little more than the personal relationships between its members and there are no formal mechanisms to prevent its breaking-up. There are no rules forcing these people to live constantly together, and most people have close relatives in a number of other local groups and are thus quite free to choose which group to join in the community.

On the other hand, there must always be enough members in the local group to ensure a sufficient production of food. If the group decreases beyond a certain level, it is easy to imagine it would disappear as a group and its members be absorbed into another local group. In relation to this, it is interesting to note that the larger groups always contain many more children than the smaller ones and that the gap in size between local groups is much narrower if we consider only the members of each group which are economically productive: the smallest group (ten members) had eight adults, while the largest (thirty-eight members) had sixteen.

One of the dominant social functions of the local group is certainly the role it plays in the process of food production. For about six months of every year each local group lives in complete isolation from the rest of society. Considering the wealth of the environment and the Cuiva techniques for hunting and gathering, the local group is no doubt quite functional: a group of less than ten adults would require the individual to hunt and gather food more frequently, whereas grouping together more than forty persons would probably strain the local resources and force the group to move more often. Being of medium size, the local group seems to avoid both excesses, and it is not surprising the Cuiva spend most of the time living in groups of this size. This should not, however, be construed as some kind of ecological or functionalist explanation for the existence of the local group, but simply as a statement that, given everything else, it obviously fits in quite nicely with the rest of Cuiva culture.

The other important function of the local group is to provide a pool of people from which the individual can find a spouse. The group is preferably endogamous and, as mentioned earlier, this is the form marriage takes whenever possible. But often enough one cannot find an available partner within the local group and is obliged to search outside. This is the point at which the concept of "band" becomes important.

THE BAND

All these local groups taken together, the grouping of respectively all 149, 179, or 211 individuals, forms the "band" or what the Cuiva call "One people." When speaking of themselves, the expression is "Our people," and when speaking of other bands "Other people." The most common way of naming a band is to indicate its geographical location: "People of the Ariporo river," "People of the Casanare river," and so on. Another way is to identify a band by the name of one of its members: "Thari's folk," "Botroum's folk," etc. By using someone's name as the identification label for a band, one feels confident that this particular man is well enough known to be used as a convenient point of reference. But this can be a debatable question: different people often use the names of different men to refer to the same band, depending on whom they personally think is the best known. Although it is usually the names of older men which are used as points of reference, this does not mean these men enjoy any special positions of privilege or influence within their band, nor does it mean they will act as representatives of their band when meeting members of other bands.

The rules concerning the membership of a band are even less defined and specific than for the local group. Membership is based on the rather vague idea of common origin of all members of the band. It is said that at the beginning of humanity each band emerged from the underground at a precise geographical location, usually within the band's present territory and where in many cases there is now a spring surrounded by a pond and a few palm trees. It was the whole band, as numerous as it is today, which came out of the ground in this way, and not simply a handful of ancestors. All those who were present at the origin of humanity are said to have died long ago and there is never any attempt to trace real or fictitious genealogical links to these people. The Cuiva see themselves as the very distant children of these ancestors, but also say they have no possible way of checking if a particular individual is or is not a remote child of these same ancestors. Thus, what is perhaps the most basic definition of the band cannot regulate its membership. Cuiva culture has only a very short genealogical memory (dead people are forgotten within two generations) and does not use it to determine who is and who is not part of "Our people."

It appears, in fact, that membership is decided by consensus and that it depends mostly on the length of time a person has been actually living with the band. For example, in the band with 179 members, who all described each other as part of "Our people," I counted twenty-eight individuals who had in fact joined this group during their lifetime. Among these immigrants, four were wives of men born in this band, three were mothers of these wives, and the remaining twenty-one had come as a group to join this band for fear of being killed by Colombian and Venezuelan settlers who were invading the territory of their native band.

Apart from marriage or fear of invaders, there seem to be very few reasons why anyone would wish to join another band. There are no economic advantages or any social prestige attached to being a member of any particular band. Even disputes, which occasionally create divisions within a band, do not seem to be sufficient reason for leaving one band to join another. Part of the reason probably is that people often look down on members of other bands as their inferiors: "they eat raw meat," "they're dirty," "nasty people," etc.

Marriage with a member of another band is never encouraged when not a matter of absolute necessity. Because of their dislike for foreigners, the Cuiva insist that whenever possible one should marry, if not within the local group, at least within one's own band. This does not mean the group is in any way equipped to impose its will on the marriage of one of its members, but simply that, as the prejudice is shared by all, one is normally reluctant to marry outside if there is any marriage possibility within the band.

When such a marriage does occur, the new spouse will normally be integrated into whichever band the couple decides to join; the rule of uxorilocal residence does not hold for interband marriages and the couple seems free to live with either group. But the integration of a new spouse is not a mere formality. It depends essentially on the opinion of every individual in the group, who remains quite free to think of any new member as one of "Our people" or not. These opinions vary from person to person, and sometimes from day to day. But even these personal opinions are not really necessary, since, loosely organized as the band is, there is very little one can actually do to prevent outsiders from joining the group. Something approaching a majority opinion is no doubt crucial, but the consensus is relevant only as an intellectual preoccupation and some people may very well lead perfectly normal lives without being considered as "Our people" by many other members. What really matters in the integration of an outsider is to be accepted at the level of "those who sleep in the same hammock" (being allowed to marry) and at the level of "those who sleep under the same shelter" (being allowed to join a residential group) and these are decisions over which the band as a whole has no control. Once these conditions are fulfilled, the granting by all of band membership seems to follow necessarily sooner or later.

If the band does not seem to occupy a central place in the minds of most Cuiva, its importance in their everyday life is not much greater. All members of a band assemble together, travelling and camping as a single group, for only one-fourth of the year, and mostly during the dry season; the Cuiva explain this by saying that only during the dry season are there camping sites large enough to accommodate all the people, whereas during the rainy season most of the ground is flooded. During another fourth of the year, which is however not so closely bound to a particular season, each band divides into two separate and independent groups of roughly equal size (from 70 to 105 persons) which will often exploit very distant parts of the band's territory. The other half of the year, we have already seen, is spent in isolated local groups. Since most of life is spent with spouse, children, members of the same shelter, and the same local group, people have in fact little to do with other members of the band. There is no obligation to join with other members and a band may well spend more than a year without ever uniting. There is never a need to gather a large working force, nor are there any ritual, festival, or other great social occasions which require attendance by all. Nevertheless, the Cuiva share a very anti-isolationist mentality and claim to enjoy nothing better than a large camp, when the band is united. Here, much of the pleasure of life comes from visiting and talking to all these people, and from sniffing drugs in a group large enough to make it worth holding a dance afterwards. In short, the band gathering is fun and one enjoys the simple pleasure of meeting people whom one does not see very often.

This means, of course, that once again the cohesion of the group depends essentially on the feelings of unity and friendship among its members; and that here again the state of relations between adults, who are all influential within their own local groups, seems to determine the degree of cohesion of the band (I know that in one case, a marital dispute involving two separate local groups kept a band from ever uniting for more than three years).

As the band is no more than the occasional gathering of independent local groups and never really acts as an integrated social unit, it would seem futile to look for a structure of leadership. The few communal decisions, such as whether to move camp, hold a dance or organize a ritual, may well be discussed by the senior members of the band, but they can follow anyone's spontaneous suggestion and always reflect the consensus of opinion within the whole group.

Should someone disagree with the decision, that person can always refuse to dance, take no part in the ritual, or move camp in another direction.

CONCLUSION: WHY THE BAND?

The band presents the simple advantage of forming a community larger than the local group. It is a greater pool of people from which to select spouses or friends. It creates a wider collective memory, it knows more stories and more songs. The advantage is obvious, but it is not sufficient: the band does not guarantee that one will not be forced to marry outside, nor does it diminish the interest of meeting newer and perhaps even greater knowledge in members of other bands.

It appears that in order to understand the Cuiva band we must first forget some of the teachings of our textbooks. Anthropologists have tended to summarize rather quickly the purpose of any social group by saying that it serves to ensure the production of material goods or the reproduction and survival of society, or both. We are also accustomed to think that to perform these tasks adequately each group must have a certain degree of cohesiveness and that the best way to achieve this is to have some form of recognized leadership. This is why the anthropological textbooks mentioned earlier, in which the authors often use "social structure" to mean structure of authority, seemed so much interested in discovering who holds power within the band. For these authors, there is a structure of authority in any social group and the band is especially important because it is the largest group in the society and as such is the centre of the highest form of political power.

As I suggested at the very beginning, an ethnographer who would catch only a glimpse of Cuiva society and then turn his experience into a permanent image, could easily confirm this view of band society. Cuiva society would appear as a series of well-structured and ever-larger social groups, with power always residing with the oldest members of each group: those who share the same shelter are dominated by the parents, the local group is run by its elders and the band by a vaguely defined council of its senior members. But anyone able to observe Cuiva society over a longer period of time and witness the remarkable flux of leadership, alliances, and associations, must reach a very different conclusion.

The Cuiva band seems important for reasons which are the very opposite of those suggested by the textbooks. Rather than being a weak instrument of political power, an underdeveloped pale copy of the "tribe" and "nation," the band seems a device to avoid authority, a means to escape the domination of power.

Although one is never free to choose one's parents, a Cuiva, thereafter, has considerable freedom in deciding with whom to live. The material and social conditions which elsewhere seem to determine this choice of where and with whom to live do not matter much for the Cuiva: there is no permanent village and no great attachment to any particular piece of land; tools and other objects are easily made and easily thrown away; the resources are abundant and any youth can master the techniques for hunting and gathering; marriage and divorce are easy; there is no debt and no obligation beyond sentimental attachment; the rules of behaviour based on kinship provide a simple code of conduct applicable to all human beings. What the Cuiva really care about is people, the family and friends with whom one spends one's life. Although one is not always free to choose in which shelter to live, it is on the basis of friendship, on the state of their relations with other members, that shelters decide which local group to join. The band provides its members with an opportunity to make this choice. It provides individuals with a community of possible associates and during three months every year, it gives them a chance to evaluate the state of these friendships and decide with whom they can best get along. It allows those individuals unhappy with their present situation to change it by leaving perhaps their spouse or shelter, but more often their local group, to go and live with other members of the band.

In this way, the band serves as a check on the relations within each local group and these can turn sour, say the Cuiva, when someone becomes stingy over things or wants to assert authority over others. Beyond the respect due to parents or parents-in-law within the shelter, the Cuiva will take orders from no one. The band is there to guarantee this freedom by allowing people to dissociate themselves from authoritarian individuals. It is in this sense that the band can be understood as a safety device against the emergence of political power. Above the level of the family, where most of the decisions in life are taken, the very existence of the band impedes the development of other levels of authority. Serving as a negation of centralized power and as a protection against its emergence, the band should never be considered a weak form of institutionalized central authority. Not only is it indeed very different from the forms of organized power represented by the "tribe," the "nation" or the "state," but it is not founded on the same political premise and its purpose is to serve opposite ends. To put it very simply, the Cuiva band gives power to the people, whereas the net effect of any centralized authority is to take it away.

BIBLIOGRAPHY

Arcand, Bernard 1976. Cuiva food production. *Rev. canad. Soc. & Anth/Canad. Rev. Soc. & Anth.* 13(4),387-396.

Harris, Marvin 1975. *Culture, People, Nature: an introduction to general Anthropology.* Second edition. New York.

Service, Elman R. 1966. *The Hunters.* Foundations of Modern Anthropology Series. New Jersey: Prentice-Hall.

Steward, Julian H. 1955. *Theory of Culture Change.* Urbana: University of Illinois Press.

ADDITIONAL READINGS

Arcand, Bernard 1972. *The Urgent Situation of the Cuiva Indians of Colombia* IWGIA Document no. 7, Copenhagen: International Workgroup for Indigenous Affairs.

Bicchieri, M.G. (ed.) 1972. *Hunters and Gatherers Today.* New York: Holt, Rinehart and Winston.

Lee, Richard B. and I. De Vore (eds.) 1968. *Man the Hunter.* Chicago: Aldine.

Sahlins, Marshall 1974. *Stone Age Economics.* London: Tavistock.

CHAPTER 11

STRATIFICATION AND CHIEFSHIP

A Comparison of Kwakiutl and Kayan

JEROME ROUSSEAU
McGill University

Social inequality is a central feature of complex societies; however, it is not generally recognized that inequality can also exist in simpler societies which lack a market economy and live in small local groupings. The Kwakiutl of British Columbia and the Kayan of central Borneo are examples of such a situation.

This paper discusses the essential features of stratification and politics in these two societies, in order to show the fundamental similarities and differences between them. There has been no attempt to describe regional variation, to analyze concrete examples or to provide detailed ethnographic information, nor is the theoretical background presented explicitly here; all these are available elsewhere. (See "References and Further Reading.") Finally, this paper analyzes only the functioning of the Kayan and Kwakiutl systems; it will not deal with the problem of historical origins and transformations. The Kwakiutl are described as they were at the time of the first contacts with Europeans; they have changed considerably since then. So far, the Kayan have retained most of their traditional system, but they are in the process of becoming part of Malaysian and Indonesian society.

THE KWAKIUTL

The Kwakiutl occupied the northern half of Vancouver island and the adjacent coastal areas, surrounded by other ethnic groups with which they shared a number of technological, cultural, and social traits. The Northwest Coast is an area of great ecological complexity and offers a variety of natural resources. The Kwakiutl practised no agriculture and relied primarily on fish for their subsistence, particularly salmon, halibut, and candlefish. They sometimes hunted sea mammals, such as seals and whales, but land animals were an occasional source of meat. At certain times of the year, women went inland to gather roots and berries, and the forest provided the timber for buildings and boats. Although food sources were relatively abundant, they were not available at all times. The quantity of fish, game, and vegetable foodstuff could vary because of the annual cycle and irregular ecological variations. Storage and preservation of food was thus a necessity. These sources of food were relatively stable over the years: specific stretches of river provided the best fishing locations, and berry bushes were productive for many years. For this reason, villages would remain in the same area for long periods. Migrations might take place because of long-term ecological changes or for political reasons, but over the short term, people stayed more or less in one place. In the winter, all community members were gathered in a central location. A village was formed by several houses made of hardwood planks which were built in a row facing the water. For the rest of the year, the community split into several sections which went to their fishing stations or were otherwise engaged in productive activities.

It is difficult to estimate the size of Kwakiutl villages; they might have ranged from 50 to 2000 people, but somewhere between 500 to 800 was probably typical. A village consisted of several social units called *numayma,* each containing about 100 individuals (Boas 1966:47). The *numaymas* (also *numaym, numima, na'mima*) were corporate groups, i.e., they acted as entities. They had a name and a chief, they held rights over fishing locations, hunting, and berry grounds and they had distinct ceremonial privileges. The *numayma* was an ambilineal descent group, which means that membership in it was acquired through either parent. The decision to include a child in the father's or the mother's *numayma* depended on several factors. For instance, if the *numayma* of one parent was significantly more prosperous, it would be advantageous for the child to belong to it. Otherwise, one child might belong to the father's *numayma,* another to the mother's. In some specific circumstances, an individual might have membership in more than one *numayma.* Each *numayma* consisted of one or more extended families occupying separate houses in the winter village. The Kwakiutl village was thus a complex social unit, divided into several groups, each of which had its own chief and controlled some natural resources.

THE KAYAN

The Kayan share the centre of Borneo with several ethnically related groups and are scattered in several river basins of Sarawak (Malaysia) and Kalimantan (Indonesia). They are shifting cultivators, and their staple food is rice. Other crops are cassava, taro, sweet potatoes, maize, Job's tears (a *graminacea*), and sago. They also grow such vegetables as cucumbers, marrows, and chilli. They plant coconut and areca palms and various kinds of fruit trees, especially bananas. Each family has a tobacco garden. The Kayan also raise pigs and chickens for ceremonial feasts, but they obtain most of their animal proteins by fishing and hunting. Kayan settlements are built beside rivers, and fish are easily available. Men regularly hunt wild boar, deer, monitor lizards, turtles, and other species of animals. They occasionally engage in trade with neighbouring nomads, exchanging trade goods they have acquired from Chinese and Malay traders for jungle produce.

Kayan villages typically consist of a single longhouse made of hardwood and divided into apartments, one for each household. Kayan communities range between 100 and 500 individuals, but most of them have less than 200 inhabitants. The basic social and economic unit within the village is the household *(amin)*, which is normally a stem family (i.e., parents with *one* married child and the latter's children), averaging ten people. At marriage, the bridegroom joins his wife's household; after a few years, his parents may pay a substantial brideprice so that he will return with his wife to his natal household, but seventy percent of marriages remain uxorilocal. The Kayan have no kinship groups besides the household, and kinship plays a minor role in their social organization.

Kayan life is regulated by rice agriculture. Every year, the village selects two to four areas of jungle which are cleared (a task which takes over two months), allowed to dry, and burned. This burning plays a double role: it clears the fields of branches and leaves that would prevent cultivation, and it transforms them into ashes which provide nutrients for the soil. This is followed by sowing (about ten days), weeding (two months) and harvest (two to three months). The soil of tropical forests is poor in nutrients, and it would be impossible to use the same land several times in succession. For this reason, the Kayan select new farm areas every year and carry out the same process annually. Land should be left fallow for ten years at the very least (twenty to thirty years would be preferable) before it is used again for cultivation. By that time, it is covered by trees and is known as secondary jungle. Because of this agricultural process, a village must control large areas of land and this means that villages are far apart. It also follows that shifting cultivators are not intrinsically attached to their land. If they are surrounded by primary (or virgin) jungle, they may wish to migrate if another area provides greater economic, strategic, or political advantages. Traditionally, most Kayan villages used to migrate every ten years, although in many cases this involved a displacement of only five or ten miles. In recent years, because of governmental pressure, the rate of migration has been reduced considerably.

In those areas of Borneo where the population density is relatively high (e.g., ten per square mile), much of the available agricultural land is utilized, and individual households have permanent ownership of the land that they have previously used. As it grows into secondary jungle, the same family or its descendants use it again for cultivation. Among the Kayan, on the other hand, the population density is low (one per square mile), and there is no individual ownership of land. Each village controls a large area and every year each household clears the amount of land that it needs; after the harvest, it maintains no rights over it. When the land becomes available again for cultivation, any member of the community may use it. Indeed, in the past, the question of land ownership was even more irrelevant, because of the frequent migrations. This is a fundamental factor, because it means that the Kayan can produce their food according to their needs and abilities without any restriction of private ownership. The same applies to fishing and hunting: the jungle belongs to no one, and everyone has access to it.

STRATIFICATION, RANKING, AND CHIEFSHIP AMONG THE KWAKIUTL

Ranking was pervasive in Kwakiutl society. Villages were ranked in relation to each other; *numaymas* were ordered relative to each other; within each *numayma*, people were differentially ranked. The various rankings formed a single system, as individuals of different *numaymas* and villages could be ranked along the same scale. The ranking of the various units was not always agreed upon, and changes in relative ranking could take place. If an individual managed to improve his rank, this could have an effect on the ranking of his *numayma*. This system of gradation theoretically implied that no two Kwakiutl individuals could be exactly equal in rank.

Articulated with this ranking system was a system of strata. The Kwakiutl were divided into nobility (or chiefly stratum), commoners, and slaves. Ranking and stratification were linked; the nobility were more diversified in terms of rank than the commoners. But, because of these fine gradations, "the distinction between low ranking noblemen and high ranking commoners sometimes became blurred." (Rohner and Rohner 1970:79) Although religious rituals contributed to marking the distinction between commoners and nobility, only the latter could become members of dance societies and hold positions which provided access to the supernatural. Each *numayma* had several ranked hereditary positions or "seats" to which were attached a series of rights and privileges, and the men who held these positions formed the nobility. The status of a person depended on the number and importance of the privileges linked to those positions he "owned." They were inherited from the father or the mother, according to the rule of primogeniture. However, if both the father and mother owned several positions, they might distribute them among their children, in which case the latter would belong to separate *numaymas* or, if they owned more seats than they had children, a child might then belong to several *numaymas* by virtue of his or her ownership of several seats linked to different *numaymas*. Marriage was thus a fundamental element in the management of rank among the nobility, as it determined what seats would be available to the children. There was thus a preference towards marrying a spouse of similar rank and even more so of the same stratum.

These ranked positions were not transmitted automatically; the transfer had to be acknowledged publicly at the occasion of a specific ritual called potlatch. Potlatches were gatherings of members of the chiefly stratum in which the claimant to a title distributed property to the guests. "Their acceptance of the gifts and their witnessing of the ceremony constitute[d] acknowledgement of the succession. If no distribution, or an inadequate one, [was] made, the claimant to a position [would] suffer loss of prestige or even total disavowal of his claims" (Rosman and Rubel 1971:201-202). The potlatch also played a role in confirming the guests' rank, because they received gifts according to their relative position. Furthermore, the rank of a given seat was not established once and for all; it depended on the number and lavishness of potlatches related to it. In other words, the continued performance of potlatches improved an individual's rank and that of his seats. Since only wealthy people were able to potlatch frequently, rank was a factor of wealth. If someone became impoverished, failure to perform potlatches would reduce the rank of his position. Eventually, he would practically become identical to a commoner. However, this does not mean that potlatches had to be performed frequently. In the nineteenth century, the number of potlatches increased for a number of reasons, one of which was a severe depopulation which left a lot of claims for seats open, thus reducing overall competition. However, even if potlatches were traditionally less frequent, they were still a fundamental element in the management of social stratification.

The system of ranking determined the political structure of the *numayma*, because its chief would be its highest ranking member. But if rank is an indirect effect of wealth, how did *numayma* chiefs obtain their wealth in the first place? The chief of the *numayma* was its administrator; with the help of other important men of his *numayma*, he regulated the use of its resources such as fishing grounds and berry fields. Food surpluses were stored under his authority, which allowed him to distribute food in times of shortage. He also accumulated surpluses so that he would be able to perform potlatches in the name of his *numayma*. The Kwakiutl chief would receive "somewhere between one-fifth and one-half, or more, of the entire food production" (Ruyle 1973:615). A proportion of the food and handicrafts (blankets, boats, etc.,) received from the commoners was not returned to them, but retained by the nobility. Similarly, the nobility would give back to their commoners only a portion of the gifts they had received in potlatches. Furthermore, even the proportion that he returned to the commoners was used in the chief's interest: this is how he managed to maintain his followers and to attract commoners who would use the *numayma's* resources (thus increasing the quantity

of products that he obtained). The need to maintain a circle of followers was one of the chief's main concerns: "as Thomas Hazard . . .
suggested, there was considerable residential mobility among the
Kwakiutl and other Northwest Coast populations, with individuals
and families moving about in response to changing economic and social conditions" (Ruyle 1973:615), and a chief could maintain his position only if he kept his followers. This implies competition between
chiefs in order to attract each other's commoners. Potlatches played a
role in that competition because they demonstrated a chief's prosperity and improved his reputation.

The chiefly stratum used some of the products collected from the
commoners for their own subsistence; thus, they did not have to
work as much as they did, nor would they perform menial tasks. Furthermore, they owned slaves which they could entirely control.
Slaves were not "persons" in the legal sense of the term, but, rather,
"property," and they could be sold or given to other chiefs. They
were obtained by capture from other ethnic groups, and their situation was hereditary. For lack of reliable data, the total proportion of
slaves cannot be evaluated with certainty. Curtis (1915:303) puts it as
low as four percent although Ruyle (1973:626) estimates Northwest
Coast class composition as twenty percent nobility, seventy percent
commoners and ten percent slaves.

Warfare was an intrinsic part of Northwest Coast life. It is not clear
how important the economic motive was in provoking wars, but the
need to maintain or restore one's honour was often an immediate
cause. "The chief had a number of warriors who obeyed his orders.
Often the younger brother of the chief was his warrior, and at the
same time, his head warrior . . . [The warrior] never accumulated
stores of provisions. Therefore, notwithstanding the property that he
acquired by plunder, he could not maintain a family. Many warriors
never married" (Boas 1966:106). Thus, among the Kwakiutl, warfare
was subordinated to the chief's authority and it was not an avenue
through which a younger brother might acquire the means to sup-
plant the hereditary chief. Chiefship was transmitted by primogeniture. However, as it had to be validated by a potlatch, the possibility
of competition between several claimants could never be discounted.
In order to prevent the disruptions that such a situation would cause,
succession to chiefship took place progressively during the lifetime of
the incumbent.

The Kwakiutl chief's position was maintained through an endless
process of negotiation and manipulation, and was based ultimately
on his control over his *numayma's* resources. He maintained his status
through potlatches; the redistribution of foodstuffs and prestigious
property allowed him to maintain and attract followers. A chief did
not have decisive authority by right. In case of disagreement, he
could impose his decisions only by force (by enlisting the help of his
slaves or commoners) or by negotiation. If serious damages were in-

flicted by members of other communities, the culprits might pay reparation, but feuds were a more common way of obtaining redress.

STRATIFICATION AND CHIEFSHIP AMONG THE KAYAN

Kayan stratification exists at two levels, one ritual, the other social. Virtually all rituals contain elements which indicate whether their beneficiaries are "refined people" or "inferior people" (kelunan jia/kelunan ji'ek). The "refined people" are deemed to have greater spiritual powers and to have the ability to come into more intimate contact with the supernatural. Thus, stratification is not limited to social interaction but extends also to unseen powers. However, these ritual categories give an incomplete idea of Kayan stratification, because each of them is divided into two social strata: the "refined people" include marens and hipuys, the "inferior people" are subdivided into panyins and dipens. The panyins form about seventy percent of the total population, and the other strata approximately ten percent each. The marens are the ruling stratum, the dipens are slaves, while the hipuys and panyins are commoners. In other words, the ritual categories cut across social distinctions by dividing the commoners into two strata and equating them respectively with strata from which they are markedly different.

Kayan strata are not groups like the Kwakiutl numaymas, but categories—which is to say that conceptual rules make it possible to distinguish between them, but they are not aggregates of people who have an internal organization and function as a body. The Kayan have no ranking scheme distinct from the stratification system, and the distinction between strata is clearly recognizable. An individual belongs to his parents' stratum. Seventy percent of marriages are stratum-endogamous, but for the children of the other thirty percent, a problem arises because an individual can belong to only one stratum. As there are no intermediate strata, this means that a child must be ascribed either to the father's or the mother's stratum. The parents' choice of residence resolves the issue: if they practise uxorilocality, as is usually the case among the Kayan, the child will be of the mother's stratum; if the family lives with the husband's parents' household, the child will be included in the father's stratum. Stratum ascription is defined entirely and uniquely by descent; the Kayan do not recognize any way in which one could improve one's rank, or where one could lose rank. Such a rigidity might create problems to the adaptability of the social system. We will see later how this is solved.

The stratification system is directly linked to the political structure, because the chief always belongs to the maren stratum. The preferred form of succession is from the incumbent to his son or nephew. If there are no suitable male heirs, a maren son-in-law or adoptee from another village takes the position. The Kayan lack an automatic rule

235

of succession: a younger son may be preferred to his elder brother, or a nephew to a son, if he is more capable of occupying the office. He is selected while the incumbent is still alive in order to allow a gradual transfer of power and to prevent the competition that might arise between potential candidates.

Each village has a single chief. He plays a limited role in the organization of productive activities. Fishing and hunting are the object of individual efforts; at most they require the collaboration of two or three men. Rice cultivation is a collective activity; work teams recruited from several households perform most of the agricultural work. However, the chief plays no role in their organization. The annual choice of farm areas is the result of a collective decision, and the chief accepts the general consensus or the majority opinion. The jungle belongs to no one, and the village territory is the collective property of the community, to be used in the general interest. Thus, the Kayan chief lacks the control over productive resources which is the basis of the Kwakiutl chief's power. However, he plays an important economic role insofar as it is his task to decide on the calendar of agrarian rituals; by doing so, he regulates the rhythm of agricultural production and he maintains the necessary conditions of cooperation. (The organization of work teams would be very difficult, probably impossible, unless all households were engaged in the same phase of the agricultural cycle at the same time.) The chief plays a major role in any decision to rebuild the longhouse or to migrate, but his wishes must accord with those of his people, as he is supposed to take decision in the general interest.

The chief also plays a judicial role. There is a strong ideology of communal harmony and whenever conflicts arise, a procedure is set in action to solve them. These may deal with marital quarrels, disagreements between agricultural teammates, and so on. The chief renders an authoritative decision; he may order the culprit to pay a compensation to the victim, and he can impose fines that he keeps for himself. However, he is not the only adjudicator; in any community, a few commoners manage to attain a prominent position because of their economic success, their knowledge of Kayan custom, their skill at interpersonal relations, and their ability to suggest reasonable courses of action. These men may chair judicial hearings in the same way as the chief; indeed, some chiefs prefer to leave this task to them. These important men may also organize meetings to discuss problems which touch upon several households. However, their position is never comparable to that of the chief; only he can make attendance to meetings compulsory. Before he makes decisions, he is expected to consult these important men, but he is not bound by their opinion.

Thus, the Kayan chief regulates the agricultural calendar and, as chief adjudicator, he is ultimately responsible for maintaining communal harmony. However, this does not seem to justify the very significant amount of work and other valuables that he obtains from the commoners. All adult commoners perform one day of corvee in the fields of the chief and other *maren* families for each phase of the agricultural cycle, i.e., four times a year. For a village of 200 people, this could amount to over 300 man-days per year. In addition, the chief owns slaves who perform domestic tasks and work in his fields. Corvees are also organized to build the chief's boats or his apartment in a new longhouse. Before the advent of outboard motors, the commoners had to provide crews for his boat when he went on official visits. The chief is also entitled to portions of large boar and fish. Finally, the commoners contribute half a *maren's* brideprice when he establishes *virilocal* residence (while uxorilocal residence is the rule among commoners, the future chief is expected to establish virilocality so that he can succeed his father), and they, along with slaves, provide most of the *marens'* subsistence.

How is this inequality possible? Within a given area, members of neighbouring communities usually visit each other in groups during the harvest festival, and individually throughout the year for minor economic exchanges. However, the villages are several miles apart along the river, and daily contacts are impossible. For a number of reasons, people are very suspicious of outsiders; they are often afraid of being poisoned while visiting other villages. Approximately one-third of all marriages take place between members of different communities because Kayan villages are too small to allow complete endogamy; but two-thirds of such unions end in divorce. Generally speaking, members of different villages find it difficult to deal with each other satisfactorily although this pattern of suspicion is characteristically absent among the ruling stratum. As these people prefer to marry a person of their own stratum, they *must* find a spouse outside their village (if there are two *maren* households in the same village, they are likely to be closely related, and marriage with them is impossible). And even when they marry a person of another stratum, they prefer to find him or her in a village other than their own. Members of the chiefly stratum are, therefore, frequent visitors to other villages and feel more at ease than would their fellow villagers of lesser strata.

All these links with other villages make it possible for chiefs to play a central role in extracommunity matters, such as boundary disputes, marriages, divorces, and theft. In the past, chiefs were active also in keeping to a minimum, or even preventing, violent clashes between Kayan communities; they regulated headhunting raids and they organized territorial expansion. Thus, the chiefs' key role in the intercommunity matters is the basis of their power, and this is how they are able to obtain a significant quantity of surplus labour. Indeed, corvees are an important factor in allowing them to play that role, as it makes time available for *marens* to visit other communities and maintain their network.

In order to preserve his position and mode of life, the Kayan chief is faced with the same problem as his Kwakiutl counterpart: how can he prevent his followers from leaving him? In order to persist, a splinter group of followers would have to establish a distinct territory and have its territorial claims acknowledged by other chiefs: but as commoners lack intercommunity contacts, they would find it difficult to do so; in the few known instances of such attempts, they were forced to return to their original community. Finally, a family cannot migrate to another village without the permission of its chief, and even if this is granted the family must pay a large fine to the chief upon its departure and so it would stand to gain little by deciding to settle in another village. In any case, a chief would refuse to welcome a household which had left its village without permission, despite the fact that he would stand to benefit by their contribution to corvees, because the chiefs of surrounding villages would put pressure on him to send them back. The *marens* are very aware that their power depends on solidarity, and they are quick to prevent actions that might endanger any chief's authority: in the long run, it could happen to them too. Competition for followers is absent among Kayan chiefs, because the negative political consequences outweigh the economic benefits.

A final problem has to be resolved in order for the system to function adequately. Chiefship is defined as the exclusive prerogative of the *marens*, and all of them expect corvees because they see chiefship as their collective property: the Kayan chief is expected to perform his duties in the interest of all the *marens* in his community. The commoners can provide for the chiefly stratum's subsistence only if the *marens* form a small proportion of the population: there are definite limits to the commoners' ability to supply their needs. But we have seen that stratum ascription is established by descent. This could create an unstable situation if there were too many *marens*, as some of them would be forced to live like commoners, thus contradicting the ideology that defines *marens* as people who do not work like commoners. Supernumerary *maren* families in fact do adopt a lifestyle similar to the commoners: they play a minor political role, they hesitate to request corvees regularly; they establish less prestigious marriages and find commoner wives and husbands. Over a few decades, their position deteriorates to the point where they are considered to be *hipuys*, not *marens*. But this means that they still belong to the ritual category of "refined people." Thus, the division of Kayan society into two categories goes hand in hand with the ideological dictum that being an aristocrat is a "natural" feature that can never be entirely lost. However, this ideology may be modified when socio-economic constraints demand it as above. Firstly, the very presence of the *hipuy* stratum makes it possible to demote *marens* without equating them with commoners. Secondly, an individual who is born a *maren* remains a *maren*: the loss of rank applies only to his or her children, and this can be easily explained away. Thirdly, semantic ambiguities help to confuse the issue: a synonym for *maren* is "big *hipuy*," while a synonym for *hipuy* is "small *maren*." Thus, by calling someone *hipuy*, one is not automatically *denying* that s/he is a *maren*.

The Kayan chief's position depends on his control over intercommunity matters. For the commoners, it justifies their obligation to perform corvees for him. From the chief's viewpoint, solidarity with his equals allows him to maintain a stable group of followers. The relative stability of Kayan political life is facilitated by the principle of hereditary stratum ascription. This principle, in turn, is workable because of the presence of an ambiguous stratum, the *hipuys*, who are socially commoners, but ritually aristocrats.

CONCLUSION

Kwakiutl and Kayan social organizations present significant similarities. Both are differentiated into three classes: nobility, commoners, and slaves (among the Kayan the commoner class is subdivided into two strata), with approximately the same proportion for each class (Kwakiutl: about twenty percent nobility, seventy percent commoners, ten percent slaves; Kayan: ten percent nobility, eighty percent commoners, ten percent slaves). In both cases, chiefship is reserved to the nobility, which receives food, work, and goods from the commoners. The slaves play a specific role in performing tasks for the nobility on a day-to-day basis, while the contribution of commoners is more limited. Rank is determined by descent, and specifically by membership in the *numayma* or the *amin*. Thus, the very reproduction of the populations maintains the basis of the stratification system. The descent principle explains the absence of debt slavery among the Kwakiutl and the Kayan, although that institution was present elsewhere in North America and Borneo. Debt-slavery is a temporary condition, as the person eventually regains his freedom after the debt has been repaid. However, such a practice clearly demonstrates the social basis of inequality, and contradicts ideologies that explain it in terms of natural, inherited differences. The two cannot be allowed to coexist. Finally, the stratification is in both cases justified by religion.

These similarities, and the fact that the two societies present two different but related modes of subsistence—hunting and gathering and agriculture supplemented by hunting and gathering—makes a further comparison particularly interesting. Kayan and Kwakiutl chiefs are faced with distinct tasks. The Kwakiutl chief plays a central role in productive activities because he supervises the use of natural resources and is the main agent of redistribution. The Kayan chief deals almost exclusively with political activities: he is the specialist in intercommunity relations, he is the ultimate adjudicator, and he has the duty to ensure that communal problems are solved in an orderly fashion. His only significant economic role, that of determining the agricultural calendar, is, in a sense, a specific case of the latter duty. This contrast between the Kwakiutl and Kayan is a consequence of the very different problems that their productive activities entail. In central Borneo, resources are fairly evenly distributed. With some significant limitations, a village can locate more or less anywhere along a river, and the jungle ecosystem does not vary significantly. On the

Northwest Coast, resources were concentrated in specific areas, and one could distinguish fishing grounds, berry grounds, etc., which were surrounded by unproductive areas. Barring important ecological transformations, these areas remained productive year after year. In Borneo, shifting cultivation implies that new land must be found every year. By itself, this does not impose a migratory existence, because land rotation can be profitably established, but other factors, some of them related to the traditional state of endemic warfare, encourage frequent migrations. At the best of times, the Kwakiutl enjoyed a much more plentiful existence than the Kayan, because the Northwest ecosystem provided more readily available resources. But they were also liable to wide fluctuations, which might occasionally create a famine situation. The Kayan are in a more stable situation. Their agricultural practices reduce the extent of fluctuations, and insufficient rice crops are rare. Even then, scarcity crops are available, such as sago and tubers. The availability of fish and game does fluctuate, but the Kayan are not completely dependent on them, and they can withstand a temporary scarcity in that domain without ill effects. (If needed, domesticated pigs and chickens can be slaughtered.)

Variations in productivity explain why the Kwakiutl chief must concern himself with economic problems. As resources were unevenly distributed, the *numaymas* felt the need to establish ownership over them. Because of his incumbency of "seats," the chief was the prime representative of the *numayma*, and he controlled these resources in its name. Food and valuables were also stored under his authority, and he could distribute them in case of need. Shifting cultivation of rice does not create the same technical problems; insofar as all village members follow the same agricultural calendar, the producers can regulate production and redistribution by themselves. Until a few years ago, the Kayan chief was needed to protect the integrity of the territory and to maintain peaceful conditions essential to the good functioning of agricultural activities.

The relation of the chief to the means of production is also a significant difference in selection procedures in both societies. A Kwakiutl could become chief only if he was able to demonstrate ownership of productive resources, and membership in the relevant *numayma* was a necessary (but not sufficient) condition of such ownership. Thus, a Kwakiutl could only be the chief of a *numayma* to which he belonged by descent. On the other hand, a Kayan needs only to be a *maren* to be eligible for the chiefly position. Of course, if descendants of the incumbent are available, they have a prior claim, but if not, it is quite permissible to seek a *maren* from another community without justifying it in terms of kinship relations. Ultimately, *maren* status is the only structural requirement for chiefship.

Kayan and Kwakiutl chiefs though, are by no means the servants of their people. They protect the latter's interests, but by doing so they are at the same time perpetuating a system from which they obtain considerable benefits. They both use indirect methods to obtain wealth from commoners. The Kwakiutl chiefs received valuables from their *numaymas* in order to perform potlatches which would reflect on the prestige of the whole group. In the long run, such exchanges enriched the nobility because the recipients of the gifts gave only a proportion of what they received to the commoner members of their own *numaymas*. Similarly, Kayan commoners help to pay their chief's brideprice, but the *maren* family which receives it keeps it all. In both cases the chiefs do not profit directly from the commoners because they give away what they obtain from them. But as this is part of a long-term series of exchanges, they stand to gain in the long run. Furthermore, they receive much of their food, lodgings, boats, and other things from their followers.

The Kayan and Kwakiutl nobilities are not totally unproductive, but they nevertheless depend on the commoners for much of their subsistence. By maintaining political or economic order, as the case may be, they not only protect their people, but they maintain a system where they profit from the work of commoners and slaves. The appropriation of surplus labour follows the logic of the respective economies: the Kwakiutl received the product of work—fish, meat, berries—in some cases keeping everything but the amount needed by the producers and their families for their immediate consumption. They then redistribute some of it when needed. Among the Kwakiutl, appropriation of surpluses can be explained as a tribute in return for using the chief's property, and as an incidental part of redistribution. The Kayan chief, however, obtains work itself, which is applied exclusively to his and his family's needs, and corvees are unambiguously recognized as a consequence of political domination. This is linked to the fact that the Kayan chief's authority is more solidly established than that of his Kwakiutl counterpart.

The degree of authority vested in the chief is indirectly related to the differences in the stability of resources between the two societies. The short-term and long-term variability of Kwakiutl means of subsistence could make it worthwhile for commoners to shift their allegiance, and this is why chiefs had to be particularly attentive to the problem of keeping their followers. A Kayan commoner, on the other hand, has little to gain by moving to another community. Resources being similar there, he will have to work just as much to obtain the same product. Individual families may still wish to move away for personal reasons, but this will be allowed to happen only if it does not create conflicts between chiefs. This is because the economic benefits obtained by the chief who would receive them "illegally" would not even begin to offset the political disadvantages of such an action. The need to maintain a stable village territory leads to cooperation between chiefs because land is sufficiently plentiful that a generally acceptable situation can be reached peacefully. In contrast, the potential instability of Kwakiutl producers forces the chiefs to compete for followers, thus the continuous rivalry between them. This explains the difference in the chief's authority in the two societies. The relation between the Kayan chief and his community is permanent and this allows him to establish a stable relationship where he is obeyed *because* he is the chief. The Kwakiutl chief, on the other hand, was obeyed because he offered more than another chief would; his power was in fact a result of negotiation.

The need for the Kwakiutl chief's generosity even penetrated the ranking system because a nobleman's rank depended, in the long run, on his performance in potlatches. Descent only gave the possibility of occupying important positions, which then had to be earned. Thus, status was something that had to be maintained, and the fact that it was pegged to generosity made possible fine distinctions of rank. This also provided a built-in mechanism that eliminated those individuals from the nobility who could not perform according to the expected standards. This can be contrasted with Kayan ranking, which is not negotiable, and where there is a clear difference between strata. In order to accommodate changing conditions, this system must provide a special mechanism, the *hipuys*, to transform superfluous noblemen into commoners.

The Kwakiutl and the Kayan then provide two examples of social inequality in societies that are based on a nonmarket economy. The similarities in their stratification systems are particularly striking if we consider that their technological and subsistence bases are distinct: while the Kwakiutl were hunter-gatherers, the Kayan are shifting cultivators. Nevertheless, in both cases, the system of stratification relates to the political and economic structures in the same way. That is, in both societies, it contributes to define chiefship and to categorize people in one of three classes: free producers, slaves, and appropriators of surplus labour.

The different ecosystems, especially the differences in the stability and availability of resources, obviously create different constraints or place certain limitations on the types of activities possible in the two societies. However, this does not mean that the Kayan and Kwakiutl social systems are produced directly by natural conditions. In order to survive, a society must, of course, adapt itself to its ecosystem, but there may be more than one satisfactory mode of adaptation and one mode relates to previous modes and so on. Natural conditions could not have compelled the presence of stratification among the Kayan, as other Borneo shifting cultivators living in similar conditions lack such a system. To be complete, a study of social organization should explain not only how a society adapts to its environment, but also why that society developed in one specific direction among the possible alternatives in that ecosystem. Thus, a historical analysis is necessary. The absence of written records in nonliterate societies does create some problems in this respect, but this is not insuperable. Firstly, we usually have some historical data ranging back a century or two, as is the case for both the Kwakiutl and the Kayan. Secondly, a comparison of neighbouring societies provides us with some of the insights that could have been derived from historical data. Thus, the next step in this analysis would consist of a comparison between the Kwakiutl and other Northwest Coast societies, and the Kayan and other Borneo groups in terms of the development of their respective stratification systems.

BIBLIOGRAPHY

The primary sources on the Kwakiutl are Boas' ethnographies. They present us with a wealth of data, as many of them were collected by George Hunt, who was himself half-Kwakiutl (e.g., Boas 1921; 1925). However, Boas was reticent about analyzing his data and about making general statements. The work of his that comes closest to a standard ethnography is *Kwakiutl Ethnography* (Boas 1966), and it owes much to Codere's editing. For this reason, it is essential to consult secondary sources. Such authors as Drucker and Heizer (1967), Rosman and Rubel (1971; 1972) and Weinburg (1965) produced general analyses based on Boas' data. The Rohners (1970) also provide a description of contemporary Kwakiutl life. Finally, Ruyle's (1973) paper on Northwest Coast stratification provides a general analysis, which is directly relevant to an understanding of the Kwakiutl. A more detailed discussion of Kayan stratification can be found in Rousseau (1978). The theoretical and conceptual background of this paper is presented in Rousseau (Ms.). I wish to thank Nels Johnson for his comments.

Boas, F. 1921. *Ethnology of the Kwakiutl. Based on data collected by George Hunt*. 35th Annual Report of the Bureau of American Ethnology (2 Vols.). Washington: Government Printing Office.

Boas, F. 1925. *Contributions to the Ethnology of the Kwakiutl*. New York: Columbia University Press.

Boas, F. 1966. *Kwakiutl Ethnography*. Helen Codere, (ed). Chicago: University of Chicago Press.

Curtis, Edward S. 1915. *The Kwakiutl*. The North American Indian, vol. 10. New York: Johnson Reprint Corporation.

Drucker, Philip and Robert F. Heizer 1967. *To Make my Name Good: A Reexamination of the Southern Kwakiutl Potlatch*. Berkeley: University of California Press.

Rohner, Ronald P. and Evelyn C. Rohner 1970. *The Kwakiutl. Indians of British Columbia*. New York: Holt, Rinehart & Winston.

Rosman, Abraham and Paula Rubel 1971. *Feasting with mine Enemy: Rank and Exchange among Northwest Coast Societies*. New York: Columbia University Press.

Rosman, Abraham and Paula Rubel 1972. The potlatch: a structural analysis. *American Anthropologist* 74:658-671

Rousseau, Jerome 1978. On Estates and castes. *Dialectical Anthropology* 3
(in Press) Kayan social stratification. Ms.

Ruyle, Eugene E. 1973. Slavery, surplus and stratification on the Northwest Coast: the ethnoenergetics of an incipient stratification system. *Current Anthropology* 14:603-631

Weinburg, Daniela 1965. Models of southern Kwakiutl social organization. *General Systems* 10:169-181

CHAPTER 12
EAST AFRICAN PEASANTS AND CAPITALIST DEVELOPMENT
The Kiga of Northern Ruanda

JIM FREEDMAN
The University of Western Ontario

INTRODUCTION

Some glaring inadequacies in the process of directed economic and social change presently taking place in precapitalist economies make it necessary to challenge the word most commonly used to describe this process: development. A specific inadequacy is that the means of development are not accomplishing their avowed objectives. Capital investment into developing countries does not always have a significant impact on such indicators of economic growth as national income. A more glaring inadequacy rests with the objectives themselves as, for example, the idea of economic growth itself.

To begin with, economic growth appears to have nothing to do with the much more pressing concern of new nations, i.e., economic autonomy. But more important is the fact that the accepted practices of investment which stimulate economic growth result in undesirable social changes. Overseas investment in developing countries results in the impoverishment of a majority and the enrichment of a minute sector, leading to the creation of antagonistic and sharply differentiated social divisions. The only real impact upon developing countries resulting from an association with developed economies has been the introduction of a very different set of principles for distributing economic wealth. And in spite of the arguments that inequalities create incentives for greater commitment to a developing capitalist economy, the reverse appears to be true. It is the creation of poverty and the destruction of a nation's cohesiveness which has been the most significant impact of overseas investments, and not the alluring of individuals to compete in a new economy with potentially greater rewards. Indeed it is, as one cogent argument has proposed, "the

245

pattern of current inequality, in particular, which tends thus to hamper a rise in productivity" (Arrighi and Saul 1973:11).

It is in part the failure to accomplish the objectives of economic development, and in particular the role of increasing social inequalities in this failure, which has led to a thorough reexamination of the concepts of development. One aspect of this reexamination has been to analyze, as Arrighi and Saul among others have done, the consequences of increasing inequalities, of unemployment and poverty, as inevitable consequences of the current patterns of investment by developed countries into African economies. These analysts have shown how increased inequality impedes the overall objective of increased productivity in African nations. They have demonstrated, for example, that the tendency for overseas industrialists to introduce capital intensive rather than labour intensive enterprises in African economies has created only a very small and too privileged labour force. The interests of growth, the authors imply, would have been better served by introducing labour intensive enterprises, giving more people access to the perquisites of a market economy, and making possible the local production of goods and the creation of viable local markets.

Another, and perhaps, a substantially more radical, reexamination has been to challenge productivity and increase in national income as objectives of development at all. Perhaps one should recommend, as has Dudley Seers, the putting up of a sign in every civil service office to wit: "Will it reduce inequality?" (Seers 1973:10). One should challenge the assumption about man's participation in economies, that they by definition must compete for scarce resources, recognizing instead that building a society with this assumption is peculiar only to the history of Europe and North America and inappropriate for exportation (Macpherson 1972).

These observations mean, among many other things, that any understanding of changing precapitalist economies in contact with a world capitalist system, must begin and end with a study of inequality. It seems to me that this should take place in at least three major contexts. A first context involves the relationship between nations participating in a world economy; here what is at stake is a growing dependence of African economies on capitalist economies by virtue of their commitment through the lack of integrated and self-sufficient economies, a lack which is perpetuated by the developed economies. A second context involves the social impact of overseas investments in African economies. Here the creation of antagonistic social classes is at stake, the differentiation of domestic elites on the one hand and a growing class of marginal, urban labourers on the other. A third context involves the impact of a market economy in exclusively rural areas. A market economy leads to private land ownership and more generally, private ownership of the means of production. Traditional inequalities, typically embedded in kinship and other forms of moral constraint, change drastically as economic activities individualize.

Access to the basic means of production is no longer mediated by such concerns as social membership and the fulfilling of the expectations of a filial relationship. Social relations no longer constrain access to wealth; access to wealth itself is the sole basis of a new style of relationship that cannot properly be called social. Traditional inequalities based on age and status become inequalities based uniquely on differences in land holdings. In a region such as northern Rwanda, whence comes the personal experience and the information on which this paper is based, land resources are scarce; this means that the progressive concentration of land holdings in the hands of a few results immediately in the progressive impoverishment of others.

I studied the Kiga society of northern Rwanda during two different periods. One was in 1970-71, and the other in 1977. My impression was that the society had changed drastically, and what follows is an attempt to describe why. It is an attempt to describe this process of impoverishment as a result of the disappearance of social constraints on relations of inequality.

KIGA SOCIAL ECONOMY

The purpose of this section is to describe, for the traditional Kiga population of northern Rwanda, how people used and gained access to two critical factors of production, land and labour, and to show the relationship between the use and acquisition of these factors of production and specific social relations. A major point to be made is that young families are dependent on older ones in ways that directly affect how these factors of production are acquired or accumulated. This dependency explains not only the "developmental" nature of the domestic group, but also at the same time, the nature of relations of inequality found among the traditional Kiga.

The Kiga have had a reputation that is aptly rendered by the French word, "montagnards" (mountain folk). They acquired this reputation by fiercely resisting any and all alien penetration into their homeland. The powerful kingdom of Rwanda to the South was among those who experienced their capacity for resistance, as the warriors of this kingdom tried unsuccessfully to dominate the Kiga mountain people for a period that lasted almost a century. The Kiga resisted with virtually equal success the academic penetration of May Mandelbaum Edel, the first social scientist to make inquiries in the area. It can honestly be said that she, like the great kingdom, never really came to grips with this society. Dr. Edel's failure can best be appreciated in an article she published in 1938, where she claimed that the Kiga were individualists to a fault, even to the extent of holding land in private property. This is a curious claim for an anthropologist whose general predilection was to suppress the uniqueness and expressive characters of individuals.

It is a fact that the Kiga have legitimately earned a reputation of jealously guarding their autonomy as a people and of treating outsiders with considerable suspicion. An outsider, such as myself, who lives for any length of time in the very northern parts of Rwanda commands respect and curiosity in other parts of the country, for what's true about the Kiga is that they like to fight and drink, and are rarely inclined to be cooperative. They give a long lasting impression of disorder to an outsider. Where May Edel failed is in not realizing that the integration of individuals into a social order, while not loudly proclaimed, exists. An individual man rejects any attempt to encroach on his lands, lands which are very well delineated, over which no one but himself has control. But he has acquired them by virtue of membership in a social group.

Marx and, following him, Claude Meillassoux have made explicit that in principle one does not have to labour to obtain the fundamental means of production, i.e., land, in traditional agrarian societies (Marx, K. 1973; Meillassoux, C. 1967). Land is ideally a "given" in one's existence. An individual need only be born to have access to land, for birth bestows membership in a social unit, and membership bestows a claim to a piece of land. It is this, Marx noted, which distinguishes agrarian economies from capitalist economies where the individual is alienated from the means of production and access can only be had by the exertions of labour. It is this also which Meillassoux used to distinguish agrarian economies. An individual obtains a long-term claim to land by virtue of a social identity which requires no greater effort than being born. This is fundamentally true for the Kiga . . . with a qualification.

A Kiga male is recruited by birth into the descent groups of his father. The smallest of these is the *inzu*, meaning house, the domestic group in which almost all aspects of the productive process are organized and adjudicated. Land is acquired, possessed, distributed, and passed on through relations within this group. There are larger groups based on descent, such as *umuryaango* (meaning door to the house), which may include a number of *amazu* (pl. of *inzu*) and which had the traditional function of defending an area . . . and the *ubwooko*, or clan, a word meaning sort or species, which includes many *imiryaango* (pl. of *umuryaango*). *Abooko* (pl. of *ubwooko*) and *imiryaango* are permanent groups, which is to say there is ideally a fixed number of them. The *inzu* on the other hand is transient, it grows and disappears with individual men, each of whom (except for those basely poor and infirm) ought ideally to be the centre of an *inzu* which receives its identity from him. The *inzu* dies, or more properly disperses, as the elder passes away, and the sons seek to build their own familial establishment. It is how land is acquired and passed on in the context of an *inzu* which is important here.

At marriage a man makes his first step toward independence, for it is then that he becomes eligible for an inheritance. At this time the father must give him a piece of land known as *ubutekeesha*, a piece of land for the kitchen. The father formally bestows the land upon his new daughter-in-law, though neither she nor her husband can dispose of the land in any way. If she leaves, she leaves the land behind. This land is explicitly for the formation of a new family, and its use depends on the continuation of the relationship of the spouses. Following marriage, but associated with it, the father may grant another field known as *umunani*, effectively a token of thanks for getting married. Lands may be informally bestowed following the marriage at any time, until near death when there is a formal distribution of remaining lands. The *ubutekeesha* lands account for about half of the lands that are acquired from a father, and the *umunani* received between marriage and death represent the other half.

This suffices to make an obvious point: land is received from patrilineal kin by virtue of being patrilineal kin. And not coincidentally, the first land is received at the moment when a member of the descent group begins to contribute to the reproduction of the kin group, the first real moment for full affirmation of membership. At the same time, however, there is a distinctly contrary point to be made, and this is the qualification. At the very moment that a young male makes a debut as an independent contributor to the group, his dependency on the group begins. It is not through membership alone, but *exemplary* membership in the father's *inzu* that a son henceforth will augment his own holdings. This exemplary membership is expressed in allegiance to the one individual through whom membership is acquired: the father or the elder of his natal *inzu*. Meillassoux traces the notion of seniority and of anteriority (1960), i.e., inequality, in agrarian society to the fact that descendants are dependent on their elders for sustenance during the nonproductive periods, the periods between harvests, which typify agrarian societies, and must perforce render constant hommage to them. One should point out, however, that it is not control over the products themselves which forms the basis of inequality, but rather control over the young man's access to the perquisites of social membership, that is, his capacity to actualize his membership in order to receive the benefits of neighbourhood and *umuryaango* membership, which is the basis of power relationships.[1] For a young man to bypass his father in acquiring land is unthinkable. A young man just married has an illusion of strength: he prances about, thrusts his spear around and may for the first time pronounce an *ikyivugo* . . . a statement of his personal worth. The illusion becomes apparent with the realization of the poverty that his new found independence has imposed. He will soon have a family, no labour and little land, and, as a result, be increasingly at the mercy of elders.

Acquiring a labour force poses a whole other set of problems for the potential household which, though quite different, are nevertheless resolved in precisely the same way: through a social relation of dependence. One can state the patent fact that agrarian societies rely heavily on cooperative labour in a number of ways. It has been said that agrarian societies have a unique capacity to absorb surplus population as labour, or, what amounts to almost the same thing except for being phrased in a more positive mode, that the productivity of agrarian households relies specifically on a greater investment of labour. This therefore permits and encourages larger families and larger cooperative work forces than in pastoral or gathering economies (Smith 1976; Boserup 1965; Faris 1975, et al.). In contrast to gathering economies, agrarian ones relate to nature by dramatically transforming it and this involves a more intensive human input and potentially a more complex social organization of production. In this situation, bearing children requires special attention as an economic activity. Not only does it perpetuate and enhance the viability of the kin group, itself a land-holding corporation which is a function hardly to be discounted, but it provides human labour. And not only does it provide human labour, but it is the *only* source of labour.

This amounts, as far as the Kiga are concerned, to one of the most fundamental equations of existence: to have children is to prosper. The Kiga women do not hesitate to remind anyone interested of the same but more encompassing principle: that poverty and being without a family are synonymous. Poverty and existence without a family (e.g., celibacy) are rendered by the same Rwandan noun: *ubukene*. Acquiring children is tantamount to acquiring land in this respect: both are essential to productivity and obtaining the perquisites of wealth. Young men, with this in mind, must consider two main elements in the building of a family, and these two elements will form the basis of our analysis of the relationship between bearing children, i.e., the reproduction of a social unit, and the social relations associated with reproduction. The first consideration is that a man must take a wife; and the second is that the whole process takes a good deal of time. Both of these end up, as with the acquisition of land, committing a beginning *inzu* to a long period of dependence.

Working out the particulars of marriage exchanges is one of the most intense moments of the Kiga social economy. The exchange of bridewealth, the sum paid by the father of the groom to the father of the bride, is the moment of greatest intensity. There is a simple, indeed a too simple, explanation given for this intensity which is that setting the brideprice sum involves a play for power and wealth on the part of the exchanging parties. It is to some extent true that the fathers of the spouses are very concerned not to be "taken" or shamed by getting a bad deal. The wife's father should ask a lot and at least get a good part of the sum, and the groom's father must not be forced to pay the whole amount that is asked. The bridewealth negotiations are filled with this concern. But too much stress on this element of competition leads to the wrong interpretation. What is being negotiated is not who is going to win or lose, but rather, some incidental features of what will be an enduring relationship. This is a subtle but important difference. By definition the parties must agree, for the Kiga recognize that maintaining the relationship is far more important than the symbolic conquest of one old man by another. The young married couple clearly articulate this fact, for the bride knows

250

that if her father has been shamed in the negotiations she will not be welcomed back into her natal home in the event of her many home-comings, or in the event of an eventual separation. Living with this insecurity, an insecurity which results inevitably in total dependence of the woman upon the man, is an unpleasant possibility for both the bride and the groom. The elders express this by saying that should the brideprice paid be insufficient, the groom's family will never be the beneficiary of the "return" brideprice. The "return" brideprice is traditionally the calf born to the cow given the wife's family as bride-price. Today it could be any number of valuables, even money. Nor do the exchanges stop with the rendering of the "return" brideprice. The reciprocity continues, and parties to a brideprice negotiation rec-ognize that they must build a sound basis for continued reciprocity.

Now where is the young groom in the course of these considera-tions? His status is subordinate to a number of other considerations, and to describe this we should see him in the context of the cere-mony. The most conspicuous feature of the ceremony is the presence of so many elders. All the important elders of the groom's local lineage and those of the wife's are present; they parade in and for-mally hand over their walking sticks to an old woman who packs them away to prevent any unintended consequences of a flare-up in tempers. They arrange themselves in clearly separate units, the groom's elders usually seated in the sun or the rain, and the wife's elders in a protected, shady spot. For a brief moment the negotiations are heated, one party for example demanding 20 000 Rwandan francs (ca. 200 Canadian dollars) and the other agreeing to pay only 8 000. The wife's group will demonstrate disgrace and demand more, and if the others refuse the wife's group may refuse to provide sufficient beer or to render the girl's box of clothes to her after the wedding. The wife's group say they refuse to be shamed, and the groom's that they refuse to be had. After the elders speak and argue and gesticulate, there is finally a long moment of silence, nods, and the money is dis-creetly exchanged. People retire to the house where there are such generous quantities of beer that no one can help but be pleased by the afternoon's deliberations.

The young groom is present but, in fact, he is so inconspicuous as to hardly be noticed. His status seems to be defined in the context of three sorts of relations. First of all, his marriage is clearly a moment in the public evaluation of a lineage's esteem. This is the interest of the body of elders who take the responsibility of demonstrating their self esteem in the presence of another body of elders. The young man's identity is both encompassed by and defined, eventually, by the per-formance of his elders. Secondly, the young man's marriage and thus his eventual capacity to build a family depends upon the setting up of a durable relationship between his and his spouse's fathers. This is the point that Meillassoux (1960) so perceptively described—that the domination of elders rests on the collusion of the elders of different lineages in controlling access to the physical agents of reproduction,

251

women. Thirdly, the groom depends directly on his father, through whom the participation of his elders as well as the agreement with his in-laws is mediated, and from whom must come the material brideprice itself.

This analysis hopefully contributes to understanding the cause of brideprice inflation after the introduction of wage labour into traditional agrarian economies. Wage labour puts a material surplus and a potential independence from familial dependence in the hands of an aspiring groom. But the dependence created by not having access to such a surplus is only *one* of the sources of subordination and dependency of the groom articulated in the exchange of brideprice. Marriage involves first and foremost a social accord resolved through the mediation of elders, and only secondly through the material means. The access that potential grooms have these days to greater and greater material means is countered by an equally greater demand by elders for their required participation in the process. This is an inflation of sorts, which Rey (1971) says is attributable curiously to a surfeit of material means rather than a scarcity. Rey is really only playing with words here since even though there is indeed an increase of material wealth there is a consequent scarcity of the real value which is being sought: confirmation of a young man's membership in a set of social relations which must be actualized in order to acquire, eventually, the material means for starting a new household.

Marriage is only the first step in creating a labour force appropriate to the Kiga economy. In marriage, a household acquires a wife, the agent of reproduction, which is far from labour itself. For labour a household needs time to reproduce, and it is during this passage of time that another dimension of the dependence of emergent *amazu* becomes manifest. Time is always in rigid and unalterable supply, and the rigidity of this aspect of the conditions of production is reflected in the unalterability of the relations associated with these conditions.

A. V. Chayanov (1966), in demonstrating that agrarian peasant households make decisions about their economy that cannot be deduced from a market place mentality, showed clearly that the different phases in the growth of an agrarian household and its productivity and decisions about what and how much to produce were related to this natural growth. At a very early stage in its development a household experiences its lowest ebb of economic activity measured in area sown and livestock kept. It is also during these years that the household suffers the most in trying to make available resources correspond to demands for consumption. The same could be said for most agrarian societies of East Africa.

Let's recall that the only source of labour for noncapitalized households such as the Kiga household, is physical reproduction. Births are greatly celebrated. After the first births, however, the need for increased production increases since the consumption increases while the resources in labour and land remain the same. As long as children are unable to make a substantial productive effort, this situation will only get worse. The ideal is for a woman to bear children every other year, and if this occurs, in the twelfth year of marriage a household may have as many as six children, none of whom are over twelve years old. This seldom occurs because of the high infant mortality rate (12.5 percent die in the first year); nevertheless a household will be in existence fifteen or twenty years before the number of producing members equals the number of nonproducing members. (This of course cannot be precisely determined since the "age of productivity" cannot be precisely determined.) During this long period of a decade and a half or more, the labour deficiency must be met with outside assistance.

Traditionally this outside assistance comes in the form of a spontaneous labour force, a group of men or women getting together for another household's benefit. There are a number of these: the *urugunga,* a group of either men or women who work without a specific reward; the *ubudehe,* a goup which works explicitly for beer; the *urobohera,* a group of women only who come together to weave; the *umuganda,* a grouping especially formed to raise the pillars of a house. These labour offerings were not pure offerings, nor purely spontaneous, in that they were more like labour exchanges. Each localized settlement had a number of developed households with surplus labour, particularly men and women who were not yet married. These households at an advanced stage of development helped those at a less advanced stage, and these offerings were to be reciprocated. Participation in these labour exchanges depended on kin or close kin membership in a settlement. No one individual controlled and organized these exchanges; exemplary membership only restricted access to them. And exemplary membership was always contingent upon the bestowal of this status through recognition by one's immediate elder.

Social membership gave access to land, women and labour exchanges by which a young household survived the first lean years. A young man was attendant upon an elder to accord this membership. It is a mistake to see the perquisites of social membership granted solely on the basis of birth and blood, for one must not only have a social identity, but must also actualize and activate this identity. This could only be accomplished by tendering expressions of loyalty, allegiance, and respect. Hence a young man did not come into his own by having a paper route and saving his pennies. He did so by tending to the relationship with his father and by accepting and operating within the constraints set by this subordination to his elders.

In developing this argument we seem to be getting closer to a central fact of Kiga society as well as some anthropological generalizations which help arrive at this fact. Patriliny, as mentioned, does exist. This kinship principle defines membership in a number of descent groups, the most important of which is the household, the basic productive unit. But it does *not* account for the enormous diversity in size, function and composition of this basic productive unit. A helpful antidote to the insufficiency of kinship rules, in describing this diversity of forms the household assumes, has been in the past to concentrate more on the developmental cycle of domestic groups (Fortes, 1962). It is obvious that the Kiga *inzu* responds readily to this approach since in truth it has no rule governing size or composition, it has *only* a development. The principle of the developmental cycle helps to comprehend the pattern according to which *amazu* diversify, but it does *not*, in the end, answer why.

The why begins with the observation that material wealth in the form of land and labour are accessible only partially through patrilineal membership. As a man matures and begins to develop his own separate patrilineal community, his needs for land and labour become urgent. Land and labour (i.e., women, labour exchanges, and large families) are all in the different senses described above collective property. There comes a moment when a man must actualize this membership, and this can only be done through his father. It is this which creates dependence of younger men on their older kin. It is only through this dependence, its constraints and the progressive discharging of these constraints made possible by accepting and operating within the dependency, that a domestic group develops into full independence.

Having stressed the relations of dependence within corporate groups as opposed to the corporate nature of these groups, it is important now to return to the corporateness to clarify an aspect of these relations of dependency. The fact that relations of inequality occur within the confines of a single *inzu* has significant implications for the nature of these relations. The relations involve individuals who are not really full individuals with respect to each other. They are both members of a patrilineal group, and both have a stake in its viability, permanence and corporateness. This fact imposes limits on the degree to which these relations can be exploitative since the pattern of dependence would be destroyed should the dependent member be alienated from the source of authority. In other words, at some level, this dependence is reciprocal, and while the limits of exploitation are difficult to define, they are clearly there. It is what happens when these limits to exploitation disappear that is the subject of the next section.

THE KIGA UNDER CAPITALISM

The fact that being born and bearing children, two sides of birth, are preconditions for acquiring, respectively, land and labour in a traditional agrarian economy, says a lot about these factors of production. For it is not just birth, but birth *into* a social collective which is involved. Birth creates a *social relationship*, and it is through actualizing this social relationship that land may be acquired. Birth reproduces not just individuals, but *reproduces a relationship*, and it is this which recruits individuals into a labour force. It follows clearly that labour

254

and land cannot be separated from social relations in a traditional economy. Land does not belong to individuals and cannot be disposed of by individuals even though, as among the Kiga, a person may have full rights over land. A Kiga piece of territory is, in a sense, as much an element of a family as a person is, since its acquisition and use are embedded in a set of relations. Nor does one acquire labour or dispose of one's own labour as an individual. Labour is one of the means of production which properly speaking is at the disposal of the community. In principle, claims by the *inzu*, or by the larger community in the case of labour exchanges, take precedence over an individual's prerogative to dispose of labour, and this gives labour its social character.

Land and labour are inalienable. They cannot be separated, by sale or bargain, from the social unit of which they are a part. A particular feature of this is that acquiring additional wealth for a household does not entail diminishing the land of another household. Acquiring additional labour does not occur by depriving another household of labour. Wealth is not increased by taking from another, but rather by increasing the total amount of wealth. Hence, if one wants to increase one's land holdings, one clears new land from the forest, or reclaims it from the swamp. Likewise, the strategy to increase a particular labour force is to bring more children into the world.

But here is where monetization of land and labour has had its impact. It makes it possible to increase one's land holdings by decreasing the holdings of another, to increase one's wealth by decreasing the wealth of another. Money recognizes only indivdual wealth and fortune since it ignores the social restrictions on the acquisition or disposition of property, work and produced goods. In losing their social character, property and work are no longer tied to the welfare of the members of a community, but to the welfare of individuals; it is only when property and work are free from their social moorings and the restrictions that communities impose on their disposition, that a new means of accumulating wealth becomes possible. One can augment one's fortune by acquiring the property and work resources of another household or individual. Exploitation of nature becomes thereby exploitation of other people. This process is what seems largely to account for the change I noticed in northern Rwanda society between 1970 and 1977.

The traditional relations of inequality differentiated between developed or elder households and developing, or younger, households. The difference was based on age and kinship status, both of which are defined and constrained socially. Now the relations of inequality are between those who have successfully manipulated the new avenues for acquiring money, and those who have not. Not only is age no longer a criterion for differentiation but in many instances, particularly among the poorer households, the relations of dependency based traditionally on age are reversed.

According to a number of cases recorded, this change has occurred as young entrepreneurs have accumulated land by acquiring cash and using this cash to acquire the lands of needy households. The young entrepreneurs are frequently members of traditionally powerful and well-endowed families. Their original accumulation has come either by virtue of a good education which has led to a political career, giving them access to a variety of sources of wealth; or it has come simply through the ability to use their surplus land to grow and market nonsubsistence crops and, when this is profitable, to invest in trucks to transport their own and other crops to more lucrative markets. In either case the original accumulation is destined to purchase additional land.

This process of accumulation does not generally affect the social relations internal to the households of the entrepreneurs or of their elders. The most severe social impact is reserved both for the relations internal to the poorer households and the relations between those households with sufficient land and those with increasingly insufficient land. This latter distinction between those with sufficient and those with insufficient land holdings is one that has assumed great significance as land accumulation on the part of some households has resulted in land impoverishment for others. The land area presently available to this northern Rwandan population indicates how really intense are the feelings toward and the impact of accumulating and alienating land. Northern Rwanda is an exception in the African continent with regard to its extremely high population density: 324 persons per square kilometre. Each household is composed, on the average, of six persons, and must subsist with an average of about 1.7 hectares. This average, however, is virtually meaningless since what has happened in recent years is an increasing differentiation between a category of those who hold insufficient land and those who are acquiring an increasing surplus of land. The process cannot be precisely documented, but the fact that it is occurring is beyond question.

The present society is divided into very distinct economic classes which are best described in terms of the average land holdings of their respective households. The Kiga perceive two different classes of households, one called *abakungu* (well-to-do) and the other called *abakene* (poor). The *abakungu* households which comprise approximately thirty-five percent of the population, hold an average of 2.79 hectares per household and the *abakene,* constituting approximately sixty-five percent of the population, hold .96 hectares per household. It is frequently noted by agricultural assistants in the area that two hectares is a minimum land holding for the average household. Some additional facts regarding fallowing and employment of household members make even clearer the nature of this growing economic differentiation among classes of households.

Without any significant use of organic or chemical fertilizer, fallowing is an important part of the agricultural cycle. Those perceived as *abakungu* leave approximately seventy percent of their holdings fallow in the course of a year as compared with twenty-four percent for the *abakene.* Along with an insufficiency of land, the *abakene* manifest a comparative underemployment of family labour. Sixty percent of resident family members contribute to agricultural production among the *abakungu,* while only fifty percent do so among the *abakene.* [2]

In short, the figures show, as does one's experience, that Kiga society is divided into two distinct groups: one group of households whose land holdings are sufficiently large that the labour force at their disposal cannot fully exploit them; and another group of households which have a critical insufficiency of land to such a degree that it cannot absorb the labour resources that the household has at its disposal. The problem of the former, if such may be called a problem, is a surfeit of land which is underexploited, while the problem of the latter is an excess of labour which is underemployed. The *abakungu* may and frequently do hire labour from outside the household, while the *abakene* are forced into seeking such employment. The relationship between the richer and poorer households has become one of predator and preyed upon with regard to land, and employer and employee with regard to labour.

As mentioned, the impact on the internal structure of social relations for the *abakungu* households is slight; but it is quite severe for the *abakene.* The problem of land insufficiency poses itself critically to the poorer households as its young descendants think about their strategy for developing their own households. All are attendant upon their elders for bridewealth and an original land grant. In twenty percent of the households in one village studied, no land grant or inheritance of any form was received. Which is to say that a large number of young men must develop households without the assistance of their kin community. Without a material base over which a social collectivity exercises some control, the dependency of a growing household, maintained by control over social membership, disappears. Social membership is meaningless without its material basis. As a rule, the men of the young and poorer households must seek employment in order to acquire by rent the lands necessary to provide a subsistence for a family. There are virtually no opportunities for employment by non-Kiga aside from a tea plantation thirty miles distant, a mission, and the occasional European research team. The prospective worker must seek employment with the wealthier Kiga households which have accumulated lands which exceed their capacity to cultivate them. The traditional filial dependency has been replaced by salaried employment; and the internal relations of filial dependency which provided the cohesion of a household have been broken; the members of young developing households seek relations outside of their kin community, in particular, among the affluent households.

The monetization of land and labour has resulted in the increasingly unequal distribution of land. The effect has been to create two increasingly distinct socio-economic classes, the so-called rich, *abakungu,* and poor, *abakene.* The impact upon the internal relations of the *abakungu* households has been minimal, but the relations of dependency within the *abakene* households have been severed. The dependency of descendants within *abakene* households now is toward employers such as those in an *abakungu* household, distant plantations, and transient whites. The most visible impact of this process is upon old men. The old men of poorer households having lost the power they retained by virtue of controlling access to the means of production, have simultaneously lost the benefits of their sons' fealty, i.e., labour. This was their only source of security. In order to survive, these destitute elders typically sell what lands remain in their possession.[3] All elders suffer to some degree this loss of filial dependency, but those of the poorer households do so to an extreme degree. They talk about this constantly and, for them, the devil word is *amataranga*, money.

An important point about this process is that the *abakene* households exist no longer as families, but as individuals. The picture, then, that one gets of the present social organization is one of the domination of privileged *households* over underprivileged *individuals*. The traditional dependency imposed on a younger member of the household in his attempts to build an independent household no longer exist; and reciprocally, the constraints upon the limits to exploitation and domination imposed on the elders have likewise disappeared. Relations of dependency go between individuals of underprivileged families and privileged households. Given the unrestrained possibility for acquiring and disposing of land and labour in a money economy, the privileged households are guided by only one principle of action: that their survival and enrichment entails the impoverishment of others. The consequence is that the underprivileged become increasingly underprivileged, and in two senses: first, by virtue of their loss of access to the traditional means of production. But also by virtue of being divorced from the traditional social relations within a household, which may have controlled access to the means of production but which at the same time set limits to the degree of exploitation. The severance of these ties not only has deprived them of the means of production, but exposed them to a form of social inequality without security and without limits to insecurity.

NOTES

1. *Rey (1973) has argued that control over land does not form the basis for elders' domination, since it is not an object of exchange. His is an interesting analysis, but it does not take into consideration the fact that there is another social domain in which a body of people support an elder and collude with him in his domination of younger men. And this is within the clan itself. The elders within a lineage share land, just as elders within a group of reciprocating lineages share women. The only difference is that the elders within the same lineage share land within, and the elders who share women do so outside their own lineage. However for the younger men, this amounts to the same thing. Whether elders restrict access to women through collusion with the elders of other lineages who supply the women, or*

whether an elder restricts access to land through the support and collusion of other elders in the same lineage does not make a lot of difference. Control over land, therefore, like control over the agents of reproduction, women, results in relations of subordination by the younger members to the elder members of the kin group. Perhaps one of the stumbling blocks of Rey's and Meillassoux's analysis in this regard is that they have tended to see the relation between the younger and the elder as a relation between two individuals. The elder does not act as an individual, but acts as part of a group. He, in fact, symbolizes the group's authority. Hence, the assymetrical nature of the relationship comes out of the fact that while the youngers are always acting as individuals, since as youngers they are not yet exemplary members of a group, the elders are always acting as group members. This seems to call attention to a more general problem in Meillassoux and Rey. Like many other contemporary economic anthropologists, they have accepted in prin-ciple *Polanyi's observation that, in traditional economies, the economy is embed-ded in social relations, but they have not accepted it* in practice. *They insist on seeing a* material *basis of deprivation or domination to define relations of exploita-tion or super- and subordination. Their search for the material basis of social in-equality has led them to ignore the fact that social relations and the reproduction of social relations are as important a value as material value and, as such, as much the basis of social domination as material production and distribution.*

2. *These figures have been presented in a study entitled:* Etude socio-economique de la Prefecture de Byumba, Volume I, La Situation Existante, Rapport Provisoire. *Société d'Etudes Pour le Development Economique et Social, 84 Rue de Lille, 75007—Paris. Fevrier, 1975.*

3. *It should be noted that the Republic of Rwanda has recently forbidden the sale of land, cognizant, no doubt, of the social impact of land sales. This does not affect the thesis of this paper which is based on past events. It is, furthermore, unlikely to af-fect the future; I have heard that land sales are continuing, in spite of this regula-tion.*

BIBLIOGRAPHY

Arrighi, G. and Saul, J. 1973. Socialism and Economic Development in Tropical Africa, IN G. Arrighi and J. Saul, eds., *Essays on the Political Economys of Africa*. New York: Monthly Review Press.

Boserup, E. 1965. *The Conditions of Agricultural Growth. The Economics of Agrarian Change Under Population Pressure.* London: George Allen and Unwin.

Dupre, Georges and Rey, Pierre-Philippe 1973. Reflections on the Pertinence of a Theory of the History of Exchange. *Economy and Society.*

Edel, M.M. 1938. Property Among the Ciga in Uganda, *Africa*, Vol XI, No. 3.

Faris, J. 1975. Social Evolution, Population, and Production. S. Polgar, ed., *Population, Ecology and Social Evolution*, The Hague: Mouton.

Fortes, M. 1962. Introduction. J. Goody, ed., *The Developmental Cycle in Domestic Groups*, Cambridge University Press.

Macpherson, C.B. 1972. Reflections on the Sources of Development Theory. Manfred Stanley, ed., *Social Development*, London: Basic Books.

Marx, K. 1973. *Grundrisse*, Transl. M. Nicolaus, Harmondsworth, England: Penguin Books.

Meillassoux, C. 1960. Essai d'Interprétation du phénomène economique dans les sociétés tradionelles d'autosubsistance, *Cahiers d'Etudes Africaines*, 4, 38-67.

Meillassoux, C. 1967. Recherche d'un niveau de détermination dans la société cynégetique, *L'Homme et la Société*, 6, 95-106.

Rey, Pierre-Philippe 1971. *Colonialisme, Neo-colonialisme et Transition au Capitalisme*, Paris: François Maspero.

Seers, Dudley 1973. The Meaning of Development, IN Charles K. Wilber, ed., *The Political Economy of Development and Underdevelopment*. New York: Random House.

Smith, Philip E.L. 1976. *Food Production and Its Consequences.* Don Mills, Ontario: Cummings Publishing Company.

Société d'Etudes Pour le Developement Economique et Social 1975. *Etude socio-economique de la Prefecture de Byumba, Volume I, La Situation Existante, Rapport Provisoire*, Paris.

CHAPTER 13

SMALL-SCALE FARMERS IN
PERIPHERAL CAPITALISM

The Huasicanchinos of Central Peru

GAVIN A. SMITH
University of Toronto

ROBERT REDFIELD AND THE ANTHROPOLOGY OF PEASANTRIES

In 1956 Robert Redfield, one of the first social anthropologists to concentrate on the study of "peasantry," published a short book of eighty pages in which he addressed himself to an issue which had concerned him for much of his career and which has since continued to concern anthropologists interested in "peasants." The issue was as follows: many social and cultural anthropologists studying "small self-sufficient primitive communities" had been able to come away with a fairly comprehensive view of their social structure. But if we use the term *social structure* to mean, "the total system of persisting and important relationships that distinguish a community from others," then, insofar as "peasantries" are only *part cultures* (Kroeber, 1948:274-6) is it really possible to study a peasant social structure in the same way as previous anthropologists had studied more "self-sufficient communities"? Redfield poses the problem in this way:

> It may be that a peasant village, related as it is to people and institutions outside of it, is so incomplete a system that it cannot well be described as social structure. (1956:23-24)

If this is so, asks Redfield, then how are we to set about the problem of conceptualizing *the peasant community?*

Despite the fact that Redfield was never very happy with the answers he could find to this queston, many anthropologists, whether consciously or not, continue to conceptualize the peasant community as Redfield had done throughout his career: as a schizophrenic system containing two relatively autonomous parts, the one based in the

261

past and founded on "tradition," the other confronting the realities of the present in the form of an incipient "urbanism."

It is a shame that few indeed have taken up his proposal that

> *Perhaps we anthropologists shall come to describe not the peasant village but the larger and more nearly complete system: the feudal society, the complex region, the nation state (1956:23-24).*

This is especially unfortunate because, despite the tremendous influence of Redfield's early work on the direction of peasant studies throughout English-speaking anthropology, there can be few intellectual figures who have subjected their entire work to such thorough self-criticism as did Redfield at the end of his career.

The task which I have set myself in this article is to give the reader a feeling for the kind of life experienced by the "peasants" with whom I lived for two years in Peru.[1] But a writer, however descriptive his or her style, always has some point s/he is trying to make, some particular axe to grind, and it is this which acts to organize the way in which s/he presents the data to the reader. So, while providing you with some data on the *huasicanchinos* of central Peru, I shall address myself to the question of whether or not *the peasant community* is a useful point of departure for the study of a group of small farmers living out their lives within the framework of the nation state.

In my view, the majority of ethnographies of "peasant communities" assume that there exist, side by side in the community, a "folk" social/cultural system and a national social/cultural system, each with its own, relatively autonomous, elements and relationships. These systems are supposed to interact with each other while in some way maintaining their own integrity, and the anthropologist's job becomes one of extricating the one "system" from the other and then examining the separate rationality of each.

In fact this dualistic view of the "peasant community" is a logical extension of the way anthropologists have gone about their fieldwork. Coming from a tradition where a small-scale society of "primitives" could supposedly be studied as a complete and easily bounded "system," those who turned attention to "peasants" had to recognize the constant presence of the nation state. The solution was to keep the idea of "community" and then place it within, alongside, beneath or against the other idea of "nation state." Although those who chose to see this interface along specifically cultural lines are most easily identifiable (Redfield and Foster), the image underlies the work of those interested in economics (Dalton, 1971; Firth, 1952) and the exercise of power (Wolf, 1966).

The problem with the image is that it allows the fieldworker to imagine the peasant community as something *sui generis* and *then* to seek out the outside influences deriving from its location in a nation state. In other words, a kind of "as if" community is set up on the laboratory bench, and then the current from the national society is turned on to see what happens. The step toward the view that the "peasant community" itself is so composed of the two systems: "folk" and "urban" (indeed in some cases: that the peasant himself has a split personality) is a small one. *Quod erat demonstrandum.*

Thus, if it were so, that the community/nation dichotomy and the duality of systems within the community, were part of the peasant's world view, it would be by a most convenient coincidence that they fit also into the world view anthropologists themselves acquired in the socialization they received from those of their forefathers who had been studying "tribal" peoples.

The problem with beginning with a hypothetical pristine folk community and *then* looking at the effects of the nation on the "folk system" is that it obviates making an enquiry into the way in which the historical development of the "folk" system relates to the *overall* structural conditions of peasants' existence over time. It must be remembered that, contrary to what most anthropologists would like to believe, nine times out of ten "peasant communities" have been interacting with larger dominant systems not just for decades, nor just for generations, but for centuries. So to look at the "folk" system "as if" it were autonomous is not unlike writing about working class culture "as if" there were no capitalists.

When this is recognized, the sheer size of the intellectual deceit, which looks at the "folk" system as if it were in some way "prior to" the larger system, becomes manifest. The fact is that in these historical circumstances it is not just the market relations of the "folk" system, nor even just all its "economic" relations, that are moulded by the larger structure: rather the entire darkened corner of "folk" values and institutions from top to bottom is shot through by the history of interaction with a larger, dominant system. It is therefore the idiosyncracies of that history in each case study which anthropologists must attempt to reconstruct, not some ideal microsystem that in most cases existed so long ago as to be merely a question for metaphysics.

HUASICANCHA IN PERU, 1970

Peru is divided into three geographical regions each of which runs from north to south. On the west coast there is a desert strip broken occasionally by rivers, along which some of Peru's largest urban settlements have grown up. Moving inland, one encounters the broad belt of the Andes which is made up of fertile mountain valleys, the high plateau grazing lands and unusable steep and craggy hillsides and mountain tops. Finally, by far the largest area of Peru comprises the jungle which constitutes the entire eastern side of the country.

Broadly speaking, Peru's development has started with the most westerly of these regions and moved towards the east: the coast continues to be the most urbanized and industrialized part of the country, while the jungle still represents the Peruvian frontier.

It is in the high sierras of the Andes that the majority of Peru's peasants live, and it is this area which concerns me here.

In the inter-montane valleys arable crops are grown, often combined with some livestock rearing especially for dairy produce near to large market towns. Large farms employing labourers (*fundos*) are interspersed here with small-scale farms varying in size from rich peasants who use some extrafamily labour during the year, to *minifundistas*-farmers whose plots are too small to provide the needs of the family.

On the higher ground settlement is far more dispersed. Depending upon the altitude (ranging from 11 500 to 16 000 feet above sea level) farmers either raise livestock together with some arable production, or depend entirely on livestock. Dominating this area has been the large-scale livestock or mixed-producton farm (*hacienda*). In some cases these haciendas have set up settlements for their own employees so that there are communities of *colonos* or *peones* with small subsistence plots located on the hacienda's land. In other cases, the hacienda draws its labour from the "indigenous communities" which border on the hacienda land. These communities may have some of their own land and hence at least theoretically a certain amount of independence. But this land is usually insufficient so that community members (*comuneros*) have to seek some income outside their own farms.

Finally, in the most remote parts of the Andes, some communities continue to exist without any direct contact with haciendas. Usually such communities have access to land which is located at a wide range of altitudes. These vertical differences provide different ecological niches for the farmers and allow them to grow a wide complementarity of agricultural produce from maize and *coca* (a leaf which is chewed for mildly narcotic effects) to wheat and root crops, to llama grazing at the highest usable lands.

Roughly then, the variety of settlements in the Peruvian Andes is as follows:

- A market and commercial town usually also acting as an administrative centre and located in an inter-montane valley. (A)
- Surrounding this town, there are likely to be a number of smaller towns which act as residences for many of the farming population as well as secondary market centres. (B)
- In the valley itself will be found large-scale fundos (C) and smaller farms varying in size and degree of commercial production. (D)
- In the higher areas are large-scale haciendas (E), sometimes together with their own communities of *peones* (E$_1$) and surrounded by older peasant communities. (F)
- Finally there remain some communities not directly connected with haciendas at all. (G)

This is shown schematically on page 265.

The community of Huasicancha (*Huasi* = house; *cancha* = corral or field) where I lived would represent a settlement of the type I have re-

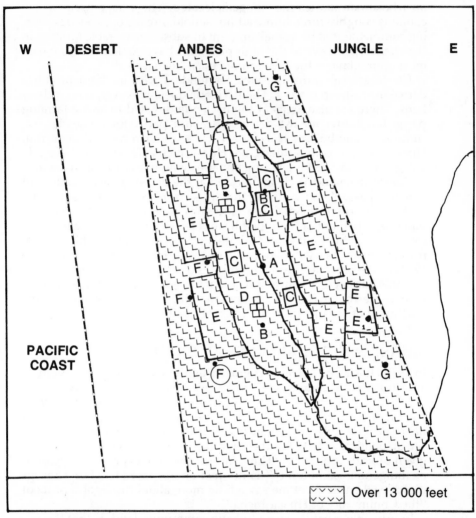

Figure 4. Forms of Settlement in the Peruvian Andes

    A. Major market town
    B. Secondary market towns
    C. Large agricultural holdings
    D. Small agricultural holdings
    E. Large livestock holdings
    E_1. Employees' village
    F. & G. 'Peasant communities'

ferred to here as (F), that is to say: it is an old indigenous community with some of its own land, but with close ties to a large-scale hacienda on whose boundaries the village is located. The village itself, which contains roughly three hundred households, relies on livestock rearing complemented by a small amount of subsistence arable farming in the sheltered valleys of the high plateau. I have circled the (F) which most approximates the position of Huasicancha.

The large-scale farm is called Hacienda Tucle. Its main products derive from sheep rearing. The hacienda does, however, have a dairy herd. There are also areas of the hacienda devoted to arable farming partly for fodder for the dairy cattle, and partly for domestic consumption. The bulk of Hacienda Tucle's labour force is drawn from Huasicancha or communities like Huasicancha. There is no hacienda village of *peones*; just a few functionaries who live at the farm itself.

Huasicancha and Tucle are located at the end of a very rough road which is passable only during the dry season, when it takes roughly six hours to reach the major local town, Huancayo. This town exemplifies a settlement of the type I have referred to as (A). In fact Huancayo is a thriving market and administrative centre of roughly 200 000 people which has witnessed a very rapid rate of growth from the 1930s to the present. We shall return to this later; suffice it to say here that this has been largely as a result of the operations of the large U.S. owned Cerro de Pasco Corporation which runs a refinery to the northwest of Huancayo in the town of La Oroya.

HUASICANCHA AS A LEGAL ENTITY

In 1930 Huasicancha was recognized by the Peruvian government as an "indigenous community" (*comunidad indigena*). This gave legitimacy to its identity as what Eric Wolf has called "a closed corporate community" (1955; 1957). As such, Huasicancha was recognized as having community lands which were not saleable to outsiders and a set of political offices for the running of the community were also given official recognition. Thus, in this case, the expression "peasant or indigenous community" is not just an abstract idea, but a recognized legal entity.[2] Let me say a little more about the legal aspects of "the Community of Huasicancha."

In principle what it means to have community land, is that the village as a whole owned Huasicancha's land rather than any individual villagers. This communally-held land was divided into three categories: community arable land; household arable plots; and community pasture. The community arable land was farmed by teams made up of household heads and its produce was used for replenishing the village coffers, whose expenses included road repairing, school building, certain *fiesta* costs and so on. In principle the household arable plots were simply communal land distributed to the households by the community authorities. Supposedly a couple, setting up house, would petition the authorities for some land and, by the same token, a household dissolved by the death of its head would return its plot to the community. In practice, however, by the beginning of this century, this was not taking place. Plots were regarded as the property of the household and were divided among its members as the household gradually dissolved during the life-cycle. There was therefore no more arable land to be distributed by the authorities (since there was none being returned to them), but household ownership was not quite complete, because the original principle of ownership by the community made it impossible for *comuneros* to rent or sell land to outsiders without the permission of the community.

The community pasture was grazed by the flocks belonging to the different families in the village. (There were some animals which belonged to the community as a whole, but these were treated essentially as the animals of one more family. They were cared for by those poorer members of the community who were given the job by the authorities.) The hut and corral (*estancia*) of the shepherd is alotted to him by the village authorities. Although this did not give households any clearly defined area of pasture they nevertheless did manage to maintain control over certain areas of the communal pasture.

In fact, despite the government's recognition of these aspects of Huasicancha as a "community," the reality of social relations within the village cannot be understood without reference to the huasicanchinos' position within a larger socio-economic system than the "indigenous community."

The presence of a large farm held by non-huasicanchinos goes back for centuries, but it was from the middle of the last century that the haciendas of the area began to expand. Tucle itself was slower than many of the others in this respect and this was partly due to Huasicancha's history of resistance to hacienda growth. But by the turn of the century Tucle did begin to expand on to Huasicancha's pasture. In some cases this was simply done by taking over communal pasture; in others a vague rental agreement was made which eventually became *de facto* possession on the part of the hacienda.

The legal dimensions of Huasicancha as a "community," i.e. communally held land, were effected by the predatory hacienda. Loss of pasture had the effect of driving pastoralists increasingly into subsistence agriculture on very poor plots of land on the hillsides. The community pasture itself became an insignificant proportion of grazing land, as comuneros turned either to employment on the hacienda in return for access to pasture (see below) or resorted to trespassing. What little community pasture there was, tended to be turned into arable if possible, and as the pressure for household plots grew, much of this in turn became divided up into individual fields.

HUASICANCHA AS A SYSTEM OF PRODUCTION

What I want to do now is take a look at the way in which production was organized in Huasicancha and relate it to the position of the *huasicanchinos* within the overall development of Peruvian capitalism.

The primary unit of production in Huasicancha was the household.

This usually contained a man and woman and their unmarried children. It often also contained the widowed parent of one of the couple. In other cases the youngest son remained in the household of his parents after marriage, gradually taking over the responsibilities of household head as his father (or widowed mother) got older. I shall refer to this as the *family economic unit*. To all intents and purposes it is far more useful to regard the household head as the person managing the property of the household on the part of its members, rather than assuming him to be the owner. Although the household head had much authority and was the legal representative of the household to the community, the success of his operation was dependent upon the cooperation of all its members, each of whom had something to gain from that success.

It is useful to begin looking at the family economic unit by suggesting that it was operated so as to provide for the perceived needs of all its members (not just those of the head) and that it began by trying to do this through using the resources and personnel of which it was made up. In other words, its first option was to seek labour for its land from within the household or, conversely, where land was insufficient to seek land to fulfill the needs of its members.

Where, seasonally or continually, the amount of labour available within the household was insufficient for the amount of land which the household possessed, labour was sought from other households in the village. Such a situation drove the family economic unit into relationships with others within the village.

In the opposite circumstance, where the amount of land was insufficient either to absorb the labour of the household (however intensively worked upon) or to produce their consumption needs, livelihood had to be gained by offering out the household's labour. As the total amount of land available to *huasicanchinos* diminished in the wake of hacienda expansion, so the opportunity of finding such work within the community diminished. So where land was scarce relative to the composition of the household in any particular year, the predicament drove the family economic unit into outside relationships not only within the village but also beyond it.

The two important elements in the question facing the manager of a family economic unit—labour (personnel) and land—have *qualitative* as well as quantitiative aspects. On the one hand, household *composition* is not the same as household *size*. If we think of the family economic unit as being made up of "labour units" and "consumption units" then there will be some who produce more than they consume, especially the mature youths, and some who do the opposite, especially the old, the sick, and the very young. Thus, since *composition* affects the equation even if *size* remains the same, the relationship between land and labour in a family economic unit is at least partially a function of the life cycle of the family (Chayanov, 1966, reviewed by Kerblay, 1971 and Shanin, 1972).

On the other hand, the ability of the land both effectively to absorb productive labour and also to produce goods more intensively for consumption, is a function of technology. Technology is made up of two parts: technique—know-how or skill on the part of the farmer—and the degree of sophistication of the inputs themselves. Put simply, the land part of the equation need not be a fixed quotient because, by using additional farming skills and applying fertilizers and irrigation, a manager can increase the ability of a fixed amount of arable land both to absorb more productive labour *and* thus produce more for the consumption of the (household) labourers. Nevertheless, both dimensions of technology invoke an investment by the family economic unit (i.e., the cost of acquiring either skills or factors of production). In peasant communities the wherewithall thus needed is both scarce and unevenly distributed. I shall show the significance of this in a moment.

But before doing this I must say something about the institutions through which extrahousehold labour was mobilized in Huasicancha. These fall into two groups: relations between the family economic unit and the community as a whole, and relations between one family economic unit and another.

It must be obvious to even the most antisocial household head that the operation of his farm is dependent upon the community as a whole, by which I mean more than just a few immediate neighbours and kin. Not only does he need the material advantages offered by the community such as its roads, sheep-dips and schools, but he also needs its entire language of social discourse—its provision of codes of social behaviour and so on. In Huasicancha this was the expression of a specific property connection: it was the community as a whole which owned the land.

Effectively then, the dictates of social behaviour within the community, which included the maintenance of a certain respectability through social performance (serving on committees, taking on *cargos* in the *fiestas,* and otherwise maintaining the honour of one's household) as well as the provision of labour on the community's arable land, acted as a form of extrahousehold payment. One representative of the family—the household head—held usufruct rights to land by virtue of being a *comunero* (a member of the community); he was a comunero partly by virtue of certain ascriptive "givens" (such as being born in Huasicancha) and partly by performing the duties of a *comunero.* Work in the *faena* (community teamwork) was one aspect of this, but it was only the most easily accountable form of social performance required in return for the benefits of community membership.

If we look for a moment at this community from the vantage point of the hacienda, we find that, by the nature of the kind of farming it was engaged in, as well as its remoteness from such public works as are usually offered by the state, the hacienda needed teams of workers for the performance of certain jobs. The crops had to be harvested, the sheep had to be dipped, the roads had to be repaired. Just across the hill in the "indigenous community" there existed the perfect institution already set up for such work: the *faena*. It was simply a matter of redirecting its labour toward the hacienda, rather than allowing it to remain captive in the community.

The hacienda did this, at least partly, by a piece of ideological sleight-of-hand: it became an ersatz community; the hacienda administrator set himself up as an ersatz community patriarch—from *padron* to *padrino* (from patron to godfather). The community *faenas* had music, drink and coca, and a meal was often served too. Initially, Hacienda Tucle did likewise. In addition, cigarettes were provided and, instead of the community dish of soup, a couple of sheep were roasted in a *paccha manca*. Furthermore, acting in the spirit of "community," the hacendado offered the villagers the services of the hacienda truck occasionally and the administrator gave the village authorities advice on farming and dealings with the government.

Of course this kind of disguising of labour-extraction through the use of an idiom of reciprocity was fraught with tensions. As time went by, Tucle began to find the music, and especially the drink, were counterproductive and therefore dropped them. By the 1950s the community was actually being offered cash to provide the hacienda with a *faena*. The point is, however, that this ideological "performance" on the part of the hacienda was by far the cheapest way of securing labour and would have remained so, just as long as the bluff of reciprocity could be maintained. The effect of this was not to dissolve the "traditional" institution of the *faena* (in fact for a time it appears even to have given it an appearance of renewed vigour) but to transform it. So the form of the institution of *faena* was not just a function of the operation of the households which made up the "community" of Huasicancha, but was also a function of the operation of the neighbouring hacienda.

The second form of extrahousehold labour was that between one family economic unit and another. A number of different institutions existed in Huasicancha for the expression of these relationships:

Uyay: This was simply the reciprocal exchange of equivalent amounts of labour between two or more households. I help you plough your field today; you help me shear my sheep next Thursday. In fact it was and is rarely measured in quite so calculating a way as this. Nevertheless, the principle of equivalence made it difficult for *uyay* to be used as a means for permanently readjusting the labour of the household: it may give you extra labour today, but only at the price of an equal deficiency tomorrow.

Minka: *Minka* offers more flexibility in this respect. Here the loan of labour is repaid in the form of produce. This means that I can use the labour of four neighbours and pay them in goods, without having to lose four days labour of my own. While *uyay* does not in fact have the effect of modifying the given composition of the household over the long run, *minka* can do precisely this.

Huaccha: In the days when Huasicancha was almost entirely a pastoral community, for a person to reach maturity without inheriting any livestock was the equivalent of being a person without any patrimony, indeed without any parents: an orphan. And that is in fact what the word means literally: orphan. It refers to the institution by which a person without livestock gives his labour to a household with animals but deficient in labour to care for them. In return, the labourer receives a certain number of the newborn calves or lambs for his services. In this way he is able—in theory at least—to accumulate some animals of his own.

Michipa: Here the shepherd cares for the animals of another household in return for some produce from their arable land.

Trueque: So far we have always talked about exchanges where labour at one point or another enters the balance. *Trueque* however, refers to the exchange of one good for another representing roughly the same equivalent in labour input. It occurs in Huasicancha most frequently between housholds which occupy different ecological levels in the Andes. Since in Huasicancha most households have access to at least some arable as well as pastoral produce, the most usual partners are those occupying the extreme opposite level of the ecology i.e., in the high jungle where maize and coca are produced. Close relationships have been built up between households in Huasicancha and others in the jungle. Trips are made to the jungle each year and equivalences between items are kept reasonably fixed and, according to the villagers, are not meant to vary with the prevailing market prices.

Each one of these institutions for the mobilization of resources between households has undergone transformations as a result of the structural position of differing family economic units among the huasicanchinos. I mean by this that the position which different family economic units have occupied in the development of Peruvian capitalism has influenced the way in which they have utilized the existing extrahousehold institutions of the community and thereby transformed them.

THE PERUVIAN ECONOMY

To understand this, we must turn to the national socio-economic structure for a moment. From the end of World War I to the end of World War II, the Peruvian economy was dominated by the export of three commodities each of which had implications for social relations in Huasicancha. These were wool, copper, and cotton.

Wool   During World War I wool prices on the world market doubled. This gave a great stimulus to the highland livestock haciendas. In particular, Tucle was rented from its owner by an amibitious busi-

nessman from the provincial captial of Huancayo: one Manuel Pielago. He was far more aggressive than his predeccessor in making
Tucle a profitable venture and, in the 1920s this was to be done
largely through the extensive use of pasture—at Huasicancha's expense.

Copper   Meanwhile, from the 1920s onwards, the Cerro de Pasco
Corporation operated its smelting plant at La Oroya, which lay to the
northwest of Huancayo, on the pass which led to Lima. The effect of
this was to stimulate the economy of Huancayo, which became a pro-
visioning centre for the mines and smelter. Pielago was also
thoroughly enmeshed in this economy: he was involved in a flax mill,
an egg business, and a leather and shoe factory, as well as his operations as an *hacendado*. So developments on Hacienda Tucle and, by
extension, in Huasicancha, were related to the fortunes of all these
various operations.

The growth of Huancayo had another effect, however. At a time
when land was becoming increasingly scarce for *huasicanchinos,* the
expansion of the Huancayo economy opened up the possibility of
jobs for migrants from Huasicancha. But this migration was quite selective. A few villagers were slightly better placed to take advantage
of the situation. A few older men, for example, held senior positions
on the neighbouring haciendas and managed to use their contacts
with the hacendado to get their sons into schools in Huancayo. These
boys later acquired skills such as electrician, male nurse, cobbler, etc.
A few other men with experience as mule traders began to get involved in small-time trade in Huancayo itself. And others simply
worked occasionally in casual jobs in Huancayo.

Cotton   Nevertheless the most frequent source of nonfarm income
for *huasicanchinos* during the 1920s and 1930s was not located in
Huancayo, but on the coast directly to the west of the village. Cotton
on the large coastal plantations demanded seasonal labour. A few
huasicanchinos had provided such labour from before the beginning of
the century. But with the expansion of Tucle in the 1920s this stream
became a river: virtually every man in the village had the experience
of working on the plantations at some time or other in his career.

Construction   During the 1930s too, the national government devoted considerable funds to construction projects throughout central
Peru, especially on roads. Many villagers went from the plantations
into these kinds of jobs. But by 1938 the bottom dropped out of the
cotton market and jobs on the plantations dried up, as too did many
government contracts. A few *huasicanchinos* drifted up the coast to
Lima, where they set up Huasicancha's first small colony of migrants.
These however were the poorest of jobs and virtually all of these first
Lima-migrants returned to the village penniless.

I should mention one final source of extrafarm income, although it
occurred after this period. From the 1950s to the mid 60s a small but
rich local mine offered a few *huasicanchinos* permanent jobs and a few
more seasonal work.

To review the prevailing economic situation during this time then: central Peru was dominated by large-scale capitalism—cotton and copper production—and the medium-sized capitalism exemplified here by the various operations of Manuel Pielago. One of the ways in which the *huasicanchinos* were involved in this economic structure took the form of the sale of their labour: to the plantations, to the mines, to the commercial operations in Huancayo or to the hacienda itself.

From 1950 onwards a different trend made itself felt. As the Peruvian bourgeoisie captured the reins of the state from the previous rentier class, so a policy of import substitution was put into effect to encourage the growth of national industry (i.e. discouraging the import of certain secondary manufactured goods and encouraging Peruvians to develop substitutes for them). This had the effect of concentrating the Peruvian economy increasingly on metropolitan Lima. As operators like Pielago began to relocate their interests from Huancayo to Lima, two new economic factors came to bear on the *huasicanchinos*. On the one hand, the vacuum left by the withdrawl of medium and large operations in Huancayo stimulated small-scale operators in that town (Roberts, 1974). On the other hand, the growth in the Lima economy converted the early trickle of migration to that city in the early 1940s to a full flow by the 1960s.

With these changing forces in mind, it is now possible to reexamine Huasicancha's family economic units and the various institutions for extrahousehold relationships which I have so far described.

TRANSFORMATIONS

I have already discussed the way the presence of the hacienda transformed the institution of the *faena*. This involved the way in which the hacienda used communal labour. But how did the hacienda use the labour of individual households? Households were most frequently used as shepherds for the hacienda sheep and cattle. The way in which shepherds were employed by the hacienda was essentially a transformation of existing extrahousehold economic relations within the village. As the hacienda began to expand onto the community pasture, what changed was that, where before there had been a few poor huasicanchinos who had access to community pasture but had no sheep, there were now increasing numbers of huasicanchinos with sheep but no pasture. The relationship of *huaccha* which I described before was therefore reversed. Before, a person who cared for the sheep of another was paid by being given some of those sheep for himself or herself. Now a household undertook to care for the hacienda animals in return for being allowed to "enter" the hacienda pasture with a certain number of animals of their own. In effect then, this shepherd rented pasture from the hacienda for a designated number of his own animals, and paid his rent in the form of labour as a shepherd for the hacienda. The animals he brought onto the hacienda land with him were referred to as the *huacchas*.

273

Because the task of shepherding for the hacienda demanded the full time labour of all the household (except a few days at harvest time), these households could not cultivate their own small arable plots in the village. (In many cases people became shepherds because they had so little of this arable land anyway.) In such circumstances they had to acquire subsistence crops somehow. In other cases, they had small plots but could not work them. In either case, the solution was found through the use of *michipa*. Hacienda shepherds (illegally) took in some of the animals of other villagers amongst their own *huacchas* and these were of course, referred to as *michipas*. In return, the shepherd received arable produce from the other villager, either from that villager's plot, or through the labour that villager did on the plot of the absent shepherd.

What we are witnessing here is the same process of transformation that I discussed earlier for the *faena*, but this time for the extrahousehold institutions of *huaccha* and *michipa*.

I have already pointed out in the case of the *faena* that in the end the rationale of capital accumulation on the part of the hacienda was in contradiction to the rationale of reciprocity in the community. The same is true for the institution of *huaccha*. From the 1940s onwards, a simple piece of capitalist economics became increasingly clear to the administrator of Hacienda Tucle. His sheep were of infinitely better quality than those of the shepherds; they produced more wool while eating no more pasture. The only way of increasing the hacienda flock would be to find more pasture. But there was no more good community pasture left to be taken by the hacienda. What there was available however was the pasture presently being consumed by the poorly bred *huaccha* sheep of the shepherds (and their illegal *michipas* as well). Why not, therefore, replace the *huacchas* with purebred sheep, and pay the shepherds a wage instead? Insofar as the hacienda sheep would produce more wool than those they replaced, the wage of the shepherds could be calculated at a little *more* than the produce of their *huacchas* while still being a little *less* than the amount gained from the better sheep which replaced them. Surely everybody would be happy?

There was in fact strong resistance to the hacienda's attempts to introduce wages. And since many villagers were involved indirectly in the hacienda's form of *huaccha* through the institution of *michipa*, the resistance included hacienda employees and "independent" peasants alike. In 1947-48 the community occupied part of the hacienda's land and managed to acquire thereby a small piece of the pasture it had previously lost. Thenceforth labour relations with Tucle declined throughout the fifties. From 1964 to 1970 an extensive campaign to recover all of Huasicancha's pasture was implemented by shepherds, villagers and migrants alike, culminating in the total destruction of Hacienda Tucle. To understand why this occurred, we must look at the changing shape of Peruvian capitalism and show how it affected small-scale production among the *huasicanchinos*.

The attempt to introduce wages which I have just described, occurred in the late 1940s and early 1950s. This was just the time when small-scale capitalist operations were beginning to develop in Huancayo and when the larger scale operations of Pielago were facing a crisis. Migrants from Huasicancha were involved in this expansion of small-scale capitalism in Huancayo (and later in Lima).

It is beyond the scope of this paper to describe the process of economic differentiation which took place in Huasicancha during this period. I simply want to point out that the different ways in which family economic units sought extrafarm income had the effect of placing each of them in its own particular position vis-à-vis the dominant economy of Peru. And this in turn led to great heterogeneity in the form of each family economic unit. If, for example, we look at one such unit, we find that in 1950, when the household head had five unproductive children to feed, he sought work on Tucle. Two years later he was dismissed for illicitly expanding his *huaccha* flock beyond the terms of his contract. He had to sell most of the flock to cover the family needs over the next year. He then found some seasonal work at the local mine. With some of this money he sent his eldest son to Huancayo to apprentice as a builder. A second son was sent to lodge with an uncle in Lima three years later and the family head now returned to full time farming in Huasicancha.

In another example over the same period, the household head left his wife and three children in Huasicancha and went to stay with the brother of his next-door neighbour who had migrated to Lima. This man taught him the trade of ambulant fruit-selling. Although the household head returned to Huasicancha twice for what he thought would be permanent stays, he ended up setting up a small hut in an inner city slum in Lima. He eventually moved his household there and they make the bulk of their living out of fruit-selling, although they continue the practice of returning to Huasicancha for a month, at least once a year.

It would be nice to go into the details of each case at this point, showing precisely the threads which relate each of these small-scale enterprises to the dominant capitalist economy of Peru. Although there is no space for quite such a detailed exercise (see Smith, 1978), I hope you will agree that for each of the units the threads are sufficiently different that the actual *form* of each unit will vary according to how it is tied into the overall economy; the variations in the development of, say fruit sales in Lima versus mining in the Central Andes, would clearly have direct implications for the developing shape of these two units as productive enterprises.

If we confine ourselves to the conception

peasant community/modern society

then our examples become two migrant peasants who, as a result of their differing fortunes in the modern society, change or do not change, become rich or poor, are achievement-oriented or not, etc. Moreover, since "peasants" themselves are taken to be a commonality we must seek out character traits, or decisive incidents, etc., to explain why some stayed while others migrated, and so on.

If, however, we concentrate attention, not on the community or on the modern(izing) society, but on the historical relationship between various forms of dominant socio-economic structures and subordinated small-scale primary producers, it is possible to suggest that there has been a long-standing heterogeneity among the latter which existed precisely because of the specific nature of this interconnection over time. And it is this qualitative heterogeneity which is the clue to the various processes of geographical and social mobility which affect "peasants" today and did so as well in the past.

Moreover, as a function of their differing form, we would expect to find the different units of production making different uses of the institutions at their disposal for the activating of extrahousehold ties. In this sense the *community* cannot be regarded as a sociological phenomenon to be studied, but only as an emergent feature of the livelihood activities of small-scale producers faced with an extractive dominant socio-economic structure. As that structure changes and as the form of small-scale production changes, so the whole bundle "traditional institutions" which constitute the *community* will change too.

Thus, in the case of the examples which I have mentioned, the institutions of *uyak*, *minka* and *trueque* continued to be used, but now within the context of a different form of involvement in the national economy. In the case of some production units, for example, the method of complementing household production at one ecological niche by the exchange of produce with a household at another level *(trueque)* was now extended to exchanges between households in different *niches* or sectors of the Peruvian economy in which the huasicanchinos' households were located. If, for example, migration from one household was initiated in an attempt to reduce the dependency of the household on the produce of the farm, later, as the life cycle progressed, the farm once more required additional labour, while the migrant was reluctant to give up his position in the city. Under these conditions, that part of the family economic unit left in the village began to activate *minkas* with others who had excess labour. Under such circumstances the reciprocal equivalent of the labour given was not always goods from the harvest, but particular services offered to the villagers by the migrants. Lodgings were provided for children at school; seasonal jobs were secured, or other "city resources" were exchanged for labour on the village plot.

If, as time went by, the migrant chose to move his entire household to the city, then in many cases this kind of reciprocal exchange continued between the village-household and the city-household. Most migrants from Huasicancha—as do peasant migrants throughout the world—survive on extremely insecure forms of livelihood. The advantage of these reciprocal arrangements to them was that it kept the farm going: always there in case disaster should force a permanent return to the village, and meanwhile producing minimal subsistence items for the household. The effect on those who remain in the village is that the more some people migrate, the more others are forced into subsistence farming on their behalf.

The result of this process over the years is that an intricate system of ties has been built up among *huasicanchinos* in such a way that the economy of one family economic unit is complemented by its close ties with others of quite different character. Moreover, insofar as these ties now form a kind of network whose node lies in the village, but whose strands spread out to the provincial capital, the mining centre, and various shanty towns and slums in Lima, the *community* of huasicanchinos means something quite different from, say thirty years ago, while nevertheless retaining for all that, something of its earlier resonances.

Indeed there are, among the *huasicanchinos*, family economic units whose members continue to hark back to older and "truer" versions of *community*. Significantly however these are the village farmers who have managed to accumulate somewhat more resources and are beginning to run their enterprises with the specific purpose of accumulation; they are less concerned with investing in institutions for staving off disaster, than in seeking out the best vehicles for good fortune. They too continue to use the institutions of the community, but in doing so they transofrm them in quite different ways. A number of farmers within the village now use the system of *minka* in order to exploit the labour of a number of labourers on a more or less permanent basis. Because these farmers have managed to gain access to the most productive land and to have bred the best sheep, and in some cases even to have invested in some advanced tools, they are able to offer the same exchange of goods-to-labour as prevails in the rest of the village, while still keeping back for themselves the surplus generated by the application of labour to their better means of production. In short, they are able to accumulate profits by continuing to use the idiom of an institution, the *minka*, which was originally part of a quite incompatible relation of production to the one they now undertake.

It is not altogether surprising then, to find these *huasicanchinos* constantly subscribing to an ideological system which serves at the same time to provide them with labour "priced" at the village level, and also to disguise the inevitable tendency of their own economic rationale, which involves the expansion of their operations and their use of increasing amounts of the village resources to do so: specifically land.

If we can successfully comprehend *both* the workings and resilience of these community institutions *and* the social forces deriving from the locating of differing kinds of small-scale producers in the national economy, we may be able to put together a sociological analysis which would explain why the attempts on the part of Hacienda Tucle to introduce wage labour in lieu of *huaccha* sparked off strong resistance from the huasicanchinos and how, from 1964 to 1970, they succeeded in conducting a campaign of attrition against the hacienda which led to its eventual destruction.

There is no space to do this here, (see Smith, 1977), but my own view is that this particular instance of what would be called "peasant rebellion" cannot be understood if we choose to assume there to be a homogeneous group called "the peasant community," which, Janus-like, faces back one way toward its "traditional past" and another way toward its integration into "modern society." What we do have to do is examine, for each specific case that interests us, the relationship between increasingly dominant social relations of production which give a certain form to the group of people we are studying, and the existing ideological apparatus which they have available to confront those changes. In this paper I have provided the raw material for such an analysis. It might be worthwhile exercise for you, the reader, to speculate on how the "peasant rebellion" of 1964 to 1970 was an expression of the processes I have here described.

CONCLUSION

At the beginning of this article I suggested that it was a misfortune for anthropology that those who followed on from Robert Redfield, borrowed his interest in peasant *culture*, and chose to concentrate the study of peasantry on the peculiar nature of their "world view," rather than taking up the challenge he was never able to respond to himself: to describe not just the peasant village but rather to concentrate attention on the forces at work in the larger system of which it is part.

In my view, one of the things which makes this task especially challenging and interesting for anthropologists is that it is plainly just as distorting to confine one's analysis solely to the uncovering of the social relations of production in the total system of which the "peasants" are a part, as it is to confine oneself to the study of peasant "culture." I use the word "plainly" because I think that those members of the Left who, like the developmentalists of the 1950s and 1960s, choose to underestimate the significance and value of the ideology of the rural poor, are guilty of the same ethnocentric arrogance as the establishment they rightly choose to scorn.

The task of anthropology then will be not a vicarious fascination with the cultural survival of a disappearing world but rather to conduct a holistic inquiry into the relationship between structure and ideology which will provide insights for the praxis of an increasingly large part of the world—the rural poor, whom, for one reason or another, we choose to call "peasants."

NOTES

1. *Fieldwork was undertaken in Peru in 1972 and 1973, and supported by the Canada Council and the Ministry of Education of the Government of Quebec, to whom I would like to express my gratitude.*
2. *The term "indigenous community" was replaced by the term "peasant community"* (comunidad campesina) *in 1970.*

BIBLIOGRAPHY

Chayanov, A.V. 1966. *The theory of peasant economy*. Illinois: The American Economic Association.

Dalton, George 1971. *Economic anthropology and development*. New York City: Basic Books.

Firth, Raymond 1952. *Elements of social organization*. London: C. A. Watts & Co. Ltd.

Foster, George 1960-61. Interpersonal relations in peasant society. *Human Organization*, 19.

Kerblay, B. 1971 in *Peasants and peasant societies* (ed.) Teodor Shanin. Harmondsworth, Penguin Books.

Redfield, Robert 1956. *Peasant society and culture*. Chicago: The University of Chicago Press.

Roberts, Bryan 1974. The social history of a provincial town: Huancayo, 1890-1972. *Social and economic change in modern Peru* (eds.) R. Miller, C. T. Smith & J. Fisher. Liverpool: Centre for Latin American Studies, The University of Liverpool. Monograph Series No. 6.

Shanin, Teodor 1972. *The awkward class*. Oxford: Clarendon Press.

Smith, Gavin A. 1977. Some factors contributing to peasant land invasions: the case of Huasicancha. *Peasant cooperation and development in Peru*. (eds.) N. Long & B. Roberts. Austin: University of Texas Press.

Smith, Gavin A. 1978. Internal migration and the farm of the small-scale enterprise. *Regional development and small-scale enterprise in Central Peru*. N. Long and B. Roberts (Eds.) Austin: University of Texas Press (Forthcoming)

Wolf, Eric 1955. Types of Latin American peasantry. *American Anthropologist*. 57.

Wolf, Eric 1957. Closed corporate peasant communities in Mesoamerica and Central Java. *Southwestern Journal of Anthropology*. 13.

Wolf, Eric 1966. *Peasants*. Englewoods Cliffs: Prentice-Hall.

CHAPTER 14

DOMESTIC COMMODITY PRODUCTION

Small Farmers In Alberta

MAX J. HEDLEY
University of Windsor

INTRODUCTION

As in the domestic mode of production described by Sahlins (1972), and in peasant production, agriculture in Canada is practised by households who own their equipment and land and provide all or the bulk of farm labour. Production is influenced by such factors as drought, hail, disease in livestock and crops, and is affected by variations in the domestic cycle. When faced with adversity, farm households are likely to reduce personal consumption, intensify subsistence production, sell their labour, and in fact do anything they can to reduce risk and retain ownership of land and equipment. Moreover, like peasant producers, they exist as part of a system of relationships which transcend the local community and incorporate them into the structure of society as a whole. It is this relationship and its effects on production that are of concern in this paper, for they lie at the root of the differences in size, capital intensity, and organization of production generally, which are held to differentiate empirically commercial farm producers from peasantry.

The general aim of this paper is to examine the position of household producers within the structure of Canadian society and to determine the way in which their position structures the transformation of rural productive organization and the rural world. The empirical focus of this study is based on a sixteen-month stay (1971-1972) in a rural area in central Alberta which I will refer to as Rossan. Despite the particular focus, I believe that the findings are directly relevant to the so-called small farm problem, rural impoverishment, and the crisis of the family farm.

The Rossan area is within the northwestern extension of the Aspen

Parkland belt which reaches north and west from southern Manitoba and southeast Saskatchewan. With considerable variations in topography, stoniness, soil types and the location of sloughs, the land rating ranges from very good to marginal for agricultural production. Rossan was settled between 1895 and 1916 primarily by pioneer families from Austria and Ontario, though a trickle of new farm households continued to enter the area until the late 1940s. Most of the forty households that I came to know were headed by the second and third generation descendants of pioneer families. The area is characterized by mixed farming in which individual enterprises specialize in the production of such commodities as milk, beef, hogs, wheat, barley, oats, and various combinations of them. Currently, the area is being subjected to a growing influx of people from the city which had led to an escalation of land prices and the loss of land from production.

Like many of the social issues in Canadian society, such as poverty, permanent unemployment, and the Indian problem, the problems of the family farm are largely hidden from our awareness. Within the perspective of our dominant ideology, we readily assume that the "problem" is a simple expression of the inadequacies of the people in question. For example, the poor are seen as having a culture of poverty which binds them happily to their condition; Indian people are seen as retaining a traditional culture which keeps them outside society and in a condition of permanent underdevelopment. In the same way, family farms suffering from low income are seen to be operated by people who are backward, apathetic or simply irrationally tied to outmoded methods of farming by virtue of their commitment to traditional rural values. Such views reflect a conservative ideology in which there is a tendency to "blame" the victim while neglecting to look at the broader structural causes underlying their particular plight. It is the counterpart to the view that upward mobility is open to all who try and are capable in what is thought to be a classless society.

The difficulties confronting the family farm first became apparent to me through a series of casual encounters with my neighbours in Rossan. In particular, I remember spending a Sunday afternoon with a part-time farmer, a person selling his labour as well as farming, who ended a conversation on farming by dejectedly saying that he had worked hard all his life but knew that he was getting nowhere and that he didn't know what to do next. The plight of this individual was reiterated many times by Rossan farmers, for over half of them were in a similar position. That is, they were working in factories and a variety of other occupations as unskilled labourers while seeking to turn their farms into viable concerns which would support them and their families without the need for a supplementary income. It became clear to me very quickly that the problems these farmers were facing as farmers could not be explained away by simply assuming that their approach to farming was traditional and backward. In fact, for the most part, these part-time farmers were well aware of many of the changes occurring in agricultural production and would have been happy to apply them to their own operation. In fact, when resources allowed, these farmers did take advantage of the technological changes available to them. However, despite doing this, despite getting larger, producing more and working with more sophisticated equipment, they were still unable to make the transition to full-time farmers. It is in light of this that the comment made above ("I do not know what to do next") has to be interpreted. Farmers do know what to do next, but many recognize that the next step, if they have the resources to take it, is very likely to leave them exactly where they were before that step was taken.

The basic difficulties faced by Rossan farmers are not unique, though the precise manifestation of them will vary in different localities and regions. In other words, it is suggested here that the problems faced by Rossan farmers reflect the crisis of the family farm in Canadian society. It is a crisis generated within a particular mode of production by virtue of its involvement in a society dominated by capitalist production. Therefore, to understand the crisis experienced by the family farm and the related questions of rural poverty, depopulation, etc., it is necessary to examine production in the context of the political economy as a whole. Through this, it will be possible to arrive at an understanding of the processes leading to, and imposing direction on, the transformation of the rural world. It is towards developing an understanding of this transformation that our attention can now be turned.

DOMESTIC COMMODITY PRODUCTION

In this section, it is necessary to introduce the basic concepts which will allow us to understand the forces shaping the evolution of rural productive organization and rural communities. What is needed is a way of conceptualizing the problem which allows us to isolate the key characteristics of production in agriculture while recognizing the significance of the involvement of farm producers in the structure of society as a whole. The immediate problem is to penetrate the empirical complexity that characterizes farm production. That is, how can we talk about the changes in the rural world when there is so much diversity to begin with? In Rossan, for example, there were grain, hog, beef, and dairy producers and various combinations of these. They had different production problems and were involved in a variety of relationships with other sectors of the economy. Moreover, they differed in such things as family size, amount of land and equipment used in production, quality of land, income and aspirations.

The most common way of ordering this diversity is to classify households on the basis of the income that is generated through farming. It is on this basis that such distinctions as small and large, viable and nonviable, commercial and noncommercial, progressive and backward, successful and unsuccessful farms are made. These distinctions are not without significance because they do point to a differentiation that has occurred in agricultural production. Moreover, they are used as a basis for organizing government policy, and therefore are imbued with practical significance. However, it is suggested here that these distinctions do not help us understand the processes underlying the transformation of the rural world. Rather, they contribute to our confusion because they tend to deceive us into thinking that groupings such as commercial and noncommercial farms are fundamentally different and have to be understood in isolation from each other. They also reinforce the tendency to believe that noncommercial farms simply are a result of a backward approach to farming, an attitudinal problem, and prevent us from recognizing the extent to which their position is a product of their very involvement in society.

To arrive at an adequate understanding of the transformation of the rural world it is important to find a starting point that does not employ these simple dichotomies. In my own research, I have found it necessary to use as a starting point the concept of productive relations. These are defined in terms of ownership, operation and control of the equipment and materials entering into the productive process. This needs to be distinguished from the organization or forces of production which refers to the *combination* of labour, equipment, and materials involved in the actual process of production. Together, productive relations and the organization of production are referred to as a mode of production, though it is recognized that this general concept may be taken to include juridico-political and ideological superstructures (Terray 1972:97).

The mode of production relevant to an understanding of agricultural production in Canada is what can be termed domestic commodity production. The defining feature of this is a relation of production in which ownership, operation, and control of the means of production are in the hands of "independent" households. This relationship is epitomized in the family farm where, as the name implies, ownership of land, equipment, and buildings rests with the actual farm family. However, as we will see, this independence is being undermined by rising levels of indebtedness. It is also important to note that the labour involved in production is derived from members of the farm family—husband, wife and children—though in practice a small portion of casual hired labour may be used. This reliance on family labour clearly distinguishes the family farm from capitalist enterprises in which there is a separation of ownership of the means of production from those actually involved in the productive process.

Defined in this way, it is apparent that the overwhelming majority of farm producers, whether commercial or noncommercial, large or small, operate within the framework of the domestic commodity mode of production. Moreover, in Rossan and in western Canada generally, this mode of production has been continuous over time. In fact, its development in the West following Confederation was deliberately engineered through Homestead policies. Put simply, these policies were directed toward the establishment of an economy of small household producers who owned their own land and equipment and provided all or the bulk of the labour required on the farm. Of course, this does not mean that there have been no changes in farm production since the settlement period. To suggest this would be to ignore such changes as massive mechanization, increase in farm size, and specialization of farm activities. Instead, it is suggested here that these are best seen as changes in the organization or forces of production which have occurred within the framework of domestic commodity relations of production. To anticipate a point that will be developed subsequently, it can be suggested that these changes have been and remain vital to the continuous survival of the mode of production.

To understand the latter point and the dynamics of the situation generally, it is necessary to recognize the way in which domestic production is articulated with other modes of production in Canadian society. Farm producers are part of a societal division of labour in that at least part of their output is destined for exchange rather than immediate consumption on the farm. Households are dependent on exchange for the acquisition of materials for immediate consumption and for producer goods that enter into the productive process. For example, when Rossan was first settled during the late nineteenth and early twentieth centuries, mechanization had already been underway in agriculture for over half a century. Draught animals, the major source of power, were used to operate a variety of mechanical implements, such as binders and mowers, which were not manufactured on the farm. These implements could only be obtained through the production of a commodity for exchange because they were not manufactured on the farm. In other words, while the satisfaction of household needs is the purpose of production, these needs, at least in part, are met indirectly through the production of commodities for exchange. Consequently, the continued existence of households as commodity producers depends on the outcome of the process of exchange.

Through the process of exchange, domestic producers unavoidably enter into relationships with other sectors of the economy. In this respect it is vital to recognize that the Canadian economy is dominated by the capitalist mode of production. The agribusiness organizations related directly to farm production, such as the implement and meat packing industries, are typical of the rest of the economy in that they primarily consist of large monopolistic corporations which are oriented towards continuous expansion and the pursuit of profit. It may be added that continuous growth and the pursuit of profit are necessary for the survival of these organizations within the competitive structure of a capitalist economic environment. The farm household, as producers of raw materials such as grain and beef, and consumers of producer goods such as tractors and combines, are a means to the profit-oriented ends of these companies. This is also true in reverse, for farm households have to be able to dispose of farm products and purchase machinery and other items for use on the farm. However, lacking economic power, domestic producers are in fact in a surbordinate position which allows agribusiness producers to transfer to themselves a portion of the surplus created by farm producers (Mitchell 1975; Warnock 1971).

As a consequence of their position, domestic producers, despite market fluctuations, are confronted with a situation in which there is a constant tendency for production costs to rise faster than prices. Consequently, income exhibits a persistent tendency to fall. Therefore, in order to meet their needs, households are faced with the necessity of making changes in the organization of production which will allow them to compensate for this decline. Individual households, as we shall see, respond to this income pressure in a variety of ways which may or may not allow them to remain in farming for the duration of the lifetime of the prime operators. However, it is only through continuous increases in output and productivity, resulting from the use of better equipment and increasing the scale of production, that the domestic unit will be able to survive as a mode of production. In turn, investment in new and more expensive machinery and in larger amounts of land heightens dependence in that it involves increasing levels of indebtedness and reliance on financial capital. Remaining alternatives are to develop specializations that do not necessitate land expansion or to transfer operations to another area.

THE TRANSFORMATION OF RURAL PRODUCTIVE ORGANIZATION

INTRODUCTION

As I mentioned earlier, it is important to recognize that the conditions of survival of particular households can be distinguished from the conditions of survival and long-run reproduction of the mode of production. Faced with a permanent tendency for income to decline, individual households are unavoidably obliged to respond in one way or another. At the very least, they must "tighten their belts" and learn to live with a reduced income. Exactly how particular households respond to this pressure will depend on the resources at their disposal, the options available, and their aspirations. On the other hand, it can be said that the only changes in the organization of production that offer a potential for continuous reproduction of the mode of production are those which allow output to increase continuously and costs per unit of output to fall. To be specific, the only way this can be achieved is through the incessant application of changes in the technology of production to the productive process. The results of this pressure, resulting from production in a capitalist society, are

clearly seen in the developing mechanization of agriculture. However, what is seldom realized is that patterns of failure and underdevelopment are equally products of process. It is to these questions
that we can now turn our attention.

MECHANIZATION: AN IMPERATIVE

It is true that changes in the amount of labour and land employed in
production at a given level of technology may offer some possibility
of increasing output. However, it must be remembered that we are
discussing a mode of production which relies primarily on family labour. Therefore, unlike a capitalist enterprise in which it may be possible to hire more labour, domestic production has to rely on the labour available within the family. This means that any expansion of
output through increments in the amount of labour use on the farm is
limited because it is dependent on changes in family size. This does
not mean that farmers do not hire extra labour but that in doing this
they exhibit a tendency towards the development of capitalist relations of production in agriculture.

An increase in the amount of land used by particular households
also holds some possibility of increasing output at a given level of
technology, though this is eventually subject to diminishing returns
unless changes are made in the technology of production. That is, it
can be said that the application of changes in technology to the productive process is a structural imperative for the continuous survival of
the domestic commodity mode of production under contemporary
conditions of production in capitalist society. It is this imperative that
lies behind the transformation of production that has occurred in
rural Canada. It acts, as we shall see, as a selective principle, for it is
only adaptations involving an increase in output and productivity
that offer some possibility for households to persist and to transfer resources (land, equipment, buildings) to a new generation of producers.

The selective effects of this imperative are evidenced by the growing concentration and capitalization of agricultural production. In
Rossan, such changes are readily seen in the changes in productive
organization which have led to the replacement of the diversified,
labour-intensive homestead by the modern capital-intensive and specialized family farm. Farming during the settlement period in Rossan
(approximately 1895-1916) was labour intensive. The major source of
power was the horse, though where farmers lacked the funds to purchase one they used oxen. Consequently, all field operations—
ploughing, harrowing, seeding, swathing, binding, stooking, haul-
ing—were done with horsedrawn implements. It was only in
threshing that an alternative source of power, steam, was in use,
though there were instances of settlers using a cradle and flail. In
other areas vital to the survival of the homestead, production was car-

ried out by hand. Buildings were rudimentary, consisting of materials that could be secured locally from the environment. For instance, dugout shacks consisted of a pit three to four feet in depth with wall of sod two to three feet high. Beams placed over the wall were covered in hay and topped by a layer of sod. Other sod-roof shacks were built of wood and chinked with mud. Fuel for heating and cooking was wood, which, like the building material, had to be cut by handaxe and hauled by horse or oxen.

The limited technology is reflected in some of the equipment brought by early settlers. For instance, a pioneer family arriving from Dresden, Ontario in 1893 had amongst their possessions: two mares and a stallion, neck yokes, reaches for wagons or sleighs, plough and harrow, and axe handles (Ardrossan 1972:165). There were also included a cow, sheep, hens, and a rooster, as well as household necessities. Another homesteader arriving in the area in 1918, who had been farming on poor soil near Leduc, brought horses and horse-drawn implements which included a sleigh, binder, plough, harrow, seed drill, and discs.

Horses were the basic source of power for field operations and transport. A consequence of this was that land had to be reserved for pasture and, when the supply of hay was reduced because of settlement, land had to be put aside for the production of greenfeed. More significant is the limitation on the productivity of labour imposed by horsedrawn implements. The physical limitation of the capacity of draft animals set limits to what could be accomplished by the labour of one man. Horses were only able to work for eleven hours, with a rest and feeding time of one-and-a-half hours at midday. This involved more labour time as the horses had to be harnessed in the morning and unharnessed, rubbed down and fed in the evening. During the eleven hours spent in the field it was possible, under good conditions, to cultivate five or six acres. The cultivation of 160 acres, therefore, would take a single producer approximately twenty-six days. Obviously, the cultivation of a large acreage would require a considerable input of labour. In fact, the largest producer in Rossan during the 1930s required a casual labour force of between five to seven farm workers during the summer months to cultivate 600 acres of land (a further 300 acres were kept fallow).

A major innovation in farm production was the development of alternative sources of power, particularly the tractor. The first tractor, a 16-30 Oil Pull Rumley, arrived in the area in 1920 and was used for breaking sod. Horsedrawn implements remained prominent through the 1920s and 1930s, and it was not until the late 1940s that work horses were completely replaced by tractors. Initially, tractor size was small, averaging 40-50 HP in the early 1950s, but by 1974 these had largely been replaced by tractors of 90-130 HP. This has been accompanied by changes in the size of implements.

The result of the adoption of tractors and their steady increase in size has been a tremendous saving in the amount of labour entering into production. It was mentioned above that one man operating a team of five or six horses for eleven hours per day was able to cultivate five or six acres. This contrasts with the 50-60 HP tractors of the early 1950s which, drawing an eight foot implement, were able to cultivate five to seven acres per hour. In other words, an hour's work on a tractor was equivalent to eleven hours spent in the field with horse-drawn implements. In eleven hours it became possible to cultivate between 55-77 acres instead of five. The trend toward larger tractors has led to further reduction in labour time as 100 HP tractors are able to cultivate approximately ten to fifteen acres per hour. An added "advantage" of tractors is that they do not have to be rested at noon but can run as long as an operator is available. Hence, it is common for farmers to work continuously for sixteen to eighteen hours during critical periods in spring. With a large 100 HP tractor this makes it possible to cultivate 160-270 acres per day. The result of this increase in productivity and in the length of the working day is that a single farmer can handle larger amounts of land than could his predecessor using horsedrawn machinery.

While the resources vary considerably, it is clear that even the smallest and seemingly most traditional households have sought to modernize and have, therefore, contributed to the general trend towards capital-intensive farming. For example, one of the smallest producers in Rossan was operating with antiquated equipment, some of which was originally designed to be drawn by horses. The resultant inefficiencies were clearly apparent for the machinery was subject to frequent breakdown which often contributed to a failure to perform field operations effectively. The reason for this was not a lack of desire to modernize but a long history of low income which had prevented the household from breaking free of the practices that undermined its own position. The necessity of modernizing was readily apparent to household members and was in fact reflected in continuous attempts to improve their operation by purchasing second-hand equipment. However, low income meant that the quality of used equipment available was extremely poor. Recent correspondence with this family (1977) indicated that after twenty-five years of trying, the attempt had failed; that household had withdrawn from agricultural production and had become dependent on wage labour as a source of income. In Rossan it is clear that both large and small producers have sought to improve the productivity and output of their operations. Larger producers have been better able to respond to cost-price pressures, but frequently express the belief that they are no further ahead and the fear that a point will be reached, especially as they get older and are less able to maintain the same intensity of work, when they too will be unable to remain in production. In other words, the pressures on households to modernize the means of production continuously are insatiable. Advances begin to be undermined from the moment they are made.

SUBSISTENCE ACTIVITIES AND REDUCED PERSONAL CONSUMPTION

The transformation of rural productive organization is not only manifest in the application of an ever newer technology to the productive process. The pressure to change cannot be resisted, but not every producer is in a position to farm in the most "rational" and productive manner. In fact, the very process of change necessitates failure, for without the expansion and effective mechanization of the more successful farmers, the investment capital necessary for investment would not become available. In this sense, success and failure are dialectically intertwined.

A common response of domestic producers to a situation of cash shortage and declining income is for the household to reduce its expenditure on food, clothing, housing, and entertainment. This may well be associated with an intensification of subsistence activities, thereby allowing commodities for exchange to be produced below the cost of production. With respect to the latter point, it is worth pointing out that the cost of production for Rossan farmers does not include any calculation of the cost of family labour or any notion of a "normal" return on capital.

Over the past three decades the level of subsistence activities in Rossan has changed considerably. Until the early 1950s, households were involved in a mixed, labour intensive pattern of farming. Typically, production on 160 acres of land involved the cultivation of wheat, oats, and barley. In addition, two to eight cows were kept to provide a source of milk to make butter and cream which, with chicken eggs, were sold or bartered locally. The skimmed milk left over from these operations was used with grain to feed hogs. In addition, there was a considerable degree of self-sufficiency in terms of personal consumption. Consumption of meat (which was canned or smoked for storing), eggs, milk, and butter was complemented by the cultivation of gardens and the collection of wild berries such as saskatoon and raspberries. Vegetables and berries were stored or canned for the winter, thereby, in conjunction with the other products, allowing households to be practically self-sufficient in the domestic consumption of food. Bread was made and baked from wheat grown on the farm and milled in Fort Saskatchewan. Other domestic activities such as quilting, making soap, clothing, pillows, as well as cutting wood for fuel made for a high degree of self-sufficiency. It is not surprising that farmers remembering those days claim that all a family needed was a quarter section of land to meet their needs.

Despite this self-sufficiency, it has to be emphasized that the reduction of personal consumption and the development of subsistence activities are not enough to guarantee the survival of the mode of production. Individual households may be able to survive for the duration of the lifetime of the primary operators. However, unless these activities facilitate saving and subsequent productivity-raising investment then they will not be adequate to compensate for the tendency of income to decline. That is, born out of capital shortage, they are an inadequate long-term response to the tendency for incomes to decline. Moreover, the increasing capital input required in agricultural production actually undermines the viability of this response by reducing the significance of the savings that can be achieved this way. In other words, the savings made available by such activities represents an ever diminishing proportion of the capital requirements of agricultural production.

The limitations of the pattern-diversified farming and subsistence activities as a response to capital shortage are reflected in the process of specialization that has occurred in Rossan. Since the early 1950s there has been a gradual specialization of existing farms, while those entering production in subsequent years have tended to be more specialized from the outset. The area as a whole remains characterized by mixed farming, because the specialization of particular enterprises has taken a variety of forms such as dairying, hog production, cow-calf enterprises and grain and beef production. The loss of functions by particular enterprises has been slow and not without some reluctance on the part of those involved. While the diversified pattern did entail a considerable amount of labour, it did offer some protection from fluctuating commodity prices and the uneven effect of such hazards as late frosts, lack of moisture, and diseases in livestock. That is, if income in one area was lost there was always the possibility that this would be compensated for by rising income in other areas. However, producers have had little choice but to accept these changes, for the overall trend is moulded in a capitalist society by the necessity of fully employing and reaping the cost advantages of expensive equipment and the greater efficiency of large-scale specialized production.

REDUCED PRODUCTIVE CONSUMPTION: A DEVELOPMENTAL PHENOMENON

The reduction of cash expenditure on consumer goods and the intensification of subsistence patterns are not the only means by which households struggle for their survival. A further set of activities used to reduce expenditure and compensate for income shortage included delaying the renewal or replacement of machinery, buildings, fences, and diminishing the application of fertilizers, herbicides and feed supplements, etc. Such practices, which are often interpreted as symptoms of backwardness, reflect a continuous dynamic response on the part of individual households to the imperatives of production in a capitalist society.

Machinery entering into the productive process is subject to wear and tear and eventually has to be replaced. Because of the high costs of replacing equipment, Rossan households seek to replace it on a cyclical basis. Ideally, a new tractor is bought one year, while in subsequent years new implements are purchased to replace old ones.

Moreover, this cyclical replacement of machinery allows households slowly to increase the size of their equipment. Thus, over a five- or six-year cycle, tractors and implements are gradually replaced with newer and larger models, thereby compensating for wear and tear and, at the same time, responding to cost-price pressures by increasing the productivity of labour.

However, the five- or six-year replacement cycle is an ideal that few Rossan households are able to live up to. Instead, lack of free capital often means that replacement of equipment has to be put off for a year or more. Even the largest Rossan households, with product incomes in excess of $40 000, delayed the replacement of equipment, though this usually allowed them to focus investment in the area of greatest pay-off. For example, a dairy producer might delay the replacement of machinery used to cultivate the land in favour of focusing investment in milking and milk storage equipment.

With smaller households, the problem is more crucial, for failure to replace equipment is likely to occur in all areas of the operation because of the chronic income shortage they experience. Moreover, if the income shortage continues, then the process becomes cumulative and a point is eventually reached where everything has to be renewed and the capital requirements of this renewal are hopelessly beyond the reach of the household. Their position is unenviable, for apart from their equipment being subject to frequent breakdown, they are faced with the impossibility of responding to declining income by improving productivity. It is households in this position who most frequently find themselves in the position of having to reduce their expenditure on elements of variable capital such as fertilizer, feed supplements, and herbicides. In doing this they enter a vicious circle because this practice leads to an immediate and predictable reduction in income and the necessity of reducing expenditure even further in subsequent years. The example of a small farm with a product income of less than $5 000 illustrates the problem. This household, consisting of two adults and four children, gained its main source of income from the sale of grain though it also marketed some beef. It operated with antiquated equipment which was subject to frequent breakdown. More important, it was in a position where low income in conjunction with the rising consumption needs of a growing family made it imperative to reduce cash expenditure even further so that farming operations could continue. This was done by reducing expenditure on fertilizer, the only option left, with the result that yields and therefore income declined even further. This farmer knew the consequences of abandoning the use of fertilizer but was compelled to take this step because no other option was available. The action was not the consequence of traditional attitudes towards farming, but reflected a chronic cash shortage which could not be overcome in any other way. For this household there seems to be no escape from the dilemmas posed by cash shortage other than actions which make their position even worse.

The final outcome of these practices is the eventual abandonment of farming, though households may well continue their operations with little or no returns on capital and labour as long as the remaining costs do not exceed income and equipment does not break down completely. The hope is always that an upward movement in fluctuating prices may make the year's work worthwhile. Reduction in productive consumption is clearly a step towards eventual loss of ownership of the means of production unless the trend can be reversed. For while the practice may allow individual households to remain in production, a point is eventually reached where further reductions are impossible and production must be abandoned. In this sense, "backwardness" and failure are generated by the very processes that are leading to the transformation of rural productive organization. They are in fact symptoms of the growing inability of domestic commodity production in agriculture to survive under present conditions of production in capitalistic society.

THE WORK-FARM PATTERN: A STEP TOWARDS THE LOSS OF OWNERSHIP OF PRODUCTIVE RESOURCES

Reductions in personal and productive consumption are often not enough to allow households to maintain themselves in farming. Under these circumstances an alternative to abandoning farming is to obtain full or casual employment while continuing to operate the farm. This is a common and growing phenomenon in Canadian agriculture.

In the Rossan area twenty-two of the forty farm households studied had at least one adult member of the family working on a full-time basis. This was usually the husband; only two wives had full-time jobs off the farm. Lacking formal education beyond grade ten, Rossan farmers find that the work available to them is limited to unskilled or semi-skilled labour. The particular reasons for entering the urban labour market vary considerably, though they are all related to low farm income. The example of a specialized grain farmer will serve to illustrate the point. This farmer started farming in the early 1950s. Because he was unable to rent 160 acres of land and lacked the equipment to cultivate it, he entered into a work-sharing arrangement with his father. In this, he simply exchanged his labour for the use of his father's machinery. Income from farming was insufficient to provide enough to support a family which included two children or to facilitate expansion of the farm. He started selling his labour on a full-time basis in 1954 at a nearby chemical fertilizer plant. However, the work-farm pattern was never enough to allow the household to accumulate enough capital to establish a full-time farming operation. When his father retired (1964) he was able to realize his ambition to become a full-time farmer, and to give up a job which offered no security, possibilities for advancement or interest. Apart from the advantages of controlling the work process, he was able to spend more time with his family and to participate more fully in community activities because he no longer had to regulate his life according to the changing demands of an industrial production schedule. Most important: it also meant that farming could be carried out more effectively. Four years after he had started full-time farming, barley prices fell below the cost of production with the result that the household could only continue farming if consumption levels were reduced drastically. Because he and his wife were not prepared to do this in the face of the rising consumption needs of their children, he once again returned to part-time farming. He now expects to continue with this pattern until his children have left home and the family's consumption needs have dropped.

This example is unique in the particular combination of events that enter into it. Yet it epitomizes the dilemmas of many Rossan and Canadian farm households. It reflects the proverbial desire of farmers to retain ownership of land and capital, their control over the organization of the work process, and the freedom to dispose of their resources and skills in any way that they see fit. This is not simply a reflection of an outmoded rural ideology because it is based on a real experience of the monotony, lack of security, and control associated with the jobs open to them, and their own experience of the advantages of the farming alternative. In addition, the example indicates that the work-farm option may be largely ineffectual. In pioneer days when land was free and production labour intensive, the casual sale of labour plus hard work was often enough to establish a farm household. Though, to avoid romanticizing the period, it is well to remember that between 1905 and 1930 approximately forty percent of homestead entries failed to obtain ownership of their land (Wood 1951:739). However, the rising capital costs of farming make it increasingly difficult if not impossible to start farming in this way today. This point is supported by the experience of Rossan farmers, for none of those who have entered a work-farm pattern during the last two decades have succeeded in becoming full-time farmers. This leads us to suspect that the adoption of this pattern is simply a step towards the ultimate loss of ownership of the means of production and the transformation of domestic producers into wage labourers.

INCREASING VULNERABILITY: THE SOCIAL DIMENSIONS OF DISABILITY

It will be remembered that the domestic commodity mode of production was defined in terms of ownership, operation and control of the tools, equipment and materials entering into the productive process being in the hands of the actual producing households. Consequently, households own the product of their labour and, therefore, have to bear the result of production or nonproduction. The former point has to be qualified with the recognition that increased indebtedness to banks, supply companies, and government agencies means that part of what is produced belongs to the owners of the capital involved. However, the latter point remains true because interest and debts have to be paid regardless of variations in income. In fact, rather than sharing the risks involved in farming with the producer, lending institutions increase the farmers' vulnerability by raising the level of fixed costs that have to be paid out of the year's work. Failure to repay these debts would mean a loss of ownership of the means of production by the household and the transformation of producers into wage labourers.

As we have seen, it is because of the private ownership of productive resources that the effects of declining income have to be absorbed by individual households. However, it is not only the price of commodities that affect farm income. It is important to recognize that illness, drought, hail, diseases in crops and livestock, and other natural hazards may reduce the value of the year's work or render it worthless. Of course, agriculture is affected by such hazards in any society. Nevertheless, it must be stressed that the way these setbacks are experienced is determined by the nature of the mode of production. To make this point clear we might compare the effects of the disability of workers in a capitalist enterprise with the effects of disabilities on domestic producers. In a capitalist enterprise, output is not threatened because the worker's labour power can always be replaced when the necessity arises. That is, labour power is simply one commodity among many which enter into the productive process, and, like other commodities, can be purchased or discarded when the need arises. The situation of fluorspar miners dying of industrial-related diseases in Newfoundland provides a tragic example of the expendability of labour. The position of the company is summed up in the words of one of the miners who is suffering from silicosis, "Well, I paid you; I never have to keep you no more" (Layton 1975:26). For the individual labourer, as in the case of the fluorspar miners, illness may have disastrous consequences, though for production in a capitalist enterprise it is little more than a passing inconvenience.

In domestic production, disability resulting from accident or illness may critically affect production because households only have access to the limited labour supplied by family members and to the voluntary help that neighbours and relatives might be able to extend. It is for this reason that domestic producers in Rossan organize themselves to extend help to households under such circumstances. For example, a recent incident involved a farmer who developed a hernia and was unable to operate farm machinery. Because his only children, two daughters, had left home and his wife was unable to drive the equipment, there was no labour available within the family to perform the year's field operations. Facilitated by a prolonged fall, relatives and neighbours were able to do all the field work in their spare time, thereby allowing the household to maintain its income and to retain its ownership of the farm. This particular farmer did not recover sufficiently to allow him to resume operations the following year. Consequently, the land was rented to another household, while the farmer took a full-time job in a nearby urban centre. Eventually, the land was sold when it was found to be more expedient to live close to the new work situation.

The help extended in this instance reflects an ethic of neighbourliness and mutual self-help that has persisted since the homestead period. It is an ethic which is frequently expressed with reference to the past and continues to be invoked as an ideal in assessing the actions of others. However, the ability of neighbours to help each other in times of need has declined with the emergence of capital intensive farming.

Mechanization has facilitated the intensification of labour and a lengthening of the working day. During spring and harvest the use of tractors and combines allows producers to work continuously for as long as the weather and physical endurance permit. Coupled with the necessity of raising output, it is not surprising to find farmers working sixteen- to eighteen-hour periods during the critical seasons of spring and fall, and cultivating as much land as time and conditions permit. For those Rossan producers who sell their labour on a full-time basis the demands on time are even greater. They have to spend nine or ten hours away from the farm, depending on the distance involved, and then find the time to complete field operations and other chores. This intensification of production unavoidably affects the capacity of households to extend help to their neighbours, because such help is dependent on households completing the tasks vital to their own survival. The situation is further exasperated in situations of indebtedness, for payments have to be made regardless of performance. In other words, it seems that households are increasingly unable to pursue effectively the ideals of neighbourliness and mutual self-help. A significant consequence of this is that the vulnerability of households to the problems confronting them becomes even more acute.

There is one further aspect to the difficulties experienced by domestic producers that should be mentioned. From the perspective of Rossan farmers, illness and accidents are a product of bad luck or carelessness. However, there is a social dimension to this question that easily remains hidden. It takes little contact with farmers to realize that they suffer from a variety of ailments, such as lacerations, broken bones, deafness, knee and back injuries, which are associated with their productive activities. Clearly, some of these injuries could have been avoided if more precautions were taken while operating farm machinery. Nevertheless, even this point has to be qualified by recognizing that the strain and fatigue resulting from long hours of work contribute to an increased susceptibility to errors of judgement. A related point is that the necessity of continuing production encourages farmers to pursue their operations without due concern for their health. For example, one Rossan farmer operating a mixed cow-calf and grain enterprise continued with his spring field work despite the pain of a broken ankle which kept him in bed one hour for every thirty minutes he spent driving the tractor. Another farmer continues to operate a tractor despite unpredictable bouts of dizziness and the threat to his safety that this poses. In both cases, to stop work would be tantamount to abandoning farming and a way of life.

The viability of domestic commodity production in agriculture is clearly threatened by these developments. The ability of households to raise the savings necessary to meet the ever increasing capital requirements of farming is thrown into doubt by the variety of difficulties experienced by Rossan farmers. Larger producers have been able to maintain and even improve their viability although indebtedness and specialization increase their vulnerability. However, even in these cases the future is questionable for the financing and operation of increasingly larger units seem likely to require a transformation to capitalist, collective or other forms of productive relations. There are additional problems for Rossan households, related to their proximity to a large urban centre, which threaten to curtail production completely in the area. A primary means of expanding production and thereby taking advantage of labour-saving equipment is through acquisition of extra land either through rental or purchase. Under the present system of private land ownership, land expansion on the part of one producer necessitates that some of his neighbours must fail. In Rossan, the stable work-farm pattern, established in the mid-1950s, has arrested this process by allowing smaller farmers to continue their operations while selling their labour on a full-time basis. More recently, escalating land prices, due to a rising demand for residential land in the area, have made it impossible to purchase land for agricultural production. It can still be rented, but retention of ownership for speculative purposes renders this form of expansion increasingly unreliable.

CONCLUSION

In broad perspective, the difficulties experienced by many Rossan households in continuously transforming productive organizations are indicative of the developing underdevelopment of the domestic commodity mode of production. The historic and continuing subordination of domestic commodity production to the needs of capital in Canada has meant that the activities of households have been harnessed to the imperatives of capitalist development. The result of this is that a contradiction is generated within the mode of production between the forces and relations of production. By virtue of their involvement in commodity production in capitalist society, domestic producers must continuously modernize the means of production. However, it is apparent that the relations of production, based on family ownership of resources and the use of family labour, are increasingly unable to provide a framework to do this. It is this contradiction within the domestic mode of production that lies behind the crisis of the family farm and the continuous generation of rural poverty.

It should be apparent that we are not simply talking of the fate of small versus large farms or of raising the output and efficiency of those producers who are deemed to have a future in farming. Rather, we are talking about the very continuity of rural life as we know it. The contradictions generated within the mode of production ensure that the large family farm of today will become the small family farm of tomorrow, or be absorbed into the corporatization of farming, and that the way of life associated with it will increasingly become a thing of the past. In this respect, farm households are like outport fishermen and Native trappers in that their mode of production and the way of life associated with it are being progressively undermined and will continue to be undermined unless the conditions of their existence can be changed.

In Rossan the process is well underway as, with the help of inflated land prices resulting from the demand for country residences, domestic production seems destined to become rapidly a part of the past. With it will disapppear the way of life that characterized the community with its mutual self-help, cooperation, and neighbourliness. We see in Rossan the tendency towards greater mechanization, the decline of diversified and subsistence farming and its replacement with specialized farming, the emergence and stability of a work-farm pattern and the difficulties of extending aid in times of need. These and other indicators reflect the changes in the organization of production that have occurred and the difficulties created by the necessity for households to counteract continuously the tendency for income to decline. The influx of people to live on acreages and developments contributes to the transformation of the area by taking land permanently out of production. Moreover, these new inhabitants tend to remain oriented towards the city in spirit and in practice.

From this analysis of domestic production it should be apparent that an understanding of the process of change requires a perspective that recognizes the embeddedness of households in society as a whole. The concept of domestic commodity mode of production makes it possible to understand the way structural pressures impinge on the autonomy of households, for, by constraining actions and shaping the outcome of actions taken, it can be seen to condition the evolution of the rural world. Finally, it is worth suggesting that the approach followed here is applicable to other situations involving domestic production, such as trapping and fishing, in capitalist society. The point is that the concept provides a means of overcoming the micro-focus of much anthropology while retaining the capacity to say something meaningful about the lives and struggles of the people concerned.

BIBLIOGRAPHY

Layton, Elliott 1975. *Dying Hard: The Ravages of Industrial Carnage.* Toronto: McClelland and Stewart Ltd.

Mitchell, Don 1975. *The Politics of Food.* Toronto: James Lorimer and Company.

Sahlins, M. 1972. *Stone Age Economics.* Chicago: Aldine.

Terray, Emmanuel 1972. *Marxism and "Primitive" Societies.* New York: Monthly Review Press.

Warnock, John 1971. The Farm Crisis. In *Essays on the Left* L. LaPierre et al., (Eds). Toronto: McClelland and Stewart.

Wood, A.W. 1962. Technological Changes in Processing, Marketing and Distribution and Their Impact on Canadian Agriculture. *Canadian Journal of Agricultural Economics* 10:54-63.

CHAPTER 15

THE CITY AND ITS INHABITANTS

The City-Dweller and Class Confrontation in
Western Capitalism

BERNARD BERNIER
Universite de Montreal

Conventional urban anthropology has focused attention on specific locales or specific issues in the city: the urban slums, shanty-towns, ethnic relations, voluntary associations, networks, and so on. This functional compartmentalization of what are seen to be "the problems of the modern city" mitigates against a thorough-going and holistic analysis of the forces of which these so-called "problems" are merely the manifestation. To overcome this, the study of the city—or any sector of the city—requires, first and foremost, that the student recognize the fundamental forces which give the contemporary capitalist city its specific character. Once we understand the forces generated by the operation of capitalism, we will see how this reduces the issues of conventional anthropology to surface "symptoms" rather than casual "problems."

STATEMENT OF THE PROBLEM[1]

In order to understand the city and the spatial organization of its inhabitants, it must be placed in the historical, economic, and social context in which it is found. As regards present-day cities in North America and Western Europe, this means monopoly and imperialistic capitalism.

The city is obviously not the creation of capitalism, but the cities of previous periods owed their existence to very different relations of production than those which characterize contemporary society. Even if the city was the centre of the power of the dominant classes in precapitalist societies, nonagricultural wealth was minimal compared to agricultural production which provided the basis of these societies. Therefore, the great majority of people lived in the countryside.

By contrast, capitalism is based on industrial production, which can be and effectively is concentrated in urban areas, and as such, it represents the first mode of production that is essentially urban. Capitalism in fact, constructs (in the case of recent cities), or modifies (in the case of older cities) the city according to its own structural requirements. In other words, the dominant class, in this case the bourgeoisie, makes the city an instrument to be used in attaining its goal: the maximization of the rate of profit.

The basis on which we must begin an analysis of the capitalist city, therefore, is the division into classes, of which two are fundamental and opposed—the bourgeoisie and the proletariat—and where the existence of other classes can only be explained by the evolution of the contradictory relationship of the first two. The extension of capitalist production has meant the multiplication of service and clerical employees, whose existence depends on, and helps reproduce, the increased extraction of value from the direct producers: the workers. By the same token, the bourgeoisie has diversified the task of management to include middle-level support staff, engineers, accountants, and planners, who organize production for capital. This stratum forms what we may call the new petty-bourgeoisie. Meanwhile the old petty-bourgeoisie—the merchants, artisans, and small-manufacturers—diminishes, while maintaining an ambivalent position toward the dominant bourgeoisie: selling goods on the capitalist market, but at the same time threatened by capitalism.

Essentially then, I will analyze the city as a product of these ever-changing class relations of advanced capitalism. But even so, two points must be emphasized. Firstly, the fundamental opposition between bourgeoisie and proletariat is, of itself, incapable of explaining the urban phenomenon; a wide variety of secondary contradictions must be taken into account: "the rural/urban contradictions"; ethnic divisions, and so on.

Secondly, we must clarify the link between the social relations of production in the city and the way in which space is utilized. In fact, the present analysis explains the manner in which the multiple contradictions of capitalism produce a necessarily contradictory use of space. What this means is that we must look at multifaceted class antagonisms and their relationship to a specific urban spatial arrangement. This is not a one-directional relationship in which classes, unconstrained, determine the use of space; rather space, the man-made urban framework, and even the natural environment (e.g., its deterioration from pollution) all exercise constraints on diverse class activities.

By recognizing these factors, two mistakes are avoided: the abstract presentation of class relationships, removed from the spatial framework in which they act; and a concentration on the appearances of the city, such as the mere description of a neighbourhood, while ignoring the underlying determining forces.

What I am suggesting is that the city be seen as a concentration of labour-power and the means for its social reproduction, in the context of the increasing concentration of the means of production and money-capital in one place.

THE CONFIGURATION OF THE CITY: INDUSTRY & PROPERTY SPECULATION

In general, the large cities of capitalist countries are industrial cities; what is paradoxical however, is that the industrial character of the city is often not immediately obvious. In effect, the central core is often thought of as the city itself. But while the city centre was largely industrial during the nineteenth century, today's central cores have been turned into commercial and administrative zones. Industry has moved away to outlying areas, to be replaced by commerce, banks, finance, state administration, company headquarters, public relations, and tourism.

This disappearance of industry from the central core serves to illustrate that space cannot be thought of as a uniform phenomenon under capitalism; locations within a certain space have quite qualitatively different characteristics. Thus commerce, industry, residence, and so on become "zoned" by reference to the diverse "resources" with unequal outputs, which certain locations offer. Thus, in almost any capitalist country, important industrial and commercial activities become concentrated in a few cities and regions, with the rest of the area being devoted to agriculture and capitalist activities of smaller scale. As I have already noted, the reason for concentration lies in the bourgeoisie's need to minimize production and especially circulation costs. For this reason those activities essential to the circulation of capital (banking, large commercial enterprise, administration) as well as major productive operations (heavy and petrochemical industries) are concentrated in the major cities. Small towns then take up the less profitable industrial sectors (textiles, clothing, shoemaking, lumbering) as well as service operations for the rural population.

Thus spatial division of tasks is the consequence of the form of capitalist accumulation. Let us examine this process more specifically for the spatial arrangements internal to the capitalist city.

The metropolitan central core has seen the disappearance of the majority of its important industries. But it is still under the control of the bourgeoisie, now more than ever. To explain this increase of capital in the central core, it is necessary, on the one hand, to describe the distinction between financial and industrial capital, and on the other hand, to present a few explanations concerning competition among firms and on the mechanisms of land speculation.

If profit as value arises from production proper, the bourgeoisie has, nonetheless, transformed all sorts of activities into means for the accumulation of capital. Thus, alongside the industrial bourgeoisie are the financial bourgeoisie (which, in Canada, is strongly concentrated), and the commercial bourgeoisie. As capitalist production has

301

developed, so have companies become much larger. The increase in the scale of enterprise has resulted in the necessity for ever-increasing the concentration of capital, which in turn must be obtained through credit. Thus major industries have established stable links with banks, resulting in the appearance of a new, more concentrated and powerful form of capital: finance capital. Despite its base in industrial production, finance capital is interested in engaging in any activity returning a profit. This increased activity means that finance capital now dominates capitalist society.

It is this finance capital which controls the central cores of contemporary metropolises, because of the profits which can be gained from the high rate of "valorization" of land produced by downtown economic activities.

It is important to recognize the "artificial" nature of profits generated in this way. The price of land is thought of as capital; rent then appears to be the profit from this capital. Yet, this capital does not exist as such. Rent does, and the capital which is represented in the price of land is really capitalized rent. And the more rent increases, the more the fictive capital represented in the price of land, increases. There is thus an increase of capital without any real production of value.

The amount of rent of a property depends on its actual use, but for certain lots there exists a potential use which could increase the rent. Land speculation consists exactly in playing upon these potential uses.

In fact, it is important to note the special nature of finance capital here. Once a building is rented, the rental value will not be determined by the price paid for the land or even for the construction of the building, but rather by rents paid for similar offices in the same area or in neighbouring areas. And these rents are themselves determined by the general economic activity of the central core, thus, in fact, by the combined actions of the bourgeoisie.[2] But what are the consequences of this practice?

The most important consequence concerns an increase in the price of all goods and services, an increase which derives from higher rental values which, in one way or another, are reflected back onto consumers. The most effected consumers are those with fixed incomes and others who cannot obtain salary increases equal to the inflation rate: the majority of workers and employees.

Elsewhere, the old petty-bourgeoisie of small merchants and small firms are also subject to a decrease in revenues if they cannot push cost increases onto saleable commodities. Finally, and this appears paradoxical at first glance, industries, which need large areas of land, leave the central core for suburban areas where rents are lower, but which are easily accessible.

What seems contradictory in this practice is that a company will keep its headquarters downtown while locating its manufacturing operations in the suburbs. Two factors can explain this apparent contradiction. Firstly, it is possible to build office buildings with forty or more storeys, while, due to machinery, it is impossible to build factories with the same configuration. Office buildings allow more intensive use of land and therefore a lowering of the rental cost of each unit. Secondly, it is easier for a company to calculate the hidden costs directly linked to production as such and compare them with the true cost of manufacturing products.

The high rental costs of locating downtown will be reflected in prices inasmuch as the labour time contained in services is incalculable; this is not the case for manufactured goods. Faced with the high rents downtown and an ever increasing need to present a solid financial appearance in order to obtain credit and sales, industries will cut production costs by relocating their factories in the suburbs while keeping their headquarters downtown. The secondary costs entailed in the maintenance of the headquarters will be reflected in the price of goods, under merchandising or administrative costs.

The downtown area then becomes the kingdom of finance-capital, large trusts, and monopoly companies. In Montreal, for example, there appears to be a division in the control of urban land: while Canadian monopoly capital (C.P.R., etc.,) linked to large Canadian banks, appropriates the central core, American capital, largely in the petroleum industry (Gulf, etc.), develops new towns in the outlying areas. Here is an obvious manifestation of an important fact: the Canadian bourgeoisie manages to keep, on the level of financial capital, a certain independence guaranteed by the Canadian state (regulation of foreign capital in the banks, etc.). This is manifested in this case by the attempt to control the central cores of large Canadian metropoli.

THE STATE INFRA-STRUCTURE AND THE HOUSING SHORTAGE

The development of capitalism has resulted in the ever-increasing intervention of the state in the economy. In fact, from its inception the state apparatus has had as its goals: maintenance of existing production relations for the benefit of that epoch's dominant class, mainly by imposing constraints on the dominated class; management of the internal conflicts within the dominant class and the periodical crises when they come to light; and parcelling out the means necessary for maintaining production. This last function means that the state must at the very least guarantee the general conditions of reproduction of productive elements, that is, the means of production and the labour force.

In advanced capitalism, the state, which in the nineteenth century administered the overall activities necessary for the maintenance of the bourgeoisie (army, police, civil service, road and harbour construction and work codes) has expanded its functions to include direct economic intervention as a promotor or owner. The state provides incentives for the construction of factories or housing; it even

303

undertakes these tasks directly as it runs manufacturing or living units.

With regard to the city, the role of the state appears in 1. zoning, 2. state use of land and 3. aiding in the reproduction of the labour force.

1. *Zoning.* Zoning consists in state regulation of land use. Zoning regulations define zones according to activities. These regulations have the effect of creating a monopoly for particular uses in a zone. Insofar as zoning aids in the valorization of land in certain areas, it regulates the use of land to the advantage of that fraction of the bourgeoisie which attempts to valorize its capital by monopolizing land and speculating on its possible uses. The state thus aids the bourgeoisie in increasing its share of wealth. Once this process is set in motion the municipalities which started it are subject to pressure by diverse speculators. And, because the municipalities are always short of funds, insofar as every increase in land value might increase the municipality's tax base, so it is favourably inclined to such pressures. Where municipalities are under the direct control of speculators, the designated zones can be modified, so as to revalorize certain lots, thus favouring some corporations or individuals over others.

2. *State Land Use.* Zoning also defines the lots serviced by the state of which the most important is what I shall call "collective equipment," by which I mean all material means necessary for capitalist production and circulation: roads, ports, airports, railroads, servicing for water and electricity, housing, parks, etc.

Collective equipment has an important role to play in the production or realization of the value of commodities. Ports, airports, railroads, roads, principally serve in the physical circulation of commodities, in their transport from production site to the place of use. They are thus the means which allow the realization of the value of commodities, i.e., their exchange for a sum of money, a realization which is evidently essential for obtaining the profit contained in this value.

Thus *collective equipment* is first linked to the efficient functioning of capitalist production and circulation. It facilitates obtaining the maximal rate of profit by the bourgeoisie by allowing an increase in the value of production and circulation (economies of scale) and a decrease in the hidden costs of commodities in circulation.

Collective equipment necessitates the use of funds and land. The funds come mainly from taxes and government loans, loans which are used towards nonproductive aims since in no way do they serve directly in the production of value and whose increase therefore reinforces inflation.

Land must be bought and serviced. The provision of collective equipment always entails a conversion in land use. Purchase of land for the development of collective equipment has several effects:

firstly, as has been shown, it valorizes land by delimiting the monopolized zones, also exacerbating tendencies towards speculation; secondly, it increases the flow of circulation towards certain zones,
especially the downtown area, mainly via highways, resulting in an
increase in sales for downtown merchants and consequently, an increase in land prices; thirdly, these infra-structural developments
often destroy residential areas where workers, welfare recipients, and
employees live, thus breaking social ties.

The role of the state in the development of collective equipment
does not equally benefit all factions of the bourgeoisie, but it
nevertheless has the overall effect of facilitating the realization of
profit. Similarly, state promotion of industrial zones has the same effect. The state thus provides the bourgeoisie with the means to counteract a lowering of profit levels.

3. *The Reproduction of the Labour Force.* The role of the state in the reproduction of the urban work force is composed of four principal
   aspects: transport, education, health services, and housing, of
   which the last is of special significance. It is worth noting that
   while these are the issues usually of most interest to conventional
   urban anthropologists, the compartmentalizing of each as a separate "problem" has prevented anthropologists from locating their
   field studies into a more holistic and historical analysis.

These aspects of the reproduction of the labour force have increasingly been taken over by the state, after a period in which certain
operations were in the hands of private capitalists. By absorbing
much of the costs of these operations, the state aids capitalism: transport is necessary for the cheap movement of labour from residence to
workplace; schooling and health services provide cheap physical,
technical, and ideological reproduction of the labour force. When I
say "cheap" I am of course speaking form the viewpoint of the individual capitalist, because the state acts to distribute these costs so that
they are incurred by society as a whole. It follows that insofar as they
are relatively cheap to capital, they are proportionately expensive to
labour—through taxes, etc.

But it is housing, above all, which is at the very core of the urban
question, because what defines the city, in the sense of constituting
its essential element (rather than its cause) is the bringing together of
the labour force: the concentration of a differentiated population
which must be housed. Although it is, first of all, a place to live, eat,
sleep, etc., in capitalist society the place of residence also constitutes a
reserve of value. So what creates the housing problem in capitalist society is this fact: that housing is a need and at the same time a commodity (Harvey 1973, Chap.5).

Under capitalism, a commodity only has an exchange value if it has
some sort of use-value. This does not mean that it is the marginal utility of commodities which determines their exchange-value. Rather,
value arises from the average quantity of labour power expended in

the production of the commodity. Nevertheless, for this value to be realized it is necessary that a demand exists and that someone be willing to pay a sum of money to obtain it. In fact, and this is crucial, it is not demand as such that allows value to be realized, but only solvent demand; that is the demand of someone who has the means to pay for the commodity. Need by itself is not sufficient unless it is backed by the ability to buy.

These considerations apply to all commodities, including housing. In this case what is important is not the need as such that people have for housing, but rather their ability to pay a certain level of rent so that the owner can obtain a sizeable profit for renting. A large segment of the population who in fact need housing because their present accommodation is overcrowded or unhealthy, cannot procure the necessary housing because they have no means of paying the rent demanded.

It is necessary to examine this in greater detail. If the rate of profit and its maximization is important to the bourgeoisie, including owners of accommodation, then rents cannot be allowed to fall below a certain minimum level. On the other hand new housing will never be built unless a high enough rent can be realized in order to maximize the profit level. But the working class and the unemployed, including a large number of senior citizens with fixed incomes, cannot afford to pay more than a certain amount of rent. This level is, for a large number of people in these classes, lower than the minimum rent necessary to ensure the profitability of adequate housing. The result is that poorer people can only rent ill-equipped apartments in older areas. And, as we have seen, these areas are being cut into by the spreading of the downtown core. Given the insolvency of these poorer people, no housing is built for them. They are thus forced to live in overcrowded, inadequate housing, with exorbitant rates for the quality obtained. These difficult conditions reinforce the effects of unemployment: misery, difficulties in social relationships, violence etc., effects which further downgrade these areas.

Faced with this situation, the state must intervene and find solutions. Police repression is one, but it is clearly inappropriate. Construction of rent-controlled buildings is another. But this too is inadequate because the number of low-rental units is always well below demand. The state, in effect, has neither the means nor the desire to remedy housing problems. With its budgetary and administrative restraints, the state can only build housing which becomes overcrowded and offers an alienating social environment (absence of trees, no stores etc.). The state only "relocates" misery, it in no way makes it disappear.

In other areas, employees and the petty-bourgeoisie see a part of their housing stock become degraded either due to the growth of the central core, or the relocation of poor people into their neighbourhoods. The only solution for many of them is to find housing elsewhere. But often available housing carries exorbitant rates, so that many are forced to move to the suburbs, increasing their distance from places of work. Others settle for less luxurious housing, or intensify the density of already occupied housing. Finally, some move to nicer neighbourhoods. Only the bourgeoisie and the upper layer of the petty bourgeoisie do not have a housing problem.

It is here that we see the effects of urban space on class relationships, which I mentioned in the introduction. Despite its position as the dominant class, the bourgeoisie, in its attempts to transform everything into a means of accumulation, encounters in the housing crisis a specific resistence. Both at the level of the production of housing as a commodity and at the level of urban politics—such as the opposition of labour organizations, who sometimes bring into question the legitimacy of the whole social order of capitalism—the dominant class faces a crisis which often finds expression in the form of the social problems encountered in the working-class neighbourhoods of the city.

THE WORKING-CLASS NEIGHBOURHOODS

The industrial proletariat's neighbourhoods occupy large areas of cities and have done so since the introduction of industry. Engels in 1844 provided a good analysis of the importance of these areas and the living conditions which have been found there since the initial phase of industrial capitalism.

During this phase the working class and the chronically unemployed subproletariat were indistinguishable, because industrial employment was illpaid and unstable (Engels 1960). It was the unions, that is, the worker's protective organizations, which were formed, despite the law, to combat the abuses of capitalists and to attempt the improvement of working conditions, which demanded salary increases, the improvement of working conditions, job security, and the reduction of working hours. One result has been the appearance of a distinction between organized and unorganized workers. The former were found in highly productive industrial sectors and appeared with monopoly capitalism after 1870 (metallurgy, heavy machinery, automobiles, petroleum) and had stable employment and higher salaries; the latter were often unemployed and worked for low salaries in older, less productive industrial sectors, (textiles, clothing, shoemaking, furniture etc.). Secondly, the "subproletariat" is really the bottom stratum of unorganized workers and includes the unemployed, welfare recipients, and periodically employed workers in underproductive industrial sectors.

Towards the end of the nineteenth century the more stable and better paid stratum of the working class developed neighbourhoods which were different from those described by Engels for the subproletariat. However, the areas they lived in were often adjacent to one another so that the boundary between them was very indistinct.

Since working people have nothing to sell but their labour power

307

they are under the sway of the bourgeoisie, either directly, through salaried unemployment, or indirectly, while they are unemployed. But it is conditions created by capitalist production which make the existence of this lower stratum of the proletariat necessary. In effect, the owners of capital need cheap labour to make sectors of low productivity minimally profitable. For this purpose they create a surplus in the work force in order to put pressure on salaries and to create divisions within the working class between effectively employed and stable workers, and unstable or unemployed workers[3]. This surplus in the work force is created in many ways: firstly by creating a new labour force through the expropriation of independent producers (peasants, craftsmen); secondly (when the level of employment rises[4] and salaries are increasing) by introducing more productive machines and manufacturing procedures permitting a reduction in the need for labour power and thus reducing labour costs; and thirdly by importing foreign labour.

The distinction between labour, properly speaking, and surplus labour is thus a distinction between factions of the same social class. It is a distinction of degree and not kind—relative differences in the extent of employment, salary, and living conditions. Nonetheless, even if it is a question of degree, it is a necessary distinction since there are neighbourhoods primarily inhabited by ill-paid workers or unemployed, who have a very specific lifestyle, and 'there are neighbourhoods where steadily-employed workers live, whose living conditions are also difficult but who enjoy a certain amount of stability and also some material advantages in relation to the poorer workers.

Inner City Slums & Shanty-towns   While the most productive factories begin to locate outside the central core, resulting in the emigration of unionized and specialized workers towards new areas, the majority of subproletariat areas in North American cities have developed on the foundations of older downtown working-class neighbourhoods. Here workers in nonproductive industrial sectors share available housing with the unemployed and welfare recipients, a large number of whom are immigrants from rural areas seeking work.

The primary characteristic of these areas is the ever-present reality of unemployment. The result is suffering. As has already been shown, these areas have lower rents because of the bad state of repair of the houses. Some could be renovated but owners prefer not to because, due to their proximity to downtown, it is the land and not the houses that are valuable. They prefer to wait for a good opportunity to sell.

From the landlord's point of view, rents are relatively low, given the dilapidated condition of these houses, even if they are high relative to the occupants' incomes and the quality of the houses. Often the only way an owner can make a profit is to refrain from renovating. Owning these hovels does not bring in a high level of profit: the majority of slum landlords are small-scale capitalists who, with only a small stock of capital, have little investment possibilities. Many have in any case bought houses only for speculative ends. For these people it is often more profitable to leave the houses unoccupied and deteriorating rather than renting them while waiting for land prices to go up.

As D. Harvey has observed (1973 p.170), it is in the slums that the worst overcrowding is found, due to the impossibility of paying higher rents coupled with the high proportion of abandoned houses. Added to this is the destruction of houses and the razing of vacant buildings to build parking lots. Lastly, due to their proximity to the downtown area, the construction of new buildings or new transport routes also disturbs the life of these areas.

D. Harvey (1973 p. 143) suggests that this construction not only is motivated by the need for services in the central core, but also acts to disrupt whole neighbourhoods (especially ethnically homogenous ones such as black ghettos in the U.S.) so that ties of solidarity among the oppressed, which might threaten the social order, are not formed. These upheavals have become a fact of life not only in inner city poor neighbourhoods but also in working-class areas generally.

The open wounds inflicted upon slum neighbourhoods can only increase the alienation of the inhabitants of these neighbourhoods. The ties of friendship, kinship, and neighbourliness which are the basis of the important social relationships in these areas, are fundamentally weakened by the necessity for constant moving. The instability of living conditions, misery, unemployment, and malnutrition result in sickness and crime. At the same time, perpetual movement of people effectively prevents the formation of new bonds of solidarity. But this is only its partial effect. In fact, encouraged by the success (limited but real) of workers' organizations and working-class neighbourhood associations, the subproletariat have sometimes rallied on a neighbourhood level to make further demands for jobs, housing, services or to protest the deterioration of living conditions. In Montreal, for example, the majority of the older downtown areas have given birth to protest movements. These organizations are often limited in size, scope and in their effectiveness, but they nonetheless constitute an elementary basis for questioning certain aspects of the social, political, and economic order of modern capitalism.

Aside from downtown areas, the subproletariat are found in the peripheral zones of large cities in squatter settlements. In North America and in England, the urban poor are concentrated for the most part in the central core of the city. Shanty-towns are thus limited in number, whether in remote suburbs or close to smaller towns. But in France, especially Paris, where Baron Haussmann's brand of urban renewal cleared the central core of factories and long established working class neighbourhoods in order to transform them into bourgeois and petty-bourgeois residential areas, low-paid labour and the unemployed have been confined to shanty-towns near industrial suburbs.

To illustrate the social and material conditions which prevail in sub-proletariat areas, I will briefly outline the conclusions reached through research with a few students in 1970-73 in such an area of a small Quebec town (population 4 500). This neighbourhood, built by two intersecting railway lines, is occupied by the unemployed, some low-paid local industrial workers (mainly in textiles), and welfare recipients and transients. The majority of these people are French Canadians in a town where French Canadians are barely in the majority. At the time of research, most houses were dilapidated, although housing had improved since 1950. Everyone was poor, even if a few owned colour televisions bought on credit. Infant mortality was three times the city-wide average; there was also a high percentage of debilitated and infirm people. Most children were not successful at school, where they were strongly discriminated against, and the majority left soon after they entered secondary school. One-third of the neighbourhood elementary school-age children were boarders at a school for retarded children, located in a nearby town. Separations, common-law marriages, and illegitimate births were common.

The neighbourhood was organized around a stable hub, comprising the members of two families, both large, who accounted for about half of its total population of 200 at any given time. The other half was composed of kin (cousins, aunts, nephews, etc.) to these two families, spouses from outside and people without kin ties to other members of the group. The turnover of people in this latter half was great. Although kinship relations were the most important social link, groups were also formed on the basis of proximity and also for some sports.

The people of this neighbourhood maintained few ties with the town of which they were part, since they were subject to strong discrimination in the job market. In fact, they were employed mostly as temporary labour in poor jobs. Many people supplied cheap temporary labour for the two local textile industries. In many cases they were used to promote divisions in the local working class solidarity (Bernier 1977 a and b).

Relationships were formed either within the neighbourhood or with people living in similar neighbourhoods within a radius of forty kilometres. These people thus only had ties with other subproletariat. Relationships with the permanent work force of the town were almost nonexistent. In fact, the division between the neighbourhood and the rest of the town was much more important than the English/French division.

Despite material and social deprivation as well as police harassment people were able to organize themselves, on a limited basis, in 1975. Helped by community workers, they succeeded in creating a "crisis centre" and in forcing the school commission to organize classes for retarded children in the local school in order to bring back the children who were boarding. These achievements, though minimal, were in large part obtained due to the push provided by community workers. The absence of clear political objectives however quickly resulted in the dissolution of the movement.

If such neighbourhoods are unorganized, they are in no way less of a base for revolutionary and reformist movements, particularly in the Third World. This is why they are often subject to being razed and their inhabitants obliged to move. The complete destruction of a "coloured" shanty-town near the Cape in South Africa in August 1977 is a striking example.

Peripheral Neighbourhoods   Working-class neighbourhoods have been created by the location of industry in peripheral urban zones, something which necessitated the provision of housing for the workers. The case of Montreal is illustrative: there these neighbourhoods were formed gradually between 1900 and 1950, when factories became located in suburbs a few kilometres from downtown. These suburbs, almost villages on the outskirts of the city, had as their centre a railyard (Pointe St. Charles, Verdun, Hochelaga, Maisonneuve), a harbour extension (Hochelaga), or quarries (Villeray). There were already railmen, dockworkers and stone workers living in these suburbs. The arrival of industries and the workers for these factories transformed the suburbs into industrial areas. During World War II a new implantation occurred in adjacent neighbourhoods, but more distant from downtown, further extending working-class neighbourhoods. In this way, Rosemont, St. Michel, Montreal-Nord, and Cartierville were developed in the north and Lasalle and Ville Emard in the southwest. These areas were merely extensions of the existing working-class neighbourhoods of the suburbs. With the locating of factories in the west of Montreal, at Dorval and along the Trans-Canada highway, it is possible that new working-class neighbourhoods will develop, even though this development is limited by the proximity of the factories to predominantly anglophone and petty-bourgeois zones. In the short run it is likely that providing commuter services for workers will take precedence over actually moving them.

The working-class neighbourhoods are isolated from the downtown area, despite access by bus, subway, and car. For the most part, in their neighbourhood, workers can find their place of work, shopping areas (where prices are often higher than those of richer areas, because of the captive market), leisure facilities and other services. They do not need, and rarely have time, to go downtown.

The housing is of average quality. The majority of newer buildings have a few storeys and have ten to thirty apartments. There are often old houses with one apartment per floor, especially in the older areas. The majority of the inhabitants rent. Given the average age of houses, most are in good shape, even if there are sporadic hovels or abandoned dwellings. In fact, the nearer the older working-class neighbourhoods are to downtown, the more the housing is ill-kempt.

Despite the generally adequate character of the environment, these neighbourhoods are subject to periodic upheavals. The building of

311

shopping centres is the most frequent form of transformation of these neighbourhoods. But in Montreal, even larger scale changes are found. In fifteen years in the east of the city, for example, there has been the alteration of Notre Dame street, the construction of the East-West throughway, the building of facilities for the Olympic games, the extension of the subway, the construction of the Lafontaine bridge-tunnel.

In such cases, what makes improvements necessary are the needs of making capital profitable, which cause the growth of urban concentration and define the central core. It is worth noting that downtown access routes are never built through the wealthier neighbourhoods (for example, Outremont and Westmount both near downtown Montreal).

In Montreal, such physical upheavals have little by little broken down the ties of neighbourliness and friendship which long existed among workers in the same craft or factory. But these ties, based on the persistence of social relations from a period where craftsmanship was preponderant, have been replaced by forms of solidarity based on class. Beginning in the factories, by attacking the poor working conditions, the workers' struggle outgrew this narrow framework to attack broader problems of daily life: housing, nurseries, opposition to the demolition of neighbourhoods, etc. Obviously many of these struggles are brief and limited, their participants do not always perceive the fundamental cause of the problems they wish to solve. The tendency to be concerned only with the immediate economic issues, such as wages, is strong. Nevertheless, practical opposition to the social order is present; it manifests itself with more and more vigour, and often prevents the state and companies from riding roughshod in their "improvement" schemes.

ETHNIC NEIGHBOURHOODS

Ethnic neighbourhoods are usually included within working-class areas[5]. Again in Montreal the Greek and Portuguese live preponderantly in subproletariat neighbourhoods, while the Italian neighbourhoods are in blue or white collar areas. In the United States the situation is similar, with the addition of another group—the Blacks—who constitute the majority of the inhabitants of the older neighbourhoods near the downtown area. It is thus evident that the characteristics of working-class neighbourhoods presented above apply to ethnic neighbourhoods too. But the ethnic neighbourhoods have some peculiarities by virtue of their ethnic character which must be explained if modern North American cities are to be understood. Firstly, the multi-ethnic composition of American societies demands a certain degree of historical analysis. The settlement of North America occurred in two stages. The first, which corresponds to the period of colonization, is dominated by European-based mercantile capital. Originally in the British Colonies, the imported European work force escaped to the frontier, so that the eventual solution reached by the bourgeoisie was the importation of a captive labour force, whose physical characteristics (especially skin colour) permitted the easy justification of their status as slave. In effect, what happened was that in the absence of the possibility of monopolizing land (i.e., closing the frontier to immigrants and thus forcing them to sell their labour), the mercantile bourgeoisie was forced to create a monopoly on labour by transforming it into a captive labour force.

The organization of plantation production, whose coexistence with petty peasant agriculture entailed the necessity of a dual process of immigration (European peasants who became smallholders, African blacks who were sold as slaves), continued without too many problems until constraints were imposed by industrial capitalism in the nineteenth century. The confrontation between the American industrial bourgeoisie (whose wealth came from using a "free" salaried work force and from the expansion of the market) and the slaveholding plantation owners (who prospered at the expense of a captive work force and wanted a closed market economy) appeared as a struggle between two factions of the dominant class, which resulted in the victory of the former.

It is notable that the victory was only possible after a virtual monopoly was established over the country's entire area. Indeed this success of the industrial bourgeoisie, on the brink of the exhaustion of the frontier marks the beginning of the second phase of migration. But before analyzing this second period we must note that the effects of the first phase remains with us today: frontier expropriation gave us the "Indian problem": race, used as an ideological tool in slavery, is the basis of the "race question"; British and French conflict over the control of trade and markets in the eighteenth century is the basis of the "national question" of Quebec.

As to the second phase, the development of industrial capitalism in Europe provoked changes in the type of immigration. While in the preceding period, immigrants either came from metropolitan centres or from Africa, beginning in 1840-50, European industrialists found it necessary to change surplus local population into an industrial labour force. The need for an industrial labour force in North America was satisfied in two ways: by transforming a part of the settled population already engaged in small-scale farming or plantation agriculture into an industrial work force; and by attracing more and more immigrants from nonindustrialized European areas, and later, from Asia and Latin America. This resulted in the arrival of the Irish, Poles, East European Jews, the Chinese and the Japanese, Italians, Greeks, Spaniards, Mexicans, Portuguese, and the West Indians. These two sources were used to create an abundant labour force which allowed the industrialists to pay low wages while fomenting divisions within an increasingly militant working class, through reference to ethnicity. In effect, and this is important, the transformation of local and foreign populations into an industrial labour force had as its primary goal the creation of the cheap source of surplus labour necessary for the maximization of the level of profit. Nevertheless, because of the expansion of the number of technical, office or service jobs, caused by industrial expansion and capitalist accumulation, a large part of the industrial labour force could leave their jobs to become employees. To counter this exodus of the labour force from industry, which was resulting in the decline in the surplus labour force and thus leading to higher wages, the bourgeoisie has to either accelerate the import of a large foreign labour force, or in some way confine a segment of the local labour force to a specific category: that of nonqualified workers.

It is by this second method that the "visibility" of physical and ideological characteristics issuing from the slaveholding period came to be important. The emphasis on physical appearance, skin colour being one example, enabled the revitalization of the ideology which had justified slavery (racial and ethnic differences) in order to discriminate against Blacks and thus maintain them as much as possible in the lower echelons of the working class. The dissemination of this racist ideology was successful inasmuch as other ethnic groups could use it to promote their own social ascendancy at the expense of Blacks. This ideology thus had another effect: that of dividing the working class according to social or ethnic divisions. This is not to say that the ethnic groups who used racist ideology for their advantage did not find discrimination being used against them.

Although its justification was based on past ideology, discrimination survives as a function of the capitalist's use of the labour force. The process is especially insidious since it is not necessary for the bourgeoisie to invent discriminatory ideology in a conspiratorial manner; it only has to use selective promotion of ethnic groups, coupled with certain educational practices, for ideological discrimination to result, be it racial, ethnic, or religious.

This history of the relationship between immigration and discrimination is essential in order to understand ethnic problems in an urban environment, but it does not exhaust the question. There is a purely urban aspect to the ethnic problem which must be considered. Because immigrants came in search of jobs; because the majority, especially those of easily identifiable ethnic background, are part of the working class; and because industries are mainly in large cities; immigrants are often in the majority in these cities.

Although discrimination is an important factor in the rural labour force, it is in urban settings that problems of ethnic interrelations are most acute. This is because of the concentration of economic activity and resulting population density. Two facts stand out clearly concerning immigrants in urban areas: active discrimination and relative isolation. On the one hand, immigrants are subjected to more or less strong discrimination, which encourages them to fall back on relations with people of the same ethnic group; on the other hand, the isolation that new immigrants experience, especially those from peasant backgrounds, encourages the same tendency. There is thus a push towards reliance on the ethnic group. In turn, there are certain elements within the ethnic group who count on this reliance to establish a basis for accumulation.

Thus, when immigrants arrive and encounter discrimination, some people from the same ethnic group undertake to offer specific services to them: in the beginning, credit, and finally, organized recreational activities. Contracting for labour is later added to these services—certain immigrants may facilitate the immigration of their compatriots in order to offer them work at a certain salary. They then contract out this labour force to an employer at a higher wage rate. Thus, a group of people is created, whose petty bourgeois position is based on traditional customs and ethnic ties, through which attempts are made to meet the needs of immigrants.

Most of these people remain members of the petty bourgeoisie, i.e., owners of small-scale grocery stores and restaurants. The few who attempt to go beyond this must increase their base of accumulation. The usual way of starting this process is by becoming a landlord. Certain immigrants buy houses and rent apartments to their compatriots. Since the latter are often recent immigrants, they wish rapidly to find housing in neighbourhoods where people from the same ethnic group live. The landlord can often also offer credit and find jobs (involving a commission) and thus add credit facilities and labour contracting to his realty operations. The purchase of apartment buildings by these people in any given neighbourhood forms the basis for the concentration of an ethnically homogenous population: an ethnic neighbourhood. Once the ethnic neighbourhood grows, an ethnic housing market develops, the neighbourhood becomes reserved for people of a given ethnic group, and if immigrants wish to live with their compatriots, they must live in these neighbourhoods. The owners, by means of their real estate property, have thus created a monopolized geographical area, which ensures them monopolistic returns given the specialized service which they offer to people of their ethnic group. But this service is specialized only insofar as the distinctive character of the group is maintained: language, customs, etc. From this come diverse cultural associations reinforcing ethnic customs, whose organizers are likely to be the petty bourgeoisie proprietors.

The point is this: the ethnic petty bourgeoisie can only transform themselves into bourgeoisie by accumulation. Discrimination actually serves a positive function in the early stages of this process. For this reason these people must maintain the ethnic identity of their group.

Once the petty bourgeoisie transform themselves into true bourgeoisie , they find themselves in a contradictory position: on the one hand, they must leave their ethnic group and blend in with the bourgeoisie, become fully "Canadian" or "American" if they wish to progress; on the other hand, by progressing, they risk losing the support of their first base for accumulation, a base which supported them as

315

members of a common ethnic group. There develops a dilemma for the ethnic bourgeoisie: either to define themselves as bourgeois and lose their ties with their group, or to define themselves ethnically and risk a failure to increase their capital.

The ethnic bourgeoisie or petty bourgeoisie are thus often the cause of the creation of ethnic neighbourhoods. But an ethnic neighbourhood can also be created through pressure from the financial non-ethnic bourgeoisie which, using the "visibility" of a certain group, create a specific neighbourhood. This creation is profitable because the arrival of people who are members of a strongly discriminated against group permits the lowering of land prices which promoters can then purchase, only for resale to members of the incoming ethnic group at higher prices. Subsequently, a concentration of people from this group in the neighbourhood then allows the renting of accommodation at a higher rate, because of the captive market represented by ethnic bonds of the group. Many Black or Puerto Rican neighbourhoods in the United States were created in this manner.

The ethnic neighbourhood, whether or not it is the product of the ethnic bourgeoisie, always appears as a monopolized residential area, as a captive market. Ethnic neighbourhoods are thus the spatial manifestation of discrimination suffered by an ethnic group, on which segments of the bourgeoisie or petty bourgeoisie base their accumulation of capital.

CONCLUSION

The analysis of the modern "urban phenomenon" under capitalism has touched upon many questions[6]. The city is a complex and multifaceted phenomenon, which is impossible to approach from only one angle. Many viewpoints must be used: the production of commodities, circulation, the valorization of money-capital, housing, transportation and the economic and ideological reproduction of the labour force. All of these viewpoints owe their explanatory principle to the class struggle which characterizes modern capitalism: the bourgeoisie attempt to increase their share of wealth at the expense of the dominated classes by any means; capitalist factions fight with each other to appropriate a larger part of this wealth, all the while relying on the state to supervise the overall process of accumulation for the benefit of the bourgeoisie as a whole, and to control the impulses of the other classes. Finally, these dominated classes continuously struggle with the bourgeoisie in battles concerned with living and working conditions.

The future of the urban scene depends in the short and long run on the outcome of the confrontation between the bourgeoisie, weakened by periodic crises, and the dominated classes, organizationally weak but in the majority. Urban problems can only be resolved when this majority controls the process of commodity production, and hence the urban scene, according to its basic interests, i.e., those of the producers themselves.

NOTES

1. *I would like to thank Chantal Kirsch who read and commented on an earlier version of this article; as well as Lise Bergeron, Andre Bouvette, Mikhael Elbaz, Gilles Lavigne, Robert Ricketts and Gilles Ritchot with whom I had many discussions on multiple aspects of urban problems.*
2. *This is an abbreviated and therefore simplified version of the various activities of speculation capital in the downtown core. It stresses the importance of profits deriving from locational rents and potential uses of space. It does not, however, cover all the possible actions of finance capital in the downtown core.*
3. *This is only a single case among the many created among the proletariat by capitalist relations of production. Among others there are the divisions between permanent and temporary or seasonal labour; between qualified and nonqualified labour; between men and women's work; between native labourers and immigrants or between white labourers and others; between office work and manufacturing work. There is also the technical division of labour within workshops.*
4. *What demonstrates without any possible doubt the necessity of a surplus pool of labour is the definition of full employment; there is full employment in capitalist countries when the official unemployment rate (that is, including only those seeking employment, excluding many nonlabourers) is around two percent. "Full employment" thus defines a situation where there is still widespread unemployment.*
5. *There are exceptions. In Canada the most striking example is the anglophone and bourgeois suburb of Westmount, an island of wealth within the predominantly French-Canadian and industrial city of Montreal.*
6. *An area of importance for which there is no space here, is the question of the encroachment of urbanism on the countryside, which eventually leads to the concentration of the population in a few huge cities, where problems of housing, transportation and living conditions are all aggravated, and a depopulation of the more distant countryside. The rural/urban contradiction of capitalism results in problems for both the city and the countryside, difficulties which are the inverse in the city of those facing the countryside; but they are alike in the ills they afford the working class. (See Bergeron; Bernier 1976.)*

BIBLIOGRAPHY

Anthropologie et Société, Numéro Spécial, *Agriculture au Québec*, Nov. 1977.

Bergeron, Lise, Bernard Bernier et André Bouvette 1977. La rente foncière et l'Agriculture dans le capitalisme actuel. *Anthropologie et Société*, Nov. 1977.

Bernier, Bernard 1976. The Penetration of Capitalism in Quebec Agriculture. *Revue Canadienne de Sociologie et d'Anthropologie*, 13.4, Nov. 1976, p. 422-434.

Bernier, Bernard 1977a. Sous-prolétaires Québécois: Analyse de classe d'un groupe défavorisé. *Manpower and Unemployment Research*, Vol. 10, no. 1, Avril 1977, p. 47-62.

Bernier, Bernard 1977b. *Bidonville, P.Q.* manuscrit.

Castells, Manuel 1972. *La Question urbaine*, Paris: Maspéro.

Castells, Manuel 1973. *Luttes urbaines et pouvoir politique*. Paris: Maspéro.

Castells, Manuel, et Francis Godard 1974. *Monopolville: Analyse des rapports entre l'entreprise, l'Etat et l'urbain*. Paris: Mouton.

Castles, Stephen, et Godula Kosack 1973. *Immigrant Workers and Class Structure in Western Europe*. London, New York, Toronto: Oxford University Press.

Chatillon, Colette 1976. *L'histoire de l'agriculture au Québec*. Montréal: L'Etincelle.

Clark, Kenneth B. 1965. *Dark Ghetto*. New York: Harper & Row.

Eames, Edwin, et J. G. Goode 1977. *Anthropology of the City*. Englewood Cliffs, N.J.: Prentice-Hall.

Engels, Friedrich 1960. *La situation de la classe laborieuse en Angleterre*. Paris: Editions Sociales (Publié originellement en 1845).

Engels, Friedrich 1970. *La Question du logement*. Paris: Editions Sociales (Publié originellement en 1872).

Ertel, Rachel, Geneviève Fabre et Elise Marienstras 1971. *En Marge*. Paris: Maspéro.

Edwards, Richard C., Michael Reich, et Thomas E. Weisskopf, (ed.) 1972. *The Capitalist System*. Englewood Cliffs, N.J.: Prentice-Hall.

Gans, Herbert J. 1962. *The Urban Villagers*. New York: The Free Press.

Granotier, Bernard 1970. *Les travailleurs immigrants en France*. Paris: Maspéro.

Harvey, David 1973. *Social Justice and the City*. London: Arnold.

Lamarche, François 1972. Les fondements économiques de la question urbaine. *Sociologie et Sociétés*, Vol. IV, no. 1, Mai 1972. p. 15-41.

Ledrut, Michel 1968. *L'espace social de la ville*. Paris: Anthropos.

Liebow, Elliot 1967. *Tally's Corner*. Boston: Little, Brown & Co.

Lefebvre, Henri 1968. *Le droit à la ville*. Paris: Anthropos.

Lefebvre, Henri 1974. *La production de l'espace*. Paris: Anthropos.

Mangin, William 1967. Squatter Settlements. *Scientific American, Biology and Culture in Modern Perspective*. San Francisco: W. H. Freeman & Co., p. 423-432.

Marx, Karl 1969. *Le Capital*, Livres I, II et III. Paris: Editions Sociales (Publié originellement en 1867, 1885 et 1893-94).

Patterson, E. Palmer 1972. *The Canadian Indian: A History since 1500*. Toronto: Collier-MacMillan.

Rey, Pierre-Philippe 1976. *Capitalisme négrier*, Paris: Maspéro.

Safa, Helen Icken 1974. *The Urban Poor of Puerto Rico*, New York: Holt Rinehart.

Suttles, Gerald D. 1968. *The Social Order of the Slum*. Chicago: The University of Chicago Press.

Vercauteren, Paul 1970. *Les sous-prolétaires*. Bruxuelles: Vie Ouvrière.

Waddell, Jack O. et Michael Watson (ed.) 1971. *The American Indian in Urban Society*. Boston: Little, Brown & Co.

Young, Michael, et Peter Willmott 1957. *Family and Kinship in East London*. London: Rontledge and Kegan Paul.

PART IV
PERSPECTIVES
ON CURRENT
ISSUES

CHAPTER 16
ON THE ORIGIN OF THE INEQUALITY BETWEEN MEN & WOMEN[1]

CHANTAL KIRSCH
Université de Montréal

Explanations offered over the past few years to account for the "social inferiority of women" have been many and largely unconvincing (see Kirsch 1976, for a review). Awareness of the realities of women's subordination, has led, on the one hand, to the rise of feminist movements and on the other, to new attempts at isolating the possible causes of this confusing phenomenon—confusing partly because previous studies have been largely androcentric, leading to the impression that everything truly human was necessarily masculine.

Many of the new attempts have come from anthropologists and, in my opinion, they are the most interesting (cf. Slocum 1975; Rubin 1975). In this paper I would like to introduce a number of points into the debate which have, however, been often overlooked by these anthropologists. It must be understood that any exploratory hypothesis offered here about the origins of the difference in status between men and women is in no way to be taken as a final or sole cause. If the social inferiority of women was established during the very process of humanization through one set of processes, still other processes might have contributed to the reproduction of the inferiority during subsequent alterations in historical conditions. It is also admitted that neither the original appearance of women's subjugation nor its degree during various epochs can be explained solely by economic causes. Nonetheless, such factors will be emphasized here as they appear to be primordial and have often been ignored by other writers.

The subjugation of women must not be viewed as a "male conspiracy," as it is in much modern feminist literature (see many articles in Ms. magazine and Millett, 1970). It does not appear to be fruitful or realistic to present men in general, both now and from the beginning of time, as a power-hungry group seeking to subjugate women. Rather than emanating from a masculine propensity to dominate, the social inferiority of women seems to be the result of prehistoric and historic conditions which remain to be identified and studied. In this paper I will dwell on processes which could have existed in the prehistoric period.

Some anthropologists, reacting against the "conspiracy theory," seem to think that the subjugation of women was inevitable simply because it happened, and do not seriously try to investigate which set of historical conditions were responsible. This view creates some problems: firstly, it may serve to justify the present social inferiority of women; secondly, it may stifle further research on the topic by encouraging the quick acceptance of partial and superficial explanations, (there are those who believe that everything was said in "The Origin of the Family, Private Property and the State," thus denying the relevance of the knowledge acquired about human evolution over the last century); thirdly, this position, being basically a-historical, ends up rationalizing the "naturalization" of historical processes. It is this latter danger which is at the root of many ecological explanations. They are merely superficial studies of the adaptation of different populations to their physical environment and ignore the historical conditions of social development. A prime example is Martin and Voorhies' book *Female of the Species* where women's inferiority is presented as adaptive with few mentions of why exactly it is adaptive in different societies and epochs.

We must avoid both subscribing to the conspiracy theory and the temptation to see women as "fallen angels." We must also avoid going too far in the other direction and placing men as a group outside the progressive social subjugation of women, making them merely passive spectators on the scene. The danger here is that women's subjugation will be seen as imposed by the physical environment, production requirements, child rearing, etc., without due consideration for the internal contradictions within the *relations* of production as a particular historical period, be it contemporary or primeval. In sum, saying that women's inferiority was inevitable merely intensifies the impression that there is an irreducible split between men and women and serves to perpetuate the *status quo.* Mechanical explanations of sexual inequalities lead to the naturalization of a complex social phenomena and hide actually existing forces from view.

I will try to demonstrate how, during the very course of humanization, women could have become socially subjugated. I will show how the process could have been an entirely *social* one rooted in productive and reproductive relations: and as a *social* process it becomes amenable to change and variation *right from the start,* something which, as a natural process, it does not. The hypothesis offered here is not to be considered a final statement: rather it is to be seen as an alternative to other explanations of the origins of the social inferiority of women based on the same kinds of data (prehistoric archaeology and the study of nonhuman primate behaviour, etc.,) but which postulate that this inferiority is "natural."

HUMANIZATION AND THE DEVELOPMENT OF SOCIAL PRODUCTION

What distinguishes human beings from animals is that they practise social production based on collective labour. This labour is planned in terms of goals conceived by a constituted social group. In addition to producing their means of subsistence, people produce a social framework within which activity is to take place, and this framework is designed with certain aims in mind. Social production, then, becomes the basis of material existence. Although the change toward this state was slow and gradual, once reached it was irreversible (i.e., it was a qualitative break with the past). My analysis assumes "completed humanization"—social production has become an integral part of the functioning of societies.

SOCIAL PRODUCTION: HUNTING AND GATHERING

Many authors believe that collective labour appeared after the invention of hunting (Moscovici, 1972). Without oversimplifying, it can generally be said that for most authors it is hunting invented by men that was responsible for cooperation, planning, etc. To maintain that hunting was the cause of humanization, then, is almost, by definition, to remove half of humankind, women, from a role in this great upheaval. Women, apparently, were strangers to this glorious accomplishment. A passage from Moscovici underlines the spirit of this theory:

> The punctual, individual and, in a manner of speaking, pre-human aspect of gathering is striking . . . Hunting involves . . . a complex series of prepared, organized, collective actions, an intellectual and technical ability requiring a prior formation of individuals. From this point of view the distance which separates a hunter from his female companion who gathers and forages, is comparable to the distance which divides a human species from a proto-human or non-human species (1972:139).

For many anthropologists, the great tragedy of women is that they failed to bridge this gap.

Many criticisms can be levelled at this kind of interpretation. Firstly, recent findings (see Teleki 1975) have demonstrated that the appearance of hunting among humans cannot be considered an "invention" as it probably already existed in an elementary form among prehumans (see Teleki 1975 on chimpanzee behaviour). Secondly, as females as well as males perform rudimentary hunting tasks in non-human primate societies, it is reasonable to suppose that such behaviour would be continued through the humanizing process (assuming humankind's ancestors resembled these modern primates in this aspect of their behaviour). Of course, one could hypothesize that females were suddenly prevented by men from hunting once the hunting process was completed, but it would be necessary to explain how. Thirdly, even if it is true that each sex is more or less autonomous with respect to the other in nonhuman primate societies, they nonetheless live in close association and constant communication. Thus there is unlikely to have been any great difference in the knowledge possessed by each sex even if we admit that each had its own sphere of subsistence activities. Studies of contemporary hunters and gatherers (Draper 1975; Goodale 1971) show that men are often aware of gathering techniques and women, even when they do not participate directly in hunting itself, possess a detailed knowledge of animal tracks and habits. The argument that both sexes were greatly separated during the early stages of humanization, thus does not appear convincing.

The assumption that hunting as such lies behind the process of social production is also suspect. This view, in part, rests on the further assumption that the first tools were "weapons" used in hunting. But as Slocum (1975) has observed, the tools discovered alongside early humans (e.g., handaxes) could have been equally suited to gathering, although they were also adapted to small game hunting. She also points out that collective labour may not have originated in hunting activity, but may have been an evolutionary tendency paralleling the development of an increasingly long maturation period. This would have lengthened the period of dependency of children and obliged mothers to increase production and share the products in a systematic manner with their offspring instead of intermittently as is the case with nonhuman primates. Further work on nonhuman primate modes of subsistence, particularly as relates to the hunting and sharing of food, and further discoveries in prehistoric archaeology may eventually allow a more solid hypothesis to be developed on the origins of social production, but for now we can at least avoid assuming the process can be attributed exclusively to one or the other sex. To assert that one of the sexes became human while the other remained animal would be to deny not only fundamental laws of genetics (see Slocum 1975, Harrison *et al* 1968) but also the relevance of the learning faculty in human development.

THE SEXUAL DIVISION OF LABOUR

Whereas there is little evidence to suggest that men's activities were exclusively restricted to hunting, and women's to gathering, there is much to support the view that women had more or less exclusive charge of children during maturation. On the first issue, among modern hunters and gatherers only *big game hunting* is exclusively male and even here women may participate by encircling the herd and tracking and beating the ground. Other tasks relating to hunting may be performed jointly or alternate between men and women. Some authors, in fact, try to separate men's big game hunting from women's domestic activities, particularly those related to child care. As they see it, women's duties in this area prevent the kind of mobility required in big game hunting as well as participation in such male activities as warfare. What these authors fail to observe, though, is that in many societies women are, in part, freed from their maternal obligations when they have important production tasks to accomplish (see Hammond & Jablow 1973). However, in certain societies, although the children are "watched" while the mother works, they do not receive full care in that they are not fed (see DuBois 1961).

HYPOTHESIS ON THE ORIGINS OF THE SOCIAL INFERIORITY OF WOMEN

Humans are social beings who must work in cooperation with others in order to survive. This cannot be an occasional collaboration among individuals based on circumstances and a haphazard distribution of the resultant product as is the case among nonhuman primates. Rather it must be a cooperation based on a capacity to plan, to forsee the long term, to produce as a group with the intention of sharing, to materially and socially support the young, the infirm, the elderly and to communicate through a complex language and symbol system. Social production, or the existing form of the relations of production, largely determines the conditions under which procreation occurs, that is, the conditions under which the human beings who reproduce the social relations of production are created.[2] If there is no social production procreation is reduced to a purely biological phenomenon as among nonhuman primates. With social production procreation becomes a social phenomenon and conscious effort can be made to reproduce productive labour at a rate which will offset any decline due to natural (or social) causes. And this labour must be reproduced as collective labour.

As we have seen, the atom of collective labour during humanization is most likely to have been mother and children, given that women actually produced and nurtured the children and that there was an extended maturation period. It is also likely that after humanization, women retained exclusive responsibility for children. Within this relationship it seems even more likely (and there is more evidence to support it) that one of women's most important tasks was to teach the children, initially, how to procure food, that is, not only show them how to find their own food individually, but how to participate in social production. Thus women had, objectively, considerably more power (potential power) than men. They could replace their own labour power at any given moment in time, with the labour power they produced themselves through procreation (impregnation is here assumed a noninstitutionalized process). Thus, at this stage, women had more chance than men of forming stable groups centred around themselves. They could reproduce a labour force which could hunt and gather and, in turn, reproduce itself.[3]

In other respects the two sexes must have been relatively equal:

both produced the same things, both cooperated in an organized fashion and were, as adults, mutually interdependent. Men were probably interested in children but only interacted with them regularly when they began producing as adolescents; women interacted with them regularly as infants and continued close ties through to adolescence because of their role as educators. As long as both sexes produced similar products, these latter differences between them were unimportant. The fact that it was women who were, in fact, responsible for the formation of the labour force did not present any particular problem for men so long as there was no specialization of tasks.

Although we do not know why specialization occurred, the evidence from contemporary hunters and gatherers indicates that it did, as almost everywhere men have exclusive province over big game hunting (if not all hunting activities) and women over child care. This was probably a very early development due to both the development of hunting techniques (including the proliferation of hunting tools) and the lengthening of the dependency period of children. It would then become necessary to socialize boys and girls somewhat differently—boys to big game hunting with adult males (something women did not participate in) and girls to child-rearing and collecting small game and hunting with adult females. A contradiction was thereby established between the division of labour and the women's control (potential control) over their children's potential and effective labour power. It was now necessary for men to train boys who were still under the control of the women (mothers) and who, in fact, still worked with them. The composition of production groups could now no longer be left to chance as was the case when men and women carried out basically the same tasks.

Although these conditions could have given rise to the social subordination of women, they would have been themselves formulated in a situation of nonsubordination—indeed of equality. Despite the contradiction, the two sexes would have continued to share their products as they had done in the past without any conflict. But now men needed male children and women, having a relative advantage in terms of power, might not have been eager to relinquish them.

Furthermore, with specialization, men found themselves more in need of the products gathered by women than women were in need of their products. Vegetable foods still formed the bulk of the diet and could be acquired more regularly. Men's problem, then, was twofold—a low productivity and lack of control over the labour force. There now appears the principal contradiction between the forces of production (the necessity of forming a labour force) and the relations of production (the mother-children collective). It is also possible here that production groups centred on women grouped together and possessed a degree of autonomy. In that case the only indispensable role played by men would have been to impregnate women.

Men, however, possessed the means of coercion (weapons) and if they were to control children's labour power they had to control women. But it is not necessary to suppose an act of physical violence here or even the use of force of any kind. Threat and negotiation could have achieved the same ends. But to resolve the contradiction men had to have control over the labour force, else they could not reproduce the relations of big game hunting by appropriating male labour.

Once male domination was established—true domination, that of one sex over another (different from the dominance found in nonhuman primates—great precautions must have been taken to protect the advantages gained. Ideological constraints would have been introduced—glorification of tasks men perform, myths justifying the new *status quo*—and the division of labour would have been institutionalized. This is not so much because it was necessary for production (women are, after all, capable of hunting) but because it was now necessary to keep women in their place—in a role newly *defined* as inferior. Taboos may also have been introduced on the use of hunting weapons by women.

This subordination of women should be seen as the end result of gradual changes in the relations of production without there necessarily occurring a violent confrontation or a battle between the sexes. The hypothesis does not imply the existence of a precise historical moment when the above-mentioned process shook human society. The process must have been a very slow and gradual one. It also does not exclude the possibility that, historically, different factors could have been important in different societies and at different points in time. It is not even necessary to assume the process itself followed the same pattern in all societies. The hypothesis attempts to show what *could have been* the material and social causes of the social subordination of women in a particular type of society based on hunting and gathering. This is one among other possible hypotheses. What I want to show here is that it is possible to build hypotheses which are nonsexist and are as logical and valid as the ones now in vogue.

It must also be emphasized that this hypothesis in no way assumes or implies the prior existence of the nuclear family, nor, indeed, any form of the family. It is not necessary to think that the social subordination of women occurred at this stage within any form of the family recorded by modern anthropology. Although certain kinds of groupings likely formed around shared "blood" ties among the first humans, as is the case for certain nonhuman primates (see Hinde 1974; Jolly 1972), there is no reason to suppose these ties were institutionalized and used as the basis for the formation of corporate groups. One would need other hypotheses to account for how such groupings eventually developed in human history. The hypothesis here, then, does not imply the existence of matrilineality as a principle of descent nor does it imply a patriarchy.

DISCUSSION

To my knowledge, the only author to have put forth a hypothesis taking account of the points mentioned above is Moscovici (1972), but he considers hunting as such the driving force in social evolution. Once men became hunters, he says, man became distinct from woman. Like myself, he believes that part of this process involved the appropriation of male labour from females by adult males. But, unlike myself, Moscovici thinks that females became "naturally" inferior to men after the "invention" of hunting. This "natural division" between men and women has persisted to the present day, he thinks, because there has remained an indestructible area within the relations of production, namely women's inferiority (the explanation is, therefore, tautological). This is despite changes in the form taken by the relations of production during the historical development of societies. Moscovici's work, while rich in detail and quite original, is nevertheless largely within the tradition of "Man the Hunter" (Lee and DeVore Eds.)—static and nondialectical, utilizing an "adaptive" model of people's relationship with their environment. Meillassoux (1975), on the other hand, although he analyzes women's inferiority in agricultural populations, assumes sexual equality for hunter-gatherers and, like many other anthropologists, does not press deeply enough into the issue.

Still other explanations of the origins of social inequality of women hold that inferiority was due to the fact that women were exchanged between men, or that subjugation was due to their being the object of acquisition through warfare. These views see women as a necessary commodity which can be exchanged, traded or captured. Women are here seen as a productive and procreative resource utilizable as mediators for alliances between men and for the acquisition of prestige items (Van Baal 1975). Although it is certainly true that the exchange and capture of women would *reinforce* the oppression of women (and therefore could be one of the precursors of modern subjugation), these factors could not, logically, be the original causes. This position assumes that women *already* existed in an inferior state—that is, they were already goods which could be disposed of and were not individuals who could dispose of themselves.

These analyses, then, start with women in a postulated inferior state and cannot shed any light on the initial causes of this inferiority.

Apart from this logical question, there is something substantively wrong about this perspective on inequality. Women are basically seen as vehicles for communication between men, that is, within the relations of production they are merely "mediators," having a lesser status than men in the productive process. But as we have seen, the role women play within the relations of production is in no way limited to the status they occupy in exchange *per se*, especially, in a hunter-gatherer context. It appears that the complexity of women's position in diverse social formations has been ignored by many anthropologists who have limited their role to "exchange between groups" within a very limited conception of the relations of production. In order to grasp the complexity of the problem of women's social subordination, the empirical and theoretical data furnished by anthropology must be reorganized according to principles which take account of all conditions of existence within which women live (economic, political, ideological).

WOMEN TODAY

Modern literature on women (Firestone 1970; Millett 1970; Mitchel 1971) demonstrates well how and why they come to be inferior in the majority of *contemporary* Western societies. Here one of the most interesting hypotheses is still that of Engels in "The Origin of the Family. . . ." He postulates that the social inferiority of women in western capitalist societies parallels the historical development of private property.

> . . . the particular character of man's predominance over woman in the modern family, as well as the necessity of and manner of establishing a true social equality between the sexes, will only blossom when men and women will legally have absolutely equal rights. Thus the enfranchisement of women has as its first condition the participation of women in public industry and this condition in turn necessitates the abolition of the conjugal family as an economic unit of society (Engels 1954:72).

This remark reveals the nature of the problem of women's social inferiority in modern capitalist societies. In a few of these societies, women now enjoy practically equal rights to men, and we may speculate that in a few years women will be legally the equal of men. (See, for instance, recent changes in Ontario Family Law.) However, they will be equal only within the bounds of capitalism—i.e., subject to the same forces as men.

Today, women have legal access to property; they may inherit, purchase real estate, invest, etc. Even though a few women may avail themselves of such rights, in reality the majority really have nothing and can look forward to having very little in the future. It is obvious that in capitalist societies this is also the case for many men: they sell their labour power from day-to-day and have no chance to accumulate. But the fate of women is even more precarious than that of men. In effect, the proportion of women in capitalist countries who have a full-or part-time job varies between thirty percent and about fifty percent of the female population of working age. There is thus a large proportion of women without any revenue: women who only perform domestic duties and care for their husbands and children. The majority of women have virtually nothing which belongs to them outright. They depend on their husbands for their subsistence.

Even if a large proportion of women manage the family budget (as in Japan, for example, cf. Okamura 1973), many others receive only the monies necessary to meet domestic expenses from their husbands. They have no material security. Usually all family possessions belong to the husband: house, car, furniture. If their husband leaves them these women are rendered destitute. They have no savings, no access to the husband's bank account, and no professional training. This economic situation can only maintain the social inferiority of women.

By the same token, as men are the usual family providers, they normally occupy a position of authority within the household. It is because women have no financial independence that many mistreated women cannot leave their husbands. In capitalist societies, the nuclear family is still an economic unit: it is the locus of procreation and of the reproduction of the labour force. It is not only the economic role of men whose wages allow the family to survive that is important to capitalist society:

> These (domestic) services allow . . . capitalists to maximize surplus-value in production; since if they had to pay a specialized labour force for these services, this would cost them much more. A larger part of social wealth would have to be devoted to this, which would entail a lowering of accumulated surplus-value. Rather than pay for two labour forces, one engaged in production and the other in services, the capitalist only pays one by including the reproduction of the worker's wife and children in the salary paid to the production labour-force (Bernier 1975:16).

But the economic importance of women's domestic labour is generally not acknowledged in capitalist societies. On the contrary, despite the "high moral worth" placed on the roles of wife and mother, domestic tasks are considered trivial and inferior. The woman who has no outside job is thus subjugated within the family—since she must bow to her husband's authority—as well as in the larger society.

The woman who remains at home often runs the risk of entering the ranks of welfare recipients and thus of the subproletariat, if she is widowed or abandoned. The laws designed to protect her have little effect: a woman who inherits from her labourer-husband cannot survive for long on the estate. Even if she inherits a house, she is often forced to sell it. Furthermore, many divorced women never receive the alimony which their husbands are legally obliged to provide.

The precariousness of the situation of women who stay at home, their relation of complete economic dependence on their husbands and, in the majority of cases, of psychological dependence, is often only realized by themselves and others when the marriage dissolves. Thus the increasing number of divorces and separations have made many women more aware of their need for economic independence.

Women who have jobs are in a less precarious economic situation than women who stay at home. Nonetheless, they have much heavier work loads: they must combine their jobs with their domestic work. They are thus in a difficult position. They most often hold badly paying jobs, which are insecure and require few qualifications (cf. Armstrong and Armstrong, 1975; Okamura, 1973; Szymanski, 1976; Sullerot, 1968). They are concentrated in a small number of activities and are only rarely unionized. Since their salaries are usually clearly inferior to their husbands', they do not fully escape the economic dependence experienced by housewives. This salary is often thought of as supplementary income—a sort of "extra" for the benefit of the working woman's family. In fact, the majority of women who work outside (their homes) do so because their salaries are indispensable to maintaining their families' standard of living. But the myth of the "extra salary" allows employers to underpay women, to fire them first, and to realize savings by making them work only part-time. In any event, the low level of women's salaries results in the inability of even working women to own much property, relative to men.

For example, few women can afford to buy a house, and even buying a car is difficult. It is men who make the larger purchases. A woman who has a job thus only rarely escapes her husband's authority, since the husband is still, by and large, the family's principal source of income. Nonetheless, a woman still may be able to scrape some savings together, to manage the money she earns, and if her relationship with her husband is too onerous, she can leave him.

If the actual tendencies of female work in capitalist societies are studied, it would seem that women will continue to enter the work force in ever-increasing numbers. They will nonetheless remain socially inferior to men as long as they remain in the slightest way economically dependent on their husbands, and as long as they remain a standby pool of labour power.

Even if every woman entered the work force, this would not mean that they would be equal to men. In effect, the exploitation experienced by women who work, their role as a reserve work force, their use by employers to divide the working class, are all characteristic traits of the manner in which minorities are treated in the capitalist system (cf. Vanderhaeghe 1975 and Bernier 1976). In the case of women, their sex serves as a criterion for discrimination which may be supplemented by criteria based on race, membership in an ethnic group, etc. This is why black women in the United States are more exploited than white working class women. One of the justifications of the economic exploitation of women is based on the fact that the nuclear family is an economic unit: women are not thought of as separate workers because it is assumed that they have husbands who "maintain" them.

If one wants to take stock, it would seem that the fate of women in capitalist countries has improved somewhat over time, since it is easier for women to become, in some measure, economically independent. This is the basis, the necessary condition, of the future liberation of women. Nonetheless, it is doubtful that such liberation can occur in a capitalist system—women are too valuable playing their double role. As I have said, they ensure that the costs of the reproduction of the labour force are kept to a minimum, they serve as a reserve pool of labour power, work for lower salaries, and they are used to further the divisions among the working class.

It is thus practically certain that even if women continue to enter the labour force, they will do so in the present context. They will remain inferior to men within the confines of the family as well as in the global society. It would seem that Engels was correct: in order for women to be equal to men they must not only secure equal *rights* for themselves but these rights must be actualized, that is, women's work outside the household must become so pervasive that the nuclear family disappears as an economic unit. This goal of independence would seem to be unobtainable in a society *based on* private property and profit. This does not mean, however, that women must stop fighting for the attainment of equal rights and free access to the labour market as it now exists, as well as for better organized social services. On the contrary, it is necessary that women struggle in order to better their living conditions and make sure that the rights they have recently gained and precariously hold are not threatened.

As Sacks (1974) has pointed out, while it is true that capitalism clearly maintains women in an inferior position, it does not appear, by itself, to be the original cause of this. There is evidence of inequality among other people with precapitalist economic systems, such as the Mbuti (Turnbull 1962), the Bushmen (Shostak 1976), and the Australian aborigines (Maddock 1972). In these societies there are few conflicts over territory, no endemic warfare, no problem of access to resources and no developed hierarchy, in short, none of the institutions associated with private property. However, it must be said that in some of these societies, (e.g., the Australians), expression of the social inferiority of women is more apparent at the level of ideology— in particular in the sphere of ritual association. Many male rituals in precapitalist societies have as their goal the consolidation of male power over women. This is the case with the Djanggawul cult of the Murngin of Australia which repeatedly attempts to affirm the superiority of men while recognizing that women as a group constitute a menace insofar as they could at any moment attempt to regain their power. Male power is thought of as having been stolen from women "in the beginning" and elaborate myths describe how this occurred and justify the fact (see Maddock 1972:152-153). Finally, despite the fact that women produce more than men in the societies mentioned above, their tasks and products are often defined as of lesser importance, and women may be mistreated (see Hart and Pilling 1960).

In our own society ideology is also one of the principal means of controlling women. It is a notably efficient instrument for restricting women to the household and its immediate environs (women's place is in the home, women are "naturally suited" to a housekeeping role, women cannot cope with the pressures and demands of the business world, etc.). It also teaches that the woman has the primary responsibility for *her* husband and *her* children and *her* household and that her tasks are individual and must be carried out alone in her place of residence. It thus strongly reinforces restricting and isolating women from other women and men and prevents them from organizing even such a simple thing as collective child care. And, as in many societies, women's activities here are still defined as inferior to men's (e.g., bringing home the paycheque is the really important thing). The sexual division of labour, then, is still a necessary part of the social inferiority of women and remains everywhere one of the material conditions upon which sexist ideology is based. But this ideology does not explain how women *came to be* subjugated—it merely explains why some women accept their "role" passively in modern society and how men maintain their dominance even though this need not be a conscious manipulation.

Neither does this ideology guarantee the maintenance of this relation in the future. It has its source in many aspects of the current relations of production, and these are changing. The sexual division of labour is part of these relations, but as important is the lack of control by females of the distribution of their products (e.g., property generated within the domestic arrangement) and the products of their husband's labour.

CONCLUSION

The above speculation on the form taken by inequality in early human societies is, of course, very hypothetical. But it does fit in well with what is now known in primatology and prehistoric archaeology as well as with ethnographic data on modern hunters and gatherers. In fact it could be expected that an elaborate comparative study of women in hunter-gatherer societies will lead to the further development of new and more precise hypotheses on the original causes of the social inferiority of women. These should, however, take account of the transformation of social relations and ideology which might have occurred between the first appearance of hunting and gathering societies and those we find still in existence today. Here I have tried to place women back into the process of humanization—as participants and not merely observers of the humanization of men. In the majority of treatments of human evolution women are excluded from the discussion and when they are included it is hard to see how they differ from female nonhuman primates (Lee and DeVore 1968 *passim*). I have formulated a hypothesis which is social and not strictly biological or ecological as an alternative to established views. In this effort two essential processes were located—social production and reproduction—which together in a hypothetical historical situation—early hunter-gatherer society—would have produced an opposition between people along sex lines.

335

NOTES

1. *Part of this paper is a revised version of Chapters 4, 5, and 7 of my Master's thesis in anthropology at the University of Montreal presented in May 1974. I would like to thank Bernard Bernier and Jacques Gomila for their comments and suggestions.*

2. *Biological reproduction of the labour force has two aspects: 1) long-term reproduction comprising the procreation of children and constitution of the labour force through maturation and 2) short-term reproduction or the day-to-day constitution of individual labour power by food, shelter, and sleep. The conditions which ensure the short-term constitution of the labour force are the same as those which serve the maturation of children (e.g., the "salary" in capitalist society).*

3. *I emphasize the importance of procreation in this paper, even though it is insufficient by itself to ensure the reproduction and survival of particular groups, because it has been largely neglected in previous analyses of social production. But as Engels remarked in "The Origin of the Family. . . .";*

> According to the materialist conception, the determinant factor in the final analysis of history is the production and reproduction of the immediate conditions of life. But this production has a dual nature. On the one hand, the production of means of existence, objects used for food, clothing, shelter and tools; on the other hand, the production of men *per se*, the propagation of the species (1954:15).

BIBLIOGRAPHY

Armstrong, Hugh and Pat 1975. The Segregated Participation of Women in the Canadian Labour Force, 1941-1971. *La Revue Canadienne de Sociologie et d'Anthropologie,* 12:370-384.

Bamberger, Joan 1974. The Myth of the Matriarchy: Why Men Rule in Primitive Society in M. Zimbalist Rosaldo and L. Lamphere (eds.). *Women, Culture and Society.* Stanford: Standford University Press.

Bernier, Bernard 1976. Bidonville, P.Q. MS 1975. *Les Femmes dans la Lutte des Classes.* Photocopied Article.

Davis, Elizabeth Gould 1971. *The First Sex.* New York: G. P. Putnam.

Draper, Patricia 1975. !Kung Women: Contrasts in Sexual Egalitarianism in Foraging and Sedentary Contexts. Rayna R. Reiter, ed. *Toward an Anthropology of Women.* New York and London Monthly Review Press.

Engels, Friedrich 1954. *L'origine de la famille, de la propriété et de l'Etat.* Paris: Editions Sociales.

Firestone, Shulamith 1970. *The Dialectic of Sex: The Case for Feminist Revolution.* New York: Bantam.

Goodale, Jane C. 1971. *Tiwi Wives.* Seattle and London: University of Washington Press.

Hammond, Dorothy and Jablow, Alta 1973. *Women: Their Economic Role in Traditional Societies.* Addison-Wesley Modular Publications, Module 35.

Harrison, G.A., Weiner, J.S., Tanner, J.M., and Barnicot, N.A. 1968. *Human Biology.* Oxford: The Clarendon Press.

Hart, C.W.M. and Pilling, Arnold R. 1960. *The Tiwi of North Australia.* New York: Holt, Rinehart & Winston.

Hinde, R.A. 1974. *Biological Bases of Human Social Behaviour.* New York: McGraw-Hill.

Jolly, Alison 1972. *The Evolution of Primate Behaviour.* New York: Macmillan.

Kirsch, Chantal 1974. *La division sexuelle de travail et l'infériorité des femmes.* Memoire de maitrese en anthropologie. University de Montreal. Non-publié.

Kirsch, Chantal 1976. Les différenciations biologique et sociale des sexes, La revue canadienne de sociologie et d'anthropologie, Vol. 13.

Lee, R.B. and DeVore, I. (eds.) 1968. *Man the Hunter.* Chicago: Aldine.

Maddock, K. 1972. *The Australian Aborigines.* London: Allen Lane the Penguin Press.

Martin, M. and Voorhies, B. 1975. *Female of the Species.* Toronto: Methuen.

Meillassoux, Claude 1975. *Femmes, greniers et capitaux*. Paris: François Maspéro.

Millett, Kate 1970. *Sexual Politics*. New York: Doubleday.

Mitchell, Juliet 1971. *Women's Estate*. New York: Vintage.

Moscovici, Serge 1972. *La Société contre Nature*. Paris: Collection 10/18, Union générale d'éditions.

Okamura, Masu 1973. *Women's Status*. The International Society for Educational Information. Tokyo.

Ontario Family Law Reform 1977. Toronto: Ministry of the Attorney General, Government of Ontario.

Rubin, Gayle 1975. The Traffic in Women: Notes on the "Political Economy" of Sex. Reiter, Rayna R. (ed.) *Toward an Anthropology of Women*. New York & London: Monthly Review Press.

Sacks, Karen 1974. Engels Revisited: Women, the Organization of Production and Private Property. Zimbalist & Lamphere (eds.) *Women, Culture and Society*.

Shostak, Marjorie 1976. !Kung Woman's Memories of Childhood in Lee, R.B. and DeVore, I. (eds.). *Kalahari Hunter-Gatherers*. Harvard: Harvard University Press.

Slocum, Sally 1975. Woman the Gatherer: Male Bias in Anthropology. Reiter, R.R. (ed.). *Toward an Anthropology of Women*.

Teleki, Geza 1975. Primate Subsistence Patterns: Collectors-Predators and Gatherer-Hunters. *Journal of Human Evolution*. Vol. 4.

Turnbull, Colin 1962. *The Forest People*. New York: Doubleday Anchor Books.

Van Baal, J. 1975. *Reciprocity and the Position of Women*. Assen: Van Gorcum.

Vanderhaeghe Andrée 1975. *Travail féminin et minorisation*. Brussels: Editions Contradictions.

CHAPTER 17
THE ECONOMICS
OF DENE
SELF-DETERMINATION

MICHAEL I. ASCH
University of Alberta

INTRODUCTION

"Dene" (pronounced de-ne or de-nay and meaning "the people" in various Northern Athapaskan languages) is the term of collective self-designation used by the descendants of the original inhabitants of the Boreal forest region of the Mackenzie River Valley in Canada's Northwest Territories. In the anthropological literature, this collectivity is referred to as "Northern Athapaskan-speaking Indians of the Mackenzie Drainage." However, the Dene are most commonly designated in the literature by their regional sub-units (once thought to be "tribes") such as "Slavey," "Chipewayan," "Dogrib," and "Hare."

The Dene recently came to the attention of the Canadian public during the debate over the planned construction of the Mackenzie Valley natural gas pipeline. Proposed by a consortium of multi-national petroleum corporation in 1971, this seven billion dollar venture to transport natural gas from Alaskan and Mackenzie Delta fields through the Valley to markets in Southern Canada and the United States was permanently halted in 1977. During the debate, the Dene as well as the descendants of the other original peoples of the Valley made clear their strong and virtually unanimous opposition to it. Once their position became known in Southern Canada through forums such as the public hearings of the Mackenzie Valley Pipeline Inquiry[1], it gained substantial support and this, in the opinion of many, was the catalytic force that led to the project's ultimate demise.

Soon another issue raised by the Dene will come to the attention of the public. It concerns their proposal to establish within Canadian Confederation a political jurisdiction within which they would have the opportunity to develop, for themselves, a modern political and economic entity, but one that is nonetheless consistent with their history and traditions.

The proposed territorial base of this entity would include virtually the whole of the Dene's traditional homeland—some 450 000 square miles in what is now Canada's Northwest Territories. In order to assert their political control over this territory, the Dene proposed in the fall of 1977, that:

> the present Northwest Territories be divided into three separate geographical boundary territories—one where the Dene are a majority, one where the Inuit (Eskimo) are a majority, and finally one where the non-native people are in the majority.

Each of these new territories was to be granted political powers that are virtually equivalent to those held by the Canadian provinces. Within each of the territories, the Dene proposed that political structures be democratically constituted and that they "recognize the political rights of all (their) citizens regardless of race," but that the specific form each structure takes would develop in accord with the history and traditions of each respective majority population (Press Release, Indian Brotherhood of the N.W.T. 1971).

The Dene have been much less explicit about how they would create a modern economy consistent with their traditions and values within the Dene Nation. Indeed, to date, they have made only one statement on this subject and it is rather vague and general. In their "Agreement in Principle between the Dene Nation and Her Majesty the Queen in right of Canada: a Proposal to the government and the people of Canada" on 25 October 1976, the Dene say:

> Clearly, we must develop our own economy, rather than depending on externally initiated development. Such an economy would not only encourage continued renewable resource activities, such as hunting, fishing, and trapping but would include community-scale activities designed to meet our needs in a more self-reliant fashion. True Dene development will entail political control, an adequate resource base, and continuity with our past. It will be based on our own experience and values. In accordance with our emphasis on sharing, Dene development will not permit a few to gain at the expense of the whole community.

But is such a proposition economically realistic? For example, do the Dene have the renewable resource base to maintain a self-sustaining, modern economy with a reasonably high standard of living? And, furthermore, given that the Dene have been under the influence of Western concepts and values since the beginning of the fur trade era, over two hundred years ago, do they have "traditional values" still in place upon which such an economy can be built?

The primary purpose of this paper is to deal with these questions. Then, in a concluding section, I will turn to another issue which requires further discussion: whether the Dene proposal is acceptable to the Canadian public.

TOWARDS AN ECONOMY FOR THE DENE NATION

As the above description indicates, the Dene anticipate that they will develop an economy that is based on the exploitation of renewable resources such as game animals, fur bearers, and fish, set within an institutional framework that emphasizes small-scale, community-centred structures founded on the principle of reciprocity or mutual sharing.

While the development of such an economy would undoubtedly be a new "creation," the general goals are nonetheless in some respects highly similar to the type of economic structure that arose during what is thought of by many as the "golden age" of Dene economic history: the fluorescent period of the fur trade during the years 1900 to about 1945. Therefore, in order to better understand the kind of economy the Dene forsee for themselves, it is useful to first consider the structure of the fur trade economy and to examine the reasons for its rather precipitous collapse in the period after World War II. Then, after outlining the current state of the Dene's economy, I will turn to an assessment of the potential for them to create at this point in their history a stable economy based on renewable resource exploitation.

THE FUR TRADE ECONOMY

As most of my readers are no doubt unfamiliar with the Dene economy, I will begin my analysis of its structure with a brief description of one typical regional variant—the fur trade economy of the grouping of Dene known as the "Slavey" Indians who inhabit the lake district to the east of the Mackenzie River between Great Bear and Great Slave Lakes.

As in the pre-fur trade era, the Slaveys sustained themselves, even at the peak of the fur trade, primarily through the consumption of locally produced and finished resources. Of these, the most significant included a wide variety of fish species, small game animals, big game such as moose and caribou, a number of kinds of edible berries, and other products such as trees and roots. From these resources, the Slaveys provided between ninety and one hundred percent of their food needs; the raw materials they used for fuel, the construction of shelters, boats, and sleds; and in the manufacturing of winter clothing as well as hand and foot wear.

In addition, the Slavey also relied on goods provided externally, mostly in Western industrial capitalist economies. From these economies, the Slaveys obtained new dietary staples such as flour, sugar, tea, and lard; luxury consumables such as tobacco, chocolate, and alcohol; most clothing; motors for their boats; and, significantly, most of the productive technology such as rifles and steel traps they used in harvesting bush resources. In return, the Slavey exchanged a single commodity of value to the Western industrial economy: furs.

The primary unit of production and consumption at this time remained as in the pre-fur era, the local band which consisted of perhaps twenty to thirty closely related individuals. In winter, these bands, in order to obtain raw materials, oriented themselves along the shores of the larger lakes (called fish lakes) which dominate the region. Here, the small game and fish, still dietary staples, could be found in most constant supply. As well, fur bearers now collected for exchange were most frequently found in habitats associated with these lakeshore microenvironments. Labour within the encampments was organized along age and sex lines with men responsible for the harvesting of big game and the collection of furs and the women, old men and children for the collection of other small game such as rabbits, berries, and fish.

In order to capture game, the Slavey still relied on a production technology dominated by tools and techniques such as snaring, netting, and trapping associated with entrapment. However, by this date, locally manufactured materials such as sinew and babiche had been replaced by goods such as wire, steel traps, and fishnet string, obtained through trade. As well, although big game was sometimes still captured by use of snares (ones now made from heavy cable), they were most often dispatched using the hunting rifle. Nonetheless, most production, even the hunting of big game, remained a labour-intensive, collective activity. On the other hand, the collection of fur bearers on traplines, although labour-intensive, was undertaken individually.

In order to obtain trade goods, Slavey men would, at least twice each winter, travel by dog team to the trading posts located along the Mackenzie River. As well, in summer, various local bands of Slaveys would encamp for perhaps two months at these posts for a period of easy living punctuated by festivities.

Finally, the institutional framework for production also remained unchanged from the pre-fur period. That is, productive technologies and labour power were considered to be controlled communally, not just by the local band but by the Slaveys (and ultimately the Dene) as a whole. Thus, exclusive control of "trapping areas" by individuals or groups never developed. Furthermore, within the local band (and, when the occasion arose between members of various local bands) produce obtained directly from the bush and indirectly through the fur trade was mutually shared by all. That is, generally speaking, all participated equally in the good fortune of the collectors and suffered equally when their luck turned bad. On the other hand, it would appear that furs themselves were considered to be the private property of the collectors and while their meat would be shared communally, the pelts remained exclusively in the possession of the individual.

Having described at some length the way in which the economy of the Dene in one region operated during the fur trade period, I would now like to proceed with my analysis of its structure as well as the reasons for its success and ultimate failure.

To begin with, it is clear that, broadly speaking, the economy of the Dene during this era fits the specifications the Dene have proposed for a future renewable resource economy in that it was based entirely on the production of locally available resources and operated within an institutional framework that stressed traditional values. Furthermore, it is also clear that the fur trade economy, with the exception of the addition of fur collection activities, operated on the ground in a manner that was quite similar to that of the pre-fur trade economy. Indeed, it might be said that the success of the fur trade as a renewable resource economy was based on its ability to raise the Dene standard of living and yet not require any major changes in the orientation of their everyday life.

Yet, if we examine the renewable resource economy of the Dene during the fur trade from a structural point of view, we find that it did not merely consist of the addition of fur collection to on-going traditional economic activities but was rather a new and distinct economic structure.

The Dene economy in the pre-fur trade era was based on a single mode of production which I will call the Dene mode of production, and consisted of a single sector which I will call the bush subsistence sector. From this economy, the Dene provided for themselves through locally produced and finished goods virtually everything they needed to survive and did so within an institutional framework in which cooperative labour, collective responsibility, communal land tenure, and mutual sharing were emphasized.

The introduction of the fur trade added a new economic sector which I will call the cash-trade goods sector to the bush subsistence sector already in place. Furthermore, the fur trade brought with it a new mode of production called capitalism and economic institutions that stressed individual ownership, private accumulation of goods, and individual responsibility. Thus, in addition to operating within the traditional bush mode of production, the Dene, in order to obtain goods from the trade, were obliged to participate in capitalism, which, as collectors of furs, they did in the role of small-scale commodity producers.

In short, the renewable resource economy of the Dene during the fur trade period contained two different modes of production and two distinct sectors. Indeed, one could almost say that it consisted, in theory, of two independent economic structures.

The success, then, of this economy rested on its ability to reduce the complexities and potential contradictions inherent in the economic structure of the fur trade into a smooth and consistent operation that differed little in its on-the-ground activities and institutional framework from the simple hunting economy that preceded it. The key to this success can be traced to three primary factors.

The first factor was the nature of the most significant product in the renewable resource economy—furs. Obviously furs were crucial as the means by which the Dene gained access to the goods available from the cash-trade goods sector. What makes them unique and pivotal in the economy, however, is the way they articulate with the bush resource sector.

Fur bearers, it must be remembered, already played a role in the

343

Dene economy even in the period prior to the fur trade. Furthermore, in most regions, fur bearers were found in the same locales as other game animals and could be harvested in conjunction with them. Finally, the fur bearer itself existed simultaneously in both sectors for it was not only a pelt to be used to obtain trade goods, it was, through the use of its flesh as food, also an aspect of the bush subsistence sector. Thus, for most Dene, the use of furs as the exchange commodity meant that they did not need to separate the economic activities necessary to participate in the cash-trade goods sector from activities needed for their continued participation in the bush subsistence sector.

The other two factors are associated with the nature of the fur trade as a business. One is its economic rationale. On one level, the purpose of the trade can be described as the exchange of furs collected by native people in return for items of Western manufacture. But such a description misses the point. The fundamental rationale of the fur trade is to make profits from this exchange. That is, the fur trade is a capitalist enterprise not only because it is organized on the basis of private property but as well because the rationale that motivates its operations is the accumulation of capital.

During the fluorescence of the fur trade, the world demand for furs was very high and, the supply limited especially after the closure of the Russian market after the Soviet Revolution. Therefore, the profitability of the trade was great. As a result, the exchange value of furs alone could provide the trader with high profits and simultaneously the Dene with enough "money" to fulfill all of their trade good needs.

The last factor concerns the fact that the fur trade was a capitalist enterprise of the *merchant* variety. This meant that unlike an *industrial* capitalist enterprise which would seek to increase profitability by reorganizing production along more "efficient" lines, the fur trade relied solely on differences between buying and selling prices of goods produced by others for its profits. As a consequence, the fur trade, broadly speaking, did not pressure the Dene to reorganize their activities to ensure high levels of production, but rather depended on the "positive" inducements of the presence of desirable trade items in order to achieve that end.

In sum, the success of the renewable resource economy during the fur trade era both as a structure and a means for obtaining increased material well-being for the Dene depended upon the continued availability of fur surpluses, high market values for this commodity in relation to the trade good needs of the Dene, and the continued dominance of the fur trade as the means by which the Dene economy articulated with the world capitalist economy.

The weaknesses that could lead to the ultimate failure of the economy can also be traced to the same sources. In the case of the Dene economy, the first concern—that of continued supplies of furs—was chronic throughout the fluorescent period and, indeed, after the influx of white trappers during the 1920s almost led to its collapse. On the other hand, the second consideration seemed, on the surface at least, to be insignificant, for profitability remained exceedingly high throughout the period and so the value the Dene received for furs stayed high enough to fulfill their trade good needs. Yet, ultimately, it was this factor that led to the economy's collapse. Due to a severe depression in the price of furs and an astronomical rise in the price of trade goods that lasted from the end of World War II to at least the middle of the Korean War, the value of furs alone could no longer provide profits for the traders and enough surplus value alone to sustain Dene trade good needs. As a consequence, the fur trade could no longer remain the dominant means by which the Dene articulated with world capitalism.

THE CONTEMPORARY DENE ECONOMY

The immediate consequences of the collapse of the fur trade economy was a gap between the value of the goods the Dene produced for trade and the value of the goods they required from it. In order to fill this gap, the Dene required "cash" income from other sources. Initially, the main sources were family allowance and old age pension payments which were introduced in the late 1940s. As these sources did not require labour, the Dene, in this period, did not have to shift their economic activities away from their fur trade era orientation and, indeed, Dene in most regions still lived in much the same manner as they had prior to the fur trade's collapse.

However, seeing that the fur trade would never return to its former prominence, the Federal and Territorial Governments began a policy in the 1950s to move the Dene from a hunting and trapping way of life and into the mainstream of Canadian life. The main thrust of this policy of directed culture change was to move the Dene out of the bush and into town where, it was argued, adults could find wage employment and the children could go to western schools and learn skills of value in an industrial capitalist society.

Although the Government pursued certain positive inducements such as new housing, improved medical services, and new schools to induce voluntary migration, the pivotal policy was rather more coercive in nature. Although family allowance payments had always been tied to school attendance, initially this was defined, for native children, as learning traditional bush skills. However, after the introduction of government supervised community education in the late 1950s attendance at community schools became compulsory and, in many regions, family allowance payments tied to attendance. Although boarding facilities, called "hostels," were available in many centres so that parents could, if they wished still live in the bush, payments in these cases would be turned over to the hostels. Thus, in order to receive essential cash, as well as remain with their children, Dene were forced to abandon their bush existence and move permanently into town.

Today, as a result of these policies, most of the Dene population, estimated in 1973 at approximately 12 000 (Berger 1978:8)[2], now re-side permanently in towns that range in size from 100 to over 600. As well, a generation of younger Dene have grown up away from the bush and have been fully exposed to Western education.

Yet, despite these pressures and the fact that the communities are situated in locales far removed from prime hunting and trapping areas, the Dene still rely for their economic well-being largely on the collection of bush resources. Thus, for example, Berger (1978:32) es-timates that in 1973, bush resource collection activities accounted for approximately $8.5 million or one-half of all Dene income. Of this, approximately thirty-nine percent with a cash equivalent value of about $7 million, came in the form of raw materials used in bush sub-sistence, while about twelve percent came from the sales of furs.

As well, bush production still provides the pivotal focus for Dene economic activities. That is, men (and except in the largest centres this is true of all men regardless of age and educational background) still participate on a regular basis in the production of big game, fur bearers, and fish. As well, old men, women, and children still pursue the collection of small game and berries, although these activities have declined somewhat in recent years due to decreasing yields as a result of their concentration in the vicinity of settlements.

Finally, it can also be said that the institutional framework and the economic rationale which arise from the Dene bush mode of produc-tion still remain dominant in Dene life. That is, labour activities asso-ciated with bush production are still undertaken collectively; where surpluses beyond the needs of the producer's family exist, they are not hoarded but are rather still distributed among members of the community on the basis of reciprocity; and finally, the Dene still hold that the land as a means of production is the mutual property of all and thus cannot be alienated by any individual or group.

This is not to say however, that the institutional framework and economic rationale of the capitalist mode of production has not in-creased its influence over Dene affairs. Without the ability to rely on furs alone to provide for their trade good needs, the Dene can no longer limit their participation in capitalism to that of primary pro-ducer in any industry that does not seek to interfere with their tradi-tional methods of production. As a result, some Dene now hold part- or full-time jobs and thus become exposed directly in the role of wage labourer in the institutional framework of industrial capitalism. How-ever, most Dene still try to rely primarily on sources of income, in-cluding transfer payments and welfare, that do not require additional labour input. Yet this does not free them from the influence of capital-ist productive relations. These payments are all made to individuals or nuclear family heads. Thus, they tend to emphasize the separate-ness of these units and to individualize ownership of capital. As such, the form of payment itself, conflicts with the institutions and values of the Dene bush mode of production. The situation is particularly stark with respect to welfare. The payments to individuals or families isolate poverty and create a division between "rich" and "poor." As such, welfare not only relieves the community of its traditional responsibility to mutually share, it actually provides a context that allows for something new: social differentiation based on relative wealth.

In short, then, Dene economic life is still oriented around renewable resource collection activities within an institutional framework dominated by the economic rationale of mutual sharing. However, because of the decline in the fur trade, they are now forced to participate in the capitalist mode of production in ways that challenge and could ultimately undermine that way of life.

THE ECONOMIC FUTURE

Clearly the Dene still have the institutional basis and economic orientation necessary to establish a modern economy based on renewable resource exploitation which is consistent with Dene traditions and values. Indeed, on a technical level, all they now lack is sufficient capital. Yet, the historical lesson is that the key to the long term stability of their proposed economy will depend at the most basic level on the method by which they obtain that capital.

The fur trade offered a near perfect solution, for as long as the price of furs was high, the economy operated as if capitalist institutions and rationales were not associated with it. On the other hand, the contemporary economy provides an example of the worst kind of answer for all that means of obtaining capital involve the Dene intimately in capitalist institutions. So therefore, the key question is whether the Dene can raise sufficient capital to operate the renewable resource economy without simultaneously undermining the institutions and economic rationale of the Dene bush mode of production.

The safest way to ensure this is through increasing the proportion of capital provided by the exploitation of renewable resources. According to estimates contained in the second volume of the Mackenzie Valley Pipeline Inquiry—the most recent and accurate source of technical data on renewable resources in the North—this sector could, with development and better management, provide a substantial portion of these needs. This can be accomplished, according to the report (Berger 1978:35-40) in three ways. First is the potential to increase production of bush commodities, especially furs—which Berger states could sustain twice the volume of production—and certain species of fish—which, according to his figures could yield, on a sustained basis, twenty million pounds rather than the seven million garnered at present. A second source would come from adding value to these commodities by processing them in the North before their export to southern markets. Among other manufacturing and processing operations, the Berger report suggests fur tanning, garment manufacturing, fish processing, and handicraft production as the most promising. A third means of obtaining revenue would derive from

347

the use of the North for sporting activities and tourism. Finally, there is also the potential to develop fur farming.

Were these operations in place, the renewable resource sector might provide enough capital to sustain a good portion of the $8.5 million Berger (1978:84) estimates is necessary to support the trade good needs of the Dene today. But, alone, they might not be sufficient. Furthermore, given the present state of the Dene economy, there is no way that renewable resource activities alone could generate the surplus funds needed to build or maintain the infra-structure required for the development of this economy. Therefore, the Dene Nation will need to secure capital from sources other than renewable resource activities in order to sustain its present trade good needs and to develop its renewable resource component to the maximum extent possible.

Under present political conditions, the sources of funds available to the Dene for this purpose are quite limited. They include, specifically, wages, transfer payments and, possibly, government grants. While, in theory, it might be possible to obtain sufficient capital from a combination of these sources, rather than extricate the Dene from the hold of the capitalist mode of production, all would entangle them ever further within its sphere. That this is true of the first two sources, I have already indicated above. The reality concerning the third alternative—government grants—shows no more promise. Government grants are made on the basis that the recipient follows standard business practices with the presumption that eventually the particular operation will show a "profit." In other words, it measures the economic potential for a venture on the basis of the institutional framework and economic rationale of the capitalist mode of production. It therefore would force the Dene to organize the development of the renewable resource economy on the very basis they seek to avoid.

On the other hand, should the Dene find themselves with provincial-type powers—especially the power to tax—within the Dene Nation, they would have available to them a vast source of capital which might prove less entangling in the capitalist mode of production: the rents, royalties, and taxes from nonrenewable resource activities now in place within the Dene Nation. The primary activity that could be taxed is mining. There are, at present, four major mining operations in the Dene Nation. These are: a lead-zinc mine at Pine Point, two gold mines at Yellowknife, a silver mine at Echo Bay, and a tungsten mine. According to figures supplied to the Mackenzie Valley Pipeline Inquiry by Arvin Jelliss, these operations yielded in rents, royalties, and surplus profits beyond fifteen percent over the costs of production in the period 1970-1974, an average in 1975 dollars of $39 million per annum. Of this figure, only about $15.5 million went to the Federal Government in the form of rents, royalties, and taxes, leaving a taxable surplus of some $23.5 million which might be available to the Dene (Jelliss 1977:64f).

The second source is crude oil production at Norman Wells. This oil well has been in operation since 1921. In the period between 1970 and 1974 it yielded approximately $6.9 million per annum of which $5.8 million remained after the Federal Government share was taken. In today's market, with higher oil prices, this figure could well be more substantial (Jelliss 1977:65f). The final source is natural gas production at Pointed Mountain. In the period from its inception in 1972 through 1974, this field produced an average surplus of over $22 million per year of which $21.8 million remained after the Federal Government had taken its portion in rents, taxes, and royalties. (Jelliss 1977:66f).

In short, the capital potentially available to the Dene Nation from Provincial-type ownership of nonrenewable resources within the Dene Nation amounts, even after the Federal Government share is taken, to over $51 million per year. With this capital alone, then, the Dene could easily meet their present day trade goods sector requirements of $8.5 million and still have enough surplus to construct the infra-structure on which to base their renewable resource economy.

This form of articulation with the world capitalist economy certainly has its drawbacks, not the least of which is that renewable resource development will be, at least for a time, dependent on an economic component that may not always be compatible with it. Furthermore, it is clear that the knowledge necessary to properly oversee and negotiate with these operations and operators requires a sophistication that may well require a lifestyle for some Dene that will alienate them from the economic life of most other Dene.

On the other hand, this form of obtaining capital is by far the best of the realistic alternatives available for the following reasons. Firstly, it is very like capital derived from the fur trade in that it does not require most Dene to participate in their everyday lives or even orient their economic activities to the imperatives of capitalism. Furthermore, it is in one respect even better than the fur trade, for the capital derived from the rents will, unlike that produced by furs, be controlled by the Dene as a whole and thus remain consistent with their emphasis on communal land tenure. Thirdly, as the funds will be controlled by the Dene, rather than by Government officials, they can be disbursed in such a way as to promote the development of the renewable resource economy along lines consistent with the institutional framework and economic rationale of the Dene bush mode of production. Finally, provincial-type power over nonrenewable resources will help ensure that the Dene on the one hand can maximize their control over the potential negative effects of the operations and, on the other, can reduce or even call a halt to their continued operation once the infra-structure necessary to run a renewable resource based economy has been put in place and sufficient funds have been amassed to ensure that this economy can sustain itself over a long period.

Of course, securing these funds will not ensure that the Dene Nation will be able to create a modern renewable resource economy consistent with their traditions and values. The potential, as I indicated above, may not be there. Also, the Dene bush mode of production in its present form is linked significantly to a division of labour based solely on age and sex distinctions. Yet, if the Dene are to develop the processing and manufacturing aspects of a renewable resource economy, new specializations and thus new parameters for dividing labour will arise. The historical question, then, for the Dene is whether—given the opportunity—they can translate their traditional institutional framework to take these new realities into account.

In short, then, the construction of such an economy is at best a gamble. But it is one that can have a reasonable chance of success only if, as a precondition, the Dene are able to gain provincial-type control in the Dene Nation.

CONCLUSIONS

In theory, as I have shown, the Dene possess the material and social resources necessary to build the kind of economy they envisage for their nation. The question is whether they will be given the opportunity to put theory into practice.

Were the Dene inhabitants of Africa or Asia, this question would, of course, not even arise. Their land, as indeed the lands of all Native Americans, have been colonized and, in principle, the Dene and all Native Americans possess a right to decolonization no less legitimate than that of the original peoples of Africa and Asia. Indeed, I would venture to say that were the Dene an African or Asian society, the majority of Canadians would support their right to self-determination and condemn those who would oppose it.

But the homeland of the Dene is not at a comfortable distance for principled stands. We, the recent settlers of North America, are not about to condemn our own presence on this continent, much less pack up and leave. Furthermore, we share with those colonists who settled in Australia, New Zealand, and Latin America, a factor unique among colonials: we are now the vast and powerful majority.

Thus, the Dene and all Native North Americans live in a reality different from that of their African and Asian counterparts. They must accept our permanent presence in their lands and also must persuade us by reason alone to grant to them the right to self-determination that we so casually extend to others more removed from our daily lives.

Whether the Dene can succeed in persuading the Canadian public is, indeed, an open question. Certainly, as in the Mackenzie Valley pipeline debate, they face very long odds, Yet, the support for the Dene's case expressed by average Canadians during that debate gives some cause for optimism. It does appear that, finally, Canadians are becoming more willing to accept that we have never dealt fairly with the original inhabitants of this land: that we may, in fact, be guilty of the same offenses we condemn so casually in others.

Thus, we may be more willing to give our sympathetic attention and even support to the notion of a Dene Nation within Canadian Confederation than the powerful interests opposed to the Dene realize.

In short, then, it is in the potential for the further maturation of our consciousness of ourselves and of the realities of our history on this continent that lie in the Dene's best hope to transform their nation from an idea into a reality.

NOTES

1. *This Royal Commission, commonly known as the Berger Commission, was conducted by British Columbia Supreme Court Justice Mr. Thomas Berger into potential social, economic and environmental impacts of the proposed pipeline.*
2. *All figures, except those noted are extrapolations from Berger and lump together native people of both the Mackenzie River Valley and the Western high Arctic.*

BIBLIOGRAPHY

Berger, Thomas 1978. *Northern Frontier, Northern Homeland: The Report of The Mackenzie Valley Pipeline Inquiry, Volume II.* Ottawa. The Queen's Printer.

Indian Brotherhood of the Northwest Territories 1976. *Agreement in Principle between: The Dene Nation and Her Majesty the Queen in Right of Canada.* Offprint Published by the Indian Brotherhood of the Northwest Territories, Yellowknife, N.W.T.

1976 Press Release pertaining to presentation of Dene position to the Federal Cabinet. Unpublished Manuscript of the Indian Brotherhood of the Northwest Territories, Yellowknife, N.W.T.

Jelliss, Arvin 1977. The Loss of Economy Rents. Watkins, M. (ed.) *Dene Nation: The Colony Within.* Toronto: University of Toronto Press.

ADDITIONAL REFERENCES

For further information on the Dene and their situation consult the Indian Brotherhood of the Northwest Territories, Yellowknife, N.W.T. Project North, 154 Glenrose Avenue, Toronto M4T 1K8

CHAPTER 18

COLONIALISM, APARTHEID AND LIBERATION

A Namibian Example

SUSAN HURLICH
University of Toronto
RICHARD B. LEE
University of Toronto

In their studies of nonwestern societies, many anthropologists have turned a blind eye to the colonial system of which they are a part. While offering detailed and often insightful analyses of the local community's kinship, ritual, and economy, they have relegated to the background the colonial administration and its array of subtle and not-so-subtle techniques of domination. This is unfortunate because, by ignoring the colonial system, social scientists fail to comprehend the most crucial social forces that are transforming the lives of the very subjects of their research.

Nowhere is this analytical gap clearer than in the study of African societies. In the early 1960s, for example, there was a lively debate among anthropologists over whether African cultivators should be called "peasants" or "tribesmen." The majority of scholars appeared to favour the latter view. Africans were "tribesmen," they argued, because they cultivated their own ground and were not plugged into a larger system of rent, taxation or markets as were the "peasants" of Europe and Latin America. However true this view of tribes may have been for precolonial Africa (and this is doubtful), the fact remained that most African tribesmen of the twentieth century *were* paying taxes—to the colonial authorities—and were marketing cash crops—cocoa, maize, coffee, or livestock—through government boards. In other words, the African peoples were in the process of being transformed by colonialism into a peasantry before the very eyes of the anthropologists!

In tropical Africa giant colonial trading companies specialized in the acquisition and export of agricultural and mineral commodities, while in Southern Africa the form of colonialism took a different turn. The influx of thousands of white settlers into South Africa, Zimbabwe (Rhodesia), Namibia, and the Portuguese colonies created a need first for land for farming and ranching and later for labour to work the vast farms and mines of the territories. The need for land and labour for the expanding economy led to two distinctive elements of the South African form of colonialism. First came the development of a system of native reserves in which the majority of the people were squeezed onto tiny islands of land thereby ensuring a cheap labour supply, and second came the legal and ideological apparatus to manage this system of exploitation and give it some semblance of justification, an apparatus which in its final form came to be known as the *apartheid* system.

The goal of this paper is twofold: to make intelligible the logic and dynamic of the apartheid system and its impact on indigenous peoples; and to introduce the student to the study of a liberation movement which has risen up in resistance to colonialism and apartheid. We argue that, just as no student could hope to understand the African societies of yesterday without a firm grasp of kinship theory, today the student must understand something of the wider system of political economy and class struggle in which millions of African people are involved.

In order to illustrate these points we focus on Namibia, a country in Southern Africa whose people have experienced colonialism and apartheid and who are now involved in a national liberation movement based on class struggle. First we look at the colonial history of Namibia and the development of apartheid there; second we study the case of the !Kung San, who in the space of twenty-five years have been transformed from an independent hunting and gathering people into an appendage of the apartheid system; third we examine the dynamics of African resistance to colonialism and apartheid, both in its early stages and then in the later development of a liberation movement exemplified by the South West Africa People's Organization (SWAPO) of Namibia.

NAMIBIA AND APARTHEID

Namibia (formerly South West Africa) is a country in the southwest corner of the African continent. The land is dry and mountainous with the Namib desert on the west, the Kalahari on the east, and with a more fertile highland area in the centre. The population of close to one million is densest in the north and falls off in the drier southern areas. The major traditional ethnic groups include the Ovambo and Kavango in the north, the Herero, Nama, and Damara in the centre, and the Basters and Nama in the south. About 20 000 San (Bushmen) live in scattered communities in the northeast, while the major urban areas and the best farms are dominated by 100 000 Afrikaner, German, and English settlers.

Namibia was a German colony from 1884 to 1915 and from 1920 to 1945 was ruled by South Africa under a League of Nations Mandate. After World War II South Africa alone of all the Mandate Powers refused to relinquish its grip on its territory and has continued to rule Namibia illegally in spite of a U.N. decision in 1966 declaring its mandate null and void.

Before the arrival of the Europeans, the African societies of Namibia lived by intensive horticulture in the north, by herding cattle, sheep, and goats in the centre and south, and by gathering and hunting in the northeast. Trade in locally-worked iron and copper was well developed but no market system or elaborate state organization had developed in the area.

European colonialism in nineteenth century Africa had as its main objective the search for new sources of raw materials for commodity production back home. The extraction of these commodities took three basic forms: through trade, through land, and through labour. In West Africa, the production of cocoa, palm oil, and ground nuts was left in the hands of the small-scale African farmer, and giant trading companies were set up to buy the goods. In East and Southern Africa, white settlers carved out farms of the most fertile lands and then set out to find cheap labour from the local African communities.

Colonialism in Namibia took the latter form: the early German settlers built their homesteads and then offered to buy some of the local livestock. At first it appeared that the transactions benefited both sides, but in fact the exchange was based on items of unequal value—a dozen native cattle for one rifle, or two native sheep for a bottle of brandy. As the Europeans bought more stock they began to fence them in, a use of the land that was puzzling to the Africans among whom land was always communally and never privately owned. One Herero chief when asked by a German farmer if he could buy a "piece" of land, placed some "land" in a bucket and offered it to the German. Since the Namibian land was vast, it was not immediately apparent to the people that allowing the settlers in would eventually result in their being ousted from their own land.

By 1904 over half the land of central Namibia had been lost to the settlers, and the Herero and Nama herders, now greatly alarmed by the shrinking land base, led a general uprising against the German colonial state. The Germans retaliated with an extermination order that by 1907 left three-quarters of the 80 000 Herero and a similar proportion of the 20 000 Nama dead—nearly one-half the entire population of the country!

After the suppression of the rebellion, German colonization expanded even more rapidly, especially when diamonds, iron, and copper were discovered after 1908. Now the need for native labour rose steadily to work the many new farms and mines. To meet this demand, various laws were enacted to impose grazing fees on the Africans so that they had to seek wage employment to raise the money for the fees. These laws had the effect of forcing Africans into the Eu-

355

ropean sectors of the economy and they illustrate how the laws of the colonial state worked specifically to benefit the settlers.

With the outbreak of World War I, South African troops invaded the colony to attack the Germans. The African people at first greeted the South Africans as liberators, buoyed by promises that their land and livestock would be returned to them. Germany was defeated in 1915 and South Africa quickly imposed its rule, but sixty years later, the black people of the territory have still not had their land and livestock returned.

South Africa was given responsibility for Namibia by the League of Nations in 1920. Under the terms of the Mandate, the population was to be prepared for eventual independence and South Africa was not to profit from the Mandate in any way. Instead, South Africa poured thousands of Afrikaner settlers into the country and allocated hundreds of new farms from the holdings of expropriated German trading companies. By 1928 there were 28 000 whites in Namibia, almost double the figure for 1913 and the Africans instead of liberation found a new colonial master in place.

During the 1920s, Namibia's economy boomed. In addition to mining and farming, a rich coastal fishery emerged as the third pillar of the economy. In the 1930s the breeding and raising of karakul sheep flourished, giving a new boost to the farming and ranching sector. The karakul pelt is a luxurious fur akin to the Persian lamb and Namibia has now come to provide over fifty percent of the world's supply. This industry is now dominated by the Hudson's Bay Company, a company that is no stranger to the fur trade in other parts of the world.

To develop the mining, farming, and fishing economy South Africa needed labour. Historically, labour has been one of the most important commodities in Namibia, for without it the settler economy could not develop. When South Africa took control of Namibia, it went about attempting to solve the problem of labour supply by speeding up several processes begun under the Germans. As early as 1922 the South African government began to allocate specific areas for African reserves. These areas consisted largely of infertile and waterless sandveld. These reserves not only barred the Africans from living on white lands but more important, they became invaluable labour preserves. Since it was impossible to obtain adequate subsistence on these overcrowded reserves, the conditions were created which guaranteed a steady supply of labour as Africans had no choice but to migrate out and work in the mining, farming, and fishing industries. And when one was no longer working, a series of iron-clad laws guaranteed their return to the reserve.

In the early 1940s the government set up a labour bureau which recruited migrant workers, dividing them into different job categories depending on their size and health. Migrant labourers were then sent to farms and mines for eighteen to twenty months at a time. They would return to their "homelands" for brief periods to see wives and families, and then sooner or later necessity would force the men back into the labour pool. Thus the system of migrant labour forced the separation of husbands from wives and fathers from children for up to three-quarters of an adult's working life. All this represented the practical application of one of the recommendations of an early South African Royal Commission which stated ". . . the Native should only be allowed to enter the urban areas which are essentially the White man's creation, when he is willing to enter and to minister to the needs of the White man and should depart therefrom when he ceases so to minister."

What kind of an economic system sanctions this inhumane treatment of human labour? Apartheid is a policy based on the idea of "separate development" for white and black. It dictates that blacks and whites must live in different areas, and all contact between the races is completely circumscribed by law. Blacks and whites cannot eat together, they cannot ride in the same buses, they cannot marry each other. These are some of the characteristics which make apartheid a policy of enforced racism. But its foundation rests on a colonial history where one group of people—mainly white settlers—aggrandized their own position of wealth and prestige at the expense of another group—mainly Africans—who were forced to work for them. It is important but not primary that the settlers were mainly white and the workers mainly black. The main point is that the settlers represented certain economic interests—the interests of foreign governments and businesses who wanted to penetrate and control for their own purposes the economies of local communities in Africa (or Asia or Latin America).

As a group which represents foreign interests, and which is united with them by their own economic aspirations, the settlers represent a *class*. In Namibia, this class comprises only ten percent of the population; it owns the farms, the mines, and the fishing industry, and also controls all positions of state power. The members of this class are mainly though not entirely white; some blacks belong to this privileged class, such as the government-appointed headmen. This class stands in sharp contrast to those who work on the farms and in the mines and fishing industries, and who own and control nothing. Although South Africa persists in viewing these workers as Ovambo or Herero *tribesmen*, the fact remains that a process of class formation is underway and these migrant workers are really a *proletariat*, or working class in the making.

Apartheid then is the policy which attempts to justify this economic and political division between owners and mere workers—between those who control and those who are controlled—by promoting the myth of white supremacy, and of the necessity for the African majority to "develop" separately from the whites because of their "special" African culture. Apartheid justifies in Namibia a situation where ninety percent of the population have been forced to live on the poorest one-third of the land—the reserves. By promoting the myth of race, the apartheid system attempts to mask the economic under-pinnings of oppression in Southern Africa.

THE SAN: A CASE STUDY OF APARTHEID IN ACTION

The last people in Southern Africa to experience apartheid are the interior !Kung San of the northern Kalahari of Botswana and Namibia. As hunters and gatherers, they are one of the few surviving representatives of a way of life which was once the universal mode of human existence. The !Kung have survived until today largely because of their extreme isolation, living at a ring of pans and natural springs around the Aha Mountain range and surrounded by a belt of waterless uninhabited country 50-150 kilometres wide. It was not until the 1950s that the interior !Kung—numbering about 1 000 people—first became known to the outside world through detailed anthropological studies conducted among the Nyae Nyae !Kung and later the Dobe area !Kung in Botswana.

The !Kung data demonstrated that the hunting and gathering way of life was not necessarily nasty, brutish, and short. The !Kung could satisfy their subsistence needs with a modest input of work (twenty hours per adult per week) and their groups were open and flexible in composition.

However, by the 1970s events had overtaken the !Kung. Having survived for thousands of years in the desert, the !Kungs' very physical survival is now threatened by the South African military machine.

THE BEGINNINGS OF DIVIDE AND RULE AMONG THE SAN

Except for a few white hunters, the main outside contacts of the San before 1930 were with neighbouring black pastoralists and agriculturalists to the north and east. In 1930 the European colonial presence began to be felt, though it was not until 1960 that direct administrative control of the interior was established with the founding of the South African government settlement scheme at Chum!kwe.

As long ago as 1884, !Kung gathering and hunting lands had been carved up by the European powers at the Berlin Conference and divided—on paper—between Germany and Britain on a line that fell between the Nyae Nyae and Dobe areas. !Kung awareness of this division, however, was not to develop until much later. Until the 1950s, the actual location of the border was unmarked, and !Kung moved freely throughout the interior. In 1954 the South Africans surveyed the border and cut a rough dirt track along its length which they patrolled monthly. But still the San could move freely back and forth to gather and hunt, and thus the border continued to remain of little concern.

In the late 1950s and early 1960s this situation dramatically changed, as South Africa began to apply its policy of apartheid directly to the !Kung, seeking first to divide the Dobe area !Kung from the Nyae Nyae !Kung, and second to divide the !Kung from the blacks. It was at this time that the !Kung themselves began to make a distinction between "Burusi n!ore" (Boer country) to the west and "/Ton n!ore" or "/Tebe n!ore" (British or Tswana country) to the east, and became acutely aware of the Botswana-Namibia border located only two kilometres west of the Dobe waterhole.

In order to strengthen its grip on the border region and establish a colonial infra-structure where none had existed before, South Africa built a series of government stations in northern Namibia during 1960-65 and lured the Nyae Nyae !Kung to come and settle at Chum!kwe with the promise of free rations and medical care. In the first few years of the settlement some 700 people came—far more than anticipated—and the South Africans were faced with the problem of whom to accept and whom to exclude. The neighbouring Botswana pastoralists were rigidly excluded, but how were they to distinguish between !Kung from Namibia and !Kung from Botswana when all !Kung looked alike, were related by kinship, and all moved freely back and forth?

The Marshall family—early anthropologists who had studied the !Kung—had turned over copies of their genealogical and census materials to the SWA Department of Native Affairs after their field work of the 1950s. The administrators later misused this data to determine who was a bona fide Namibian !Kung and who was not by checking individual !Kung against the Marshall data when they reported to the settlement's office for their weekly ration of maize meal. If the !Kung were recorded as residents of Namibian waterholes, metal numbered dog-tags were issued which had to be presented each time food was handed out. If no names were recorded in the Marshall books, they were denied rations and told to return to Botswana.

The strong !Kung institutions of sharing and gift exchange initially foiled this crude attempt at divide and rule, and a lively trade in dog-tags sprang up on both sides of the border. Later when South Africa instituted a system of wage payments for labour, food hand-outs were phased out and the trade in dog-tags declined, though visiting and sharing among the !Kung continued.

In the mid-1960s other techniques of domination were introduced. A Dutch Reformed Church missionary-linguist was sent to Chum!kwe. After gaining the people's confidence through free food and medical care, this missionary later turned openly hostile to !Kung traditional healing dances, calling them the work of the devil. Next a primary school was opened in which !Kung was the language of instruction with only Afrikaans offered as a second language. The exclusive use of !Kung and Afrikaans further entrenched the isolation of the !Kung from other black peoples while providing a channel of communication with only the Afrikaner ruling party.

Economically the !Kung were introduced to the value of wage labour and consumer goods such as transistor radios, western clothing, powdered milk and commercial baby formula became popular items in the Chum!kwe store. Much of the remaining !Kung income went into ingredients for brewing home-brew beer, and in the late 1960s the Chum!kwe settlement became the site of marathon drinking bouts, brawls, absenteeism, and child neglect caused by drinking. Politically, "leaders" were appointed from the native community by the South African authorities. But these new leaders had little credibility with the people because in traditional !Kung society there were no chiefs or headmen who were seen as having any authority.

THE BIRTH OF THE LIBERATION STRUGGLE IN NAMIBIA

In order to understand what happened next to the !Kung San we have to look at the wider context of Namibian society under South African rule. Although the !Kung enjoyed relative autonomy from the colonial state until 1950, most of the other people were not so fortunate and their hardships are reflected in their long history of anti-colonial struggles. Even after the submission of the Herero and Nama in 1907 the people of Namibia continued to resist. The Bondelswart Nama in 1922 and the Ovambo in 1932 rose up in rebellion. Both were forcefully suppressed by the South African administration and land expropriations and forced labour continued unabated. By comparison, the !Kungs' initial experience of colonialism and apartheid was relatively benevolent.

Although the government got the upper hand militarily this early resistance had important consequences for the people; it challenged the traditional parochialism of Namibians and helped them to see that the injustice of the seizure of land and the migrant labour system was not a problem of the Herero or Ovambo alone, but was common to all the indigenous people of Namibia. It was this growing awareness that served to forge the beginnings of a national consciousness and later a class consciousness among Namibians.

In the era of decolonization following World War II, colonial powers such as Britian and France dismantled their African empires. This was partially in response to the emerging nationalism in their colonies which had as its aim the end of oppression and the institution of governments under majority rule. Portugal and South Africa, however, dug in their heels and ignored the anti-colonial resolutions of the U.N. In the former Portuguese colonies of Mozambique, Angola, and Guinea-Bissau, this intransigence eventually led to the development of popularly-based revolutionary movements committed to the total transformation of society.

In Namibia, the people's desire for an end to domination has given birth to a similar revolution, one which has its roots in the earlier resistance to German colonialism but particularly in the nationalist up-surges of the 1950s. At this time, Namibian students and workers began organizing against the domination of the South African regime. In 1959 massive demonstrations and boycotts met the forced removal of Africans from the capital of Windhoek to a barren location five miles away. South Africa again responded with violence, killing twelve and wounding more than fifty.

By 1960 nationalism in Namibia had gained a popular base, and SWAPO was formed as a broad-based national liberation front. Then followed a wave of arrests, detentions, and exile of SWAPO leaders, and when in 1963 public meetings were banned, SWAPO went underground. Finally, after years of peaceful appeals to the South African authorities being met by violence and hundreds of petitionings to the U.N. met by an increased entrenchment of apartheid, SWAPO decided that only through armed struggle could the country be freed. On August 26, 1966 the first armed SWAPO militants entered the Caprivi Strip from neighbouring Zambia and engaged in their first combat against South African soldiers. In the same year, the U.N. terminated South Africa's Mandate over Namibia, a ruling which was confirmed in 1971 when the International Court of Justice declared South Africa's continued presence in Namibia illegal.

With the onset of the armed struggle, South Africa's tactics vis-à-vis the Namibian people entered a new phase. Namibia is today an occupied country with 50 000 South African soldiers in the north alone. The army and police in Ovamboland have virtually unlimited powers of arbitrary arrests and indefinite detentions against the local population—a situation which has existed since February 1972 when the ruling authorities enacted Emergency Proclamation R17 as their answer to a massive strike involving over 15 000 migrant workers.

With the San, South Africa foresaw a different scenario. Through the application of counter-insurgency warfare techniques, the South African occupation forces have been attempting to draw the !Kung and other San deep into the morass of their illegal war as unwitting participants on the side of apartheid. This story is eerily reminiscent of the use that the American Green Berets made of the Montagnard tribesmen of the strategic central highlands of Vietnam.

Some of the major techniques of counter-insurgency warfare being used against the !Kung include, quarantine, dividing the people on ethnic lines, terror tactics, and psychological warfare.

The most dramatic impact, however, has been the wholesale incorporation of some of the most isolated bands into paramilitary tracking units directly involved in the anti-guerrilla war. These units have been set up in isolated border posts where they are "protected" against outside influences, and are virtual prisoners of the army, dependent on them for their water and their weekly rations and for other supplies.

The units make daily patrols along the Botswana border fence looking for fresh tracks. Any signs are reported to the police within hours.

The trackers also frequently visit !Kung villages inside Botswana where they have been instructed by South Africans to observe closely any unusual behaviour and say nothing. The result is that the trackers now enter !Kung camps and sit silently at the perimeter. This is bizarre behaviour by !Kung standards; just as !Kung place a high value on sharing and reciprocity of food, so they emphasize sharing and reciprocity of information. Ironically, Dobe !Kung now refer to the !Kung South African puppet troops as "shumbus," a term meaning ghosts which they used to apply to the earlier freedom fighters!

Until recently, much of the information about the manipulation of the San was unknown to the outside world. Then in late 1977 the South African Defence Forces made known the existence of secret San military bases in the Caprivi Strip and took South African newsmen on a tour of some of them. A typical report on these bases in the *Windhoek Advertiser* of 22 September 1977 reads,

> *Deep in the dense Caprivi bush a colony of Bushmen are being taught a new culture and a new way of life by the White man. More than a thousand Bushmen have already discarded the bow and arrow for the R1 rifle and their wives are making clothes out of cotton instead of skin . . .*
>
> *A handful of South African soldiers started the colony some time ago, attracting the children of the veld to a secret Army base where they are teaching them the modern way of life . . .*
>
> *The men are being trained as soldiers while their womenfolk learn how to knit, sew and cook . . .*
>
> *It is an open camp and the people may come and go as they please, but most of them prefer to stay.*

But are these camps really open? In reality these military bases are really nothing more than "protected villages" or "strategic hamlets" of the kind set up by the Americans in Vietnam and more recently by the Ian Smith regime in Zimbabwe ostensibly to "protect" the inhabitants from the guerrillas, but in reality to prevent the inhabitants from giving support to the freedom fighters.

The parallels to Vietnam can be carried further. In the central highlands of Vietnam and in Laos entire tribes of Montagnards, numbering thousands of people, were wooed by the Special Forces and by CIA operatives during the 1960s. Some like the Mnong Gar were badly displaced by the war and their forest environment repeatedly bombed. Others were herded into refugee camps. In both the Montagnard and the San cases whole communities of women and children are brought into the war zone, thereby subjecting not only men but entire societies to the threat of injury and death.

Theo-Ben Gurirab, SWAPO's Chief Representative at the U.N., has commented on these press reports saying that the San are being misused by South Africa as "landmine sweepers" in a war against their will and best interests. He goes on to say:

The Bushmen being traditionally hunters are being used by South Africans as trackers. In the process they become victims of land-mines and guerrilla ambushes . . .

These ancient people . . . are lured with tobacco, dagga (mari-huana) and meat to do the dirty job . . . Since they always walk in front of patrolling soldiers in most cases they receive much of the punishment intended for the racist soldiers. Their population being small, our concern is that they might be exterminated. [3]

The attempt of South Africa to use the politically unsophisticated San in its illegal aggression against Namibia represents only one case of what the apartheid regime is trying to do elsewhere in the country. It also represents the desperate act of a regime which is now facing its most serious challenge to date: a people united and determined to fight for their liberation. As SWAPO is the national liberation movement which is leading this struggle against apartheid, it is to SWAPO that we now turn.

SWAPO: A PEOPLE'S MOVEMENT

What does a liberation movement look like and how are we to understand its organizational basis and principles? Not all liberation movements develop in the same way, nor is it inevitable that they develop at all. In Namibia—as in the former Portuguese colonies—it was partially the intransigence of the oppressive regime itself which led to the development of SWAPO. But oppression and the anger it causes do not in themselves make a revolution. People must understand what they are fighting for, how to fight effectively, and how to organize among their own ranks. In Namibia it was not until the formation of SWAPO that the people were able to implement these prerequisites of a national liberation struggle.

A liberation movement such as SWAPO is first and foremost a people's movement. Its membership as well as its leadership is composed largely of workers and peasants and a smaller number of intellectuals or others who have received education under the apartheid regime. SWAPO differs from the earlier nationalist movements of the 1950s in several respects, one of the more important being that it operates simultaneously on two fronts: the political and the military. These two fronts are interrelated, as one of the cardinal principles of guerrilla warfare is that the militants must educate and win the allegiance of the people while attacking military targets of the enemy.

There is also another way in which SWAPO differs from the earlier nationalist upsurges. Wheras in the 1950s resistance was mainly local or tied to specific issues like the migrant labour system, with the formation of SWAPO political action became nationally coordinated for national objectives. More recently, among the more militant cadres, there is an increasing awareness that the struggle is twofold: for national independence *and* social liberation, the latter having to do with the creation of a new society and the development of a new political consciousness among the people for this task. But this process is not a mere spontaneous occurrence. Just as the apartheid system has techniques of domination through which it attempts to control the local population, so too does a liberation movement have principles around which it educates and mobilizes the people to combat this domination. We will here consider three principles fundamental to SWAPO's policy of action:

1. combining guerrilla warfare with political mobilization;
2. uniting the people along national rather than ethnic lines;
3. identifying the enemy within.

COMBINING GUERRILLA WARFARE WITH POLITICAL MOBILIZATION

To be a member of PLAN—the People's Liberation Army of Namibia, the armed wing of SWAPO—it is not enough to just pick up a gun. Before this, each SWAPO militant must go through an intensive process of military training and political orientation. In these orientation programmes militants learn among other things that the enemy is not the white race which must be destroyed but a system of oppression which must be dismantled. In teaching this lesson SWAPO is preparing the ground for the emergence of a genuinely nonracial society in Namibia. Kakauru Nganjone, a Political Commissar with PLAN since 1972, has described the objectives of PLAN in the following terms:

> We are waging a war, a liberation war which must be fought arms-in-hand by the Namibian people themselves. Therefore, our first task is to build a party capable of mobilizing the masses . . . The demands on us are extraordinary. We must be extraordinary ourselves . . . By building the People's Liberation Army, we are also building a core of political cadres who will act as catalysts within the country during the armed struggle and after independence. These cadres will be the ones to educate the people about the way we want Namibia to be. They will fight for the well-being of our people and educate the young ones towards a revolutionary spirit . . .
>
> When we go into a region where there has been no previous PLAN or SWAPO activity we first engage in political education. We tell the people what our objectives and programs are. We are very careful about how we act, to counteract the Boers' propaganda that we are bandits and thieves. We help them in their work, and sometimes teach them other things. Working with them, we win their confidence, and they are willing to help us with food or whatever they can to help free Namibia. (1976:20, 27)

When PLAN militants first entered the Caprivi region, the local peasants not only helped them by giving them food, but refused to betray their location to the South African police. In some cases, they knew the militants personally because they had come from the same family or village. In other cases, they knew that because the militants had themselves experienced the injustice of having their lands taken away and being forced to work as migrant labourers hundreds of miles from home, they would understand the suffering of the people. There was thus a common bond between them, which the militants helped to articulate because of the political education which they themselves had undergone. In response to this situation, the administration began to retaliate against the local people by arresting them and often torturing them to get information. Because of this intimidation thousands of Namibians have fled the country to neighbouring Zambia, Angola or Botswana. Since 1968 many of these same people have returned to Namibia as PLAN militants.

The armed struggle in northern Namibia has not only further politicized the peasantry by drawing them into the struggle as active partners of the militants, it has also involved people in a basic reorganization of their lives as more and more areas come under SWAPO control. As early as 1972 SWAPO was speaking of areas in the north where militants were working along with the people to provide a rudimentary medical service and mobile schooling system where none formerly existed. By 1977 SWAPO had areas in the north where over 100 000 people had been organized under the semi-administrative authority of PLAN, and where structures of health care and basic education were being established and production reorganized. Though still subject to air attacks by the South African forces, these semi-liberated areas are important for two reasons: firstly they provide people with the concrete experience of social, economic, and political reconstruction and secondly they have an invaluable spin-off effect in mobilizing and educating people elsewhere in the country about the reasons and objectives for the struggle.

TO DIE A TRIBE AND BE BORN A NATION

The policy of divide and rule, which has been the characteristic policy of colonialism everywhere, creates an insoluble contradiction for the colonial power. In order to keep people divided along cultural and ethnic lines, and to try to create class allies from within the ranks of more traditional authorities and leaders, it is necessary to "preserve," at least to some extent, the integrity of the traditional social structure and culture. On the other hand, colonialism can only ultimately survive if it has destroyed, at all levels, the capacity of people to unite for common action. The preservation of traditional social structures, even if robbed of their economic base, provides one channel through which people can mobilize against the colonial power.

In order to mobilize however, the traditional leaders must first transcend their ethnic self-image and move to a new level of national consciousness. This step is a critical transformation in the ideology of every mass-based liberation movement. For example, in October 1976 the traditional leaders of the four most important Nama communities in southern Namibia, which together represent over three-quarters of the 32 800 people living there, after long deliberations issued a statement announcing their decision to formally unite with SWAPO in the national liberation struggle. In assessing the reaction of the South African state to their move, these Nama leaders state:

> . . . We will especially face a lot of attempts to create tribalist divisions, but no one will fool us with this any more. We say to those false advisers: Any attempt to create minority rights is nothing else than defining the quality of a Namibian by his colour, language, religion, social or ethnic origin or sex. There are no minorities, there are no special rights or duties for any section of the people of Namibia. We are all Namibians, with the rights which our work confers on us, with the same duty to build a united, peaceful and democratic nation. [4]

This statement—to die a tribe and be born a nation—has been made not only by the Nama but by many other peoples as well. During 1976, organizations representing the Baster and Damara peoples also disbanded their separate status and merged with SWAPO. And in April 1977, the Association for the Preservation of the Tjamuaha/Maharero Royal House—an organization representing the traditional chieftainship of the Herero and to which more than 17 000 people belonged—joined forces with SWAPO. The reasons are spelled out by Reverend B. G. Karuaera, former chairman of this Association:

> First of all, this decision was borne out of the conviction that the South African government was busy dividing the people inside Namibia and putting them one against the other—the different tribes—using the ethnic leadership. We didn't want the South African government to have the chance of using us as an ethnic group against SWAPO.
>
> Secondly, we thought that only by unity can we strengthen the struggle of the oppressed people in Namibia, and as SWAPO is now the leading liberation movement of the Namibian people, any unity politically or otherwise outside of SWAPO will be eventually used by the South African government to oppose SWAPO. [5]

"Only by unity can the struggle proceed" is the theme in statement after statement. The decisions of these local organizations and traditional councils represent an important development in the Namibian struggle for two reasons. Firstly, they show the clear rejection by the people of any attempt to preempt the struggle by dividing them along "tribal" lines. By uniting with SWAPO not as Nama or Herero but as Namibians, these groups have dealt a serious blow to South Africa's divide and rule policy. Secondly, in the case of particularly the Nama and Herero organizations, they represent the potential for the traditional leadership to actually serve as a mobilizing rather than as a conservative force in the resistance against oppression. In the south it is actually the traditional chiefs and headmen who are leading the struggle, and who in some cases have been appointed to important leadership positions within SWAPO itself. A comment from one of these leaders brings home the tremendous strength of culture and tradition when they become merged with a genuine liberation struggle.

> The most powerful weapon we have is our history and our culture. Our forefathers failed to fight colonialism successfully simply because they were not united soon enough. But nothing remains static. In the process of the struggle you learn new methods. Today you do a thing one way, and tomorrow you learn other ways of doing it. [6]

KNOWING THE ENEMY WITHIN: FROM NATIONALISM TO REVOLUTION

So far we have outlined the class structure of Namibia in terms of two classes: the *ruling class* and the *workers and peasants*. But there is also a third class, numerically small but politically very important, which is comprised largely of Africans who have received what education the regime offers: teachers, nurses, traders, and civil servants connected with government-appointed "tribal" authorities and departments. This class—the *petty bourgeoisie*—plays an interesting role in colonial situations. It is from the needs of colonialism itself that this class develops, for its members represent the people from among the oppressed who are being trained to service the oppressive system itself. The petty bourgeoisie represents an attempt by the colonial power to create a class of local people who have a stake in the colonial system and who have been educated to see the world the colonialists' way.

However, under apartheid, this petty bourgeoisie is subjected to the same constraints which control the majority of the people. They cannot own land. A teacher is not simply a teacher, but is a Herero teacher or a Damara teacher or an Ovambo teacher who must teach in the "appropriate" ethnic school located in the "appropriate" reserve. So in an important way, the petty bourgeoisie is never quite separated from the workers and peasants.

It is largely from the petty bourgeoisie, rather than from the peasants, that the first stirrings of nationalism arise. In Namibia in the 1950s, nationalism was first expressed among the students and only later was broadened to the workers. Even when the workers were being mobilized, it was largely the intellectuals who were doing the organizing.

In SWAPO, the existence of this petty bourgeoisie creates a potentially double-edged sword, and an understanding of this issue is absolutely critical for an understanding of liberation movements today. The intellectuals, teachers, etc. provide leadership, but they also represent a potential elite capable of being co-opted by the enemy. However, if the gap between the leadership and the mass of workers and peasants is closed, the formation of an elite can be preempted. The petty bourgeoisie is thus faced by two choices: it can either become more bourgeois, and try to co-opt the liberation struggle for its own ends, or it can identify fully with the working people and the peasants. This means, among other things, that the leadership lives and works with the people, and that the skills of the petty bourgeoisie are turned to the needs of the masses rather than to self-aggrandizement.

These aspects of the petty bourgeoisie are being noted here to bring out two points. Firstly, it is important to understand that the struggle in Namibia is not just a class struggle between the forces of colonialism/imperialism and the forces of liberation. It is also a class struggle within Namibia and even within SWAPO itself. Secondly, the potential for dividing the movement is one of the major assets of the colonial state. For example, South Africa has lost no time in attempting to play these potentially divisive strands within SWAPO off against each other, thereby attempting to undermine the struggle. This became most evident during 1975, when there was an attempt made to split SWAPO from within. At this time, several SWAPO members in senior leadership positions were able to spread propaganda among some of the PLAN militants and members of the SWAPO Youth League the intent of which was to precipitate a leadership crisis. Later investigation revealed that these same individuals had been in direct collaboration with South African police.

SWAPO of the late 1950s and early 1960s represented a broad-based united front whose main aim was independence from colonial rule. But in the course of struggle people change, and their understanding of what they are doing also changes. With the beginnings of armed struggle in 1966, a process was set in motion where some people—particularly the militants—began to rigorously test their political understandings against the practical tasks of military struggle and mobilization of the masses. This process of education by combining theory and practice has a built-in corrective, which eventually leads to a deeper and qualitatively different understanding about the very nature of what one is fighting for.

This new understanding has led to sharp differences within SWAPO about goals and long-term strategy. On the one hand, there are those who see the struggle as being fundamentally anti-colonialist, with few questions being asked about the nature of the society which will be brought in after independence. On the other hand, there are those who see the struggle as not just anti-colonialist, but as anti-capitalist and anti-imperialist, meaning that the enemy is not just South African domination, but also those foreign governments and businesses which, through trade and corporate ties, support the continuation of apartheid.

This struggle within SWAPO is taking place at all levels and among all sectors of the population. During a visit to Namibia, in 1976-77 it became clear that there is emerging a strong move away from the old-style nationalist politics towards a much more revolutionary and socialist orientation. Among the more militant SWAPO members—particularly the young—the struggle is seen as fundamentally a class struggle *against* capitalism and *towards* the creation of a new social, economic, and political system based on the principles of scientific socialism, a system typified by collective ownership of the means of production, a popularly-based government, the liberation of human relationships particularly between men and women, and universal literacy, etc. To bring this struggle to fruition requires not only a correct theory and understanding of the situation, but a leadership which has fully merged with the people. We are not suggesting that this has as yet fully occurred within SWAPO, but only that the conditions for it to occur are coming rapidly into existence. How this struggle is resolved will say much about the direction in which SWAPO—and ultimately a free Namibia—will move.

NOTES

1. R. B. Lee, fieldnotes, October 1968.
2. Jean Fischer, 1977. South West Africa: Tightrope Walking in a Terrorist War. In To the Point 6:38, 56-57.
3. Office of the Commissioner for Namibia. 23 September 1977. Bushmen being used as landmine sweepers. In Namibia in the News. 1-2.
4. The full statement of the Nama chiefs is found in Namibia News. Dec. 1976. 9:12, 3-4.
5. One Nation, One Namibia: An Interview with SWAPO. 1977. TCLSAC Reports, 5 (Sept.), 1.
6. S. Hurlich, fieldnotes, November 1976.

SUGGESTIONS FOR FURTHER READING

Cabral, A. 1969. *Revolution in Guine.* R. Handyside (ed.). New York & London: Monthly Review Press.

Cabral, A. 1973. *Return to the Source.* Africa Information Service (ed.). New York & London: Monthly Review Press.*Selected texts by one of Africa's greatest revolutionaries.

First, R. 1963. *South West Africa.* Middlesex: Penguin Books. *A useful readable introduction to the history and economic situation of Namibia.

Hamutenya, H.L. & Geingob, G.H. 1972. African Nationalism in Namibia. *Southern Africa in Perspective* (ed.) C. P. Potholm & R. Dale. The Free Press. 85-94. *A brief history of the rise of nationalism in Namibia and the formation of SWAPO.

Hurlich, S. 1975. Up Against the Bay: Resource Imperialism and Native Resistance. *This Magazine* 9:4, 3-8. *A study of the Hudson's Bay Company's fur operations in Canada and Namibia. EDUCATION

Lee, R.B. & DeVore, I. (eds.). 1968. *Man the Hunter.* Chicago: Aldine. *A world survey of hunting and gathering societies.

Lee, R.B. & DeVore, I. (eds.). 1976. *Kalahari Hunter Gatherers: Studies of the !Kung San and their Neighbours.* Cambridge: Harvard University Press. *Intensive studies of the San by fifteen scientists.

Lee, R.B. (in press) *Ecology and Society of the !Kung San.* *A detailed study of the Dobe area !Kung 1963-73.

Magubane, B. & O'Brien, J. 1972. The Political Economy of Migrant Labour: A Critique of Conventional Wisdom, or A Case Study in the Funtions of Functionalism. *Critical Anthropology* 2:2, 88-103. *Two anthropologists analyze the logic and impact of South Africa's migrant labour system.

Marshall, L. 1976. *The !Kung of Nyae Nyae.* Cambridge: Harvard University Press. *An excellent study of the Nyae Nyae !Kung before they were settled at Chum!kwe.

Mercer, D. (ed.). 1974. *Breaking Contract: the Story of Vinnia Ndadi.* Richmond: LSM Press. *The life history of a migrant labourer who turns to SWAPO and the cause of liberation.

Namibia News *A monthly magazine published by SWAPO, now appearing as a fortnightly information digest available from SWAPO, 21/25 Tabernacle St., London EC2, U.K.

Nganjone, K. 1976. An Army to Serve the Exploited Masses. *LSM News,* 11 & 12, 18-27. *An eloquent account of SWAPO's method of combining military work with political mobilization.

One Nation, One Namibia: An Interview with SWAPO. 1977. *TCLSAC Reports,* 5 (Sept.). *Two Namibian leaders explain why their organization joined SWAPO. Available from TCLSAC (Toronto Committee for the Liberation of Southern Africa), 121 Avenue Road, Toronto, Ontario.

Rogers, B. 1976. *Divide & Rule: South Africa's Bantustans.* London: International Defence & Aid Fund. *A concise introduction to South Africa's bantustan policy.

Saul, J.S. & Woods, R. 1973. African Peasantries. *Essays on the Political Economy of Africa.* G. Arrighi & J. S. Saul. New York & London: Monthly Review Press. 406-416. *A clear exposition of why African peoples are best considered peasants and not "tribesmen."

CHAPTER 19

THE NATIONAL QUESTION

The Making of the Canadian Nation State[1]

BERNARD BERNIER
Université de Montréal

In the middle of the present debate about Canadian unity and Quebec's national independence, it is to my mind important that we analyze the historical formation of the Canadian nation state. To do this, it is necessary to examine the class system of the Canadian state and its relation to ethnicity. For this purpose, one must look at the different stages of the development of sovereignty in Canada, from the 1840 Union Act to the 1867 British North America Act. It is, indeed, during this period that Canada's political and judicial structures were established. Although complete political sovereignty will be acquired only in the twentieth century, it is clear that with the accession to a responsible government in 1847-48 (Chatillon 1976:32; Ouellet 1966:536; Stevenson 1977:74), the Canadian state came into existence. The process whereby the Canadian nation state was established will be examined in the third section of this paper.

In the first section I will go into some detail about the formation of nation states the world over, from the end of the Middle Ages to the beginning of the twentieth century. This phenomenon can be related to the development of capitalism. I will then examine the stages through which the native British bourgeoisie established control over the territory that became Canada. At this point, the various forms of ethnic domination which characterized that period will be analyzed. Finally, in the fourth section, I will examine briefly the constitution of the labour force in Canada in the nineteenth and twentieth centuries, its ethnic composition, and its development to the present day. Nevertheless, the conclusions drawn in this paper must not be considered final: they are rather a programme for subsequent research.[2]

HISTORICAL ASPECTS OF THE FORMATION OF NATION STATES

Nation states were born with capitalism. But their constitution did not come at the same time in different countries. The formation of France, Britain, and the Netherlands goes back to the era of merchant capitalism during the latter stages of the Middle Ages when the rigid bonds of feudalism were burst under the pressure of newly found markets (Anderson 1975; Wallerstein 1974; Moore 1969, chapters 1, 2, and 7; Hardy 1974, chapters 2, 3, and 5; and Bourque 1977, chapter 1). What characterized the breakdown of feudal society was, above all, the dismemberment of territorial sovereignty between various lords as owners of land (Anderson 1977:159 *seq.*, 211 *seq.*; Postan 1972:89 *seq.*, Duby and Mandrou 1948:43; Duby, ed., 1975:377 *seq.*). This break-up both made possible and was a function of the formation of a merchant class which could escape, to a certain extent, the lords' control. From the lords' point of view, trade was necessary if essential commodities were to be brought to their fiefs. Merchants could thus move from region to region. This partial independence of the merchants gave rise, in turn, to commercial towns and a degree of political autonomy was achieved through dues paid to the lords (Duby and Mandrou 1968:87-88).

An agreement based on mutual profit was then arranged between some lords and some merchants: the lords collected taxes from the merchants' profits and, in exchange, the merchants were free to trade as they wished. Naturally the *entente* was never that cordial from the start and many setbacks followed. But by the end of the European Middle Ages the new relations had become a basic factor to be reckoned with by all.

According to the terms of this *entente*, it was to some lords' and all merchants' advantage to increase trade. In the interests of this, some feudal lords, with or without the support of the merchants, tried to unify an increasing amount of land at the expense of bordering territories. To justify ideologically their efforts in consolidating territory, some lords tried to use their filiative links, real or fictive, with monarchs who, after the fall of the occidental Roman empire, had attempted to form kingdoms or regional empires (Charlemagne, etc.). But, in spite of these ideological claims, the tendency was not to restore the monarchies and their ancient empires, but rather, without knowing it, to unify territories, ultimately in the interest of the bourgeoisie (Anderson 1975).

For a few centuries, the feudal lords, backed by absolute monarchies and court nobility, exercised a political control that seemed even more secure than during the Middle Ages. But this control was based on the existence of an internal market, that is, on commercial wealth. The absolute monarchy, the ultimate political manifestation of the feudal system, impeded the growth of this market and, hence, of the merchant class. Because of this, numerous crises came about in the seventeenth and eighteenth centuries ending up in civil wars, revolutions and finally the seizure of political power by the new bourgeoisie (Moore 1969: chapters 1, 2, 7, and 9).

It is thus the feudal aristocracy which, at least in France and England, made up the political structure of the nation state, took control over the territories of previously independent fiefs and set up a centralized administration. In doing so, it eliminated a few dissident groups (the Albigenses in France, the Catholics in England, etc.) and tried to impose a certain religious, cultural, and linguistic uniformity within its jurisdiction. This, however, was only effectively implemented after political power was achieved by the bourgeoisie itself.

The boundaries of national territories so established were relatively arbitrary and subject to disputes as is clearly demonstrated by the example of Alsace-Lorraine. Nevertheless, despite certain instances of uncertainty about boundaries, the nation state acquired control over an ever more clearly defined territory within which there was implanted an internal market system. This process was first completed in France, England, and the Netherlands[3]. It is interesting to note that it is in these countries that manufacturing and, later, industrial capitalism first appeared.

The advent of industrialization in England and in France, and the massive export of manufactured products which followed, forced the German and Italian bourgeoisie, in concert with what was left of their national aristocracy, to unify their national territory. In effect, the German and Italian bourgeoisie had to control their own internal markets as quickly as possible so as to prevent their fragmented principalities from becoming the colonies of the new industrial powers of Britain and France. In Germany, national unification, achieved between 1848 and 1871, mostly under Bismarck's influence, was so successful that around 1900, Germany became the most powerful industrial state in the world (Rodes 1971: chapters 2, 3, and 6; Braverman 1974: chapter 7; Lénine 1917: chapters 3 and 4).

The making of nation states outside Europe was also tied to the expansion of capitalism but through historically and politically different processes[4]. In the case of Japan, it was European imperialist expansion in the nineteenth century that forced Japanese feudal lords to transform state control into an autocratic and centralized nation state, based more and more on industry and imperialist expansion (Halliday 1975: chapters 1 and 3; Norman 1840; Lockwood 1954, chapter 1).

In the United States—a settlement colony—the making of an independent country was the result of the rise of a local merchant bourgeoisie frustrated by metropolitan controls (Hardy 1974:190 *seq.*; Wahlke 1973). Similar trends were observed in Canada during the same period, but were easily suppressed. Canada was sparsely populated, and mainly French speaking: the French-speaking *élite* owed its survival to the maintenance of the seigniorial system by the

British administration and was therefore opposed to independence or to union with the United States (Bourque 1970; Ouellet 1966:116 *seq.*).

It was, in fact, only when the United States became a capitalist power through exporting agricultural products (cotton, tobacco, wheat) and through industrial production, that the merchant bourgeoisie established in Canada, wishing to preserve for itself a territorial base for accumulation, decided to create a sovereign state (Ryerson 1968; Ouellet 1966:27). This process will be looked at in detail in section three. I will only mention here that Canada was created in the interests of the French and English local bourgeoisie as a means of preventing the North American British Colonies from becoming part of the United States.

It is interesting to note that the last three countries to follow the pattern of "classical" capitalist development, Canada, Japan, and Italy, established their nation states in 1867, 1868, and 1870 respectively, that is, at the onset of monopoly capitalism, before the division of the world between the Great Powers. After that process was complete, world wide economic and political constraints, tied to monopoly capitalism and imperialism prevented further national development. Thereafter, every country wanting integrated economic development has had to isolate itself from the world capitalist market; this was the case for the U.S.S.R. and China.

STAGES OF CONTROL OVER CANADIAN TERRITORY

The principal process by which the bourgeoisie has established control over the Canadian territory has been the expropriation of lands belonging to indigenous populations. It is beyond the scope of this paper to detail this process which began in the seventeenth century and which is still continuing today. Many sources provide pertinent information on the matter (Patterson 1971; Morris 1971; Price 1950:55-86; Newcomb 1950; Zlotkin and Colborne 1977; Rouland 1977; for a résumé of the entire process, see Bernier 1977 and 1978b).

I will just mention that the arrival of Europeans in the settlement colonies led to the expropriation of the lands of the original peoples. In North America the expropriation started around 1610 on the New England coast and the motivation was the desire on the part of European settlers for the best agricultural lands. In fact from 1520 to the present the appropriation of agricultural land by colonists at the expense of indigenes has been characteristic of White expansion in America, from north to south and from Atlantic to Pacific.

But agriculture was not the only activity that led to expropriation. The search for furs and timber also played an important part. Later, in the nineteenth century, the laying down of the railroad motivated by the desire to export grains and cereals led to massive land expropriations. Finally, with the advent of industrialization in the era of monopoly capitalism, the search for ore, oil and hydroelectric energy has completed a process tied inextricably to the search for profit, first in the form of trade, then industry.

There have been different kinds of expropriation: illnesses transmitted by Whites have decimated indigenous populations; treaties, agreements, or conventions were entered into to relieve the indigenes of their lands. In all this, military constraint was always present, either indirectly or directly, and, in the case of treaties and land transfers, the native people were faced with the presence of government agents and Northwest Mounted Police, ancestor of the RCMP (Morris 1971). Inasmuch as all the might of the state was used to confront a few hundred or thousand indigenes, it is reasonable to assert that the Canadian territory was acquired by force.

At first, that is, in the seventeenth, eighteenth, and the beginning of the nineteenth century, it was the monarchy (French and then English) which nominally took possession of Canadian territory. At the outset, the objective in establishing colonies was profit, and the beneficiaries were the merchant and industrial bourgeoisie. Then, as now, profit remained the primary motivation for expropriation.

But force was not applied only against indigenes. Other groups have been subject to similar constraints. Acadians, occupying good agricultural lands desired by English colonists and posing a collective threat to English domination, were summarily regrouped, hoisted in boats, and sent to sea.

In general, the descendants of the French settlers to *Nouvelle France* before the conquest of 1760 have experienced similar treatment. The peasants who formed the majority of the French-speaking population saw the new British administration reinforce the control of the seigniorial class of landowners, associated with the church, and place limitations on the use of free lands for the purposes of their agricultural expansion.

The internal contradictions of the seigniorial system, deriving from its antagonistic relationship to the merchant economy, combined with the abuses of the English merchant bourgeoisie to drive the Quebecois peasants to insurrection in 1837-38. Similar revolts occurred in Upper Canada as well, but were put down by military force (Bourque 1970, third part; Ouellet 1966, chapter 14; Whitaker 1977:38 *seq.*).

With control retained by the bourgeoisie, the excess rural population, mostly French speaking, was transformed into a cheap industrial labour force. Although this labour force was first employed in the textile factories in New England from 1840-50 (Ouellet 1966:288 *seq.* and 348), it was eventually localized and contained, to be utilized within the factories of Quebec. Since 1850 the French-speaking population has provided the Canadian bourgeoisie with a low cost industrial labour force which could be effectively employed or kept in reserve at will (Hamelin and Roby 1971:261 *seq.;* Bélanger *et al.* 1973: chapter 1). This containment of the French-speaking Quebeckers accounts for their extremely low income up to now, compared with other "ethnic groups" in Canada.

The Red River Métis to whom a certain regional autonomy had been promised also saw their territory invaded and conquered by the Canadian militia. Their chiefs were executed in 1885 and they themselves were forced to submit to the government of Manitoba—this in the interests of creating a united Canada for the proper operations of the Canadian bourgeoisie (Stanley 1963; Waite 1971:63 *seq.* and 150 *seq.*).

All these instances of appropriation of territory have been justified by European ideologies relating to superiority and progress and, particularly after 1760, with an ideology of British superiority. (See among others Sellar 1907.) Force was justified by diverse, discriminating ideologies all of which increased control by the Canadian bourgeoisie over the territory, resources, and population of Canada.

THE FOUNDING OF A SOVEREIGN STATE IN CANADA

The formation of Canada as a nation was motivated, on the one hand, by the rapid growth of economic power in the United States after the War of Independence and, on the other, by the changeover of British imperialist policy from protectionism to free trade after 1846.

After 1776, the United States, free from metropolitan impediments, experienced a spectacular economic development. In the south, the plantation system, based on slavery, produced tobacco and cotton sold in Europe. In New England a flourishing bourgeoisie developed and controlled external trade. Furthermore, as of 1800, the establishment of settlers in the midwest led to a massive output in the production of cereal which was sold mainly in Europe.

At the beginning of the nineteenth century a fair percentage of the cereals hauled from the midwest en route to Europe was shipped down the St. Lawrence River. But with the construction of the Erie Canal in the United States in 1825 and of the railroad after 1831, cereals, including those produced in Upper Canada, could be channeled through the United States towards New York and Portland. The Canadian merchant bourgeoisie, benefiting from the wood and wheat trade, now saw its chance of profit diminishing.

On the other hand, since 1780 England had developed an unequalled industrial capacity. After 1815, English industrialists, experiencing little competition, pressured the British government into eliminating preferential tariffs on colonial products and implementing free trade. This free trade policy had a double objective: on the one hand, cereals could be imported at a lower price thus lowering the costs of feeding the British labour force and thus lowering their wages too. On the other hand, foreign markets could be invaded with products manufactured in England.

The results of this policy for the Canadian merchant bourgeoisie could have been disastrous. The Canadian merchants were threatened with loss of their main source of income and of becoming dependant on the American bourgeoisie. The only possible solution appeared to be the establishment in British North America of a sovereign nation state.

The first step in this endeavour was the building of a maritime transport route linking the Great Lakes and the St. Lawrence River. The Lachine and Rideau canals opened in 1825 and 1832 respectively allowing commercial traffic to flow increasingly between Upper and Lower Canada (Ouellet 1966:362 seq.). But two canals were insufficient. During the years 1830 to 1840 English-speaking merchants in Montreal and Upper Canadian administrators tried without success to convince the assembly of Lower Canada to vote credits for the canalization of the St. Lawrence River. It was only with the Union Act in 1840 that it was agreed that Lower Canada would pay fifty percent of the canal costs. But the St. Lawrence River canal system, once completed, still did not allow the Canadian bourgeoisie to divert an important portion of American cereal traffic towards the St. Lawrence. At the same time, better railroad networks were being built in the United States which made it easier and cheaper to carry cereals from the midwest to New York.

The canalization of the St. Lawrence River, financed by public funds, had nevertheless allowed numerous contractors, financiers and speculators to prosper. But the return was insignificant compared to that obtained from the construction of the railroads.

At first, railway lines were directed towards the United States. Far from solving the Canadian problems of the time, they reinforced Canada's dependence on its southern neighbour. A railroad line going from east to west, from the Atlantic to Montreal, the Great Lakes and even further west became necessary in order to break this dependency. Such a project was formulated in 1849 but only later became a reality.

From a political point of view, the first step in the formation of Canada was the Union Act of 1840, followed by the accession to responsible government in 1847-48. But the crucial step was in 1867. Then, the British North America Act unified the territories previously called Upper and Lower Canada and joined them to the Maritimes. Confederation simply consolidated the formation of a sovereign state which had been developing between the years 1840-50 (Stevenson 1977:74). The British North America Act in fact extended the jurisdiction of the new Canadian state over a much larger territory by allowing for the annexation of other British territories.

Confederation only makes sense if it is seen in relation to the consolidation of the Canadian bourgeoisie and their interest in building a national railroad. This railroad, which began to be built after 1850, was to be the means of establishing an internal market, making possible commercial exchanges on an east-west axis between the British colonies of North America. It therefore gave a real economic basis to the new country reducing its dependency on the United States. In other words, it was the means by which the Canadian bourgeoisie could secure itself an economic foundation.

Not only did the railroad make possible the development of a certain internal market but it also gave the bourgeoisie the ideal way of becoming rich. As a matter of fact, the building of the railroad, financed mostly by state subsidies, allowed the financiers of the Bank of Montreal to make loans at very favourable rates, the contractors to obtain lucrative contracts, and the owners of the railroad to have guaranteed profits.

Furthermore, land grants to the railway companies allowed them to make large profits by selling the unused lands to settlers. Although the railroad showed a deficit for a long time after it was built this did not prevent the owners from accumulating large profits—the state had guaranteed them a certain rate of return. This transportation network was thus a most effective way of diverting a good part of the national wealth toward the national bourgeoisie. It was therefore a privileged means for primitive accumulation. Confederation, in fact, proved the culmination, at the political level, of the territorial unification of Canada via the railroad (Stevenson 1977:74).

As Stevenson (1977:80 *seq.*) points out, this episode of Canadian history illustrates the leading role played by the Canadian state apparatus in establishing Canadian capitalism. Neither in the United States, nor in England, nor in France has the state played such an important economic role. As I outlined in the first section, the economic role of the state in Canada, as in Japan, Germany, and Russia was necessary because the take-over of the internal market by the local bourgeoisie had to be accomplished after other national bourgeoisie were well established and were simultaneously trying to widen their economic influence in other regions.

But what is probably unique about the Canadian "case" is the artificial nature of the formation of the country through the conscious efforts of local merchants and financiers to transform themselves into a national bourgeoisie. Of course, the making of every capitalist state has had a certain arbitrary aspect; but in Canada's case, the bourgeoisie had to unify territories previously quite autonomous in order to compete with their American counterparts.

The Canadian nation state was therefore created in reaction to an exterior threat. It has been, from the beginning, under the control of a relatively small and weak national bourgeoisie. To defend themselves the bourgeoisie have always counted on the state and on controlling their financial institutions. As expected, the bourgeoisie have invested in industry but they have had to deal with strong competition from the American bourgeoisie. So attempts were made to protect, at least, its control over the banks.

By Confederation, the English Canadian bourgeoisie had resigned themselves to the fact that the Quebecois would not assimilate to English-Canadian society and authority. Instead, Canada had incorporated into its constitution important ethnic or national disparities directed particularly at the French-speaking indigenes. Confederation placed an official stamp on Quebeckers' subordinate position, economically and politically, while the bourgeoisie encouraged an ideology of Anglo Saxon ethnic superiority. (See amongst others, Sellar 1907.) Although some French-Canadians have been able to join the Canadian bourgeoisie, the vast majority have been relegated to the ranks of the industrial labour force, either employed or kept as a reserve.

The development of Canada into a capitalist power, albeit one of secondary importance, then, perpetuated certain divisions which were to later play an important role in the internal structure of the labour force.

ESTABLISHING THE CANADIAN LABOUR FORCE

The development of Canadian capitalism after 1867 was characterized by the further acquisition of territory and by the establishment of industries. Use of the new territories required the immigration of a population of small farmers ready to cultivate the land. In fact, until about 1900 most of the immigrants were British (including Irish), German, and Scandinavian, and most settled on the Prairies.

Following this wave came people from Eastern Europe, China, and Japan. The Greeks came from 1920 on, then Italians, followed by Indians and Pakistanis, the Portuguese and, more recently, the East Indians.

Canadian immigration has always been divided into two main types. Firstly, there have been the people with only their working power to sell; then there have been those with property, trades, or professions. Before 1900, the "others" were mainly peasants though there were a number of craftsmen, professionals, and bourgeoisie. After 1900, the great majority of "the others" were those with better skills. Since 1920, about seventy percent of all immigrants to Canada have been workers or employees. At present, it remains this way despite changes in the immigration regulations (Bernier 1978 (a); Inquiry Commission . . . , 1972, Vol. III and Malservisi 1973).

A few figures about immigration in Canada give us a fairly accurate picture of the purpose of immigration for the state—that is, creation of a cheap industrial labour force, usually in the worst paid factories. This meant that the state would not have to cover education costs and upkeep during the period prior to immigration. Needless to say, quite a few people born in Canada are also used as workers and employees. But the percentage of immigrants holding low paying jobs in industry is far higher than the percentage of people in those industries of British descent. It is, however, more or less equal to the percentage of French-speaking people in such jobs. There is thus, inside Canada, an inequality in occupation and income based on ethnic differences.

The fact that recent immigrants and members of such a long established ethnic group as French Canadian have less qualified jobs and lower income is not specific to Canada: immigrant workers in Europe and in the United States, as well as Blacks in the United States, share the same characteristics (Castles and Kosack 1973; Granotier 1970; Ertel *et al* 1971; Adler 1969; and Jacobson, ed. 1968). The major difference between America on one side and Europe on the other is the recent phenomenon of mass immigration to the former continent. In America, as well as Canada, immigration was, from the start, one of the major factors responsible for the establishment of the labour force.

All through the process of immigration in Canada, ideologies pertaining to ethnic differences have been present. This has allowed certain groups to be taken advantage of more easily and with fewer pangs of conscience. Avery (1972 and 1975) gives a few eloquent examples pertaining to the Chinese and to people from Eastern Europe. We immediately grasp that these ideologies, which are still apparent in attitudes toward Indians, Pakistanis, and West Indians in Toronto and Vancouver carry the same message as those that were used to expropriate the lands of the native people and to ensure the containment of French Canadians within the proletariat.

In fact, these ideologies are integrated into the Canadian scene and are essential components of the class system. Multiculturalism policy, far from eradicating them, seems rather to reinforce them, insisting on the ethnic specificity of these groups. It is not that insisting on ethnic culture is wrong; rather, insisting without making real efforts to abolish inequalities leads to further confrontations such as those encountered in the Pépin-Robarts Commission meetings on national unity.

Ethnicity has been used ideologically in Canada, as in other capitalist countries, to contain and segment certain groups within the working class, to divide the working class, to stop the creation of a united workers' movement and in general to ensure the continued domination of the bourgeoisie in economic, social, and cultural life. The fact that, objectively, this works against the establishment of the very internal commercial economy which is so necessary to the continued prosperity of that class seems only now to be in the process of realization. That is, for the bourgeoisie, the need to divide the work force conflicts with the positive features of a self-contained economy. Thus the emphasis on unity or diversity in Canada, as elsewhere, is determined by the concrete situation of the class antagonisms in various historical periods.

NOTES

1. *This is a revised English version of a paper presented to the plenary session of the Canadian Ethnological Society, February 25, 1978.*
2. *This paper is the result of research on ethnicity and the national question carried out in collaboration with Mikhael Elbax (Bernier, Elbaz, and Lavigne 1978). The*

leading authors who have written on this subject are Bourque 1970, Naylor 1972, Panitch 1977, Ryerson 1968, Stevenson 1977, and Whitaker 1977. One may also consult Chatillon 1976, chapter 2, Ouellet 1966, and Hamelin and Roby 1971 who give in detail the economic context of that period especially relevant to Quebec.

3. *As far as Spain is concerned, it is less obvious. As a matter of fact, for a long period of time, the Spanish monarchy tried to gain political control over numerous territories (the Netherlands, Germany, a part of Italy) without trying to integrate them into a common market. In fact, even the regions of the Iberian penninsula were not integrated into such a market. The reason for this particular development was the weakness of the national bourgeoisie which, with the New World's gold, attempted to transform itself into a landowning nobility (Wallerstein 1974:191 seq.).*

4. Here I make a distinction between three different phases: first a colonial expansion phase, starting in the fifteenth century and tied to merchant capitalism; a second phase related to the beginning of industrialization in Europe (end of the eighteenth century) which was characterized by its quest for new markets; finally, a third phase, the imperialist one that accompanied monopoly capitalism, starting around 1860-70.

BIBLIOGRAPHY

Adler, Franklin Hugh 1969. Les rapports entre le travailleur noir et le capitalisme américain. *Les temps modernes*, Janvier: 1213-1269.

Anderson, Perry 1975. *Lineages of the Absolutist State*. London: NLB.

Anderson, Perry 1977. *Les passages de l'antiquité au féodalisme*. Paris: Maspéro.

Avery, Donald 1972. Canadian Immigration Policy and the "Foreign Navy", 1896-1914. *Historical Papers*, Canadian Historical Association, Ottawa, pp. 135-155. F 5000 C19

Avery, Donald 1975. Continental European Immigrant Workers in Canada, *Revue canadienne de Sociologie et d'Anthropologie*. Vol. 12, no. 1:53-64. HM1 C212

Bélanger, Noel et al 1973. *Les travailleurs québécois*, Montréal: Presses de l'Université du Québec.

Bernier, Bernard 1977. La *"question autochtone" au Canada: une analyse de classes*, Ronéo, Anthropologie, Université de Montréal.

Bernier, Bernard 1978a. L'utilisation de la main-d'oeuvre immigrante au Canada. Dorais, L.J. (ed.), *Perspectives anthropoligiques*, Montéal: Editions du renouveau pédagogique, à paraître.

Bernier, Bernard 1978b. Classes sociales et idéologie raciste dans les colonies de peuplement. *Compte-rendu du colloque de la Société canadienne des Etudes ethniques*.

Bernier, Bernard, Elbaz, Mikhael et Lavigne, Gilles, 1978. Ethnicité et lutte de classes. *Anthropologie et sociétés*, Vol. 2, no. 1

Bourque, Gilles 1970. *Classes sociales et question nationale au Québec, 1760-1840*. Montréal: Parti Pris.

Bourque, Gilles 1977. *L'Etat capitaliste et la question nationale*, Montréal: Presses de l'Université de Montréal.

Braverman, Harry 1974. *Labor and Monopoly Capital*, New York: Monthly Review Press.

Castles, Stephen, et Kosack, Godula 1973. *Immigrant Workers and Class Structure in Western Europe*. London: Oxford University Press.

Chatillon, Colette 1976. *L'histoire de l'agriculture au Québec*. Montéal: l'Etincelle.

Commission d'enquête sur la situation de la langue française et sur les driots linguistiques au Québec 1972. *Rapport*, vol. III, Les groupes ethniques. Québec, Gouvernement de Québec.

Duby, Georges (ed.) 1975. *Histoire de la France rurale*. vol. I (Des origines à 1340). Paris: Seuil.

Duby, Georges et Mandrou, Robert 1968. *Histoire de la civilisation française*. Tome 1. Paris: A. Colin.

Ertel, Rachel, Fabre, Geneviève et Marienstras, Elise 1971. *En marge*, Paris: Maspéro.

Granotier, Bernard 1970. *Les travailleurs immigrés en France*. Paris: Maspéro,

Halliday, Jon 1975. *A Political History of Japanese Capitalism.* New York: Pantheon.

Hamelin, Jean et Roby, Yves 1971. *Histoire économique du Québec, 1851-1896,* Montréal: Fides.

Hardy, James, D. Jr. 1974. *Prologue to Modernity: Early Modern Europe.* New York: Wiley.

Jacobson, Julius (ed.) 1968. *The Negro and the American Labor Movement.* New York, Doubleday.

Lénine, V.I. 1917. *L'impérialisme, stade suprême du capitalisme.* Paris: Editions sociales.

Lockwood, William M. 1954. *The Economic development of Japan.* Princeton: Princeton University Press.

Malservisi, Mauro F. 1973. *La contribution des Québécois des groupes ethniques autres que français et britanniques au développement du Québec.* Etude pour la Commission d'enquête sur la situation de la langue française . . . , Québec, Gouvernement du Québec.

Moore, Barrington Jr. 1969. *Les origines sociales de la dictature et de la démocratie.* Paris: Maspéro.

Morris, Alexander 1971. *The Treaties of Canada with the Indians.* Toronto: Coles Publ. (Réédition).

Naylor, Tom 1972. The Rise and Fall of the Third Commerical Empire of the St-Lawrence Gary Teeple (ed.). *Capitalism and the National Question in Canada.* Toronto: University of Toronto Press.

Newcomb, W.W. 1950. A Reexamination of the Causes of Plains Warfare. *American Anthropologist.* 52:317-330. GN 1 A51

Norman, Herbert 1940. *Japan's emergence as a Modern State.* New York: Institute of Pacific Relations.

Norris, John 1971. *Strangers Entertained.* Vancouver: Evergreen.

Ouellet, Fernand 1966. *Histoire économique et sociale du Québec.* 1760-1850, Montéal: Fides.

Panitch, Léo 1977. The Role and Nature of the Canadian State. Leo Panitch (ed.), *The Canadian State.* Toronto: Universtiy of Toronto Press. Under JL 65 1977 C22

Patterson, E. Palmer 1972. *The Canadian Indian: A History since 1500.* Toronto: Collier MacMillan.

Postan, M.M. 1972. *The Mediaeval Economy and Society.* London.

Price, A.G. 1950. *White Settlers and Native Peoples.* Melbourne: Georgian House. HT 1523 P99

Rodes, John E. 1971. *The Quest for Unity: Modern Germany, 1848-1970.* New York: Holt, Rinehart & Winston.

Rouland, Norbert 1977. *Le règlement du statut juridique du Nouveau-Québec et la Convention de la Baie James et du Nord Québéquois.* Ronéo: Faculté de droit, Université d'Aix-en-Provence.

Ryerson, Stanley B. 1968. *Unequal Union.* Toronto: Progress Book.

Saxton, Alexander 1971. *The Indispensable Enemy,* Berkeley: University of California Press.

Sellar, Robert 1907/74. *The Tragedy of Quebec,* Toronto: University of Toronto Press.

Stanley, George F.G. 1963. *Louis Riel.* Toronto: McGraw-Hill Ryerson.

Stevenson, Garth 1977. Federalism and the Political Economy of the Canadian State, Leo Panitch (ed.). *The Canadian State.* Toronto: University of Toronto Press.

Wahlke, John C. (ed.) 1973. *The Causes of the American Revolution,* Toronto: D.C. Health Canada.

Waite, Peter B. 1971. *Canada, 1874-1896,* Toronto: McClelland & Stewart.

Wallerstein, Immanuel 1974. *The Modern World-System,* New York: Academic Press.

Whitaker, Reg 1977. Images of the State in Canada, Leo Panitch (ed.), *The Canadian State.* Toronto: Universtiy of Toronto Press, 1977.

Zlotkin, Norman, et Colborne, Donald R. 1977. Internal Canadian Imperialism and the Native People. Craig Heron (ed.). *Imperialism, Nationalism and Canada.* Toronto: New Hogtown Press. FC97 I34

GLOSSARY OF
CONCEPTS

The arrangement of the glossary reflects the organization of the argument as set forward in the book.

Way of life: the totality of relations through which people set out and create their material/conceptual existence.

Society: a system of organized, interpersonal relations.

Culture: the symbolic, intellectual construction of a people.

History/Prehistory: literate vs. nonliterate tradition/period of a people.

Production/Reproduction: through activity, creating and/or sustaining the cultural and biological conditions of a way of life (i.e. population, symbols, means of living).

Economy: production of material conditions of life.

Mode of production: relations and techniques with which a people are organized to produce their means of existence.

Forces of production: the combination of wo/man power and machinepower used in the productive process.

Relations of production: the social relations people enter into as a result of the process of production.

Ecology: the environmental components upon which production takes place.

Social Organization: the way in which a people organize or are organized to deal with the problems of living in a society.

Social Relations: the way in which people effect the network of inter-effective action and interactions of people in a society.

Social Structure: relations governed by rules or principles.

Reciprocity/Exchange: a means of establishing social relations between people through mediation of material goods, symbols, and people.

Kinship: the culturally defined relations of reproduction within a society.

Descent: selection of various kinship linkages for the purpose of transmitting property, resources, knowledge, etc.

Locality/Territoriality: principle of organization based on position in space and by space.

Family: a self-contained economic and reproductive unit formed around the basis of primary kinship ties.

Domestic Group: a residential group that lives together and is oriented to its own support.

Corporate Group: a group that regards itself and is regarded by others as if it were an individual.

Ethnic Group: a group which defines itself in reference to common kinship/residence/territory.

Hierarchy/Domination: the framework/ability to impose rules of general conduct upon a group.

Class: a specific grouping defined in terms of distinct socio-economic position, cutting across other kinds of group formations.

Symbolic Organization: the way in which a people conceptualize, interpret, and manipulate their way of life.

Symbolism: a means of defining, understanding, and communicating experience by words, distinctive features, analogies, identities, or images.

Myth/Folktale: an imaginative, traditional construction of a people.

Ideology: a set of interpretative abstract ideas assumed to be true.

Language: the speech, acts, and underlying structure of rules through which a people communicate.

Social Change: the quantitative and qualitative alterations of social and cultural patterns through time.

Opposition: a relation of mutual exclusiveness.

Contradiction: a situation in which two or more oppositions are being asserted at the same time.

Transformation: when a contradiction becomes so severe that social change takes place.

Evolution/Development: theory of fundamental gradual/directed change which is inherent in the social formation.

Schools of Thought

Functionalism: the study of how a society is maintained in terms of how it maintains itself through the inculcation of a set of norms/rules, values/ideals, beliefs/ideas.

Marxism: the study of society in terms of the interplay of opposing forces and interests.

Structuralism: the study of society through the analysis of its symbolic representations.

INDEX